NY

LITHUANIA
(annexed by U.S.S.R.)

RUSSIAN ADMINISTRATION
East Prussia

BALTIC SEA

Memel
Tilsit
Königsberg
Pillau
Insterburg
Eydtkau
Goldap
Allenstein
Lyck
Orteisberg

Gdynia
Danzig
DANZIG
Elbing
Marienburg
Bromberg
Marienwerder
Osterode
Groudenz

Bornholm
Stolp
Lauenburg
Köslin
Rügenwalde
Cammin
Neustettin
Dramburg
Stargard
Schneidemühl
Deutsch Krone

Pomerania

POLISH ADMINISTRATION

POLAND

Thorn
Bromberg
Posen
Kalisz

Landsberg
Küstrin
Schwiebus
Sagan
Glogau
Liegnitz
Liegnitz
Görlitz
Breslau
Hirschberg
Brieg
Kreuzburg
Waldenburg
Ohlau
Glatz
Oppeln

Silesia

Hindenburg
Gleiwitz
Ratibor
Mor. Ostrava
Olmütz

PRAGUE

Tabor
Brünn

CZECHOSLOVAKIA

BERLIN
OUTER MUNICIPAL DISTRICTS

PANKOW
REINICKENDORF
WEISSENSEE
SPANDAU
CHARLOTTENBURG
LICHTENBERG
WILMERSDORF
SCHÖNEBERG
ZEHLENDORF
STEGLITZ
NEUKÖLLN
TEMPELHOF
KÖPENICK

BONN
Rhine River

THE RUHR
DORTMUND
ESSEN
DÜSSELDORF

THE UNITED STATES
IN GERMANY

1944-1955

---

by

HAROLD ZINK

Former Chief Historian
U. S. High Commissioner for Germany;
Professor of Political Science
Ohio State University

D. VAN NOSTRAND COMPANY, INC.

PRINCETON, NEW JERSEY

TORONTO　　　　　　　　　　　　　　　LONDON

NEW YORK

D. VAN NOSTRAND COMPANY, INC.

120 Alexander St., Princeton, New Jersey
257 Fourth Avenue, New York 10, New York
25 Hollinger Rd., Toronto 16, Canada

*All correspondence should be addressed to the
principal office of the company at Princeton, N. J.*

PRINTED IN THE UNITED STATES OF AMERICA

Preface

It seems appropriate in introducing this book to say something about its purpose. To begin with, it must be stated that it makes no claim to be a definitive analysis of the tangled events of the American occupation of Germany arising out of World War II. There may be some doubt whether a truly definitive single study of the extremely complex and widely ramified aspects of the occupation will ever be forthcoming. In any event, it is likely to require a decade or so before a serious attempt can be made to produce such a work. Nor does this book pretend to furnish detailed and technical coverage of the occupation. Such an undertaking would require for one thing several times the space available here. Studies of such a character are likely to be the responsibility of official historical agencies or contracted to semi-official organizations or private research foundations. The more modest purpose of this book is to present an overall account of the American role in the occupation of Germany for the use of general readers, university students, and others who desire to have a carefully drafted and authoritative study of what went on in this most important undertaking. It is hoped that despite the nontechnical character of the book certain of its conclusions may be of interest to those with a more specialized interest.

Although this book does not essay to be definitive, it is based on a great array of authoritative material. It will be noted even by a casual reader that it makes generous use of the monographs of the Historical Division of the Office of the U. S. High Commissioner for Germany (HICOG). This is no accident. Indeed one of the chief reasons leading to the preparation of the book was the feeling of the author who served as the first chief historian of HICOG and participated as consultant of the State Department in the initial planning of the project that the significant conclusions of this series of monographs should be brought together as far as possible within the confines of a single volume. At one time it was hoped that this could be done as part of the official project, but for various reasons this did not prove feasible. And even now the classified status of several of the monographs precludes a complete summary.

The principal source of the data on which the book is based is not, surprisingly, official documents and reports. In the preparation of the monographs of the Historical Series access was had to what might be described as large quantities of such materials. The files relating to the military government phase of the occupation alone ran to approximately 70,000 square feet. Those sections of the study which incorporate the findings of the Historical Series involve therefore large numbers of official papers. Other sections, it is fair to note, have a lesser base of this character, but they too make considerable use of such materials.

One of the strong impressions which the author carried with him out of both military and High Commission service in Germany was that, essential as official documents may be, they do not tell the whole story. This is not only because certain important matters are handled through personal contacts and may never get recorded on paper, but because much of the highly important background material which throws a great deal of light on events is not preserved. Notes, memos, early drafts, comments on tentative drafts, revisions of drafts, and the like, have a significant bearing on many developments in such an undertaking as the occupation of Germany; yet most of them are destroyed, leaving only the final directive, policy statement, etc., for the files and the future historian. The Historical staff of HICOG had the great and perhaps almost unique advantage of carrying on its work during the most active period of the High Commission phase of the occupation. Since its staff was assigned as specialists to the subdivisions of HICOG and recognized the importance of supplementing official papers with more or less constant contact with those directing and administering, its monographs include much material not to be found in official papers alone. In sections of the book which are not based on the Historical Series, the author has drawn on his experiences as a military government specialist officer, member of the staff of the Interior subdivision of the German Country Unit of the Supreme Headquarters of the Allied Expeditionary Forces (SHAEF), American representative on the board of editors which reviewed and coordinated plans of the German Country Unit, executive officer of the Political Affairs subdivision of the U. S. Group, Control Council for Germany, chief of the Reorganization of German Government Section of the same agency, and visiting civilian expert

iv

Preface

in Office of Military Government of the United States for Germany (OMGUS), as well as on numerous visits in a private capacity to Germany during the occupation.

Finally, substantial use has been made of the numerous books, monographs, collections of papers, articles, and so forth, which have been written by scholars, participants in the occupation, journalists, and others. These represent a wide variety of backgrounds and points of view and many are based on personal observation arising out of association with the events of the occupation.

June, 1957.   HAROLD ZINK

v

Acknowledgments

The author desires to express appreciation to various persons who have contributed either directly or indirectly. First of all, thanks are due to G. Bernard Noble, chief of the Division of Historical Policy Research of the State Department. The wisdom which he displayed in planning for an historical project in HICOG and the most generous support and personal attention which he gave to the work in the field deserve a high rating. In contrast to the strained relations which frequently characterized agencies in Germany and their counterparts in Washington, the Historical Division of HICOG enjoyed the most cordial and intimate relations with the Division of Historical Policy Research of the State Department and this was in large measure due to Dr. Noble. The author acknowledges a great debt to his associates both American and German in the Historical Division of HICOG and to his successor, Roger H. Wells. Special mention should be made of Elmer Plischke and Henry P. Pilgert who have read various chapters and helped strengthen the study through numerous suggestions. The author expresses his warm appreciation to John J. McCloy and Shepard Stone for taking the time, despite heavy demands made on them elsewhere, to go over the manuscript of this book. It should be emphasized that though much assistance has been given in the form of comments, suggestions, and additional material by those who have read the manuscript, responsibility for the views expressed must be borne solely by the author—indeed it is fair to say that in various instances the readers have not agreed with the conclusions reached.

The author is also indebted to the State Department, the United States Information Agency, the Roy Bernard Company, the Department of the Army, and Mr. John J. McCloy for the loan of photographs.

Finally thanks are due to Miss Ruth Martin who typed the greater part of the final draft of the manuscript and to Miss Shirley Fisher who assisted in the preparation of the bibliography.

Contents

	Preface	iii
	List of Illustrations	viii
	Abbreviations	x
1	THE SIGNIFICANCE OF THE AMERICAN OCCUPATION OF GERMANY	1
2	PRELIMINARY PREPARATIONS AND PLANNING	5
3	AMERICAN MILITARY GOVERNMENT ORGANIZATION IN GERMANY	26
4	OFFICE OF THE U. S. HIGH COMMISSIONER FOR GERMANY	43
5	MILITARY GOVERNORS, HIGH COMMISSIONERS, AND OTHER OCCUPATION STAFF	66
6	THE THORNY PROBLEM OF POLICY	86
7	RELATIONS WITH THE RUSSIANS, BRITISH, AND FRENCH	103
8	CIVIL-MILITARY RELATIONS	121
9	THE PERSONAL IMPACT OF THE AMERICANS	132
10	WAR CRIMES TRIALS	145
11	THE DENAZIFICATION PURGE	150
12	CONSTRUCTING A NEW GERMAN GOVERNMENT	169
13	AMERICAN ACTIVITIES IN THE EDUCATION FIELD	193
14	THE EXCHANGES PROGRAM	215
15	BRINGING INFORMATION TO THE GERMANS	234
16	AMERICAN PARTICIPATION IN ECONOMIC RECONSTRUCTION	251
17	PUBLIC FINANCE, CURRENCY, AND BANKING	269
18	MANPOWER AND ORGANIZED LABOR	280
19	FOOD AND AGRICULTURE	293
20	PUBLIC SAFETY, LAW, AND THE COURTS	304
21	YOUTH AND WOMEN'S ACTIVITIES	311
22	RELIGIOUS AFFAIRS	320
23	THE PROBLEM OF DEMOCRACY FOR GERMANY	326
24	THE SPECIAL PROBLEM OF BERLIN	340
25	THE OCCUPATION IN RETROSPECT	352
	Bibliography	362
	Index	367

List of Illustrations

Germany: Zones of Occupation   22
Organization of the Office of the U. S. High Commissioner for
    Germany   47
Organization of the Allied High Commission   57
Office of U. S. Land Commissioner   60
Office of the U. S. Land Commissioner for Württemberg-Baden   61
Berlin Element—Office of U. S. High Commissioner for
    Germany   62
Land Hesse-Kreis Resident Officer Administrative Districts   64
General Dwight D. Eisenhower, first American Military
    Governor   86
General J. T. McNarney, second American Military Governor   86
General George S. Patton, Jr., District Military Governor   86
Lt. General Alexander M. Patch, Jr., District Military Governor   86
General Lucius D. Clay, American Military Governor, with the
    British Military Governor and German Ministers President   87
U. S. High Commissioner John J. McCloy with Chancellor
    Konrad Adenauer of the West German Federal Republic   87
Allied Control Authority for Germany   108
U. S. High Commissioner James B. Conant, with Prof. Otto
    Hahn   118
President Theodor Heuss of the West German Federal Re-
    public   118
The Farben Building at Frankfurt   119
An America House at Stuttgart   119
Organization of the Federal Republic of Germany   189
The Henry Ford Building of the Free University in West Berlin   214
U. S. High Commissioner John J. McCloy strikes the corner-
    stone of the American Memorial Library in West Berlin   214
High Commissioners of Britain, France, and the United States
    signing the Occupation Statute   215
The signing of the European Recovery Program agreement with
    West Germany   215
The historic Brandenburg Gate in Berlin   246

List of Illustrations

Nuremberg after the German surrender in 1945   246
A typical street scene in Berlin during the early period of the
  occupation   246
The new Esso oil refinery at Hamburg   247
Hamburg University Hospital after war devastation   247
Hamburg University Hospital after reconstruction   247
Allied Kommandatura, Berlin   342

Abbreviations

ASTP	Army Specialized Training Program
CATS	Civil Affairs Training Schools
EAC	European Advisory Commission
ECA	Economic Cooperation Administration
FSOs	Foreign Service Officers
FSS	Foreign Service Staff Corps
GARIOA	Funds appropriated by Congress for occupied areas during the early period of the occupation of Germany
GYA	German Youth Assistance
HICOG	Office of the U. S. High Commissioner for Germany
JCS 1067	Joint Chiefs of Staff paper, number 1067, the early basic directive relating to Germany
JEIA	Joint Export-Import Agency
MSA	Mutual Security Agency
OMGUS	Office of Military Government of the United States for Germany
OSS	Office of Strategic Services
OWI	Office of War Information
SHAEF	Supreme Headquarters of the Allied Expeditionary Forces
SWNCC	State, War, Navy Coordinating Committee
USFET	U. S. Forces, European Theatre

1

The Significance of the American Occupation of Germany

The United States has had many experiences of greater or less significance involving the outside world during its more than a century and a half of existence. Perhaps the most striking of these have been in connection with military operations—certainly on the basis of numbers of men involved and expenditures, World Wars I and II stand in a unique position. Of the experiences not directly involving national defense, though of course closely related to World War II and the "Cold War," one of the most important, and in some respects the most important, has been in connection with the occupation of Germany during the momentous years 1944-1955.

Germany is not, it is true, the only country in which the United States has found itself confronted with the necessity of assuming occupational responsibilities. After the Spanish-American War both Cuba and the Philippines were occupied by the United States for a time. After World War I the United States agreed to take over a portion of the Rhineland area of Germany for occupation purposes and for several years maintained forces there. But Cuba and the Philippines and the German Rhineland represented comparatively small populations and relatively simple problems. In the case of Japan after World War II, the United States had an occupational experience of great significance. The Japanese occupation involved a more numerous population than its counterpart in Germany, but it covered a shorter period of time and seems, to many observers at least, more simple in character. The Japanese surrendered before an invasion of their main islands was undertaken and this eliminated the early phase of administering an occupied territory required in Germany. Since the Japanese government was intact at the time of surrender, it could be used as an instrument of military government

1

and consequently it was not necessary to construct a new system of government from the ground up as in Germany. Although formally an Allied undertaking, the Japanese occupation was, in reality, largely an exclusive responsibility of the United States, with virtually complete authority exercised by General Douglas MacArthur. In contrast, the German occupation presented the almost incredibly complex problem of four-power cooperation and agreement; and the United States, despite the difficulties arising out of this division of authority, learned lessons which were never necessary in Japan.

It is perhaps not an undue exaggeration to state that the United States entered upon the occupation of Germany as a rather immature and inexperienced nation in the international field. The lessons learned in Germany were so far-reaching and the experience gained so maturing that few would give the United States such a rating in 1955, and a good many would place the United States in the top category of nations on the basis of knowledge of world affairs and expertness in handling difficult international situations. So great was the immaturity of the United States in 1945 that many of the experts apparently failed to recognize the deep-seated and indissoluble connections between Germany and Europe. It was proposed by the influential White-Morgenthau group that Germany be de-industrialized and reduced to a pastoral economy, that a strict quarantine be established to isolate Germany from the rest of Europe and indeed the world. If there were wise men in the United States who at the initial stage realized the impossibility and futility of this policy and were aware of the necessity of getting the German economy back on its feet if the other European nations were to be self-supporting, they were not numerous and in general were not in a position to control action. The United States therefore had to learn the hard way, but the immensely valuable lesson was learned eventually. Thus the early period of the occupation saw a great deal of fumbling and many costly mistakes, while the record of the later years, if not perfect, certainly put the United States in a light which occasioned respect.

American experience in the occupation of Germany is also of great significance because it was in that area that the United States came into closest contact with the Russians and, after a great deal of effort to get along, found that the expectations held by President Franklin D. Roosevelt and others could not be realized. It was out

2

of the experience in Germany, therefore, that the United States proceeded to the position of founding its foreign policy in large measure on a Western European defense community which, it was hoped, would furnish protection against Russian aggression.

Although the United States had maintained far-reaching relations with the British during World War II, these contacts were largely of a military character and did not survive the fighting very well. Thus, after the intimate relations during the war, contact between the United States and Britain became rather formal during the early postwar period. So shortsighted were some of the top authorities in Washington that a reliable source reports that the Civil Affairs Division of the War Department intimated to General Lucius D. Clay that it was undesirable to maintain close contacts with the British in the occupation of Germany. Be that the case or not, the bitter experiences of the early months of the occupation proved beyond much doubt that the United States could not stand alone. The postwar alliance of the United States and Britain may be said to have developed then in large measure out of the occupation of Germany.

It was in Germany that the United States tested its foreign-aid programs perhaps more effectively than in any other single place. Although larger amounts have been expended in an effort to get French economy strengthened, the economic assistance activities of the United States in West Germany have produced far more spectacular results. Indeed outside of the United States and the USSR it is probably fair to state that no other large nation has achieved as great a proportionate increase in its industrial output as West Germany since 1948. Obviously the Germans themselves claim much of the credit for what has been accomplished, but the more than three billion dollars of direct aid from the United States, together with an unknown but undoubtedly large indirect contribution arising from expenditures of American personnel in Germany, have played an important role. Moreover, as a result of various experiments in Germany where there were fewer restraints than in most of the other countries receiving economic aid from the United States, it was possible to develop techniques that could be used elsewhere.

The information, cultural relations, and exchanges programs of the United States in occupied Germany have been the largest and most developed to be found anywhere—indeed at one period these

3

programs in Germany exceeded in proportions those in all other countries put together. As a result not only have more Germans been brought into contact with American books, films, periodicals, people, institutions, and enterprises through American libraries and centers and visiting the United States in person than in the case of any other people, but many valuable lessons have been learned that could be advantageously applied to similar programs elsewhere.

Finally, the occupation of Germany has been of unusual significance to the American people because so many Americans, both civilian and military, have participated. The exact number who have served the occupation in one manner or another during the years stretching from 1944 to 1955 cannot be fixed with any degree of accuracy for various reasons. Much, for example, would depend upon whether one included the military forces stationed in Germany for security purposes. But at the very least some hundreds of thousands of persons have been involved altogether and, if all the military personnel are counted, the total mounts into the millions. Some of these Americans have had their outlooks broadened immeasurably by such experience; others have not been able to survive the stresses and temptations of the occupation. Many thousands have taken German brides who have returned to the United States with their husbands and thus have become a part of the American people and mothers of young Americans. A very small number have been converted to communism and a few have sought refuge with the Russians. But the vast majority came away from Germany with tangible evidence that communism is a snare and a delusion, having little to offer humanity other than misery. It will never be possible to ascertain the full impact of the occupation, constructive and negative, on American people and the American way of life, but, with such large numbers involved, it is apparent that the net result has not been negligible.

2

Preliminary Preparations and Planning

Some observers of the spectacular activities of the United States in Germany during the years 1944-1955 have expressed disappointment at what they regarded as serious weaknesses. It has been implied that had careful preliminary preparations and planning been undertaken, the mistakes and wastages might have been avoided in large measure. No responsible person can deny that errors were made by the United States in the occupation of Germany during the years following 1944. And most of those who have had even a casual glimpse of the occupation in action have probably felt that American activities in Germany were at times being carried on haphazardly, on a day-to-day basis without much attention to long-range objectives.

To those however who have attempted to familiarize themselves with the history of other occupation experiences of the United States—during the Civil War, the Spanish-American War, World War I,[1] and the recent occupation of Japan—the unique feature of the occupation of Germany lay not in its casualness, but in the elaborate preliminary preparations and efforts to plan. Perhaps it is not too much to say that all occupations, by their very nature, are characterized by imperfection, frequent poor judgment, and the like. The complex problems to be encountered, the emergency character of many of the activities, the pressure to take action without delay, and the abnormal atmosphere surrounding an occupation, all combine to promote haphazardness, mistakes, and extravagance. In earlier occupations, the United States had depended upon non-specialized tactical forces which happened to be available to perform

---

[1] For discussions of these earlier occupations, see D. Y. Thomas, *A History of Military Government in Newly Acquired Territory of the United States* (Columbia University Press, New York, 1904); E. Fraenkel, *Military Occupation and the Rule of Law: Occupation Government in the Rhineland, 1918-1923* (Cornell University Press, Ithaca, N. Y., 1944); L. L. Hunt, *American Military Government of Occupied Germany, 1918-1920* (Government Printing Office, Washington, 1943); R. H. Gabriel, "American Experience with Military Government," *American Political Science Review*, June 1943.

the necessary tasks involved in military government. Any planning that was done was of a perfunctory character. Even though possibly more preliminary preparations and planning were carried on looking toward the occupation of Japan than in the case of Germany, their actual role was probably less in Japan, though this may not be admitted in some quarters.[2] Preliminary preparations for the occupation of Germany were far from perfect, and plans drafted frequently proved impractical or at least required substantial modification. But anyone who wants to understand the American occupation must pay some attention to the preparations covering a period of some three years prior to the German surrender and they should also know something of the planning efforts which were made.

SETTING UP AN ORGANIZATION

Shortly after the United States entered World War II a Military Government Section of the Office of Provost Marshal General and a Civil Affairs Division were set up in the War Department. Thus, recognition was given at an early stage to the significance of the problem of administering German territory after it had been taken over by American military forces. There were still numerous officers who saw little or no need for any specialized occupation machinery, maintaining that the old arrangement of assigning tactical troops to handle military government tasks was good enough. However, the more progressive military leaders realized that the far-reaching developments which had brought about the use of specialists in many strictly military areas dictated, or at least made desirable, special arrangements for the administration of occupied areas.[3]

It was not ideal that two agencies should have been set up in the War Department to give attention to such a problem, but conflicting interests and points of view made this unavoidable. Since the Office of Provost Marshal General had responsibility for military police and since the maintenance of order among the civilian population

---

[2] For discussions of the Japanese occupation, see P. W. Buck and J. W. Masland, *The Government of Foreign Powers* (Holt, New York, 1950); E. M. Martin, *The Allied Occupation of Japan* (Stanford University Press, Stanford, Calif., 1948); R. A. Fearey, *The Occupation of Japan* (Macmillan, New York, 1950).

[3] For a discussion of the general problem of basic organization, see G. C. S. Benson and M. D. Howe, "Military Government Organizational Relationships," in C. J. Friedrich and others, *American Experiences in Military Government in World War II* (Rinehart, New York, 1948).

of a vanquished country is a primary task of military government, it was not surprising that the Provost Marshal General argued that his office must have a role in the administering of occupied territory. But military government is far more than merely the agency for maintaining law and order among a civilian population, and consequently it would have been unfortunate had the entire responsibility been left to the Office of Provost Marshal General. Military government, in its broader aspects, was therefore the responsibility of the Civil Affairs Division. With two agencies, there is invariably the problem of defining limits, eliminating friction and duplication of efforts, and the like; and this unhappy situation arose in the case of preparations for the occupation of Germany. The Office of the Provost Marshal General conceived of the task of occupation as a somewhat routine one which was subordinate to the job of military policing; it displayed comparatively little imagination in making preparations, but it zealously guarded its claim to a share in the field. The Civil Affairs Division was in a more favorable position to give adequate consideration to the important task of the problems arising out of the occupation of conquered territory. To begin with, it could focus its attention on this job, since it had no other assignments. Not being a military police agency, it naturally had a broader outlook, a different psychology, and more imagination.[4]

The main task of both the Civil Affairs Division and the Military Government Section of the Office of the Provost Marshal General during the early stage was to set up organizations designed to handle occupational duties in the enemy territories taken over by American military forces. Since no trained personnel was available in a field where there had previously been so specialization, steps had to be taken not only to find suitable persons but to train these officers and men for their jobs.

It was no easy undertaking to find any considerable number of men who had the qualifications desirable for service in this field. There had been a lively scramble for promising human material on the part of Army and Navy agencies responsible for staffing the tactical units. So voracious were the demands of the tactical units that the

---

[4] For an account of this Washington preparation by one who participated, see H. Holborn, *American Military Government: Its Origins and Policies* (Infantry Journal, Washington, 1947).

number of suitable, vigorous, intelligent, and experienced persons was extremely limited when the time came for the Civil Affairs Division and the Military Government Section of the Office of Provost Marshal General to set up an organization to handle the assignment of administering occupied Germany. And as the need was demonstrated for military government and civil affairs specialists in North Africa and requests came to the War Department for expanded numbers of these persons, it was an increasingly thorny problem to locate the manpower needed.

It shortly became apparent that manpower available within the armed forces usually did not possess the qualifications which specialists in the administering of occupied areas should have. The able, well-adjusted, adequately educated, and hard-hitting men had been put to good use by the tactical and existing staff agencies and their supply was always short. Obviously it could hardly be expected that these units would give up their good men for a new organization, particularly for one primarily concerned with the post-surrender period. The various efforts on the part of the Civil Affairs Division and Office of the Provost Marshal General did reveal a considerable number of officers who were available, but their past records did not show them to be particularly valuable. It is not fair to conclude that all of those officers transferred from other military organizations to the new military government-civil affairs setup were either worthless or rather poor material. Actually some of those transferred were square pegs in round holes, so to speak, and while they had not established enviable records in their previous assignments they had a good deal to offer as prospective officers in administering occupied territory. Quite a number of such persons proved their real worth in Germany.

However, there can be no question that some of the later headaches of military government in Germany resulted from the basic weaknesses of the officers who had been taken over from other military units. The embarrassing notoriety given to the military government personnel as living exponents of the slogan "wine, women, and song" grew to no small extent from the original errors in recruiting personnel from the misfits of military service. There were among this group officers who had reasonably high IQs, fairly adequate professional training, and agreeable personalities but little self-control,

8

indifferent moral standards, and a record of failure in their domestic relations and social groups at home. To certain of the officers assigned to military government duties in Germany, the primary motive of military service was an opportunity to get away from the dullness of home and office. From an early stage military government had an unenviable reputation in the more conservative military circles because of the character of the officers assigned to it from other branches of the service. However, it is one thing to be critical of the record of the Civil Affairs Division and the Office of Provost Marshal General in this respect, and quite another to suggest a course that might have avoided the difficulty. By the very nature of the case, the tactical units are going to have first claim on manpower. In addition, it is unlikely that attention would be given to setting up an organization to administer occupied areas until the pressing tactical needs had been met. Here is one of the most serious weaknesses inherent in a staff of military character to administer such territories; it is a principal argument for a civilian organization to handle the job.

Not all of the officers assigned to military government staffs came from the surpluses of officers noted above. It became apparent that the background needed for occupied areas duty was not to be found in sufficient measure within the military services, and a program of recruiting from civilians was undertaken. An attempt was made to find specialists in various fields that had some relation to the administration of an occupied territory and who possessed the vigor and adaptability essential to army life. Thus business executives, public utility engineers, public safety experts, court officials, agricultural specialists, and others were sought out. The difficulty here, of course, was to decide what specialists were needed in an organization designed for administering an occupied area and in what numbers.

Almost at once it became apparent that political and personal pressures were developing which would seek to influence the selection of these specialists, particularly at the higher levels. Commissions as captains might be relatively free from such pressures; but in the case of majors and particularly of lieutenant colonels and full colonels (there were very few of the latter), pressure might be exerted by important politicians and military-politicians to have their friends and followers appointed. Then, too, greater emphasis was sometimes placed on recruiting "big names" than on obtaining specialists,

9

with the result that some of those selected had little professional expertness in the fields which they were supposed to represent. While the commissioning of specialists has much to recommend itself on paper, careful analysis is not needed to perceive that it has certain fundamental weaknesses. In addition to those already mentioned, attention should be focused on the conflict between military and civil demands during the period when the service is to be performed. Granted that the direct commissioning of officers for duties arising out of administering occupied areas can secure the specialist skills needed to a greater extent than any other method—and there will be some difference of opinion here—is it sensible to commission people who will be needed at home as soon as the fighting is over and whose business associates and relatives are in a position to bring strong pressure to have them returned home very shortly after hostilities cease to assume their responsibilities in connection with conversion to a peacetime economy? Anyone even casually familiar with the German occupation will admit that most of the specialist officers in military government had to be returned to the United States long before the main job had been accomplished, and in many instances almost at once after the German surrender, because of the irresistible pressures brought to bear on the military services.

It is apparent, too, from examining the record that more careful attention should have been paid to age and to general physical vigor in commissioning from civil life. No specialist can serve a useful purpose unless he can adjust to military life, and a number of those commissioned from civilian status fell by the wayside after the government had expended what was commonly reported as in excess of $10,000 on their training and maintenance. Some of those in the age group above fifty admirably demonstrated their ability to stand up under military rigors, but the number that had to be sent home on account of bad hearts and other serious maladies before their duties had commenced raises a grave question as to the wisdom of taking specialists beyond the early fifties. The program of commissioning direct from civil life was ended in September 1943.

TRAINING OF PERSONNEL FOR OCCUPATION DUTY

It might have been logical to provide a single system of training occupation staff for service in Germany and elsewhere, but with the

10

divided authority noted above in the case of the Civil Affairs Division and the Office of the Provost Marshal General this was not feasible. A School of Military Government was established on the campus of the University of Virginia at Charlottesville in 1942. Another program was inaugurated later in connection with the Provost Marshal General's center at Fort Custer in Michigan. The latter was supplemented by Civil Affairs Training Schools set up on various campuses, including Harvard, Yale, Pittsburgh, Boston, Michigan, Chicago, Northwestern, Western Reserve, Wisconsin, and Stanford Universities.[5]

The ranks of those sent to the School of Military Government at Charlottesville were in general somewhat higher than those ordered to Fort Custer and the CATS (Civil Affairs Training Schools), and there was some disposition to regard the former as the training center for the top group of military government officers and the latter as the place where the rank and file went.[6] The School of Military Government at Charlottesville had a longer life and certainly received more attention from the top brass than Fort Custer and the CATS—but the preference of top brass for Charlottesville may have resulted at least in part from the proximity to Washington and the superior facilities of the campus of the University of Virginia. As it worked out in practice, there was not a sharp dividing line between the two training systems. Some of the Fort Custer trainees eventually also spent time at Charlottesville. And when it came to the period of operations, there were Fort Custer officers working at the highest levels alongside of Charlottesville graduates and Charlottesville people in the military government detachments along with CATS graduates. Charlottesville had the reputation of being a "gentleman's" school, since lectures and exercises did not start until 8 A.M. and there was no early morning reveille, which at Fort Custer got the trainees out at 6:20 A.M., even in the dead of the winter. Charlottesville officers lived in hotels and private houses which contrasted sharply with the G.I. barracks with their single huge dormitory rooms at Fort Custer.

---

[5] For a discussion of these programs by one who participated in administering them, see C. S. Hyneman, "The Wartime Area and Language Courses," *Bulletin of the American Association of University Professors*, Autumn 1945; and by the same author "The Army's Civil Affairs Training Program," *American Political Science Review*, April 1946.

[6] For additional information relating to this school, see H. C. Beukema, "School for Statesmen," *Fortune*, Jan. 1943, and "Prepare to Occupy," *Fortune*, Feb. 1943.

Considering the limited literature and few official records relating to American occupation experiences in other wars, the training program for officer personnel, as far as lectures and courses went, was not too bad. Colonel L. L. Hunt's report on military government in the Rhineland became a sort of "bible" and, had it been more carefully heeded in practice, at least some of the later mistakes in Germany might have been avoided.[7] Since it was felt that it was not feasible to separate those destined for Germany from those intended for civil affairs assignments in France, Holland, and the liberated countries and military government work elsewhere, much of the training was very general in character rather than focused on Germany. At Charlottesville there were more lectures by university professors who were drawn from the field of public administration and from top brass visiting or stationed in Washington.

At Fort Custer particularly there was a miscellaneous assortment of instruction which may have been justifiable but which covered so large an area in so short a time that much of it probably made little or no impression on the trainees.[8] Thus one or more lectures had to do with the army postal service, airplane identification, military law, army correspondence rules, security, military courtesy, and supply. Since the trainees were army officers, it was expected that they have some knowledge in many fields which often seemed to have little or no bearing on their main assignment. The lectures on military government by Major Charles J. Turck, President of Macalester College, in St. Paul, Minnesota, were, however, not only meaty but interesting. Fort Custer subjected its trainees to instruction in the care of machine guns, rifles, and other weapons—this perhaps resulted from the military police influence—though there was little occasion for more than a very few military government officers to disassemble and care for such weapons later. In both Charlottesville and Fort Custer there was target practice, but in the latter the trainees had to march for several miles to the range while in the former they were driven in vehicles.

Perhaps the greatest weakness of the courses, which at Fort Custer

---

[7] Colonel L. L. Hunt, *American Military Government of Occupied Germany, 1918-1920* (Government Printing Office, Washington, 1943).

[8] This instruction was under the control of Provost Marshal General Allen W. Gullion. Some of his ideas are set down in an article entitled "Military Government," *Coast Artillery Journal*, March-April 1943.

12

consumed six 9-hour days per week and at Charlottesville and the Civil Affairs Training Schools ran to many hours each day, was that the trainees who had entered with only a smattering of knowledge of German history, political, economic, and social institutions, and psychology left with not a great deal more. True, at Charlottesville the teams set up to simulate field or staff detachments might know a good many details about a particular city or district of Germany or about some special problem, but few indeed of the finished products had an adequate knowledge of the people, institutions, or geography of the country which they were to occupy. This lack of a broad and fairly detailed acquaintance with the German problem constituted a serious handicap to the United States efforts throughout the occupation.

The instruction in the German language was a great disappointment.[9] Army representatives extravagantly praised the new scheme of imparting knowledge of foreign languages. By eliminating grammar, concentrating on the spoken language, using native Germans as informants, and so forth, it was claimed that any ordinary person could be given not only a good working knowledge of German but an expert skill in the time allotted. Responsible persons who had the opportunity to observe the records of military government officers in Germany estimated that not more than 5 per cent had sufficient knowledge to understand the German officials with whom they had to deal, to read the German newspapers and reports, and to carry on even the simplest conversation in German and that, for the most part, this 5 per cent had had a knowledge of German before they entered military service. This lack of even a rudimentary understanding of German language was a major handicap to the effective operations which the United States wanted to carry on; but, despite language instruction in the field, the obstacle was never overcome. The American personnel in charge of the occupation of Germany remained little islands apart while they operated in Germany, unable to communicate with the Germans except through interpreters who

---

[9] For various points of view on this instruction, see a series of articles in the *Bulletin of the American Association of University Professors:* R. A. Hall, Jr., "Program and Reaction in Modern Language Teaching," Summer 1945; C. S. Hyneman, "The Wartime Area and Language Courses," Autumn 1945; M. A. Pei, "A Modern Language Teacher Replies," Autumn 1945; and J. S. Diekhoff, "The Mission and Method of Army Language Teaching," Winter 1945.

13

in general were not only inexpert but infrequently unreliable. Many of the errors resulted from this lack of knowledge of the language.

The close-order drill and physical training devised for the prospective military government officers did not represent American military common sense at its best. Most of the officer trainees, who averaged some forty-five years of age, had long passed the stage where they had the muscular coordination essential for superior performance in close-order drill; hence they were usually embarrassed or humiliated at the spectacle they made. They were not to use the familiarity acquired in their work. The argument that any army officer should know the essentials of close-order drill seems a specious one in light of the demeaning effect on the trainees. The physical training program was even less satisfactory. Men whose energy should have been conserved were forced to do miles of marching in January under the frigid conditions existing at that season in Michigan, while young G.I.s rode blithely by in army vehicles. Physical training which was obviously important should have been suitable for men between the ages of 38 and 58, not planned for young men in their late teens and early twenties. Exercises that had men in their fifties struggle under the load of carrying one another about were hardly wisely conceived. It was not surprising that various older officers and some not so old had to be shipped back to the United States because of heart conditions after they reached Britain and France.[10]

THE ARMY SPECIALIZED TRAINING PROGRAM

The Army Specialized Training Program (ASTP) was set up on various university campuses to provide a highly selected group of enlisted men for special programs. The emphasis placed on area studies and languages seemed to indicate that one of the chief purposes was to supply adequate enlisted personnel for occupational duties. Many have attested to the quality of the boys selected for the ASTP units. The course work both in the area studies and in foreign languages was for the most part in charge of the regular staffs of the universities on whose campuses the units were located, and in

---

[10] For a retrospective analysis of the entire training program, see J. B. Mason, "Lessons of Wartime Military Government Training," *Annals of the American Academy of Political and Social Science*, Jan. 1950; and by the same author "Training for A.M.G. Officers," *American Journal of International Law*, July 1944.

general the instruction was more organized and the time allowed more adequate than at Fort Custer or other strictly military camps. A good many of the boys acquired a working knowledge of the language which they studied and, in addition, became reasonably familiar with the geography, institutions, and people of a particular country. The weakness inherent in the program shortly became apparent, however. The group was too good to be reserved for assignments in occupied areas; there were too many pressing demands for their immediate use in tactical units. The net result was that comparatively few of the rather large number of young men trained in the ASTP for service in Germany ever became a part of military government detachments or staffs in Germany. Those who, by some accident, did get to Germany proved distinctly valuable on various scores: their own ability, their knowledge of the German language, and their familiarity with German institutions and psychology. The chief criticism which one heard relating to the ASTP boys in Germany was that they were "too good and knew too much," indicating that in some instances they were superior to the officers in their units.

WAITING FOR ACTIVE DUTY OVERSEAS

Because shipping facilities for sending military government personnel across the Atlantic seemed to be uncertain and to some extent doubtless because the Germans appeared to be softening for speedy collapse, the bulk of the officers trained for occupying Germany were sent overseas early in 1944. Under an arrangement with the British, the extensive facilities of a military college at Shrivenham on the borders of Wiltshire and Berkshire were taken over for military government and civil affairs personnel destined for Germany and elsewhere in Europe. Here training of a sort continued, but it was for the most part so poor in quality that it probably did more harm than good. Language instruction was provided under the direction of amateurs who were themselves members of the group and usually had German origins. These instructors took themselves more seriously than professional teachers and had their own strong likes and dislikes in such matters as pronunciation. After the military government officers had been exposed to several of these, they were often so confused that they gave up any serious thought of mastering the

15

German language. Perhaps the most valuable part of the instructional program at Shrivenham was carried out under the direction of Major Arthur Bromage, a professor of political science before and after the war at the University of Michigan. The officers were organized into "American" and "enemy" teams in order to try their hands at simulating action after arrival in the field.

Perhaps the most important development during the stay at Shrivenham was the drawing up of a system of military government detachments and staff units and the assignment of individual officers to these units. Many changes were of course made from time to time, and detachments for specific *Länder*, *Regierungsbezirke*, cities, and counties were later increased or decreased in size. Also individuals once assigned to the detachment designed for *Land* X might be transferred to the detachment responsible for *Stadtkreis* W. However, despite changes which were later made, here was an organization, largely on paper it is true, for occupying the states, districts, cities, and counties of the American Zone in Germany. To begin with, many of the units, planned as mixed units, were made up of both British and American personnel. American officers were tentatively assigned to units under British control, and British officers were assigned to units under American control. The American units were brought together in an organization known as the ECAD, the European Civil Affairs Division, which was to serve as an agency for keeping personnel records and furnishing supplies, though not as a command headquarters.

With most of the officers assigned to detachments by the late spring of 1944, there was an exodus from Shrivenham to Manchester and Eastbourne. The American-commanded military government units took over a building in downtown Manchester and here they continued their training, focusing attention on the particular state, district, city, or county in Germany for which they had been pinpointed. American officers assigned to work with the British joined similar units in Eastbourne. As the Allied invasion forces moved inland from the beaches in France, civil affairs detachments assigned to duty in France crossed over, and some of the units earmarked for eventual service in Germany were given temporary assignments in France. By the fall of 1944, transfer of military government detachments earmarked for Germany to the Continent had been completed,

16

and those with no immediate responsibilities in France were sent to an old chateau some distance from Paris to await developments in Germany. Here they spent a miserable winter and early spring. Officers over fifty years of age were quartered on the bare floors of the unheated chateau; those under fifty lived in tents in the grounds of the chateau, enduring the cold and wet weather as best they could. Due to the exposure which some had undergone during a period of a month or more in moving from England to France, a number of the officers did not survive these hardships and had to be sent home. As a part of a military organization, such an experience was not unusual, but it raises the question as to whether it would not have been wiser to set up teams for administering occupied areas on a civilian basis following the pattern of the Office of Strategic Services (OSS). Military personnel could then have been employed along with civilians, and the entire organization could have been closely aligned to the military by the appointment of a military officer as head. With an age group averaging in the mid-forties, such an arrangement might have avoided much of the waste which characterized the existing setup, and it would have permitted a flexibility which might have served a useful purpose.

The chief problem of military government personnel during this waiting period was, however, not one of enduring a cold French winter but rather one of general morale. Military government-civil affairs, in their infancy, had been the "bright-haired boy" in the United States. Widespread publicity had featured the exciting and crusading work to be done; and a good many had entered with the idea that, after somewhat prosaic lives at home or in other military organizations, they would be plunged into the midst of highly stimulating, if not romantic, activities. The training period belied these promises to some extent, but it could be argued away as a sort of novitiate which would lead to better things. Moving across the Atlantic these "better things" were expected to materialize shortly if not at once, but instead there was the long wait. The training program was a stale and inferior replica of what had already proved rather dull at home. The process of screening to determine assignment to specific detachments required some weeks, and many were disappointed at the results in their own cases. Then there was additional waiting which sometimes went on month after month for a

17

year or so. Had the officers been free-agents and able to use this period of waiting to see the country, they might have whiled away the time without too great difficulty, but they were military bodies and subject to military discipline. Conditions in England and France were far from normal, and large numbers of military personnel should not be roaming about and exploring the countryside. So the military government officers, accustomed to more than ordinary activity as men of affairs at home and a large measure of freedom to determine their movements, found themselves in a more or less impossible situation.

Had the top brass in charge of the military government officers had more imagination and experience, some of the trouble might have been avoided. Certainly the close-order drill, the elaborate parades before visiting generals, the long marches with packs under officers who could command little or no respect because of their weak characters and poor professional attainments did little to improve the morale. General Eisenhower made an important contribution by taking time from his heavy duties shortly before "D-Day" to visit Shrivenham and talk to the officers in an informal fashion about their significant role, explaining the necessity of putting up with the long waiting period.

But in the last analysis the situation, by its very nature, was bound to result in badly damaged morale. After weary months of twiddling their thumbs, many officers lost all interest in any service in Germany and could think only of getting back to their real work in the United States at the earliest possible time. In many cases this attitude became a fixed one which was never altered and which of course had anything but a good affect on the record in Germany.

THE GERMAN COUNTRY UNIT

Attention thus far has been given to setting up a military government organization in the War Department and recruiting and training officers and men for the task of administering occupied Germany. The work to be done by this organization had to be planned, since military government personnel could hardly be expected to proceed without instructions after arriving in Germany. Some attention was doubtless given to the job to be done in Germany by the Civil Affairs Division of the War Department and to a lesser extent by the Military Government Section of the Office of the Provost Marshal General, but these offices were primarily concerned with setting up the machinery already noted. Perhaps the most important contribution made by Washington was the Army manual dealing with military government. This was not specially focused on Germany and, being a manual, did not contain many details, but it did offer general guidance.[11]

Much of the specific planning for the occupation of Germany was left to the field rather than undertaken by Washington. A Combined Civil Affairs Committee and the Supreme Headquarters of the Allied Expeditionary Forces (SHAEF) through its G-5 division had given only slight attention to the planning of the occupation of Germany due to insufficient time and staff. The fact that SHAEF was primarily an operating agency for ousting the Germans from Western Europe made it difficult for its G-5 (civil affairs-military government) division to spend a great deal of time on planning for the occupation. To meet this situation the German Country Unit, at times a special staff of SHAEF and again an organization more or less dangling in thin air, was set up.

Early in 1944 the German Country Unit started its work in Shrivenham, the center for military government-civil affairs personnel noted earlier. With approximately 150 American and British officers and a corresponding complement of enlisted men, the German Country Unit was organized to parallel the structure of the German government. Its function was to draft plans to control the various German ministries as well as regional and local German governments. To begin with, it proceeded on the assumption that the occupation would be a joint Allied affair, using the German government as an instrument. This was before the decision to divide Germany into national zones: at a time when it seemed that there would be a going German government to control. There was little in the way of policy directives from either Washington or London, and queries frequently went unanswered because of preoccupation with the winning of the war and the approaching "D-Day."[12] Never-

---

[11] War Department, *Field Manual 27-5 Rules of Land Warfare* (Washington, 1940).

[12] For a discussion of the problems encountered by one who participated, see Dale Clark, "Conflicts over Planning at Staff Headquarters," in C. J. Friedrich and others, *American Experiences in Military Government in World War II* (Rinehart, New York, 1948).

19

theless, it made a very serious effort to perform its work and actually succeeded in drafting a series of plans which had a considerable bearing on the actual occupation of Germany. Many modifications had to be made due to the breakdown of the Allied Control Authority,* the more or less autonomous role of the national military governments, and the fanaticism of the Nazis which led to the destruction of the German government apparatus. However, it is significant to note the degree of similarity between what was planned by the German Country Unit and what actually was done by the western occupying powers after the initial period.

The plans prepared by the German County Unit were constructive rather than negative in character, though certainly not based on an "easy" concept of occupation.[13] Recognizing the futility of a revenge policy, the plans followed a middle course designed to liquidate war industries but also to get German economy back on its feet to the extent necessary to feed and otherwise support the German population. A food ration of 2,000 calories per day for the German people was set as a goal; food experts regarded this as the minimum caloric intake for an individual not engaged in unusual activity.

The experiences of the German Country Unit can contribute much to those concerned with the general problem of military government or administering occupied areas. To begin with, they illustrate the difficulties of attempting to get policy decisions from top-level political authorities in periods of war. Despite their professions of interest and their promises to furnish policy guidance, presidents, prime ministers, and other top political officials find it difficult, if not impossible, to consider what comes after the fighting during actual conflict. Much can be said about "We won the war only to lose the peace," but the very nature of a major conflict seems to make it impossible for top political officials, who must finally decide such matters, to give serious consideration to postwar problems. Thus, planning for an occupation tends to be like work done in a vacuum—it takes on too much of the artificial and is too far removed from the scene of reality. Such planning usually makes little allowance for political pressures such as were brought by the White-Morgenthau group on the President and Congress and consequently

---

* See pp. 98, 107.
[13] These are set forth in *Handbook for Military Government in Germany.*

20

may be put aside more or less completely. However, since military occupations have to deal with concrete situations even when home-lands are more or less gripped by a Morgenthau Plan, such plans, even if formally set aside, may have considerable practical influence. Of less consequence, perhaps, the experiences of the German Country Unit indicate how little skill corporation executives, prominent law-yers, and other men of affairs have in preparing papers, organizing data, and getting their thoughts down on paper in a form intelligible to others. Perhaps there has rarely been a reasonably high-level organization where low-ranking university professors were more ap-preciated and sought than in the German Country Unit. This obvi-ously had nothing to do with any love for university professors as such, but their ability to sift data, organize reports, and write papers which could be understood made them distinctly valuable in an organization made up so largely of men of affairs accustomed at home to have subordinates to do such work for them.

The *Handbook for Military Government in Germany*, prepared by the German Country Unit, went through three editions before it was "cast aside" by President Franklin D. Roosevelt, as far as the United States was concerned, after a "little bird" in the form of the White-Morgenthau emissary, Colonel B. Bernstein, had flown a copy of the last revised edition to Washington. Nevertheless, it was shortly issued unofficially for the use of military government personnel after a few minor changes had been made by G-5 of SHAEF. In addition to this general basic set of plans, various subdivisions of the German Country Unit got out functional manuals dealing with public safety, local and regional governments, etc., which served a useful purpose.

THE EUROPEAN ADVISORY COMMISSION

Since the German Country Unit was strictly a military agency and had neither a political division nor representatives of the Amer-ican State Department or the British Foreign Office on its staff, ar-rangements had to be made for political planning elsewhere. For this purpose a smaller body known as the European Advisory Com-mission (EAC) was set up in London in 1944. Ambassador John G. Winant represented the United States on this commission; the British government was represented by Sir William Strang; and the Russian

GERMANY: Zones of Occupation

government by Ambassador F. T. Gusev. Each representative had a political adviser to assist him and a number of staff members furnished by State Department or Foreign Office. Much of the work for the American delegation was in charge of Philip E. Mosely, later a professor at Columbia University.[14]

Although many matters relating to the occupation of Germany by the Allies were discussed, concrete accomplishment was difficult, particularly because the Russian attitude differed from that of the Americans and British.[15] Only three basic agreements were finally completed by EAC. The first, entitled "Declaration Regarding the Defeat of Germany," was the most comprehensive and was intended to be issued in Berlin by the Allied Commanders in Chief after victory had been assured. It provided for four zones in a defeated Germany rather than a joint Allied administration and contained numerous provisions for the recognition on the part of the Germans of unlimited control by the Allies in political, military, economic, financial, and other matters.[16] The second, also in the form of a proclamation to be issued by the military commanders in Berlin, provided for the almost absolute authority of the national commanders in the national zones subject only to their unanimous agreement in matters involving Germany as a whole. The third dealt with the boundaries of the zones and the setting up of Berlin as a little island within the Soviet Zone to be administered by the military forces of the occupying powers.

The three agreements drawn up by the EAC were discussed at Yalta and approved by the Russians, British, and American representatives. French participation in the occupation of Germany was provided at Yalta. Though small in number, the agreements worked out by the European Advisory Commission prior to the German sur-

---

[14] For valuable articles by Mr. Mosely, see "Dismemberment of Germany," *Foreign Affairs*, April 1950, and "The Occupation of Germany: New Light on How the Zones Were Drawn," *Foreign Affairs*, July 1950.

[15] In his autobiography published in London in 1956 Lord Strang expresses a more favorable view, maintaining that the gulf separating the Russians from the West was less formidable at this time than later and that the general prospects for agreement were more promising than at any other period in his career. See *Home and Abroad* (Deutsch, London, 1956), p. 208.

[16] For a critical discussion of the plan to divide Germany into four zones, see J. Viner, "Treatment of Germany," *Foreign Affairs*, July 1945.

render were of great significance and had an important bearing on the occupation record following 1945.[17]

THE U. S. GROUP, CONTROL COUNCIL FOR GERMANY

With the winding up of the German Country Unit in the late summer and early fall of 1944 and the decision to set up national planning groups to take over its work, the United States authorized the establishment of the U. S. Group, Control Council for Germany. General Cornelius W. Wickersham was sent to London to head this organization and it began to function in the late summer of 1944, though not formally activated until October. It took over many of the American officers and enlisted men who had served with the German Country Unit and in addition received a number of State Department personnel. Unlike the German Country Unit, it had a political affairs subdivision staffed by the State Department. Starting out with some 150 officers and 250 enlisted men, the U. S. Group, Control Council for Germany took over planning where the German Country Unit left off. Although the European Theatre of Operations had recommended to Washington that the new American planning and eventual military government headquarters group should be organized to parallel the structure of German government, as had been the case in the German Country Unit, this was not done by the Joint Chiefs of Staff. Difficulties resulted which interfered with effective operations for many months and indeed plagued the group throughout its existence. For example, no provision was made for subdivisions dealing with regional and local government, civil service, and so forth, despite the considerable importance of such fields.

When the U. S. Group, Control Council for Germany moved from near London to Versailles in the spring of 1945, it had some 250 officers and more than 400 enlisted men. As the time came for it to assume actual administrative duties in Germany instead of simply planning for the occupation, it increased its staff, and after moving to Höchst, near Frankfurt, in May and June 1945, it shot up to the point where it had some 2,000 officers and more than 4,000 enlisted

---

[17] The problems confronting this body are dealt with in *Report on the Work of the European Advisory Commission* (London, 1945), and State Department, *Foreign Relations of the U. S., Diplomatic Papers, 1945*, "The Conferences at Malta and Yalta," (Washington, 1955).

men. Large numbers of colonels were added as well as some general officers, and many civilians were brought in from the United States to join such subdivisions as those dealing with trade and industry, food and agriculture, and legal affairs.

3

American Military Government Organization in Germany

In the preceding chapter attention has been given to the military-government-civil-affairs machinery set up by the United States at home and in Great Britain and France prior to the actual occupation of Germany. Not all of this of course was designed or intended for use in Germany, but Germany bulked large in such preparations. At the planning level there was the U. S. Group, Control Council for Germany which operated for some months in London and in Versailles before moving to Germany shortly after the German surrender. Below there were the military government detachments designed to take over occupational duties in specific localities in Germany, though last-minute shifts actually prevented many of these from being used where originally intended. In this chapter an attempt will be made to survey the elaborate American military government organization which was developed from these foundations during the years 1945-1949. It may be stated, at the outset, that it is not a simple matter to present anything like a clear picture of this structure because of the many changes that took place from time to time.

U. S. GROUP, CONTROL COUNCIL FOR GERMANY AND G-5, USFET

The U. S. Group, Control Council for Germany, activated in London in the autumn of 1944, was intended for a dual purpose: to serve as an American planning agency prior to the actual occupation of Germany and subsequently to assume a place as the top-level military government headquarters of the United States in Germany. With this in mind, it was built up from a rather small organization of a few hundred, suitable for planning, to a large organization of several thousand designed to supervise the military government of the United

26

States in Germany. In its earlier phase it was commanded by General C. W. Wickersham; but, as it moved toward operational responsibilities, General Lucius D. Clay took over command in his capacity as Deputy Military Governor. Located first at Höchst, a suburb of Frankfurt, the U. S. Group, Control Council for Germany moved to Berlin in the summer of 1945.

In its operational phase the U. S. Group, Control Council for Germany was a rather untried and over-large agency which had been transformed in a brief period from a comparatively small planning group. Even General Clay at this time did not quite know what his position and responsibilities were. As noted earlier, it was constructed to suit the fancies of arm-chair experts in Washington rather than in accordance with the recommendations of officers in the European Theatre who had had experience in dealing with operations in the field. Thus, while it had three sizable subdivisions labeled "Army," "Navy," and "Air Force," respectively, it had no subdivision charged with the main job of dealing with the German governmental structure. The latter responsibility was supposed to be handled by sections of the Internal Affairs and Communications Division which also included education, religious affairs, the post office, telephones, telegraph, and so forth. But a Political Affairs Division representing the State Department also had a role here. There was a sizable Economics Division, despite the limitations imposed by JCS 1067. A Legal Division not only gave attention to the obliteration of Nazi legislation but advised the other divisions and of course the Military Governor on legal questions. A Manpower Division was intended to assist in the building up of democratic German labor unions and a Transport Division had the responsibility of seeing what could be done to get the badly damaged transportation services into operation again. A Finance Division dealt with the complicated currency problem as well as such matters as taxes, the banking system, and insurance. A Prisoners of War and Displaced Persons Division handled the emergency problems presented by prisoners of war and the multitude of displaced persons in Germany. Finally, there was an Information Control Division.

A large part of the U. S. Group, Control Council for Germany had little, at least directly, to do with military government. An Administrative Service Division at times seemed to overshadow the subdivisions charged with dealing with German affairs. A Chief of Staff, a Personnel Officer (with many assistants, of course), a Control Officer, a Secretary General, an Adjutant General, an Intelligence Division, and a Public Relations Division all enjoyed substantial authority and usually had sizable staffs. Some of them seemed indeed to be able to get personnel even if the subdivisions directly in charge of the occupation went without.

With the U. S. Group, Control Council for Germany in Berlin and consequently at some distance from the American Zone, there was pressure to build a separate military government organization as part of the American military headquarters in Frankfurt. G-5 of the U. S. Forces, European Theatre (USFET), shortly came to a position where it looked upon itself as the chief military government agency of the United States in Germany, regarding the U. S. Group, Control Council for Germany as a rival, an interloper, and even something of an enemy. It was the contention of G-5, USFET that it had full responsibility for military government matters within the American Zone and that the U. S. Group, Control Council for Germany was limited to relations with the Russians, British, and French and to those aspects of military government which would be handled on a uniform basis throughout Germany by the Allied Control Authority. The U. S. Group, Control Council for Germany did not, of course, accept such an interpretation of its role, and indeed its organization was far more elaborate than was required for such an assignment. During the early months of the occupation, friction between the two agencies developed which had a serious effect on the operations of both. Instead of concentrating on the main job to be done, both groups expended great amounts of energy on attempting to offset the other and to gain the upper hand. There was much duplication of effort, and the fight raged so furiously at times that the field organizations were more or less left to their own devices at a period when their problems were pressing and they needed all of the guidance and assistance they could obtain.

This unfortunate situation was permitted to go on for several months, though it must have been clearly apparent to Generals Eisenhower and W. Bedell Smith, as well as to the top-level people in Washington. The early months of the occupation were of course hectic ones, and there were many pressing problems demanding the attention of the top brass. The fact that there was a sort of vacuum in Washington resulting from the death of President Franklin D. Roosevelt doubtless contributed to the lack of attention to this important problem. The rather indefinite character of the appointment given to General Clay played an important part in this involved situation—he of course was fully aware of the conflict, but until he could work out his own relationship to the complex military headquarters which the United States maintained in the European Theatre it was difficult to do anything about it. However, by the fall of 1945 General Clay was sufficiently established to exert his influence, and the general situation was such that something had to be done. The result was that the G-5 section of the USFET was, except for small subdivisions necessary to be on the spot in Frankfurt, moved to Berlin and merged with the U. S. Group, Control Council for Germany into an Office of Military Government of the United States for Germany, ordinarily known simply as OMGUS.[1]

OMGUS

The Office of Military Government of the United States for Germany (OMGUS) had a life of approximately four years, remaining until it was supplanted by the Office of the U. S. High Commissioner for Germany (HICOG) in the latter part of 1949. It had the dual responsibility of representing the United States in relations with the other Allies in the Allied Control Authority and of supervising military government activities in the American Zone. Its headquarters remained in Berlin until the summer of 1949, but, as the Allied Control Authority demonstrated its inherent weakness and it was increasingly apparent that little could be accomplished on a quadripartite basis, more and more of the work of OMGUS was done in the American Zone. This necessitated shifting some of the personnel from Berlin to Frankfurt, Nuremberg, and other places within the American Zone.

Although never as sizable as the British Control Commission,* OMGUS was a large organization, made up of some 12,000 officers and enlisted men from the American military forces and increasingly

---

[1] For a discussion of the organization problems at this period, see H. J. Heneman, "American Control Organization in Germany," *Public Administration Review*, Feb. 1946.

* It was reported to have some 25,000 members at its peak.

of civilians brought in from the United States.† Because of the distance involved and the high level of salaries in the United States, more reliance was placed on the use of German staff than was the case with either the British or French military government in Germany. This must be taken into account in estimating the size of OMGUS. American officials frequently boasted of being able to do the job in Germany with distinctly smaller staffs than their Allies,

OFFICE OF MILITARY GOVERNMENT FOR GERMANY (OMGUS)

AS OF MARCH, 1946

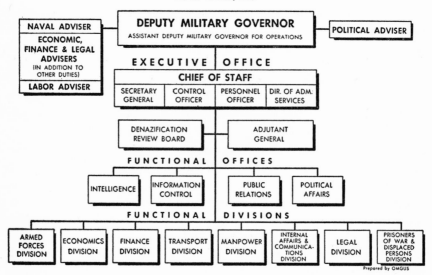

and certainly the American staff in OMGUS was perhaps no more than one half the size of the British staff in the British Control Commission for Germany. But the United States employed substantially larger numbers of Germans in its military government in Germany than did its Allies, and if these are added to the total strength the difference becomes much less. The larger population of the British Zone and particularly its highly industrialized character also entered into the picture. It may be added that the American use of German civilians throughout the occupation was not the result of any prefer-

† At the end of December 1945, its highest point, it had some 12,000 members, but was later reduced in size.

ence for Germans but rather the outgrowth of what appeared to be necessity. Funds available for bringing American civilian personnel from the United States were not adequate to meet the needs; hence German civilians paid for out of occupation costs or counterpart funds had to be depended upon for many services.[2] A strict application of the security rules of the United States would have precluded any such wide-scale use—foreign employees were not supposed to be employed in offices where documents classified higher than "restricted" were used. But necessity prevailed over security regulations and Germans were depended on in all except the few offices where security considerations were paramount.

Although civilians became more numerous than military personnel before OMGUS came to an end, it should be borne in mind that this organization remained a *military* organization throughout its existence. It was commanded by a professional military man, General Clay, except at the very end when it was being wound up— during this interim period Mr. John J. McCloy held the post of Military Governor. Its administrative and control staff was largely made up of military personnel. Even if high posts in OMGUS were held by civilians, papers ordinarily had to pass up through the channels which were controlled by military regulations and staffed by military men. Many of the policies of the United States in Germany were more intimately related to the State Department than to the armed services and SWNCC, the State, War, Navy Coordinating Committee, which formulated many of the policies, was headed by an Assistant Secretary of State. However, the policy decisions were not transmitted directly to the American Commanders in Germany: they had to be sent to the War Department where their contents were incorporated into military directives to be sent from the Pentagon to the field commander. In this process there was opportunity for modification and it was frequently alleged that the directives sent to Germany were different not only in wording and detail but in important aspects from the policy decisions arrived at in SWNCC and its successor and approved by the State Department. Moreover, it had become the established tradition to accord high-ranking military

---

[2] For further discussion, see J. F. J. Gillen, *The Employment of German Nationals by the Office of the U. S. High Commissioner for Germany*, in the Historical Series of the Office of the U. S. High Commissioner in Germany (1952). Chap. 1 deals with the military government period.

commanders in the field a considerable degree of leeway in interpreting directives from Washington. This gave General Clay an opportunity to follow his own discretion to an extent which could hardly be imagined in the case of a nonmilitary administration.

Apparently some persons assumed that since there was no change in name of the American military government organization in Germany from late 1945 to the latter part of 1949, the internal structure remained static. Actually it is quite erroneous to imagine that the internal organization remained unchanged. Indeed the changes were such that it is difficult to obtain anything like a clear overall picture—one may know the organization chart in early 1946, for example, but be quite unfamiliar with the setup in 1948 or 1949. In a military government organization such as OMGUS, fairly frequent modifications in structure are inevitable even if there is continuity in direction, as under General Clay. After a major defeat conditions may be expected to change rapidly in an occupied country; and such changes are, to some extent at least, likely to be reflected in the structure of the military government organization. Pressures at home may lead to political sensitiveness which, in turn, will necessitate modifications—the radical change made in the status of education may be cited as an example. Even international developments may play a role in effecting changes in organization: deteriorating relations with the Russians and the desire to cultivate the Germans as allies certainly had a bearing on the reconstruction of American military government in Germany. In looking back it is difficult to reach any definite conclusion as to whether the changes made in OMGUS were about what one would expect under the circumstances or whether they went beyond that point. At the time, many of those who served on OMGUS staffs had the feeling that changes were too frequent if not too drastic in character: the personnel in a certain subdivision would no sooner become familiar with their duties than a change would require new patterns. This seemed wasteful and a serious obstacle to efficiency. However, it must be admitted that personnel involved in changes often do not see the entire picture and consequently do not fully realize why modifications have to be undertaken.

Like its predecessor, the U. S. Group, Control Council for Germany, OMGUS, to begin with, was handicapped by its failure to

32

base its organization on the job to be done in Germany. Thus, while it had the ubiquitous Legal and Economic Divisions, it lacked a governmental affairs subdivision and an education and cultural relations subdivision with major status. An Armed Forces Division, an Intelligence Division, and the usual complex administrative services, control, personnel, and secretarial subdivisions were invariably provided. But at the beginning, there was a most unsatisfactory Internal Affairs and Communications Division which violated almost every canon of public administration.

Throughout its life OMGUS maintained a Political Affairs Division. But the precise division of authority between this and the Office of the Political Adviser was, at least at times, not well defined and in general not too satisfactory. The Political Adviser was supposed to represent the State Department, while the Office or Division of Political Affairs was theoretically a more integral subdivision of OMGUS. Since the staff of the latter were very largely drawn from the State Department and the Foreign Service, it was actually difficult, if not impossible, to differentiate between the two. The staff of neither had too much freedom from the eagle eye and strong opinions of General Clay, but at the same time they never became quite the captives which corresponding officials on General MacArthur's staff in Japan were said to be. The representatives of the State Department in Germany, for example, might have little influence on General Clay, though on occasion they were able to ward off some particularly unwise decision; but they at least had direct communications with the State Department and could keep that department acquainted with developments. In Japan General MacArthur insisted that all communications from State Department personnel pass across his desk and only those were transmitted which he approved of—thus Washington might have little factual knowledge of what was going on in American military government in Japan.

Perhaps the most important developments within OMGUS during 1945-1949 were those setting up new major divisions to handle governmental affairs and education and cultural relations and the gradual transformation of the personnel from almost exclusively military to numerically civilian predominance. The most serious weakness of the U. S. Group, Control Council for Germany and of early OMGUS was probably the lack of a major subdivision to give

33

attention to German government reconstruction. The step to set up a Governmental Affairs or Civil Administration Division in OMGUS was thus of first-rate significance. Critics of the U. S. educational program in Germany may well feel that it was not necessary to have a major subdivision of OMGUS to handle educational and cultural relations. However, if one admits the more than nominal importance of education and cultural relations as military government activities, then it is clear that the addition of an Education and Cultural Relations Division to OMGUS was desirable.

REGIONAL MILITARY GOVERNMENT ORGANIZATION

During the first months of the occupation the Armies which the United States maintained in Germany were used as the basis for a regional military government organization. Before that, Army Group headquarters had some importance, but they were very shortly dismantled and the Armies, through their G-5 sections, then handled military government in their territories. The American Zone was divided into an eastern and a western district, with the Third Army in charge of the former and the Seventh Army responsible for the latter. The commanders of these Armies held positions as district military governors along with their tactical titles. The headquarters of the eastern district was located in or near Munich, and that of the western district at Heidelberg.

These were the days when great emphasis was placed on using tactical command channels, and military government therefore did not have its own channels. Orders relating to military government had to be routed from the U. S. Group, Control Council for Germany or OMGUS through the Office of the Commander of USFET to the headquarters of Army Groups (as long as they existed) and on to the Armies. Each step permitted redrafting of directives and some modification in content. The directives relating to military government which finally reached military government units in the field were sometimes not only delayed but quite different in content from the original policy. Field units had to follow the same round-about and time-consuming route, sending a request for assistance through their local tactical military commanders, up through division, possibly corps, to Army headquarters, from thence to Army Group and

34

USFET and to OMGUS. It is no wonder that many such requests never reached their destination and that the field relations with military government headquarters were far from intimate. Nor could personal representatives from OMGUS ordinarily accomplish a great deal, since they too had to observe the cumbersome traditions of getting permission from Army Group and Army headquarters to visit within the areas of the latter and clearing every step taken with these headquarters.

This almost impossible arrangement fortunately came to an early end—otherwise the tribulations of American military government in Germany would have been far greater than they were. The closing of the Army Group headquarters brought the Armies more closely into relationship with OMGUS. The provision that the Army should be the lowest tactical unit for control of military government eliminated the corps and the division at least in theory from the channels. The last days of 1945 saw the abandonment of command channels in military government and the establishment of technical channels which permitted direct communication between military government agencies. The deactivation of the Seventh Army and the moving of the Third Army out of Germany made it possible for OMGUS to set up regional offices of military government directly under its own control in Bavaria, Württemberg-Baden, Greater Hesse, and Bremen.

The *Land* military government offices remained vital units in the administration of military government from late 1945 until the end of military government in 1949. There was too great a distance between OMGUS and the local military government units to permit direct administrative control, and the military government offices at the *Land* level consequently served as an intermediary. They received directives, materials, and the like from OMGUS and transmitted these, where appropriate, to the local detachments. They also received reports, requests for information, and so forth, from the latter to be forwarded to OMGUS. In addition, they performed the very useful function of supervising and coordinating the work of military government at the operating level. Finally, they were the instruments through which OMGUS maintained contact, issued directives, and gave oversight to the German system of government. To begin with, the local military government detachments had been permitted to give orders to the German governments which they paralleled, but this made it impossible to establish an effective system of German government up through the *Land* level and consequently OMGUS decided that orders for the various German governments should be transmitted only through the *Land* military government offices to the German *Land* governments. The latter then sent orders down to the lesser German governments.

The military government offices at the *Land* level were under *Land* military governors and their organization in general paralleled that of OMGUS. Since the populations, areas, and problems of the *Länder* varied considerably, it was necessary to take this into account in setting up the *Land* offices of military government. Bavaria, with some eight million people, obviously required a larger and more specialized *Land* office of military government than Bremen with its half million or so inhabitants gathered together within the confines of a single city. In addition to the usual administrative offices, the *Land* offices of military government always included subdivisions dealing with political affairs, economic matters, legal problems, education, food, intelligence, and public relations. Except in Bremen, agriculture was provided for. Labor might be separate or included with trade and industry under economic affairs. Special provision might be made for finance or it might be placed under economic affairs. As the exchanges program got under way, each *Land* office of military government had an exchanges officer. At least to begin with, there were usually, if not always, subdivisions dealing with the special problems of refugees and displaced persons and archives, monuments, and fine arts. In Bremen provision was made for ships and fishing. Ordinarily there were to be found specialists in the fields of public safety, public works, public utilities, religious affairs, transportation, posts, telegraph, and telephone, public welfare, and the like. While the size of the *Land* offices of military government varied from period to period, the largest one for Bavaria at its height had a staff of several hundred persons.

MILITARY GOVERNMENT ORGANIZATION IN THE FIELD

As pointed out in the preceding chapter, plans were made before the German surrender to organize the rank and file of military gov-

36

ernment personnel into detachments. Such detachments were actually formed in large numbers, at least on paper, with attention being given plans for taking over a specific German city, county, district, or state. Many changes of course took place after this job had been undertaken in England about a year before the actual surrender. A good many replacements were necessitated as officers transferred to other areas, failed to survive the rigors of the winter spent under canvas in France, or for other reasons were not available for service when the time came to take over a German "pinpoint." And after the surrender, when great pressure resulted in large numbers of the military government specialists being returned to the United States to resume civilian status, wholesale replacements and reorganizations were required. Nevertheless, the work done in organizing field detachments before the German surrender served a useful purpose.

To begin with, four types of military government detachments were provided for: A, B, C, and D. Later it was found desirable to organize five different types of detachment and these were labeled "E," "F," "G," "H," and "I".

The A (later E) detachments were the largest and most specialized. Their number was never large, since they were intended to take over the sizable units of German government, including *Länder* (states), *Provinzen* (provinces of Prussia), and in a few instances large *Stadkreise* (cities). Although some of these detachments finally had several hundred officers and enlisted personnel assigned or attached to them, they were originally organized on the basis of approximately 30 officers and 50 enlisted men. A senior military government officer, holding the rank of colonel, commanded each of these detachments. Each A (E) detachment also had a deputy to the commanding officer, an executive officer, administrative officers, officers to handle displaced persons and enemy property, and various functional officers to deal with the administrative agencies of the German government to be supervised. Since each of these detachments was tailored to fit a particular German government, there was naturally some variation among the functional officers. Thus, a detachment earmarked to take over a port city had an officer or officers who were specialists on harbors; a detachment intended to control a *Land* where forestry was an important industry was given a forestry officer; a *Land* where

37

mining played an important role was assigned one or more mining specialists; and so forth. The A (E) detachments invariably included specialist officers in the fields of public safety, public health, government and administration, food, public finance, banking, insurance, public works, public utilities, courts and legal system, education, religious affairs, transportation, communications, trade and industry, and monuments, fine arts, and archives.

The expertness of the specialist officers assigned or attached to the military government detachments varied a great deal, but many of the original assignees at least possessed a high degree of competence in their fields. The education officer usually had to take on religious affairs as a sideline, it is true; and monuments, fine arts, and archives did not always have well-trained personnel because of the difficulty of finding persons with such background in the military services. As the detachments mushroomed after V-E Day and doubled and tripled in size, the general level of competence deteriorated because of the use of surplus tactical officers and others with little or no specialized training and the departure of many of the specialists for home.

The B (F) detachments did not differ a great deal from the A (E) detachments in size and specialization. Originally consisting of some 25 officers and about twice that number of enlisted men, they, too, increased rapidly in strength after V-E Day and at the top frequently had from 50 to 75 officers assigned or attached and 100 or more enlisted men. Designed to take over *Regierungsbezirke* (districts) and large *Stadtkreise* (cities), these detachments had the same provisions for commanding officers and executive and administrative officers as the A (E) detachments, but their functional officers were somewhat less numerous. Tailored to fit the needs of a particular German district or city, they might or might not include a specialist to deal with a specific major industry, but they always included trade and industry officers. In addition to displaced persons and enemy property officers, they, too, had specialists on food, education, finance, public utilities, public safety, public health, courts and legal system, and so forth. Their specialists might be somewhat less experienced than those assigned to the A (E) detachments.

The C (G) detachments marked a considerable drop in strength and specialization from the A (E) and B (F) detachments. They started out with approximately a dozen officers and perhaps 20 enlisted men and jumped to 30 or so officers and 50 or more enlisted men after taking over. Intended to administer medium-sized *Stadtkreise* (cities), smaller *Regierungsbezirke* (districts), and a few of the largest *Kreise* (counties), they had the same general organization as the larger detachments but fewer functional officers. They ordinarily claimed specialists in public safety, public health, trade and industry, finance, and legal matters; but they were less likely to have other specialists, though being planned to meet the needs of a given German government there was some variation among them.

The smallest and by far the most numerous detachments were originally designated "D" and later broken down into two types known as "H" and "I." H detachments ordinarily had six officers and perhaps ten enlisted men assigned, while I detachments consisted of four officers and half a dozen or so enlisted men. As in the case of the other detachments, they increased in size after taking over, but usually shot up less spectacularly, generally doubling in strength. One officer in both types of detachment served as commanding officer, while a second had the responsibility of being assistant to the commander, performing administrative duties, and handling government organization problems. Detachments of this size could of course do little in the way of specialization, and each officer other than the two noted above found himself confronted with several areas of the German government controlled. One ordinarily devoted himself to public safety and possibly denazification; in rural areas food and agriculture usually occupied the full attention of one officer. As the strength increased, more attention was given to denazification, and one or more officers might devote themselves to displaced persons and refugees. Both the H and I detachments were designed to take over the rural counties (*Kreise*) and the small cities (*Stadtkreise*), the H being earmarked for those of larger size.

The military government detachments described above performed essential services during the early days of the occupation, but they did not prove as lasting as OMGUS or the *Land* offices of military government. When they arrived at their destinations, they usually found emergency conditions prevailing. The German government had collapsed and there was no provision for performing government services. Within a few hours, they were expected to select a *Landrat* (county manager) to head a *Kreis* government or a *Bürgermeister*

39

(mayor) to head a city, together with officials to deal with public safety, public utilities, public works, public health, and the like. The job of getting a skeletal government organized and of coping with such emergency problems as public order, water supply, sanitation, lighting, food, and public health was far from simple under any circumstances and, considering the fact that few members of the detachments staffs could speak German or had more than casual knowledge of German psychology and institutions, their assignment was a very difficult one indeed. Although they had been promised assistance by OSS (Office of Strategic Services) in determining which local inhabitants could be regarded as dependable and which were to be avoided as Nazis, they found all too often that they had little to go on except their own ingenuity. The result was that they made many mistakes in picking out Germans to start new governments, but their record in getting water supplies, providing emergency food, starting the electric current, and arranging for a few streetcars to operate amid the ruins was often impressive.

Within a few weeks the detachments usually had the emergency job well in hand, but the long-term task of reconstruction was beyond their competence and often their interest. In many instances these local detachments had to depend very largely on their own resources, since they were so cut off from the higher military government organization that they had little or no direction as to policy, little assistance in meeting special problems, and indeed slight contact of any kind. At the same time they were more or less continuously harassed by American tactical units in their neighborhood who often did not know what military government detachments were charged with doing and sometimes seemed to care less. Again and again they found that their energy had to be directed primarily at maintaining some sort of working relations with American tactical units rather than at dealing with the Germans. American tactical forces often saw no reason why they should not seize for their own use any German property or supplies which they happened to desire, and the task of military government in maintaining some sort of law and order under such circumstances was far from easy. The military government detachments even faced serious problems in connection with their own food and supplies. Dependent on the European Civil Affairs Division for their commissary and other supplies, the confusion in this organization during the early period was such that supplies frequently were long delayed in arriving. Consequently the military government detachments had to beg from tactical units or scrounge elsewhere.

Although the military government detachments performed highly important services and frequently in a commendable fashion, it was not long before they constituted a problem in the reconstruction of German government. Their work in getting a skeletal German government set up in their areas was essential, but as a system of German government up to and including the *Land* began to operate, the military government detachments often "got in the way" so to speak. They regarded the German governments which they had set up as their own children and naturally not only supervised and assisted but gave orders. Yet anything more than an emergency system of German government required an arrangement under which one level of German government would be geared into another and orders would go from the *Land* to the *Regierungsbezirke* (if provision was made for the district, as in Bavaria), thence to the *Kreis*, either rural or city, and finally down to the village or *Gemeinde*. With the American military government detachments giving orders to their local German government, such an integrated system was impossible.

With the establishment of *Land* offices of military government, there was no need for military government detachments at the *Land* level and these were merged with the former. Military government detachments at lower levels were transformed into liaison and security teams during the winter of 1945-1946, with a certain amount of telescoping under which several military government detachments might be joined together into a single liaison and security team to maintain contact with two or more rural *Kreise* or perhaps a *Stadtkreis* and a *Kreis*. Under this arrangement American orders to German governments were transmitted only through *Land* offices of military government to German *Land* governments which then sent them down the line to the districts, rural counties, and cities. The liaison and security teams had no authority to give orders to German officials; their responsibility was to report on local developments to the *Land* offices of military government, to assist the Germans without interfering or giving orders, to carry on American programs of information and the like, and to serve as a go-between in the case of American

41

tactical units and German officials. This assignment was not without its importance, but it represented a drastic change from the original concept of a military government detachment with far-reaching responsibilities of a direct character for the control of German local affairs. Many of the American military government officials were quite unhappy about such a limitation and found it difficult to adjust to the new regime. The military government specialists who had not already gone home often found little to attract them unless they had become wedded to life away from home, had few prospects in the United States, or had entered into domestic arrangements of various sorts with European women in preference to returning to their families at home. Thus the type of personnel engaged in military government duties at the local level after 1946 became quite different from that originally assigned. A good many changes were made from time to time in the local military government setup, but it remained at least in some sort of attenuated form until military government gave way to the High Commission period in 1949.

4

Office of the U. S. High Commissioner for Germany

Prior to the surrender of the Germans it had generally been assumed that the military government phase of the Allied occupation would be relatively brief and that, after a short period, a civil administration would be set up in the American Zone under State Department control. The State Department representatives assigned to the U. S. Group, Control Council for Germany held such a belief and looked forward to the early acceptance of responsibility from the Army. But events developed otherwise and the military government phase, as has been noted, stretched over a period of more than four years.

General Eisenhower recommended the termination of Army responsibility for the nonsecurity aspects of the occupation soon after the surrender, indicating that in his opinion it was not appropriate for military services to be charged with political duties, such as were involved in the occupation of Germany, except on an emergency basis.[1] But Secretary of State James F. Byrnes and other Washington officials felt that the State Department was not prepared to assume such a major task at this time.

The State Department had mushroomed during the years following 1938 from a small informal organization to a sizable agency having some thousands of persons on its staff and, despite all the efforts to provide administrative support, it faced the period immediately after World War II with many internal problems. Moreover, its experience had been mainly in the field of foreign affairs and foreign policy; consequently, it had developed little expertness in handling difficult administrative problems such as would be inevitably part of a civil administration in Germany. The chief factor

---

[1] See his *Crusade in Europe* (Doubleday, New York, 1948), pp. 434-435.

explaining the reluctance of the State Department to take over the primary responsibility in Germany was not however its lack of preparedness in the administrative field, but rather the deteriorating relations of the United States with the Russians. It was apparent soon after the German surrender that the occupation following World War II would not be a "normal" one and that the security aspect would consequently be far more important than was ordinarily the case.

Although the State Department did not implement its take-over plans of 1945, no specific statement was made as to when a civil administration might be established. Thus the question remained an open one and, even after the announcement by Secretary of State Byrnes in 1946 that his department was not prepared to take over from the Army, it was expected by some at least that the delay would not be a long one. Plans were made in 1947 for a civil administration in Germany, and in 1948 some very comprehensive plans were jointly drafted by the State Department and the military agencies. However, the great difficulties confronting the United States in Germany led to the postponement of making any actual use of these plans—the 1948 plans were shelved when the Russians undertook the blockade of Berlin. It is interesting to note in this connection that Secretary of State George C. Marshall informed Senator Henry Cabot Lodge of the Senate Foreign Relations Committee that his department hoped that it would be able to complete a transfer of occupational responsibilities in Germany other than in the security field by June 30, 1948.

Decisions of the London Conference of 1948, in which the United States, Great Britain, and France participated, made it necessary to reopen the entire question of the establishment of a civil administration in Germany despite the far from satisfactory situation as regards the Russians. Developments during the period 1945-1948 accentuated the fact that further delay in establishing a central German government in the western zones would have serious consequences. The vigorous efforts by the United States and Britain in Bizonia were not sufficient to meet the basic problems confronting western Germany, and at the London Conference this was recognized by these two countries as well as by France.

The objective of setting up a central German government necessi-

44

tated a fusion of the three western zones, the establishment of a new Allied organization to control the German government, an Occupation Statute defining the relations between the Allied organization and the German central government, and authorization to the Germans to draft a constitution or at least a basic law as a foundation for their new government. Tripartite committees which represented the military governors of the three western powers worked on some of these problems during the summer and autumn of 1948 and in the early months of 1949. In the latter part of 1948 a German group assembled at Bonn to draft a constitution. The Washington Three-Power Meeting in April 1949 brought final agreement on most of these matters.[2] All of this made it necessary for the United States to consider the reorganization of its own setup in Germany.

Planning for a new American occupation agency in Germany was carried on both in Washington and by OMGUS. A Committee on Planning for Germany, representing the State Department, Army, and ECA, started work in the spring of 1949. Although it held only three general meetings, it produced a considerable number of reports and papers on the various aspects of the problem and authorized various working committees that reached some agreement as to what should be done. At the same time, under directives from the Army, OMGUS was engaged in putting its ideas down on paper. Two OMGUS committees, a Committee on Tripartite Military Government Organization and a Committee on State-Army Reorganization, gave attention to the basic aspects of a transition from military government to a civil administration, but neither made much progress, though they did occasion the preparation of preliminary reports and papers. Most of the planning was therefore actually done in Washington.

On May 18, 1949, the Secretary of State sent a letter to the Secretary of Defense which formally announced an agreement to transfer nonmilitary responsibilities for the occupation of Germany from the Army to the State Department. On the same day the appointment of John J. McCloy as U. S. High Commissioner for Germany was made public. On June 6 an executive order providing for the Office of the U. S. High Commissioner for Germany (HICOG) was issued.[3]

---

[2] For the agreements reached at Washington, see State Department, *Germany, 1947-1949; The Story in Documents* (Washington, 1950), pp. 88-97.

[3] For its text, see *ibid.*, p. 182.

During the summer and early fall the text of a directive to the High Commissioner was drafted, circulated, and revised, and finally sent out as of November 17, 1949, several months after Mr. McCloy had assumed office.

Despite the great amount of planning by Washington and OMGUS since 1945, the actual job of constructing the headquarters office of the U. S. High Commissioner was done largely on the spot. There is little evidence that much attention was paid to any of the plans which had been drafted on earlier occasions, though certainly some of the staff work served a useful purpose. Mr. McCloy went to Germany during the first week of July 1949, taking with him Chauncey Parker as special adviser and Colonel H. A. Gerhardt as special assistant, as well as representatives of the State Department, Army, ECA, and Bureau of the Budget, Arthur Kimball, Colonel van Wagoner, Alden Boyd, and Mr. Lawson, respectively. He at once took over the position of Military Governor, using the dual title for the time being of U. S. High Commissioner and Military Governor. A provisional office of administration was set up in July under Glenn G. Wolfe who had preceded Mr. McCloy to Germany in May and this, with the addition of James L. Sundquist, the former OMGUS control officer, constituted the kernel around which a new American organization in Germany was built.

Mr. Parker was entrusted with considerable responsibility and recommended that the High Commissioner appoint as many acting division heads as possible at once, giving them the job of drafting definitions of functions, organizational structure, staffing requirements, and the like within certain terms of reference. After a review of these proposals by Wolfe and approval by McCloy's deputy, Major General George P. Hayes, he proposed that they be authorized to make tentative selections of staff from OMGUS. Parker emphasized the budgetary limitations and the desirability of keeping the staff small. As Military Governor, Mr. McCloy approved the Parker recommendations and issued General Order No. 27 to put them into effect. Mr. McCloy apparently indicated his desire that his headquarters office should have a small enough number of principal sub-

ORGANIZATION OF THE OFFICE OF THE
U.S. HIGH COMMISSIONER FOR GERMANY

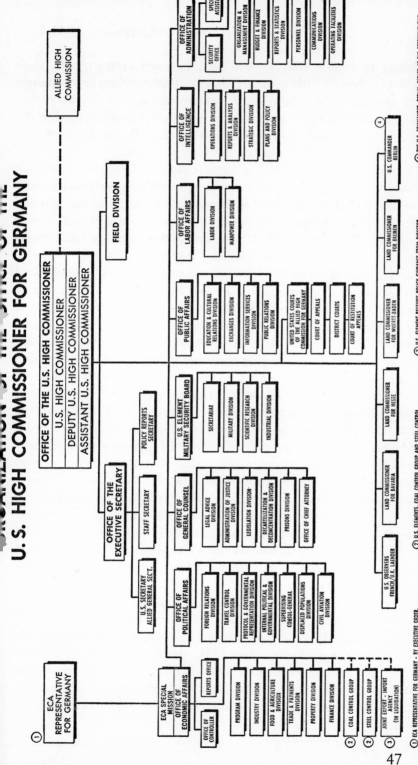

REVISED FEBRUARY 8, 1950

Prepared by HICOG

divisions to enable him to maintain personal contact with their heads, but there is little evidence that he displayed any great interest in the details of the administrative organization. Under the Parker recommendations General Hays was given the job of overseeing the establishment of such a structure, and much of the actual work was done while Mr. McCloy was in the United States.

Some specialists in public administration have expressed surprise at the character of the administrative organization which eventuated. It consisted of eight major subdivisions as follows: Economic Affairs, Political Affairs, General Counsel, Military Security Board, Labor Affairs, Intelligence, Public Affairs, and Administration, all directly responsible to the High Commissioner and his deputy. An Office of Executive Secretary was to handle secretariat work and a Field Division was to serve as a link with the field organization. A special subdivision to handle Berlin problems was also authorized. One of these subdivisions was more or less outside the discretion of General Hays—the three western Allies had agreed on the establishment of a Military Security Board to give attention to German activities which might have military significance and an American section of this was therefore more or less stipulated. Perhaps the conglomerate Office of Public Affairs occasioned the greatest criticism, but it was probably mainly the brain child of the special mission sent from Washington to recommend steps to be taken in the information, exchanges, and related fields. With education not included in the reserved powers under the Occupation Statute, there was little basis for continuing such a function as a major subdivision. Most of the subdivisions, such as Economic Affairs, Political Affairs, Administration, and General Counsel, were so traditional that it was virtually decreed that they be included. Whatever one's reactions may be to the initial organization scheme, it is fair to acknowledge the comparative simplicity of its main outline.

In August 1949 the acting heads of these new divisions moved from Berlin, where OMGUS had been located since 1945, to the Farben Building in Frankfurt where HICOG headquarters were to be until the move to Bonn in late 1951. After spending several weeks in Germany in mid-summer of 1949, Mr. McCloy returned to the United States to confer with the State Department and to select top staff. Announcements of key appointments were made during August

48

and September, and the headquarters of HICOG was ready to function in September when the West German Federal Government came into operation under the control of an Allied High Commission.

It was contemplated in some quarters that HICOG would be a much smaller organization than OMGUS, and the Parker recommendations had stressed keeping the size down. However, the usual pressures became active as the organization was built and started to operate, with the result that the size exceeded that anticipated. Education which had been omitted from the reserved powers seemed more or less doomed, for example; but, after professional education groups in the United States had expressed their indignation, a fairly sizable education staff was added to HICOG, despite the responsibility which had been turned over to the Germans. Even so HICOG did manage to keep its size somewhat below that of OMGUS. At the end of 1950 before cutbacks were made, it employed 896 Americans and 2,298 Germans at Frankfurt headquarters, and a total of 1,431 Americans and 6,282 Germans throughout Germany.

One of the chief criticisms directed at the establishment of HICOG arose out of the employment of large numbers of OMGUS officials and staff. Screening boards were set up to interview those OMGUS employees who wished to be retained by HICOG and, in general, preference seems to have been given those already employed in Germany by OMGUS. However, except for General Hays, none of the top officials of HICOG were taken over from the high-position holders of OMGUS, at least not more than temporarily. The executive secretary had, it is true, served in a subordinate position in OMGUS; and N. H. Collisson, who held the top ECA position, had held a ranking position under OMGUS, but the latter did not stay long. E. H. Litchfield, the director of Governmental Affairs in OMGUS, remained for a brief period. In general, the major positions were given to new people brought from the United States.

At the second level, however, the situation was different. Here there was a considerable number of persons who had been closely identified with OMGUS, sometimes in both a military and a civilian capacity. Such individuals were familiar with certain aspects of the American program which continued without much change throughout the occupation. This was obviously of no slight importance, since people brought from the United States would, in most cases

49

at least, have had to go through a breaking-in period. Moreover, by taking people on the ground all the delay and red tape so characteristic of recruiting new personnel could be avoided, and heavy travel and moving expenses eliminated. On the other hand, most of those who had worked for military government had established patterns of thought and action which could not be easily changed. As a result of their absence from the United States for several years they had often lost touch with current developments at home, which made them less valuable. Some had taken on the ways of victors in a conquered land, which, it may be added, was almost impossible to avoid after a few months' sojourn in Germany. This occasioned an attitude which constituted a liability for the sort of work which HICOG wanted to do. The general result was that critics sometimes said that HICOG was more or less OMGUS under another name and that one could not distinguish between the two in attitudes, approaches, activities, and the like. This was doubtless an exaggerated point of view, but there was enough truth behind it to raise the question as to whether it was not a mistake for HICOG to take over so many of those who had served under OMGUS.

The general system of organization under HICOG varied a good deal from that of OMGUS. Not only were the major subdivisions somewhat different, but the channels varied significantly. OMGUS was primarily a military organization even after its staff became predominantly civilian: its head was a professional military man and below him were a military chief of staff and a control unit which embodied military methods even if some of the personnel serving in these agencies were civilians. The path up from the working levels to the office of General Clay was a long and devious one, and the bottleneck created by the chief of staff and the control office made it difficult for many of those at the operating level to reach General Clay. In any event, some time was required to pass papers through the various levels.

In contrast, HICOG, despite its holdovers from OMGUS, was essentially a civil organization. It did have a Deputy High Commissioner who was a professional military man and might have held up papers, but in reality General Hays was not a deputy in the traditional sense. Having his office in the Bonn area, he was normally in charge of the part of HICOG located at Bonn before the great move

50

from Frankfurt took place in late 1951. Consequently, except during the absence of the High Commissioner, the deputy had little to do with the main HICOG offices. In the reorganization in 1952, the position of deputy was dropped entirely. Since the directors of the major subdivisions of HICOG reported directly to the High Commissioner, business moved more freely and with less delay than had been the case under OMGUS. That is not to say that Mr. McCloy personally gave his attention to a great deal of the routine business of HICOG—many matters could be disposed of by others—and his special assistant, Colonel Gerhardt, and his efficient secretary, Miss Patricia J. Dermody, were expert at channeling unimportant matters away from the desk of the High Commissioner. Nevertheless, there was an informality in HICOG which could never have been expected in a military organization such as OMGUS.

It will be no surprise to those familiar with modern developments in public administration to learn that the Office of Administration was the largest subdivision of HICOG headquarters, employing more than 300 Americans and in excess of 1,500 Germans at its height. Subdivided into divisions dealing with organization and management, budget and fiscal, personnel, operating facilities, communications, reports and statistics, and security, it performed many essential services and some not so essential. As in many other public agencies, it seemed to other sections of HICOG that the Office of Administration was somewhat overorganized and that it could get staff and facilities when others could not. Thus, fairly low-ranking personnel on its staff had publicly owned automobiles assigned for their use, in which they drove to and from their homes, while higher ranking personnel in other sections had to depend on the motor pool for transportation for official business and had to provide their own transportation otherwise.

The Office of Public Affairs was perhaps the most extensive of the operating subdivisions of HICOG and necessarily had a large staff, although well below the office of Administration. It employed 142 Americans and 3,345 Germans at the end of 1950. During its most active period it was organized into divisions as follows: information services, press and publications, publishing operations, radio, motion pictures, exchange, education and cultural relations, community activities, America Houses, governmental institutions, and

51

public relations. While some of its activities related to the Allied High Commission and the West German Federal Government, to a large extent it was engaged in carrying on programs inherited from American military government aimed directly at the German people. But unlike its predecessor in OMGUS, the Office of Public Affairs of HICOG regarded all of West Germany and Berlin as its field rather than simply the American Zone.

Another subdivision of HICOG with elaborate setup and sizable staff was of course the Office of Economic Affairs which also handled ECA programs in Germany. It had a staff of 181 Americans and 306 Germans at the end of 1950. While its internal organization varied a good deal from time to time, during its most active period it maintained subdivisions dealing with program review, industry, food and agriculture, finance, trade and payments, property, statistical standards, east-west trade, and policy guidance to steel and coal groups and to JEIA (Joint Export-Import Agency). Much of its energy was directed at administering the ECA program in West Germany and at stimulating German economic reconstruction. But it also was interested in the larger problems of European recovery through its trade and payments division. Its property division was a holdover from OMGUS, giving its attention to the administration and disposal of German property still held by the United States.

The Office of Political Affairs was always an office of great importance even when its staff was smaller—it employed 301 Americans and 317 Germans at the end of 1950—and its scope perhaps more restricted than that of some other offices. In contrast to the other subdivisions staffed largely by takeovers from OMGUS and persons recruited on a temporary basis into the Foreign Service Staff Corps (FSS), the Office of Political Affairs had most of the Foreign Service Officers (FSOs) to be found in HICOG and, as time passed, the State Department attempted to send more and more Foreign Service Officers for this purpose. Of course, not all of the persons working in the Office of Political Affairs were professional career men, but they received the chief assignments in the main divisions dealing with policy and government, consular affairs, and protocol and foreign representation. In the displaced persons, civil aviation, and combined travel board divisions, holdovers from military government, staff members were rarely Foreign Service Officers. After the reorganization which was effected in 1951 and 1952 and the Office of Political Affairs took over certain functions formerly handled by the Office of Public Affairs, various temporary Staff Corps people were transferred to it. But it always retained a sort of inner circle, so to speak, of the elite Foreign Service Officer Corps.

Although inferior in size to certain other subdivisions—it had a staff of 139 Americans and 255 Germans at the end of 1950—the Office of the General Counsel never admitted for a moment its inferiority in any other respect and without doubt exerted great influence. Organized into divisions dealing with legal advice, legislation, administration of justice, decartelization, and deconcentration, its staff was, except for the usual secretaries, administrative assistants, clerks, and so forth, made up of attorneys. As in many other public agencies, the Office of General Counsel surrounded itself with somewhat of a shroud of mystery and secrecy to safeguard it from the encroachments of curiosity of those not members of the legal fraternity. Other sections of HICOG at times felt that the Office of General Counsel took itself too seriously, though at the same time they respected it.

The Office of Labor Affairs was the baby among the HICOG offices and maintained a total staff smaller than that of major subdivisions of the big offices, such as those of Economic Affairs and Public Affairs—its staff consisted of 20 Americans and 38 Germans at the end of 1950. Divided into three divisions: international labor activities, U. S. labor practices, and relations with German labor organizations, it concentrated on reporting on labor developments in Germany to Washington agencies and serving as a liaison between organized labor in the United States and Germany.

The Office of Intelligence, with divisions of reports and analysis, operations, and plans and policy, occupied a rather isolated position in HICOG. While its staff members were seen about—they included 75 Americans and 14 Germans at the end of 1950—its operations were naturally carried on more or less behind the scenes rather than in the limelight. The Military Security Board also was somewhat removed from the main scene in HICOG. Actually a carry-over from military government, it was a tripartite agency with headquarters near Coblenz. It was represented in HICOG by its American chief, but for practical purposes its operations were only distantly tied in with those of the other offices.

The Office of Executive Secretary was given a somewhat different place in the HICOG organization chart than those subdivisions thus far mentioned. As far as the Office of Administration saw things, this office was a violation of basic canons of public administration and more or less of a reproach to the Office of Administration which should have been given the job of providing secretarial services. However, despite such lack of appreciation on the part of the powerful Office of Administration, the Office of Executive Secretary survived. It had a staff of 91 Americans and 70 Germans at the end of 1950 and was subdivided into divisions as follows: multi-partite secretariat, policy reports, and historical. Thus it provided the expert American secretariat staff at the Petersberg, the Allied High Commission headquarters, on the Rhine; got out the *Quarterly Report* of the U. S. High Commissioner as well as special reports; and gave a niche to the group of scholars charged with preparing a series of monographs dealing with various aspects of the record of HICOG. Whether it violated administrative principles or not by being permitted to exist, it provided services which were essential and could not have been easily supplied by the large Office of Administration.

Finally, there was a Field Division, which, like the Office of Executive Secretary, did not fit into the organization chart on the same basis as the other offices. This subdivision was never a large one—it had a staff of five Americans and three Germans at the end of 1950—and was wound up in 1952 when the field organization of HICOG was discontinued. While it functioned, it performed the important service of maintaining liaison between the HICOG headquarters and the regional and *Kreis* offices.

During the first two years of its existence the organization of HICOG remained more or less stable, though certain internal changes were made from time to time within the major subdivisions. However, by 1951 the policy of the United States pointed in the direction of giving sovereignty to the West German Federal Republic and winding up the Allied High Commission, thus ending the occupation as far as the western Allies were concerned despite the lack of a peace

54

treaty. Negotiations were carried on with the West German Federal Government looking to this end and it was expected that this step could be completed in 1952—actually it was not until May 1955 that the long-drawn out process was finally ended. But looking toward German sovereignty and the end of the occupation in 1952, it was of course necessary to make arrangements to bring about the transformation of HICOG to an American Embassy or status of "normal mission," as the official jargon put it.

This of course involved dropping many of the functions performed by HICOG, taking on a few other functions or at least modifying certain sections already in existence, and reducing the size of the staff drastically. It was estimated that an American embassy in Germany would require only about one third as large a staff as HICOG. Commissioner McCloy borrowed his old friend, Chauncey Parker, who had helped set up HICOG, from the World Bank to advise on the radical overhauling. In order to make the process as orderly as possible, it was planned to do the job by steps, three main steps being fixed at intervals of a few months apart.

Offices such as those of Labor Affairs, Intelligence, and General Counsel were to disappear entirely, though their functions might be taken over in part by sections of other subdivisions in the new embassy. Important shifts were made in such subdivisions as those of Political Affairs and Public Affairs. Though far-reaching changes were effected during 1951 and 1952, the delay in bringing West Germany into the Western European Defense Alliance, and consequently giving her sovereignty, slowed up the process of transforming HICOG into an embassy. For example, the actual reduction in staff was less than had been anticipated earlier. Nevertheless, the latter period of the Allied High Commission marked a change on the part of the attitude of the western Allies toward Germany which resulted in giving the West German Federal Government more or less complete freedom in managing internal affairs despite the delay in achieving a legal bestowal of sovereignty. This change was naturally reflected in the activities of HICOG.[4]

---

[4] The headquarters organization of HICOG is dealt with at length in a monograph of the Historical Series of the Office of the U. S. High Commissioner for Germany prepared by G. A. Lee under the title *The Establishment of the Office of the U. S. High Commissioner for Germany* (1951). At the time of this writing it retained a "Restricted" classification.

MAJOR HEADQUARTERS FUNCTIONS

The headquarters staff of HICOG was charged with varied responsibilities. To begin with, it supported the High Commissioner, giving him advice and rendering such assistance as he called for. The directors of the offices were in frequent consultation with the High Commissioner and, as a group, attended his staff meetings which were held at one period once each week and later at less frequent intervals to give attention to general problems confronting the United States in Germany. The Executive Secretary and the directors of the Offices of Political Affairs, Economic Affairs, Administration, and General Counsel usually briefed the High Commissioner in preparation for the sessions of the Allied High Commission held thrice monthly and accompanied him to these formal meetings.

In the second place, the HICOG staff served as American representatives on the numerous tripartite committees and in the secretariat maintained by the Allied High Commission. An agency such as the Allied High Commission obviously required a fairly elaborate secretariat to keep records, arrange sessions and agenda, provide papers and information, furnish interpreter and translator services, and maintain the quarters of the High Commission with offices, conference rooms, restaurant facilities, and so forth. HICOG furnished the American complement of the secretariat and this required a number of full-time officials stationed in the Bonn area.

An uninformed person may imagine the work of an international agency, such as the Allied High Commission, to be handled largely, if not entirely, by formal meetings of the High Commissioners. Actually a vast amount of work has to be done outside of such meetings. It is perhaps not an exaggeration to say that the greater part of the work of the Allied High Commission was performed by its tripartite committees, the formal meetings of the High Commissioners being rather routine and of the rubber-stamp variety.

The Allied High Commission charter provided for six main committees as follows: political affairs, foreign trade and exchange, economics, finance, law, and the Military Security Board. Acting under its own authority the Allied High Commission organized additional committees, such as a general committee and a review com-

56

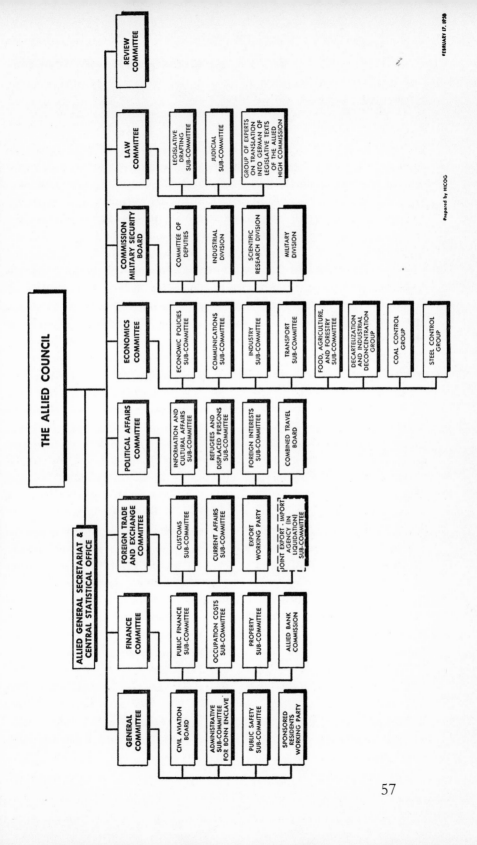

ORGANIZATION OF THE ALLIED HIGH COMMISSION

THE ALLIED COUNCIL

ALLIED GENERAL SECRETARIAT &
CENTRAL STATISTICAL OFFICE

GENERAL COMMITTEE
- CIVIL AVIATION BOARD
- ADMINISTRATIVE SUB-COMMITTEE FOR BONN ENCLAVE
- PUBLIC SAFETY SUB-COMMITTEE
- SPONSORED RESIDENTS WORKING PARTY

FINANCE COMMITTEE
- PUBLIC FINANCE SUB-COMMITTEE
- OCCUPATION COSTS SUB-COMMITTEE
- PROPERTY SUB-COMMITTEE
- ALLIED BANK COMMISSION

FOREIGN TRADE AND EXCHANGE COMMITTEE
- CUSTOMS SUB-COMMITTEE
- CURRENT AFFAIRS SUB-COMMITTEE
- EXPORT WORKING PARTY
- JOINT EXPORT - IMPORT AGENCY (IN LIQUIDATION) SUB-COMMITTEE

POLITICAL AFFAIRS COMMITTEE
- INFORMATION AND CULTURAL AFFAIRS SUB-COMMITTEE
- REFUGEES AND DISPLACED PERSONS SUB-COMMITTEE
- FOREIGN INTERESTS SUB-COMMITTEE
- COMBINED TRAVEL BOARD

ECONOMICS COMMITTEE
- ECONOMIC POLICIES SUB-COMMITTEE
- COMMUNICATIONS SUB-COMMITTEE
- INDUSTRY SUB-COMMITTEE
- TRANSPORT SUB-COMMITTEE
- FOOD, AGRICULTURE, AND FORESTRY SUB-COMMITTEE
- DECARTELIZATION AND INDUSTRIAL DECONCENTRATION GROUP
- COAL CONTROL GROUP
- STEEL CONTROL GROUP

COMMISSION MILITARY SECURITY BOARD
- COMMITTEE OF DEPUTIES
- INDUSTRIAL DIVISION
- SCIENTIFIC RESEARCH DIVISION
- MILITARY DIVISION

LAW COMMITTEE
- LEGISLATIVE DRAFTING SUB-COMMITTEE
- JUDICIAL SUB-COMMITTEE
- GROUP OF EXPERTS ON TRANSLATION INTO GERMAN OF LEGISLATIVE TEXTS OF THE ALLIED HIGH COMMISSION

REVIEW COMMITTEE

FEBRUARY 17, 1950

Prepared by HICOG

57

mittee in 1949 and a labor affairs committee and a special committee in 1950.[5] The review committee was terminated in 1951 when the modification of the Occupation Statute provided that German legislation would no longer be subject to Allied review. Certain committees were consolidated with others or dropped—foreign trade and exchange was eliminated in 1951, and the finance committee was combined with the economics committee in late 1951; the special committee finished its work and came to an end in 1952. Despite these changes, the system of tripartite committees remained very important. Indeed, a listing of the main committees gives no true picture of the role of the committee system of the Allied Control Commission since the main committees were broken down in many cases into several subcommittees on such matters as foreign interests, steel control, civil aviation, information and cultural affairs, and decartelization and industrial deconcentration. There were more than 40 of these subcommittees; even as late as May 1952, when the Contractual Agreements were signed with the Germans, there were 30 such subcommittees.[6]

These tripartite committees usually met every week for several hours and, in addition, their members exchanged papers and discussed matters over the telephone. The General Committee could go so far as to dispose of certain matters referred to it by the Allied High Commission when full agreement of its members could be reached. The other committees had less complete authority in theory; but, in actuality, if they reached full agreement on matters within their scope, it was probable that the Allied High Commission would follow their recommendations as a matter of course. The American representatives on these committees were drawn from HICOG, and the HICOG staff spent a great deal of its time preparing papers for the use of these committees.

The third major activity of HICOG involved the direction of certain American programs directed at the German people. Some of the subdivisions had little of this to do—the Office of General Counsel for example; while others, such as the Office of Public Affairs, were mainly engaged in such activities. The information pro-

---

[5] This material is drawn from Elmer Plischke, *The Allied High Commission for Germany*, a monograph in the Historical Series of the Office of the U. S. High Commission (1953), Chap. 8

[6] *Ibid.*, p. 108.

gram, the exchanges program, the efforts to assist German education, and the community services programs may be cited as examples of such activities which required the time of large numbers of HICOG staff members.

The fourth activity of HICOG, providing services for the operation of HICOG and for the support of its staff, was less exciting perhaps than the other three; but it required a large staff and a considerable expenditure of time and money. Personnel administration, budget preparation, and the like, are familiar to anyone who has an acquaintance with a public agency; but when that agency is located in an occupied area there are many other functions, such as housing for staff, a sizable motor pool, and supply facilities, which have to be undertaken. HICOG depended on the Army for PX and certain other facilities, but it had to provide other services for itself.

HICOG ORGANIZATION IN THE *LÄNDER*

In addition to the headquarters office located until 1951 in Frankfurt and thereafter at Mehlem in the Bonn area, HICOG found it desirable to maintain offices of various sorts throughout West Germany and in Berlin.

The most important of these were the offices of the *Land* Commissioners located in each of the states of the American Zone. There were four altogether: at Munich in Bavaria, at Wiesbaden in Hesse, at Stuttgart in Württemberg-Baden, and at Bremen. These were the outgrowth of the former *Land* Offices of Military Government, but under HICOG they were headed by *Land* Commissioners instead of *Land* Military Governors. Since there was a great variation in the population and area of these states, the offices of the *Land* Commissioners varied considerably, the one at Munich being the largest. *Land* Commissioners reported directly to the High Commissioner and attended his staff conferences. In addition, they headed staffs which at their height ran into the hundreds in the larger states—the Munich office had a staff of 175 Americans and 1,762 Germans. The *Land* Commissioners' Offices together employed 524 Americans and 4,374 Germans at the end of 1950. The organization of the offices of the *Land* Commissioners paralleled that of the headquarters offices of

59

OFFICE OF U.S. LAND COMMISSIONER
(FOR BAVARIA, HESSE, WÜERTTEMBERG-BADEN AND BREMEN)

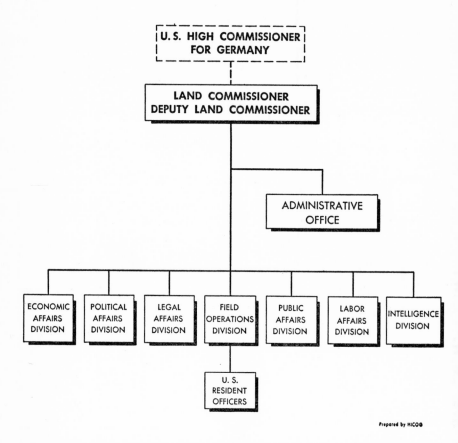

Prepared by HICOG

HICOG, with provisions for administration, political affairs, economic affairs, public affairs, intelligence, legal counsel, and so forth.[7] Each of these offices had a field division to supervise the work of the *Kreis* resident officers.

The offices of the *Land* Commissioners performed various functions. They maintained contact with the German governments in

---

[7] Guy A. Lee, *Field Organization of the Office of the U. S. High Commissioner for Germany*, a monograph in the Historical Series of the Office of the U. S. High Commissioner for Germany (1952), deals at length with the field organization of HICOG, but at the time of this writing it retained a "Restricted" classification.

CHART OF THE U.S. LAND COMMISSIONER FOR WÜRTTEMBERG-BADEN

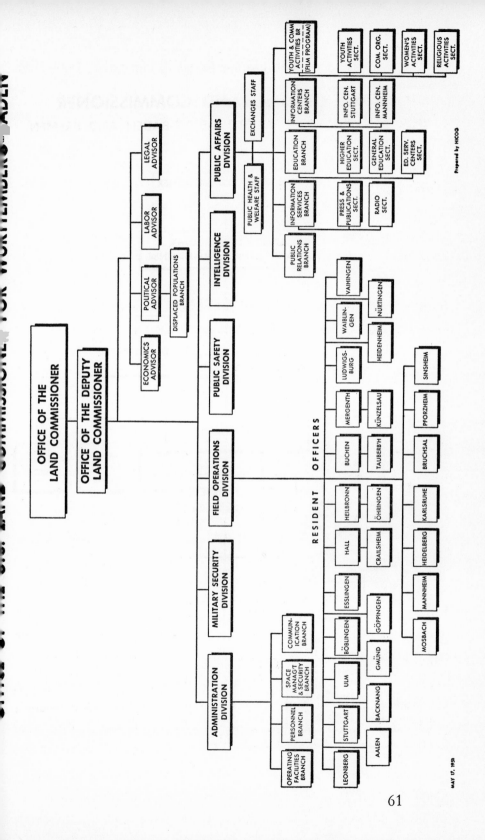

Prepared by HICOG

MAY 17, 1950

61

their areas and with business, educational, and other German circles. They reported to the main HICOG office on local developments and gathered information requested by the latter. But their main job was to administer American programs directed toward the German people. Consequently their work in the field of public affairs was particularly important. In the reorganization started in 1951 looking toward converting HICOG into an embassy these offices were dropped and necessary functions transferred to American consulates in the area.

In the states of the west which belonged to the former British or French Zones, HICOG maintained liaison officers or observers, often

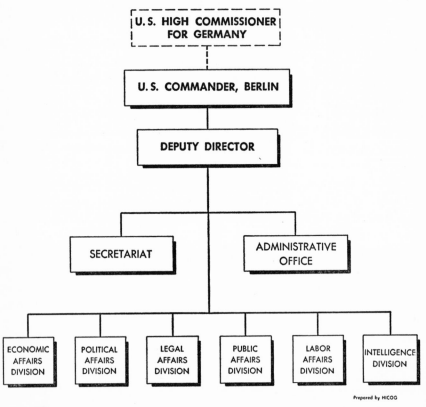

BERLIN ELEMENT
OFFICE OF U.S. HIGH COMMISSIONER FOR GERMANY

Prepared by HICOG

American consuls in such places as Hamburg and Düsseldorf, to report on local conditions, to interpret American aims to the French, British, and German officials of those states, and to represent the United States in such programs as the exchanges of persons, America Houses, and education centers. These officers had small staffs consisting of several persons. They attended one of the High Commissioner's staff conferences each month to report on developments in their areas and to confer with various headquarters officials.

Since the United States had a great interest in the western sectors of Berlin, a special subdivision of HICOG was maintained for the Berlin Area, and at the end of 1950 it included 119 Americans and 492 Germans. Headed by the American military commander in Berlin, it also had a civilian deputy director, usually the head of the economic or political affairs sections, who assumed charge of the nonmilitary aspects of the HICOG organization in Berlin. The organization of the Berlin Element was similar to that of an office of *Land* Commissioner except for the military head. Like the *Land* Commissioners, the U. S. Commander in Berlin attended the staff conferences of the High Commissioner. The work of the Berlin Element resembled that of the offices of the *Land* Commissioners, but it included in addition certain activities directed to eastern Germany, such as RIAS, the radio broadcasting station, and an information gathering and disseminating service. Unlike the offices of the *Land* Commissioners, the Berlin Element was continued after 1951 and indeed in another form survived HICOG itself.

Before the main HICOG offices moved to Mehlem in late 1951, a branch of HICOG was maintained in the Bonn area. This included the American personnel in the Allied High Commission secretariat and certain sections of the Office of Political Affairs particularly interested in maintaining contact with the West German Federal Government. Under this Bonn element there was a special liaison office for keeping in close and continuing contact with the West German parliament and the various German executive and administrative offices.

KREIS RESIDENT OFFICES

The approximately 150 *Kreis* resident offices were sometimes referred to as the "eyes and ears" of HICOG and were indeed in closer

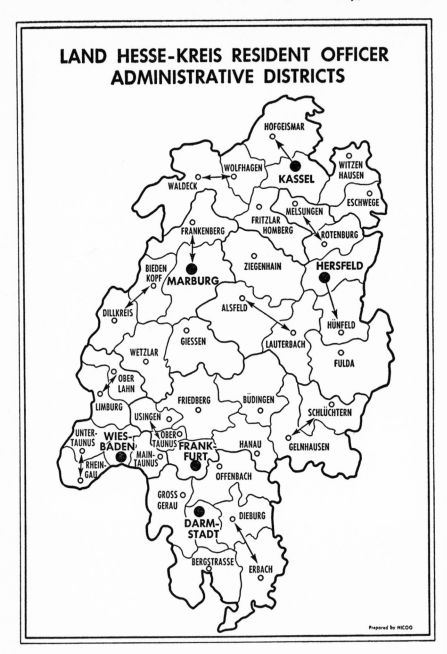

LAND HESSE-KREIS RESIDENT OFFICER ADMINISTRATIVE DISTRICTS

HOFGEISMAR

WOLFHAGEN

WITZEN HAUSEN

WALDECK

KASSEL

ESCHWEGE

MELSUNGEN

FRITZLAR HOMBERG

FRANKENBERG

ROTENBURG

BIEDEN KOPF

ZIEGENHAIN

HERSFELD

MARBURG

ALSFELD

DILLKREIS

HÜNFELD

GIESSEN

LAUTERBACH

WETZLAR

FULDA

OBER LAHN

FRIEDBERG

BÜDINGEN

LIMBURG

SCHLÜCHTERN

USINGEN

UNTER-TAUNUS

WIES-BADEN

OBER TAUNUS

FRANK-FURT

HANAU

GELNHAUSEN

MAIN-TAUNUS

RHEIN-GAU

OFFENBACH

GROSS GERAU

DARM-STADT

DIEBURG

BERGSTRASSE

ERBACH

Prepared by HICOG

contact with the German population than any other elements of HICOG. They succeeded the military government liaison and security offices and performed something of the same functions, though greater emphasis was placed on carrying out a public affairs program under HICOG. About half of the liaison and security personnel of military government were taken over by HICOG and made *Kreis* resident officers. But the KROs were on the whole considerably younger and more intelligent than their predecessors—the new additions being in large measure young Foreign Service Officers on first assignment or young men selected out of the universities on the same basis. In some *Kreise*, these officers had to spend a great deal of their time in trying to keep American military groups in good humor and out of the hair of the Germans. But the emphasis was placed on reporting to higher levels of HICOG on local developments and particularly on implementing the public affairs programs in youth work, adult education, public affairs, forums, and the like.[8] The KROs were expected to maintain close relations with local German officials, though they had no authority to give them orders. In the reorganization started in 1951 looking toward transforming HICOG into an embassy, the *Kreis* resident offices were closed.

---

[8] Additional information relating to the work of the *Kreis* resident officers is available in letters written by various of these officers reproduced in Guy A. Lee, ed., *Documents on Field Organization of the Office of the U. S. High Commissioner for Germany, 1949-1951*, a volume of the Historical Series of the Office of the U. S. High Commissioner for Germany (1952), pp. 27-70.

5

Military Governors, High Commissioners, and Other Occupation Staff

It goes without saying that the personnel serving in the administration of an occupied territory is of the utmost importance, probably in the last analysis more important than organization and perhaps almost as important as policy. A staff of well-trained, intelligent, resourceful, and interested persons can do a great deal to make a weak structure work fairly effectively, but not even the best machinery will produce results if the staff is inadequate. While an able staff is by no means a substitute for a carefully drafted policy which embodies consideration of present and future objectives, it is true, nevertheless, that a superior staff can do much to strengthen what might seem to be a weak policy and indeed, in the absence of a workable policy, as was the case for a time in Germany, may use its own judgment in some matters and make at least a fair amount of progress.

The staff employed by the United States to administer the occupation in Germany has been variously viewed. It has received very high praise in certain quarters; it has been held up to ridicule by certain journalists as a remarkable example of addiction to "wine, women, and song." Others have mixed a measure of commendation with substantial criticism. It is of course not a simple matter to evaluate the large body consisting of many thousands of men and women, both military and civilian, of a great range of ages and experience and responsibilities, who have served the United States in military government or in its successor, HICOG. It would not be a simple matter to make an evaluation of those employed at any one time and the task is complicated by the rapid turnover and the consequent fact that what might be true at one period would not necessarily hold true at another.

66

Military Governors, High Commissioners, Occupation Staff

MILITARY GOVERNORS

The United States had four military governors in Germany during the period 1945-1949: General Dwight D. Eisenhower, to November 1945, General Joseph T. McNarney, from November 1945 to March 1947, General Lucius D. Clay from March 1947 to May 1949, and Mr. John J. McCloy from May 1949 to the end of the military government phase in September 1949. The first two and the last of these incumbents require little attention here.

The Supreme Commander, General Eisenhower, carried heavy responsibilities of a tactical nature both before and after the German surrender. He displayed an interest in military government-civil affairs and indeed as Allied commander in North Africa had a good deal to do with the recognition of the important role of military government and civil affairs in World War II. Even during the hectic days before the invasion of France, he found time, as noted elsewhere, * to visit the Shrivenham center and urge the military government officers awaiting action there to be as patient as possible until their big chance for service should arrive. General Eisenhower was not particularly active in the military government aspect of the postwar period in Germany, though he bore the title of "Military Governor" as well as "Commander of American Forces." With General Clay as Deputy Military Governor, General Eisenhower could devote himself largely to the pressing problems of a strictly military character arising out of the German defeat.

General McNarney, like General Eisenhower, did not assume a very active role in the military government area, despite his title as "Military Governor"—indeed in his biography in *Who's Who in America* he did not even report such an assignment, contenting himself with the entry "Commander of U. S. Forces in Europe." General McNarney had to cope with the enormously arduous and complex problems of returning huge American military forces to the United States, disposing of vast quantities of military stores, and at the same time constructing as adequate a security force as possible in Germany. Since General Clay was handling military government effectively as

---

* See Chap. 2.

Deputy Military Governor, General McNarney, like General Eisenhower, could leave these matters largely to him. General McNarney did display an interest in the problems confronting the OMGUS and in general his role was a constructive one.

Mr. McCloy served as a Military Governor during the interim between the departure of General Clay in mid-May of 1949 and the activation of the HICOG in September 1949, but his big job was that of U. S. High Commissioner.

General Clay was just under fifty years of age when he was rather dramatically transferred from Washington to serve as Deputy Military Governor in Germany. A product of West Point, he joined the engineers upon graduation and prior to his service in Germany his military experience had been almost entirely in the engineering and materiel fields. He had received assignments to various rivers and harbors jobs, had taught engineering at West Point, and had been in charge of the defense airport construction program just prior to Pearl Harbor. His only foreign assignment prior to World War II had involved service with General MacArthur in the Philippines in 1937. During World War II his main job prior to 1945 was to assist Director Byrnes of the War Mobilization Board in getting supplies turned out in sufficient quantities. But he also established excellent records in constructing air fields in Brazil and in opening a badly needed harbor in France for Allied shipping. The *New York Times* branded him a "stormy petrel" as he left the War Mobilization Board. A conventionally minded person would perhaps have seen comparatively little in the background and experience of General Clay to suggest him for the job of Deputy Military Governor and subsequently Military Governor of Germany.[1]

With almost no background in political matters, even in the United States, General Clay undertook as difficult a politico-military assignment in Germany as could be imagined. His lack of experience in dealing with international problems is indicated by the fact that, despite the character of his new responsibilities, he made no effort to contact the State Department before leaving Washington.[2] And

---

[1] For General Clay's account of his appointment, see his *Decision in Germany* (Doubleday, New York, 1950), pp. 4-5. See also J. F. Byrnes, *Speaking Frankly* (Harper, New York, 1947), p. 47, who states that the selection was made by the War Department and that the President did not know Clay at the time.

[2] See *Decision in Germany*, p. 6.

it is a significant commentary on the rather haphazard manner in which American foreign affairs were being handled at the time to note that it was not indicated to him that this would be appropriate.[3]

A clean-cut, slender-built man, General Clay had little of the physical front sometimes associated with top brass, but his piercing eye and self-confidence suggested decisiveness and force. Very few human beings in any walk of life work as hard as General Clay: he frequently arrived at his office well before anyone else and not uncommonly remained after the normal closing hour far into the night. Sundays and holidays meant little to him. He was more informal than most men who bear his responsibilities and had little liking for red tape. Rather quiet and on the surface mild, he developed what some regarded as imperious mannerisms as the years passed by in Germany. His memory was excellent and detailed and served him well.

Military officers are frequently accustomed to working closely with and depending heavily upon a staff, and this was certainly the case with General Eisenhower and others. However, General Clay had been an engineer and in solving engineering problems there is apparently less scope for staff work—more depends on the judgment and decisiveness of an individual. At any rate General Clay was not a good example of the military officer who places great emphasis on staff deliberations and advice. With as large a staff, both military and civilian, as anyone could want in Germany—at the peak in December 1945 there were approximately 12,000, many of whom had impressive professional backgrounds, in his military government organization—General Clay necessarily entrusted routine duties to his subordinates, but he depended less on his top associates than is ordinarily the case. Though he had had almost no experience coping with most of the political problems confronting the United States in Germany, General Clay rarely was at a loss and, rather than delay action until he could consult his experts, he often made an immediate decision. If he did listen to his numerous advisers, including his political adviser representing the State Department, there is not much evidence that he relied heavily on their counsel.[4] That is not

---

[3] See *ibid.*, p. 6.
[4] For a typical example of this, see B. U. Ratchford and W. D. Ross, *Berlin Reparations Assignment* (University of North Carolina Press, Chapel Hill, 1947).

to say that he was overbearing, waiving the opinions of others rudely aside, for indeed he ordinarily displayed a courteous manner toward associates, and his relations with such staff members as General William H. Draper and E. H. Litchfield were quite cordial. It was simply that by his very nature and past experience he was accustomed to deciding problems himself. If the almost impossibly involved issues of postwar Europe were substituted for the engineering problems of his earlier career that did not change his ways perceptibly.

Fortunately General Clay possessed a shrewdness, and at times it almost seemed a sort of uncanny sixth sense, which made this way of proceeding less hazardous than might first appear to be the case. A man of his type and impetuosity might have gotten so bogged down in the mires of European troubles that he would have been engulfed and his country would have suffered grievously. It has seemed unfortunate to many observers that General Clay did not use his staff of experts more fully and often rushed in where even angels could hardly have been expected to venture; on occasion he made foolish moves. Nevertheless, his record as a whole was good.

General Clay's seizing of the bit in his own teeth must be viewed against the background of his time. Had President Franklin D. Roosevelt lived and enjoyed his one-time vigor, it is improbable that General Clay could have carved out an empire for himself in Germany or perhaps that he would even have tried. But President Truman was immersed in domestic problems, and the White House was almost unaware of Germany when General Clay was establishing his pattern. A stronger State Department or at least a State Department in a stronger position might have successfully challenged the way things were being done in Germany. As it was, General Clay's actions were not infrequently looked upon askance by the State Department and his disregard or perhaps neglect of that department was the occasion of considerable resentment. His quite magnificent record in breaking the Berlin Blockade went a long way toward neutralizing the mistakes which he had made and caused his position to seem almost invulnerable.

An objective evaluation of so controversial and colorful a public figure as General Clay is almost, if not entirely, impossible. So much depends upon the background of the person doing the evaluating. Some of those who were close to General Clay literally idolize him

70

and honestly feel that his service as American Military Governor was brilliant to the point of being matchless. Others give General Clay a low rating, regarding him as a very dangerous man with a lust for power and a disregard for anyone except himself and his own opinions. Neither of the extreme estimates seem entirely tenable. It was hardly ideal that a man with such limited knowledge of German history, German institutions, and German psychology should have been named Military Governor. Nevertheless, General Clay was not indifferent to these and he actually learned a great deal about these matters after arriving on the scene. His early distrust of the British and his failure to understand the French suggest a weakness which one cannot excuse. His inability to make good use of his staff of experts was one of his most serious limitations. Nevertheless, when the entire record is examined, it seems justifiable to conclude that the United States was fortunate in having General Clay as its chief military government representative during the critical years 1945-1949. Ideally the United States might have done better, but it is not easy to name one who would have promised more. Had the United States not had an officer like General Clay in Germany during 1945 and 1946, when there was little or no direction coming out of Washington, a heavy price might have been paid.

THE MILITARY GOVERNMENT STAFF

It is more difficult to obtain a clear picture of the military government staff, not only because of their large number but because they came and went. To begin with, there were the commanding generals of the Third and Seventh Armies, Generals George Patton, Jr., and A. M. Patch, who served as military governors of the areas covered by their forces. Both generals established outstanding records as tactical commanders and also left a distinct impress on military government in Germany, though this aspect of their careers is less well known.

General Patch deserved much credit for any success which military government achieved during the early period. Less colorful than certain other high-ranking military leaders, he combined the best qualities of a soldier in himself. Living austerely and working incessantly, General Patch had little time for the small amenities.

71

He did not seek publicity; yet he let his ideas be known with a frankness which sometimes startled observers. Few men have been as indifferent to currying favor—when a group of U. S. Senators visited his headquarters he served them with spam sandwiches in contrast to the succulent repasts set before them by other commanders. General Patch stood as a source of great strength to military government. He believed that military government had a vital role to perform, and he gave military government personnel assigned to him and operating within his area great responsibilities.

General Patton, in contrast to General Patch, never really understood the function of military government. He probably in all sincerity considered it an innovation which served no useful purpose and merely cluttered up the scene. He did, of course, recognize the necessity of performing some of the functions assigned to military government, but he did not seem to rate these very highly. Instead of having military government specialists at his headquarters, he preferred to use tactical personnel. When the latter's record proved so unsatisfactory that outside pressure compelled him to bring in the military government specialists, he gave the latter very slight support. His subordinates followed the same course, and it is not surprising that many of the military government detachments in his area found themselves so checked that they almost threw up their hands in despair.

The district military governors who succeeded Generals Patch and Patton were less involved in tactical matters and hence more able to give their full attention to occupation problems. The War Department attempted to recruit former state governors and others with similar experience from the United States to serve in these posts and actually brought to Germany several of these officials. In general, they were political dead-ducks who, for various reasons, had little or no future at home and were willing to adventure in Germany at a price. Their background in German institutions and life was virtually nil and, what was worse, all too often they displayed little interest in acquiring any such knowledge. Their chief interest too frequently seemed to be in hunting game, drinking copiously of alcoholic beverages, living well, and having as exciting a time as possible. Their indifference to developments in Germany was at times almost beyond belief. Thus one might attempt to discuss various current problems with certain of them and find them almost completely uninformed and even uninterested. Upon being asked about an important German election in his district, one damned such nonsense and said that he expected to have a poker party the night before and to be drunk the day of the election. Two of these district military governors in Württemberg-Baden stood out as notable exceptions. One of the original military government specialist officers, Colonel William Dawson, came as commander of the military government detachment assigned to the *Land* Württemberg-Baden. A professor of law at Western Reserve University in civil life, Colonel Dawson made a highly valuable contribution to military government in his district. His knowledge of Germany and German problems was substantial, and his personal character and professional qualifications combined to make him an admirable choice for the position. A very hard and effective worker, he died in the harness while serving as district military governor. Charles M. LaFollette, a former member of Congress from Indiana, also served with distinction as a *Land* military governor.

General Clay's senior staff members at headquarters varied a great deal in ability and record. Some stood up well by any standard; many others were reasonably effective; and there were those who had little to recommend them. General William H. Draper, Jr., like his chief a man who usually worked at least a twelve-hour day, was mistrusted by some because he had been an officer of Dillon, Read and Company and was regarded as a representative of Wall Street in Germany. However, there is little if any evidence to back this up and, though not a specialist on the Germany economy, he handled the difficult task of economic adviser about as well as could be expected under the circumstances. General Henry Parkman and Edward H. Litchfield gave very good accounts of themselves in the governmental affairs field. Parkman was an unusually composed and fair-minded officer who had served with distinction in the field operations of military government before coming to OMGUS. Edward H. Litchfield, one of the youngest if not the youngest of the OMGUS senior staff, came as a civilian to work on civil service matters, having previously been a member of the Michigan Civil Service Commission. He shortly attracted the attention of General Clay and moved to a top position on the OMGUS staff. A human dynamo

73

and an expert on administration on a large scale, Litchfield could take on almost unlimited responsibilities which he pushed along more rapidly than most of his associates. The result was that his division took over programs which others felt belonged to them, and this led to resentment in certain quarters.

The Political Affairs Division and Office of the Political Adviser represented the State Department in OMGUS, but the former at least constituted an integral part of OMGUS on the organization chart. Both actually reported to the State Department in Washington and also advised General Clay. Robert D. Murphy, the Political Adviser, was a veteran Foreign Service Officer who had served in a junior capacity in Germany before the war. As an Irishman who knew all of the ways of smiling, handshaking, and saying pleasant things to the people who counted at the proper moment, Murphy made an excellent front for the State Department in Germany. But he was often very reluctant to take a stand on controversial matters—and most of the situations confronting military government in Germany were of this character. In those instances where he brought himself to take action, Mr. Murphy's judgment frequently did not prove sound. The ousting of Dr. Fritz Schaeffer, later the able Finance Minister of the West German Federal Government, as head of the Bavarian State Government may be cited as an example of his lack of good judgment. General Clay's statement that he could recall no instance during four years when Mr. Murphy disagreed with his decisions would seem to indicate that the latter did not effectively present the views of the State Department.* Donald R. Heath, John J. Muccio, and James Riddleberger of the Political Affairs Division, all experienced Foreign Service Officers who later served as career ambassadors, were in general less averse to taking stands on important issues and more willing to present and argue for State Department views. Unfortunately they were not always given adequate support by their senior colleague, Mr. Murphy, and this served to make their positions difficult at times. Nevertheless, their contributions were considerable.

Among other senior staff members were Charles Fahy, Judge Joseph W. Madden, Alvin Rockwell, and Colonels John Marsh and John Raymond who served at various times as legal counsel to

---

* See *Decision in Germany*, p. 58.

General Clay. The judgment of Mr. Fahy in extending the denazification program to include vast numbers of Germans outside the party[5] seems questionable in retrospect, but in general OMGUS was fortunate in its legal counsel. Calvin Hoover of Duke University who offered expert counsel during the early period on economic matters, David Morse in the field of labor problems, Orlando Wilson in public safety, and James K. Pollock who performed valuable service in connection with the *Länderrat* may also be mentioned as able specialists at the senior level.

In the case of the numerous staff members at lower levels and in the field, there was naturally greater variation than in the higher positions. Here were to be found military men and civilians of the highest integrity, seriousness of purpose, and ability, not infrequently with a greater knowledge of German problems than those higher up. Any country could well be proud of this group of hard-working, poorly compensated men who, for the most part, received little in the way of public recognition. They did many of the routine tasks which had to be attended to and, though not outstanding, were responsible, honest, and faithful agents of the United States who made a substantial contribution.

Unfortunately there were, in addition, two groups who brought little credit to themselves or to their country. One of these included representatives of business firms in the United States who had somehow managed to bore into official employment in military government and whose chief effort was to look after the interests of these private enterprises. More numerous in the same group were those who wandered into military government through no fault of their own because they were either surplus in a military replacement depot or civilians needing a job. As the military government specialists were returned to the United States in increasing numbers beginning in the fall of 1945, these "bodies," who usually had little to recommend them for military government assignments, were infiltrated in wholesale lots into field detachments and to some extent into headquarters jobs. Most of them had neither the capacity nor the personal interest required and only wanted to draw their pay and, in the case of many military persons, to get home as soon as possible.

---

[5] See W. E. Griffith, "Denazification in the United States Zone of Germany," *Annals of the American Academy of Political and Social Science*, Jan. 1950, p. 69.

The second of the two problem groups embraced the "wine, women, and song" boys who were so notorious in their exploits that they often brought a bad name to the entire military government organization. How many of these there were it is impossible to estimate; doubtless they were more numerous than they should have been, but it also seems fair to conclude that they were a comparatively small minority. However, they, like the man who bit the dog, received the attention of the press, when the more responsible and hard-working members of the military government staff worked in obscurity. The depraved manner in which some of these openly flaunted their mistresses in their contacts with their fellows as well with the German people was almost unbelievable. Their fantastic efforts to attract feminine followers from among the Germans and refugees would make a lurid story. The alcoholics were of course a pitiful group and life in many of the out-of-the-way places where military government officers were stationed was so dull that there was more than the usual temptation to seek solace in the bottle. How the "wine, women, and song" staff managed to hang on is difficult to explain. It is hardly surprising that there should have been this blot on the escutcheon of military government during the early days when confusion reigned, but it is hard to account for the fairly numerous cases of this sort at the end of the military government period in mid-1949 when HICOG screened military government personnel in the transition process. One might have supposed that General Clay would have been well aware of the situation and that with his own fine personal record he would have taken decisive steps to clean house. On the military side, at least, perhaps the explanation was the scarcity of personnel available and the pressure to take any one offered.

HIGH COMMISSIONERS

During 1949-1955, when the occupation had moved from a military government to a High Commission stage, the United States was presented in Germany by High Commissioners rather than Military Governors. Three incumbents of this office, John J. McCloy, Walter J. Donnelly, and James B. Conant, may be noted, but only

76

the former and latter require more than passing attention here, since Mr. Donnelly held office briefly.

John J. McCloy was selected as High Commissioner even before the Allied High Commission came into existence and indeed was sent to Germany to supervise the transition from military government in the early summer of 1949 as the last Military Governor. Unlike some of the officials whom the United States selects for its most important assignments, Mr. McCloy had an impressive background of a specialized nature. During the long and difficult years from early 1941 to late 1945, Mr. McCloy had held the post of Assistant Secretary of War and was in charge of military government planning, preparations, and operations throughout the world. Thus he came to the job of High Commissioner with as much or more knowledge relating to the task of administering occupied areas as anyone in his country, since he had not only been "exposed" to what went on but had taken a very deep personal interest in the problem. As a member of a well-known New York law firm, he was familiar with the business world, but his interests had not by any means been limited to the problems of law and business. Before his appointment as High Commissioner he had headed the World Bank, and this of course involved many significant international contacts.

Those who gained their impression of Mr. McCloy from his public utterances usually tended to underestimate the man. He was not very articulate and his speaking style was not particularly impressive. But he possessed sound judgment, worked effectively with his staff, and usually moved ahead only after careful preparation. While not especially interested in the routine job of administration, he commanded general respect from his staff.

High Commissioner McCloy regarded his assignment in Germany as primarily directed at the Germans rather than as the administrative head of a fairly large American organization in Germany. He spent a good deal of time in his office and held regular staff meetings, but senior employees sometimes complained that they never saw their chief. But if his own staff did not always see much of him, Mr. McCloy devoted a great deal of time and attention to the Germans, both official and unofficial, and at this stage it seems fair to conclude that this was more important than his job as head of an

77

American organization. He spent long hours on frequent occasions conferring with Dr. Konrad Adenauer and the leaders of the West German Federal Government, and he made a strong impact on them, not only because of his constructive ideas but because he could, with his conservative background in law, banking, and business in the United States, "speak their language." At the same time it would be a mistake to conclude that he gave himself wholly to the Christian Democrats and the conservative leaders in Germany, for he found the occasion also to discuss matters with Dr. Kurt Schumacher, the Social Democratic leader, and others, though here there was less meeting of minds.

The High Commissioner and his wife, a personable and intelligent woman of German ancestry, appeared frequently before various groups throughout Western Germany and in Berlin, sometimes together and sometimes singly, addressing their audiences in German and displaying deep concern for the future of Germany. A special fund, contributed by the McCloy family and friends, made it possible to purchase sewing machines for this church group, sports equipment for that youth group, and various other needed equipment, but above all it was evidence of the genuine interest of the McCloys in the welfare of Germans.[6] Mr. McCloy remained as High Commissioner until 1952, when he returned home to become chairman of the board of the Chase National Bank in New York City.

During several months in 1952 Mr. Walter J. Donnelly, a Foreign Service career Officer who had had much experience in Latin America and had recently been the minister and first civilian High Commissioner of the United States in Austria, held the post of U. S. High Commissioner for Germany. But he found the situation difficult and, desiring to leave the public service and enter the field of business, he shortly returned to the United States.

The third and final incumbent of the HICOG was Dr. James B. Conant who assumed office in 1953 and remained until the end of the occupation in May 1955, becoming the first American ambassador. Although not a specialist on German affairs, Mr. Conant

---

[6] For a more detailed account of such activities, see J. F. J. Gillen, *The Special Projects Program of the Office of the U. S. High Commissioner for Germany*, in the Historical Series of the Office of the U. S. High Commissioner for Germany (1952). The McCloy fund projects constituted only a part of the above program.

had had wide contacts with foreign scientists and educators as a professor of chemistry at Harvard University, as President of Harvard, and as one of the most active scientists in advising the American government on various problems. He retired from the presidency of Harvard to take over this most important assignment in Germany. With a reputation for impetuosity as President of Harvard, Mr. Conant, as the years passed, acquired a great understanding of the ways of men and his counsel was listened to with more than ordinary respect. As one of the world's leading educators and scientists, Mr. Conant brought a distinction to the Office of the U. S. High Commissioner which was particularly appreciated by German educators and more valued by German leaders than would perhaps be the case in the United States. His background was not such that he could step into the duties of a High Commissioner with the ease that Mr. McCloy had done, but Mr. Conant was not only highly intelligent but willing to learn and he mastered the job in a way as to command the respect of his staff. His influence on the Germans was also good and in certain circles probably beyond that of Mr. McCloy. However, his relations with Dr. Adenauer and the political leaders, though cordial and correct, were not as close as those of Mr. McCloy, largely perhaps because his background was more divergent and he could not meet them on their own level as easily.

OTHER HIGH COMMISSION PERSONNEL

During the period 1949-1952 the United States maintained a *Land* commissioner in each of the states within its area and a liaison officer or *Land* observer in the several states in the British and French areas. These officials naturally varied in background and ability, but by and large it seems fair to say that they were superior to the district military governors during the earlier period. Two of them, General C. P. Gross and Captain (Navy) C. R. Jeffs, were professional military men who had retired and a third, J. R. Newman, had been a military government officer. The outstanding *Land* commissioner was Dr. George N. Shuster who was loaned by Hunter College where he served as President to fill the post in Bavaria. An expert on German affairs, with a fluent knowledge of the German

79

language, and a leading Catholic layman, Dr. Shuster made a considerable impression on Munich and indeed on Bavaria as a whole.[7] The *Land* observers varied more widely than the *Land* commissioners, both in experience and ability. At least two carried out the difficult duties attached to their positions quite well; one seemed weak indeed on almost every score.

General George P. Hays and Benjamin Buttenwieser served as Deputy High Commissioner and Assistant High Commissioner, respectively, under Mr. McCloy. Hays, a regular Army officer, had seen service in Europe in World War II and had been in the military government organization in Germany. A Lincolnesque sort of man despite his ordinary height, he represented the High Commissioner in the Bonn area before the Office of the U. S. Commissioner moved from Frankfurt to Bonn. Mr. Buttenwieser, a partner in the Wall Street firm of Kuhn, Loeb, and Company, gave his attention to various special problems relating to the Germans rather than to the internal administration of HICOG. A man of broad experience, distinct ability, and much vitality, Mr. Buttenwieser was not the conventional sort of Wall Street banker and broker by any means. His ideas were frequently exciting and his addresses to various groups of German officials were often given a careful hearing. Colonel H. A. Gerhardt, the special assistant to the High Commissioner, made a very valuable contribution to HICOG because of his extraordinary combination of intelligence, sound judgment, tact, and force.

The heads of the major subdivisions of HICOG presented a fairly diverse picture, though perhaps less diverse than in the case of OMGUS. To begin with, there was probably less coming and going, despite changes which were inevitable. James E. King, Jr., the executive secretary, had been trained in political science at Oxford, Harvard, and Duke and had served earlier in military government in Germany. He was almost, if not absolutely, a perfect executive secretary, with intelligence, tact, imagination, and reliability. Glenn G. Wolfe, in charge of administration, was the sort who believes in a rude approach as an indication of strength and his "bark" pained many people; but, despite a limited professional background prior to coming to Germany, he possessed a considerable

---

[7] Dr. George N. Shuster with A. Bergstrasser contributed *Germany, A Short History* (Norton, New York, 1944).

amount of ability in the administrative field and it may be said that his "bark was much worse than his bite."

Samuel Reber, Jr., James W. Riddleberger, John Paton Davies, and John Hay headed the Office of Political Affairs at various times. The first three were experienced Foreign Service Officers who were assigned to this post in Germany. Riddleberger and Reber had had more extensive contact with European affairs than Davies, but Davies made a considerable impression on various associates as a result of his efforts to familiarize senior staff members of HICOG with the basic factors in German political life through a staff seminar. John Hay joined the State Department as late as 1949 and came to his post in Germany after service in the subdivision of the State Department in Washington handling German affairs. Robert M. Hanes, a banker and industrialist from North Carolina, and Jean Cattier, a New York financier, headed the Office of Economic Affairs until succeeded by a younger man, M. S. Harris, who had had considerable experience in the Economic Cooperation Administration in Europe.

The Office of Public Affairs had various chiefs, but perhaps the most effective was Dr. Shepard Stone who had served briefly with military government in 1945 and earlier had taken a Ph.D. at the University of Berlin, marrying a German girl during his student days. Stone had a broad knowledge of German problems and displayed a keen interest in German youth and information services, the latter to some extent arising no doubt from his association with the Sunday edition of the *New York Times*. Harvey W. Brown, director of the Office of Labor Affairs throughout its existence, came to Germany from long service with the A. F. of L. in the United States, having been one of its vice-presidents. He rarely if ever missed an opportunity to report on labor activities in contrast to many of his colleagues who usually had little to say about the work of their offices. B. H. Shute was the chief of the Office of Intelligence during the early years of HICOG. His work was naturally not performed in the limelight, but he gave the impression of being effective.

Chester A. McLain, Robert R. Bowie, and E. W. Debevoise occupied the post of General Counsel at various periods. Bowie had been a professor in the Harvard Law School and had had extensive experience in military government as assistant to General Clay.

81

Debevoise came to Germany from the senior partnership in a well-known New York law firm and from a very active role in the civic life of his city. All were first-rate lawyers.

Some of the heads of the major divisions of HICOG devoted themselves primarily to directing the work of their staffs. Others including McLain, Stone, Bowie, Reber, and Hanes were particularly close to Mr. McCloy and in addition to their work as division heads spent much time and energy in assisting in the formulation of general policies. Reber and Bowie gave much of their time at one period to negotiations relating to the Schuman Plan.

In Berlin the United States was represented by a military commander who held both military and HICOG status and a civilian who headed the Berlin Element of HICOG. Military commanders came and went, but the outstanding one among a generally able group was doubtless General Maxwell D. Taylor, later Commander of American Forces in the Far East and Chief of Staff of the Army in Washington. It may be added that few military officials or civilians in Germany or elsewhere combined greater force, hard work, interest, and intelligence than General Taylor. Among the civilian heads in Berlin, Howard P. Jones, Cecil Lyon, and Henry Parkman stand out, though for different reasons.

The remaining HICOG staff may be divided into two general categories: those serving in the headquarters and those doing work in the field. The former included a fairly large group which was gradually reduced by about two thirds during the years 1951-1955. Here were chiefs of divisions and sections dealing with education, the exchanges program, the information services, fiscal matters, personnel, religious affairs, and a wide range of other matters and specialists or supposed-specialists assigned the basic work to be done. Some gave an excellent account of themselves; others were reasonably effective but not outstanding. Some were not impressive at all and one could only wonder on what basis they had been selected and how they managed to hang on after they joined the HICOG staff. In general, however, the number in the last category tended to shrink under HICOG and there were those who attributed the existing weaknesses to the fact that HICOG had taken over a good many OMGUS employees.

This may be an appropriate place to note the problem of Ameri-

82

cans who remain too long away from home. Many members of the HICOG staff had come to Europe in military capacities, they remained in military government, and then civilianized to take jobs with HICOG. Having been away from home for half a dozen years or longer, they had largely lost contact with American developments despite leaves taken at home. Some of these expatriates did their official jobs well enough, but others were more or less dead weight. Not a few of these persons had more or less tragic experiences when the time came for their ultimate separation from work in Germany and the necessity of finding a job in the United States. One may wonder whether it is wise to permit Americans to hold jobs, such as those in organizations like OMGUS and HICOG, for periods exceeding four or five years.

The HICOG staff in the field was almost wound up by 1952, but during 1949-1952 fairly large numbers of persons were employed in the offices of the *Land* commissioners and as *Kreis* resident officers. The offices of the *Land* commissioners more or less paralleled the HICOG headquarters but, of course, on a more modest basis and with staff members of somewhat lower grades. It is probable that there were more holdovers from OMGUS in these offices. Like the HICOG headquarters staff, there was wide variation among these employees: some were outstanding; a good many were reasonably able; and too large a number were misfits and incompetents.

The *Kreis* resident officers had the assignment of representing the United States in the various *Kreise* or counties in the American area of Germany as well as that of serving as liaison officers between American military installations and local German populations. Many of these resident officers were young Foreign Service Officers and other young men selected on the same basis who were sent to Germany without previous professional experience. They were in general an intelligent, personable, and ambitious group. Some of these youngsters found their assignments as resident officers challenging and, in the short time during which they held these jobs, gave an excellent account of themselves under rather trying circumstances. Others felt that their efforts were wasted on anything lower than political reporting or political policy-making. Among the older *Kreis* resident officers were many who had served with military government, and some of these handled their assignments in a highly effective manner.

83

GERMAN EMPLOYEES

Before passing on to another topic some attention must be given to the large number of Germans who served both OMGUS and HICOG. Many of these performed routine tasks, such as driving motor pool cars, caring for buildings, staffing restaurants and cafeterias, guarding properties, and the like. Numerous others served as stenographers and typists, file clerks, messengers, and research assistants. But a fairly sizable number advised various divisions of both OMGUS and HICOG on legal matters, economic problems, and other technical fields. And the information services program, the operation of America Houses, the film programs, and radio broadcasting were largely dependent upon German employees. It is hardly too much to say that neither OMGUS nor HICOG, but more especially the latter, could have managed without their German employees who, in the case of HICOG, far outnumbered the American staff. It was not easy to draw conclusions about these Germans because much of their work was done behind the scenes. Some of them were undoubtedly highly intelligent, professionally able, and anxious to contribute as far as possible to the work of their organizations. Others were neurotics who constituted more or less constant problems. A number of those engaged in routine work seemed inferior on almost every count and did not bother to work when they could avoid it. The majority probably did their more or less monotonous jobs about as effectively as such work is ordinarily performed inside of Germany or without.[8] In many instances it was unfortunate that so great dependence had to be placed on the German employees, but lack of dollar appropriations and the high costs of American salaries and traveling expenses made their use essential. Their salaries varied widely, but in general they were paid a small fraction of what their American associates received for the same work.

CONCLUDING COMMENTS

Any attempt to pass definitive judgment on or to evaluate authoritatively the thousands of Americans who served with military government or HICOG must be tentative. However, a few general

---

[8] For a detailed monograph dealing with the German employees of HICOG, see J. F. J. Gillen, *The Employment of German Nationals by the Office of the U. S. High Commissioner for Germany*, (Restricted) in the Historical Series of the Office of the U. S. High Commissioner for Germany (1952).

conclusions may be valid. In the first place, it seems fair to say that the United States was distinctly fortunate in its Military Governor and High Commissioners. General Clay, John J. McCloy, and James B. Conant would be unusual in any roles and they served the United States in a distinguished manner in Germany. They were not perfect, but they were so much better than those ordinarily available, even for top places in public service, that it is truly remarkable that such appointments were made.

The men who served at the second level were in general less able and uniform in quality. Some of them were men of first-rate caliber who handled their assignments in a very effective manner, but many were mediocre in attainments and service. Too many had little specialized knowledge of German affairs, were primarily interested in empire building, and spent too much of their time and energy in waging feuds with associates in Germany and with the authorities in Washington. There were some downright failures at this level, but their number was not large.

Finally, it was hardly surprising that the many lower level and operating employees at headquarters and in the field were as a whole less outstanding than those in the two upper levels. The very numbers of positions involved and the lower ratings and remuneration would explain this disparity to a large extent. Insufficient credit has been given to the high quality work done by many of the members of this category, largely perhaps because of the widespread publicity given the ne'er-do-wells, the alcoholics, the sex maniacs, and other misfits. Actually the work of both OMGUS and HICOG could not have been performed with anything like the success achieved had it not been for the large number of hard-working, reliable, and reasonably competent persons holding the operating positions. They have received little publicity and far too little appreciation of any kind. However, no responsible observer can ignore or justify the group of persons who did little or no work at all, who handled miserably those tasks assigned to them, and who gave the military government setup of the United States and, to a lesser degree, HICOG a bad name because of their dishonesty, alcoholism, sexual exploits, and the like. How so many of these ever got into the armed services or the civilian employ of the government may be difficult to explain. It is even less apparent how and by what means they were able to remain in public positions in some instances during a period of several years.

6

The Thorny Problem of Policy

A study of the policy of the United States as regards Germany during the period of the occupation throws considerable light on the general problem of foreign policy-making. Perhaps not every facet of the general problem is represented in the occupation of Germany, but certainly most phases are. Indeed it would be difficult to select a single American experience which reflects so well the basic factors which enter into the shaping of the foreign policy of the United States.[1]

Here one notes the almost insuperable difficulty of looking ahead and viewing in anything like proper perspective the many ramifications of present-day international relations. A great deal of preliminary attention was given to the planning of the occupation of Germany by the State Department, the War Department, and to a lesser extent by other agencies of the United States government. Most, if not all, of this served a useful purpose and prevented certain errors later; but, as one reviews at the end of the occupation the analyses and proposed policies to be followed, it is apparent how many matters were not clear to those experts in charge of the early planning. It is almost incredible as one looks back to see how little understanding there was of the indissoluble ties binding Germany to the rest of Europe. It was more or less assumed that Germany could be regarded as a problem in a vacuum, so to speak, and that little if any attention was required to the overall effect of postwar conditions in Germany on France, the Low Countries, the United Kingdom, the Scandinavian countries, Italy, and so forth and vice versa. Experience indicated how mistaken such a procedure was and how tremendously important the situation in Germany was to the rest of Western Europe.

---

[1] For a discussion of the general policy, see A. Wolfers, *United States Policy Towards Germany*, Institute of International Studies, Yale University (Yale University Press, New Haven, 1947).

General Dwight D. Eisenhower, Supreme Allied Commander Europe, Commander of U. S. Forces European Theatre, and first American Military Governor, standing at his desk.

General J. T. McNarney, C. G., U. S. Forces European Theatre and American Military Governor.

General George S. Patton, Jr., C. G., U. S. Third Army and District Military Governor.

Lieutenant General Alexander M. Patch, Jr., C. G., U. S. Seventh Army and District Military Governor.

General Lucius D. Clay, American Military Governor, and General Sir Brian Robertson, British Military Governor, shown with Ministers President of the West German *Länder* Bavaria, North Rhine Westphalia, Hamburg, Schleswig-Holstein, and Lower Saxony.

Dr. Konrad Adenauer, Chancellor of the Federal Republic of Germany, presents to John J McCloy, U. S. High Commissioner, a letter announcing the Federal Government's forma ratification of the ECA agreement between the West German Federal Republic and th United States.

The Thorny Problem of Policy

In a democratic country such as the United States, the making of foreign policy is intimately tied up with political pressures of one kind and another. Not even the President can afford to ignore the more powerful of these pressures, though a strong national leader with definite goals relating to foreign policy can of course do something at least in building up public opinion which serves to neutralize or counteract some of these political pressures. Even if a President may be inclined to minimize political considerations, which is quite unlikely, Congress is bound to be sensitive to them. And since the President has to depend upon Congress for financial assistance and Congress has its own responsibilities in connection with the foreign relations and affairs of the United States, powerful political winds are almost certain to be influential in shaping the policy.

This is illustrated in the case of the occupation of Germany by the insistent demand for a punitive policy which was represented in the so-called Morgenthau Plan drafted by Harry Dexter White, Henry Morgenthau, the Secretary of the Treasury, and others.[2] As one looks back, it seems almost unbelievable that such large numbers of Americans could have been gullible enough to subscribe to the unrealistic proposal to de-industrialize one of the most highly industrialized countries of the world. But emotions are blinding and the dastardly conduct of the Nazis involving the Jews, those advocating world peace, many of the clergy, American airmen, and others stirred up resentment and bitterness on an enormous scale in the United States. Many citizens ordinarily reasonably mature were swept off their feet by this emotional appeal. As a result they gave their strong support to demands aimed at Washington that would have the effect of quarantining Germany and reducing the German people to a position of misery. The force generated by this movement was so powerful that even President Franklin D. Roosevelt, Secretary of State Hull, and other top officials bent before it for a time. The plans of the State Department and War Department specialists had to be shelved in the face of such political pressure, though they later proved of some value when the movement had subsided and the German problem still remained to be settled.

American policy toward postwar Germany also is of interest because it throws light on the difficulty of getting decisions at high levels.

---

[2] See H. Morgenthau, *Germany Is Our Problem* (Harper, New York, 1945).

It is generally known that a great amount of preparatory work has to be done before a specific policy can be formulated. The State Department and, to a lesser extent, other agencies of the government have expert staffs which devote themselves to the research work, the drafting of working papers and memoranda, the reviewing, the formulating of proposed policies, and the like, upon which policy must be based. But these specialists, despite their essential character, can go only so far as to propose or recommend. The President, the Secretary of State, and a few other top-ranking officials are too involved with other duties to give close attention to the preliminary work of foreign policy-making, but they must find time to go over the proposals and recommendations of the lower level specialists, since only they have the constitutional responsibility for deciding what shall be the foreign policy of the United States.

Considering the far-reaching importance of foreign policy in major areas, it might be supposed that it would be comparatively easy to secure the attention of the President and the Secretary of State to items of first-rate consequence in this field; but, as the German experience indicates, it is frequently most difficult. In principle, the officials recognize the imperative character of the responsibility which the Constitution has conferred on them, but they are confronted with so many other demands, many of which involve domestic matters that may seem to have political implications beyond those of foreign relations. Some of those who must bear this constitutional burden may have little background or first-hand knowledge of international affairs and this may cause them to display reluctance in making decisions. Or there may be enormously demanding national efforts, such as fighting a world war, which seem to dwarf every other activity and push even the weighty problems of the postwar period into the background.

In the case of establishing a policy for postwar Germany all of these complications may be noted. To begin with, President Roosevelt and his associates were so immersed in the winning of the war that they could be approached only with great difficulty in connection with policies relating to the occupation of Germany. It was not that they were indifferent to what came after, and criticisms to the point that they won the war only to lose the peace are rather meaningless. The explanation was that they were human beings of only so much capacity and energy, and the tactical aspects of the conflict were so engrossing, so demanding, so identified with the national thinking that they simply could not find the time and energy to devote to the postwar situation.

When postwar problems were taken up, as at Quebec and Yalta, they tended to be subordinated to the immediate military considerations of a war not yet finished, with the result that all too frequently far-reaching matters were passed over with hardly more than a moment's consideration and with little understanding of the full implications. With the end of fighting, the United States had a new President in the person of Harry S. Truman who had had little experience in foreign affairs and, consequently for a time, was very hesitant to get involved in even those situations which were the most pressing. The result was that for about a year following the German capitulation it was virtually impossible to get the White House to give attention to policy matters relating to Germany.

Although the United States occupies a position as a world leader, with international relations being of utmost importance, domestic issues sometimes seem to dominate the field, leaving foreign items more or less unattended for the time being. Here too the German experience throws light on the general problem. Domestic problems were particularly in the limelight after the end of World War II because they had been put into the background to a considerable extent by the concentration on winning the war. Emphasis on demobilization and conversion of the economy to a peacetime basis was overwhelming. The American people were thoroughly tired of the war and wanted their husbands, sons, brothers, and boy friends home. Moreover, American business felt that it deserved a break after some years of regimentation, and exerted great pressure to have the government focus its attention on conversion.

There was almost complete indifference on the part of the American people or of American political leaders to the problem of the occupation of Germany for many months after V-E Day. One American news service which recognized the stakes of the United States in Germany discovered this to its loss when it put a number of its ablest representatives in Europe on a project of reporting in some detail and as authoritatively as possible on the German situation in the autumn of 1945. Among its several hundred newspaper subscribers only a handful made any use of the features, and the expenditure of a considerable sum of money had to be written off as a complete loss. When editors and publishers were approached during this period in an effort to persuade them to give a reasonable amount of space to the German problem, they almost invariably replied that their hands were tied because the newspaper public had no interest in such matters. Aside from the *New York Times* and the *Christian Science Monitor*, there was very little reporting of German developments for at least a year after May 1945.

The State Department has the traditional responsibility for handling foreign affairs in the United States, but modern developments have brought about a situation where various other agencies of the government expect to participate and be consulted. Particularly during a period when a legal state of war continues though the fighting has ceased, the defense departments and the Joint Chiefs of Staff occupy very important roles. Although the National Security Council had not yet been established when the American occupation of Germany began, it played an important role during the latter years of the occupation. The Treasury Department is interested in monetary and credit aspects of international problems. The Commerce Department displays an interest in international trade. The Labor Department feels entitled to a voice in international affairs involving labor. And so it goes. The formulation of foreign policy is therefore considerably more complicated than was once the case. A number of departments have specialists who are planning for various foreign relations of the United States and these want a finger in the making of foreign policy, even if they admit the primary responsibility of the State Department in this field. Hence, interdepartmental committees have to be set up to discuss and coordinate proposals and recommendations to be submitted to the President for approval or to take more or less final action in minor matters which have been delegated to them by the President.

In the handling of the German problem, various agencies in Washington felt that their interest was sufficient to justify their participation in drafting policy. Committees of one sort and another resulted, of which the most publicized was the State, War, and Navy Coordinating Committee, commonly known as SWNCC. The policy of the

United States relating to Germany was therefore not the work of a single agency; it was the result of compromise on the part of agencies with somewhat varying points of view. Even when prepared by a single department, American foreign policy cannot ordinarily be as crystal clear as some would like, but when it emerges from the joint efforts of a number of departments, it will obviously be less consistent.

One of the phenomenal developments of recent years in the United States has been the expansion of the military beyond the narrow limits of defense activities. Many matters relating to foreign relations are now considered to have an important bearing on national defense and as such are of vital concern to the Department of Defense. The role of the National Security Council and, during an earlier period, of the Joint Chiefs of Staff in foreign affairs has been highly important. During the early years of the occupation of Germany it was impossible to make headway in understanding American policy without taking into account the Joint Chiefs of Staff. Since the American occupation authority was military in character and since a civil administration was delayed until late 1949, policy directives were sent out by the Joint Chiefs of Staff to the American Commander in Germany who was also the Military Governor. The Joint Chiefs of Staff were of course not given the entire responsibility of formulating American policy as regards Germany: they were expected to be guided by the decisions of the coordinating committees representing the various interest agencies noted above. At the same time they were by no means limited to transmitting such decisions to Germany. They discussed the situation among themselves, drafting a directive which was supposedly based on the decisions representing the State and other interested departments but incorporating their own interpretations. The emphasis to be placed on a particular item was something which they determined in large measure. The American occupation authority in Germany was generally bound to follow the policies as interpreted and laid down by the Joint Chiefs of Staff, though it might have information indicating that these did not reflect the thinking of the State Department or even of the President.

A spectacular example may be cited in the case of the basic directive known as JCS 1067 which legally controlled American activities in Germany from May 1945 until the middle of 1947. This famous, or as some would regard it "infamous," directive reflected in large measure a philosophy of quarantine and revenge, embodying a very harsh economic policy and emphasizing denazification. As a mirror of Presidential and high Washington attitude of the period of the second Quebec Conference held in September 1944, it was impressive. But by the time it was issued in April 1945 President Roosevelt and other high officials had seen the folly of their earlier position and no longer supported the unrealistic policy of de-industrializing a highly industrialized country such as Germany. Had President Roosevelt lived, perhaps JCS 1067 would have been withdrawn shortly or at least thoroughly revised. As it was, JCS 1067 remained the basic policy directive for two long years, despite the drastic change of thinking in official circles in Washington.

Finally, it is apparent that American foreign policy is often the result of indirect as well as direct influences. The course in a given matter may be determined by various factors, some of which may seem to have little direct bearing on the immediate situation. In other words, there are policies and there are policies, some of which are overriding and others subordinate. An overriding policy in one field which may seem to be far removed from another may determine in large measure the policy in the latter. It would be difficult to find a more striking example of this than the United States policy relating to Germany during the later years of the occupation. The overriding foreign policy of the United States during this period was one of building up a defense against the Soviet Union. American policies relating to Germany were to a considerable extent then the result of such an overriding policy rather than based on the immediate situation in West Germany. It is to be noted of course that the experience with the Soviet Union in the Allied Control Authority of Germany and particularly in the Berlin Blockade entered into the overriding policy of the United States based on defense against the Soviet Union.

THREE PHASES OF AMERICAN POLICY TOWARD GERMANY

It is possible to classify American policy relating to Germany on various bases, but perhaps as convenient a system as any for the purpose here is one which makes use of three phases. Under such a classification the first phase was that extending from the German surrender in 1945 to mid-1947.[3] The second phase covered the period from mid-1947 to the Berlin Blockade (1948-1949). The third and final phase extended from the Berlin Blockade to the end of the occupation. Further subdivisions might be made which would split the first phase into two parts, one extending from the beginning of the occupation to the address by Secretary of State Byrnes at Stuttgart in September 1946, and the second from that time until mid-1947, when a new Joint Chiefs of Staff directive was issued. The third phase could be subdivided into a preliminary period ending with the establishing of the Allied High Commission and the West German Federal Government; a second period concluding with 1952, when the Contractual Agreements designed to end the occupation had been completed; and a third period covering the years from 1952 to 1955, when the long-drawn efforts to get ratification of the agreements to bring the occupation to a close were being made. But the division of the occupation into three main phases has the advantage of some simplicity and is sufficient for most purposes.

The first phase of American policy covering the period from April 1945 to July 1947 has usually been designated the JCS 1067 phase, taking its name from the Joint Chiefs of Staff basic policy directive to the U. S. Commander in Germany. This directive was received in the European Theatre in April of 1945 and remained formally in effect until supplanted by a second policy directive from the Joint Chiefs of Staff in July 1947. Although JCS 1067 underwent a number of drafts, reference is usually to JCS 1067. The version issued in April 1945 was technically the sixth and therefore designated JCS 1067/6.[4] It was approved by President Truman early in May and formally issued as a top secret document on May 14, 1945.[5]

JCS 1067 was a detailed policy directive covering twelve large double-columned printed pages. It was divided into three parts deal-

---

[3] For contemporary discussions of the first phase, see Dean Acheson and others, "Our Military Government Policy in Germany," *Department of State Bulletin*, Sept. 2, 1945, J. J. McCloy, "American Occupation Policies in Germany," *Proceedings of the Academy of Political Science*, Jan. 1946; Henry Morgenthau, *Germany Is Our Problem* (Harper, New York; 1945); State Department, *Occupation of Germany, Policy and Progress* (1947).

[4] For its text, see State Department, *Germany, 1947-1949; The Story in Documents* (Washington, 1950), pp. 22-33.

[5] A detailed analysis of the genesis and development of this directive has been made by Professor Walter L. Dorn in a manuscript which had not been published at the date of this writing.

ing with general and political matters, economic matters, and financial matters, and further subdivided into 52 paragraphs. In general, it was a harsh and stern set of instructions largely negative in character. It forbade fraternization on the part of American personnel with the German people, ordered a very strict program of denazification extending to both public life and business, emphasized agricultural reconstruction, and prohibited American aid in the rebuilding of German industry. Under this directive the German people were definitely considered a menace to humanity and guilty of crimes against other people; as such they were to be dealt with very firmly though properly. Punishment was to be meted out by reducing their standard of living drastically and by preventing them from regaining economic strength. Along with its negative and punitive provisions, JCS 1067 stipulated the preparation of the German people for democratic political institutions, but it may be fair to conclude that such preparation was of the sort which penal institutions are supposed to furnish in the making of good citizens. This directive showed the United States as a shortsighted country, motivated largely by revenge, and with little appreciation of the fundamental problems of an occupation. It constituted what may be called without undue exaggeration a heavy millstone around the neck of the American military government.[6]

Although JCS 1067 was a severe handicap to American efforts in Germany, it should be noted that its impact was rather less paralyzing than some have imagined. American character is such that in an impossible situation there is a tendency to overlook formal laws and orders and to make use of common sense. Even General Clay, brought up as he was in a strict military tradition with great respect for such a body as the Joint Chiefs of Staff, increasingly found himself interpreting the policy as set forth in JCS 1067 to meet military government needs and when necessary bypassing its provisions. On occasion, especially in the economic field, he resorted to the terms of the Potsdam Agreement, which, though far from liberal, represented a less negative policy than JCS 1067.[7] But perhaps more frequently he made his own policy. The occupation of a country such as Germany presents a multiplicity of detailed questions to be settled, and even

---

[6] For a first-hand reaction to such impact, see M. M. Knappen, *And Call It Peace* (University of Chicago Press, Chicago, 1947).

[7] See L. D. Clay, *Decision in Germany*, p. 72.

a detailed policy directive such as JCS 1067 cannot possibly cover them all. Had the situation in Washington been less confused, General Clay might have found it difficult to make his own policy; as it was, the State Department might grumble but could do little to challenge him. The White House was indifferent to Germany or at least immersed in domestic problems during the formative period. The American people were wholeheartedly devoted to conversion to a peacetime economy. General Clay could do more or less as he pleased in Germany, as long as he observed the formalities and accepted JCS 1067 as the general guide. What happened was that American military government increasingly followed the middle-of-the-road course anticipated by the planners in the German Country Unit, in the U. S. Group, Control Council for Germany, and in Washington.

This departure from the policy as laid down by JCS 1067 was encouraged by an address which Secretary of State Byrnes delivered in Stuttgart on September 6, 1946.[8] After more than a year of occupation the general situation confronting the United States in Germany was far from bright. The Germans seemed to be doing less than might be expected to help in supporting themselves. Secretary of State Byrnes consequently came to Germany to address an assemblage of German political leaders and others in the presence of General Clay and major officials of OMGUS in the early autumn of 1946. In this address he pledged continued American interest in European affairs, expressed a more liberal attitude toward economic reconstruction in Germany, and stated the American view as favoring the economic unification and as soon as possible the political unification of Germany. He made a hit by declaring that "It is the view of the American Government that the German people throughout Germany, under proper safeguards, should now be given the primary responsibility for the running of their own affairs," and adding that the United States did not regard the Oder-Neisse line fixing the eastern boundary between Germany and Poland as final. One of his concluding statements: "The American people who fought for freedom have no desire to enslave the German people," naturally aroused a very favorable response from the Germans. As one looks over the words of the Stuttgart address today, it may well be that they do not seem particu-

---

[8] For the text of this address, see State Department, *op. cit.*, pp. 3-8.

larly generous, but, coming as they did at a time of great national discouragement on the part of the Germans and in reference to the harsh JCS 1067, they made a favorable impact on the Germans. Perhaps it was not so much what Secretary Byrnes said as how he said it that was significant.

In October 1946 shortly after the Byrnes address, General Clay made a trip to Washington to discuss the revision of American policy. In his *Decision in Germany*, he states that his ideas in regard to revision of policy were favorably received and that he found the various interested agencies in substantial agreement as to what should be done.* But, despite the generally propitious situation in Washington, there was what now appears an almost incredible delay in revising the basic policy directive. General Clay apparently expected a revised directive late in 1946 or at least early in 1947—it was actually July 1947 before JCS 1067 was supplanted by JCS 1779. During this interval General Clay, knowing that Washington official thinking had moved a long way toward a more liberal policy for Germany, was naturally freer from the terms of JCS 1067 than had been the case before. Nevertheless, it can hardly be denied that this long delay was unfortunate. It is indicative of the confusion and inability to operate effectively which continued to prevail in Washington after the war came to an end.

The second phase of policy extending from July 1947 into the period of the Berlin Blockade was somewhat briefer than the first, covering a period of less than two years. The new directive, JCS 1779, much less well known than its predecessor, was not as detailed, covering some eight printed pages of double-column type.[9] It consisted of six parts subdivided into 27 paragraphs and, while it continued certain restrictive policies, such as those relating to militarization, it was more positive in character than the earlier directive. Its economic provisions were more liberal and its emphasis on cultural activities, education, information program, and so forth, represented a considerable shift from the provisions of JCS 1067. It recognized the system which had developed under which the American Military Governor exercised a considerable amount of discretion by providing: "Your authority as Military Governor will be broadly construed and empowers you to take action consistent with relevant international agreements,

---

* See *Decision in Germany*, pp. 72-73.
[9] For its text, see State Department, *Germany, 1947-1949*, pp. 34-41.

general foreign policies of this Government and with this directive, appropriate or desirable to attain your Government's objectives in Germany or to meet military exigencies."

Acting under this liberalized policy directive, General Clay moved ahead to encourage German economic reconstruction and, indirectly through Bizonia, political reconstruction. Denazification had been turned over to the Germans during the first policy period and, while the German denazification tribunals continued their work into the second phase, there was less emphasis on this aspect of military government. Perhaps the greatest practical impact during the second phase arose out of the vigorous and decisive action on the part of the United States looking toward the breaking of the Berlin Blockade. Secretary Byrnes had said that the United States would continue to maintain interest in European affairs, but words are not always to be taken at face value. The bold and courageous efforts of the United States to deal with the emergency in Berlin went far to convince Germans, not only in Berlin but elsewhere, of the American interest in German affairs and of the constructive character of its policy. More than that, it enormously added to the prestige of the United States. Many Germans had not been favorably impressed by the early record of American military government. The Russians had sometimes appeared in a better light than the Americans because of their vigorous efforts in the economic field, their immediate recognition of German cultural needs, and so forth. But the American record in connection with Berlin went far to counteract any such feeling on the part of certain Germans. The Berliners naturally reacted most favorably, but Germans in the West were greatly impressed too. The success in relieving Berlin doubtless did more to add to the hope of eventual freedom of the East Germans than any previous action.

It was during the second phase that General Marshall as Secretary of State delivered his famous address at Chicago on November 18, 1947, during which he stressed the importance of a European community bound together by close economic and cultural ties and concluded: "The restoration of Europe involves the restoration of Germany. Without a revival of German economy there can be no revival of Europe's economy." [10] Here at last was the recognition which should have been one of the principal foundations of American policy

[10] For the text of this address, see State Department, *op. cit.*, pp. 9-13.

relating to the occupation of Germany from the very beginning. This clear-cut reversal of the policy embodied in JCS 1067 aided in putting Germany on a self-supporting basis. The significant inclusion of Germany in the ECA program and in the world of nations as a member of the Organization for European Economic Cooperation and the European Payments Union grew in large measure out of this new American policy.

The Blockade of Berlin and the final breakdown of the Allied Control Authority convinced the United States that there was no possibility of cooperating with the Russians in Germany. The result was a third phase based on an American policy of going along with Great Britain and France in dealing with West Germany as a political and economic unit. Steps were taken in concert with the western Allies toward the establishment of a West German Federal Republic after a trizonal fusion had been agreed upon. An Occupation Statute was drafted to define the authority of the West German Federal Government, and an Allied High Commission was organized to supervise and assist such a government. Most of the limitations were removed from the German economy, and vigorous encouragement in the form of ECA aid and moral support was given toward rapid economic reconstruction. The policy of regarding the German people as human beings who might have been led astray under Hitler but were still likely prospects for membership in a world of nations, which had been inaugurated to some extent during the second phase, was greatly extended. Elaborate information programs, exchanges projects, and the like, were supported in order to bring the Germans into closer touch with recent developments in the United States and other western nations. The American policy during this third and final phase was very largely constructive in character. There was little or no emphasis placed on the earlier efforts in the direction of denazification, dismantling, and the like.

The cold war following the Blockade of Berlin convinced the United States of the threat to world peace offered by the Soviet Union. Consequently a basic, if not the most important, element of general American foreign policy was to build up a defense against the Russians. This was implemented the world over, but Europe was regarded as the most important area for defense measures. It was frequently said that the defense of the United States rested not on the

Atlantic nor on Great Britain or France but on the Elbe. West Germany was a vital link in this defense, and the policy adopted was aimed at bringing Western Germany into a European union of friendly powers and into the North Atlantic Alliance. No longer was Germany to be dealt with as a defeated country. She was to be given all-out assistance to enable her to regain strength; she was to be released from the occupation as soon as arrangements had been made to bring her into the European defense organization. As a member of the latter, West Germany not only would be permitted to rearm but would be given substantial assistance through American funds and supplies toward this end.

The first year of the new policy saw the end of American military government and the establishment of HICOG under State Department control. The basic policy did not change as a result of such a move; but, with the indirect channels of conveying policy through the Joint Chiefs of Staff giving way to more direct channels, it was perhaps easier to put the new policy into effect. A civilian High Commissioner was in a considerably stronger position to give assitance to a West German Federal Government and to supervise a cultural and information program than a Military Governor. Certainly great progress was made in strengthening both the West German political and economic institutions during the middle period of the third phase: the autumn of 1949 to early 1952. Steps were taken under the new policy to draft Contractual Agreements which would make it possible to end the occupation as soon as West Germany could be admitted to membership in a European defense group.

There were unexpected delays in achieving West German membership in the European defense group. The first arrangement, devised only after long and very protracted negotiations, was not ratified by the French Parliament. A substitute arrangement, under which West Germany would be brought into the Western European Union set up earlier at Brussels and made a member of the North Atlantic Treaty Organization, was then proposed and finally ratified by all the governments including West Germany in 1955. During the three-year period 1952-1955, after the Contractual Agreements had been drafted, the American staff in Germany was reduced, and various programs were eliminated or drastically curtailed. But the basic American policy of rearming West Germany as part of a western defense alliance never wavered. Attention was given to German unification during this final period, with the United States favoring unification on general principles, but only if a free Germany emerged which would remain an active participant in the western alliance.

CONCLUDING COMMENTS

Evaluations of American policy relating to Germany run the gamut from extreme criticism to high praise. J. P. Warburg, representing the severe critics, has written at least eight books and numerous pamphlets since 1944, in which he indicts the United States and its leaders for the policy relating to Germany.[11] In his eyes almost every possible mistake has been made. Indeed it seems to be his contention that if the United States had set out to devise the worst possible policy, it could hardly have committed more serious errors. He goes so far as to predict the collapse of the western world unless a complete about face is ordered. To Mr. Warburg and other critics it is nothing short of criminal to rearm the Germans: he proposes a unified neutralized Germany which would stand as something of a buffer between the West and the Soviet Union.

Other less critical students of American policy relating to Germany question the rearming aspects and the admission of Germany to the North Atlantic Treaty Organization. There are various bases for such doubt, but one of the most important is the feeling that the Germans will never rest until unification of West and East Germany has been achieved and may well push on to regaining the some 47,000 square miles of lost territory beyond the Oder-Neisse line. It is argued that these goals cannot be attained unless the Germans meet the Russian terms and that this will involve the possible use of German arms against the West or at least make the American investment in German rearmament a complete loss. Some critics are disappointed that the United States has not given more careful consideration to the deep feeling on the part of the Germans in favor of unification, maintaining that in the desire to set up defenses against the Russians the United States has neglected what may turn out to be very serious loopholes.

---

[11] His views can be found in detail in his *Germany: Key to Peace* (Harvard University Press, Cambridge, 1953), and his *Germany—Bridge or Battleground* (Harcourt, Brace, New York, 1947).

The Thorny Problem of Policy

Those who find no fault with American policy relating to Germany seem few in number. If observers approve the latter policy, they usually regard the early policy as distinctly unworthy of the United States. If they approve the negative policy of JCS 1067, they do not find it possible to support the rearming of Germany and the American support which has gone into making West Germany the strongest economic nation on the European continent, if the Soviet Union be excluded.

It will require many years before anything like a full evaluation of American policy in Germany can be made. Those responsible for the later policy admit that there is a risk involved in rearming the Germans and that, under ideal circumstances, it would not be desirable to take such a step so soon. But they feel that the stakes are so high that this risk is worth taking. They are convinced of the sincerity of the West Germans and believe that a sell-out to the Russians at some critical stage is unlikely. They do not seem to have an answer to the unification issue and may go so far as to admit that it will require a miracle to bring about unification on terms satisfactory to the United States. Yet, when pressed, they admit that it does not seem probable that the West Germans will surrender their objective of unification.

In looking back, it is difficult for most serious students of the occupation to justify the American policy embodied in JCS 1067.[12] This seems to them the sort of policy which could have led nowhere except to trouble. In their opinion it represents the United States in one of its weaker endeavors. On the other hand, they cannot accept the denunciations of such writers as James P. Warburg. They find his arguments worthy of consideration and useful in calling attention to the difficulties, but they are of the opinion that Warburg and others oversimplify the German problem, viewing everything in terms of absolute right and wrong, black and white, and ignoring the complexities or alternatives presented. They see little if anything in the Russian record, at least prior to the end of the occupation, which would suggest, as Mr. Warburg maintains, that the Soviet Union would be willing to make a satisfactory agreement if the United States

---

[12] See, for example, the comments of M. Fainsod, "The Development of American Military Government Policy During World War II," in C. J. Friedrich and others, *American Experiences in Military Government in World War II* (Rinehart, New York, 1948).

were not so unwilling to meet it halfway. They are troubled at some of the aspects of the resurgence of German industry, the ultra-nationalistic attitudes of certain of the Germans, even if few in number, the existence of anti-semitism in some quarters of Germany, and the prospect of German rearmament. However, they find it difficult to envision Germany as a neutral state in Europe. They hope very strongly that the policy of the United States during the latter years of the occupation will prove to have been a sound one.[13]

[13] On the complexity of the issues, see O. Butz, *Germany: Dilemma for American Foreign Policy* (Doubleday, New York, 1954).

7

Relations with the Russians, British, and French

In occupying foreign territory the United States has usually had a lone hand. The occupation of the Rhineland following World War I was of course an exception, but this was a comparatively small operation. Even in Japan, where the occupation was under an advisory Allied Commission, the United States actually had a relatively free hand. However, the occupation of Germany in its entirety following World War II was definitely an Allied responsibility, both in theory —and in fact. The United States was but one of the occupying powers and found itself faced with a situation complicated by the necessity of working with its Allies. Accustomed to doing things in its own way to a large extent and laying down its own policies, the United States was confronted with Allies, some of whom were just as independent and were far from willing to accept an agreement on basic policies.

No one can get even a glimmer of the tangled skein of events during the years following 1944 without keeping the inter-Allied character of the occupation uppermost in mind. Nor can one expect to understand even the main outlines of American policies and activities in Germany without giving careful attention to the Russians, French, and British, for in large measure, particularly as the tactical phase receded into the past, the record of the United States in Germany was determined by relationships with Russia and to a lesser degree with France and Britain. Indeed, as stated in the previous chapter, it is not too much to say that Germany became the European focal point of the cold war with the Russians, rather than merely a country under occupation by the United States. Consequently much of what was attempted by the United States in Germany was conditioned not so much by the Germans as by the Russians. The American occupation of Germany therefore can hardly be regarded as a conventional case

103

of occupation. Instead of proceeding along the courses which were mapped at the beginning, however dim and twisted some of these may have been, the United States made a drastic shift which changed the latter part of the occupation to a point hardly reconcilable with the initial course. Such a spectacular turn of events was due, of course, primarily to the difficulties with the Soviet Union.

THE UNITED STATES AND THE SOVIET UNION

After the many years of unwillingness on the part of the United States to recognize the Soviet Union as a legitimate government and the coldness of the relations between the United States and the Soviet Union after formal recognition was finally accorded, it was one of the glaring anomalies of history that the two countries should have been thrown into each other's arms as allies during World War II. It is not the purpose of this study to analyze the curious if not grotesque character of the military partnership of the two countries during the mighty struggle which finally led to the surrender of Germany. Some Americans, as the investigations of congressional committees and other publicity have revealed, apparently became convinced that the wartime alliance was based on a solid foundation which justified mutual trust and a friendly attitude. Even in high places, as seems to be indicated by President Franklin D. Roosevelt's position at Yalta, there was at least some measure of belief that the alliance between the United States and the Soviet Union could be cemented to the point where it would prove enduring and useful in the postwar world.

At a time when there is much interest in Yalta, it is worthwhile to analyze as carefully as possible the early relations between the United States and the Soviet Union in planning for the occupation of Germany. In general, it is clear that those (at least those in the field) who carried the responsibility for such planning on the part of the United States did not see concrete evidence that the Soviet Union would collaborate on more than a nominal basis after the surrender of the Germans. That is not to say that everyone among the Americans assigned to the German Country Unit of the Supreme Headquarters and the subsequent U. S. Group, Council for Germany and the European Advisory Commission regarded the Russians with hostility, but their experience in these agencies was not such as to lead

104

them to expect a great deal of cooperation from the Soviet Union. The attitude of President Franklin D. Roosevelt and his associates must therefore have been based on inner hope or at least on evidence not available to those at the working level in the field.

The Russians did of course send representatives to the European Advisory Commission in London, and certain basic agreements were finally concluded by the EAC. But the sessions were often of a stormy character and the attitude of the Russian representatives seemed far from cooperative and cordial to various observers, though British representative, Sir William Strang, took a more hopeful view.[1] Even after prolonged discussion and much patience and compromise on the part of the British and Americans, it was impossible to reach an agreement with the Russians on various matters. It therefore seemed to some of the Americans involved that, since the Russian attitude was one of belligerence, distrust, and unwillingness to cooperate at a time when lend-lease aid was flowing from the United States to Russia and military exigencies still welded the alliance into some sort of cohesiveness, the outlook for the future was far from promising.

Although Russian representatives participated in the European Advisory Commission, they did not join the other agencies charged with making the detailed plans for the occupation of Germany. The German Country Unit which was preparing a *Handbook for Military Government in Germany* expected Russian officers on various occasions, but none ever arrived. The British and Americans had to shoulder this task alone. It was understood that the Russians looked with disfavor on the German Country Unit because it was on occasion attached to the Anglo-American Supreme Headquarters (SHAEF), but even when a different arrangement was made no Russians presented themselves.

The dissolution of the German Country Unit in the latter part of 1944 was to some extent perhaps the result of the Russian unwillingness to participate in an Anglo-American endeavor. Through national occupation planning groups for Germany, as set up by the United States and Britain in the latter part of 1944, Russians would allegedly have an opportunity to associate themselves with the work of planning. It was reported that the Russians did not want to see

---

[1] See his autobiographical work, *Home and Abroad* (Deutsch, London, 1956), pp. 199-225.

105

such agencies operating in England. One of the factors in the moving of the U. S. Group, Control Council for Germany to France early in 1945 was the hope that contact with the Russian planners for the occupation of Germany might be achieved. But during the several months that the American group carried on its planning at Versailles the Russians still maintained their aloofness. The result was that prior to the surrender of the Germans in May 1945 there had been outside of the European Advisory Commission and the Yalta Conference little or no collaboration on the part of the Russians in the preparations for the occupation of Germany, despite the decision for an Allied Control Authority to deal with the highly complicated overall German problems.

With the collapse of Germany, the American military government organization moved as rapidly as possible into Germany—the U. S. Group, Control Council for Germany setting up headquarters near Frankfurt in late May and June of 1945. It was not until strong pressure was brought on the Russians that agreement was reached to have at least part of the American and British control groups establish themselves in Berlin, and there was evidence of great reluctance on the part of the Russians to countenance any such arrangement. When, after certain delays, American and British occupation personnel reached Berlin in July 1945, the Russians were not prepared to start the Allied Control Authority operations.[2]

After waiting for several weeks, the Americans took the bit in their teeth and insisted on meetings between themselves, the Russians, the British, and the French. But at the first date set for certain meetings no Russians appeared. When sessions finally did materialize, it was apparent that the Russians were not prepared to do more than stall. As the directorate personnel and the working committees of the British, Americans, French, and Russians met together to deal with the very pressing problems of the occupation, little or no progress could be made because of the Russian attitude. Paper work that could be handled in a few hours by the Americans required days on the part of the Russians—whether because of unwillingness to move ahead or lack of typewriters and typists was a moot question. After such preliminaries had finally been completed, the Russians were usually in

---

[2] See F. L. Howley, *Berlin Command* (Putnam, New York, 1950).

no position to make any decision even on minor matters and insisted on referring every question to Moscow.

It is true that personal relations among Russian and other Allied personnel were sometimes friendly during the beginning period of the occupation. General Eisenhower and Marshal Grigori Zhukov apparently established genuine regard for one another. The Russians were fond of participating in social events sponsored by the Americans and British, especially if there was drinking and eating to be done. It was not uncommon for Russian officers to come up to unknown American officers on the streets of Berlin and to slap them so vigorously on the back in their good humor that the latter sometimes staggered from the impact. Russian officers who drove around Berlin in large numbers in commandeered German vehicles frequently stopped and offered rides to American officers who, in many instances, had to depend on their legs for transportation. But such good fellowship came to an end shortly, when orders were issued to the Russians to refrain from social contact with their Allied associates except at specified official functions.

The Allied Control Authority was finally ready and went through the motions of functioning until 1948.[3] Many hours were spent by the working committees and the directorate staffs in performing the vast amount of spade work necessary before the Coordinating Committee and the Control Council itself could function. Despite the generally uncooperative attitude on the part of the Russians, some agreements were reached and certain recommendations were passed up to the Coordinating Committee. The number of Control Council laws, directives, and orders that were issued was larger than has sometimes been realized, though the fundamental steps of organizing German agencies to deal with finance, transport, post office and telegraph, economic matters, and so forth, as provided by the Potsdam Agreement, were never taken. However, the relations with the Russians were never what might reasonably be expected on the part of an ally.

From the very beginning, even before the German capitulation,

---

[3] For additional details of this organization, see E. E. Nobleman, "Quadripartite Military Government Organization and Operations in Germany," *American Journal of International Law*, July 1947; R. W. Van Wagenen, "Cooperation and Controversy Among the Occupying Powers in Berlin," *Journal of Politics*, Feb. 1948; A. Whyte, "Quadripartite Rule in Berlin," *International Affairs* (London), Jan. 1947.

the Political Affairs subdivision of the U. S. Group, Control Council for Germany had concluded that genuine collaboration between the United States and the Soviet Union was unlikely. Probably the chief activity of that subdivision was thereafter devoted to watching and

ALLIED CONTROL AUTHORITY FOR GERMANY

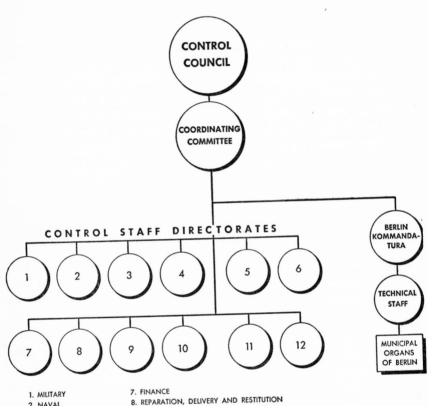

1. MILITARY
2. NAVAL
3. AIR
4. TRANSPORT
5. POLITICAL
6. ECONOMIC

7. FINANCE
8. REPARATION, DELIVERY AND RESTITUTION
9. INTERNAL AFFAIRS AND COMMUNICATION
10. LEGAL
11. PRISONERS OF WAR AND DISPLACED PERSONS
12. MANPOWER

checking the Russians. Some idea of the lack of trust of the Russians on the part of the Americans may be given by citing the incident involving the German Foreign Office archives. Many tons of these records were discovered in Thuringia which was first occupied by American military forces, but, being in the part of Germany assigned to the Russians, shortly had to be turned over. Instead of communicating this discovery to the Russians and arranging a plan of joint use, American military personnel under the direction of Political Affairs representatives from the U. S. Group, Control Council for Germany and the British Control Commission for Germany worked day and night prior to the turnover in order to move these valuable records to the American Zone.

Experience with the Russians in the Berlin *Kommandatura* was similar to that recited above in the case of Allied Control Authority. This agency attained an operating status earlier than the Allied Control Authority, perhaps mainly because of the smaller scope of its activities and the emergency character of its assignment. For a time it seemed that working relations of a sort might be achieved, despite the great fondness of the Russians for long-drawn-out oratory, their disposition to criticize their Allies in a caustic fashion, and their insistence on having their own way. But it became increasingly apparent that they regarded Berlin as their monopoly and that they would not consider any arrangement other than a Communist regime for Berlin.[4] After many deadlocks, spectacular displays of verbal fireworks, and other dilatory tactics on the part of the Russians, the Berlin *Kommandatura* ceased to function on a quadripartite basis in 1948 and two city governments were subsequently organized, one for the three western sectors held by the British, and the French, and the Americans, and the other for the Russian sector.

After the blockade of Berlin by the Soviet Union and the audacious and amazingly successful airlift, in which the Allies brought supplies including fuel to some two million people in West Berlin, any pretense of cordial relations of an intimate character between the United States and the Soviet Union ceased. Limited formal contacts were maintained: American representatives in Berlin sometimes paid official calls on their Russian opposite numbers, there was a slight exchange of formal courtesies, and it was not uncommon for representatives of both countries in Germany to lodge formal protests with each other on the occasion of some action which was considered improper. But the Allied Control Authority ceased even to go through the motions of carrying on business. The United States moved closer to its western

---

[4] For a first-hand account by an American representative, see F. L. Howley, *Berlin Command* (Putnam, New York, 1950).

Allies and proceeded with the establishment of a West German Federal Republic, and the Russians concentrated on the east and the setting up of the puppet German People's Republic.[5] The main aspect of the relationship between the two countries took the form of the cold war, and as the United States and the Soviet Union considered Germany the main scene of such a struggle for power in Europe, both expended great amounts of energy and ingenuity in seeking the upperhand.

THE UNITED STATES AND BRITAIN

If the relations of the United States with the Soviet Union in Germany represented the lowest level of cooperation and trust, it may be fairly stated that Anglo-American relations reached the highest level. However, this does not mean that the United States and Britain always saw eye to eye in matters involving the occupation of Germany or that there was the degree of cordiality, intimacy, and confidence that might have been desirable. The United States regarded Great Britain as a genuine ally to be sure, in contrast to the Soviet Union, but British methods and motives were sometimes suspected and there was a tendency to ignore Britain on occasion. Relations between the two countries varied from period to period.[6]

To some Americans, particularly of Irish extraction, British motives are hardly ever, if ever, to be trusted. Even if everything seems unexceptionable, these Americans look for a hidden selfishness or lack of honesty on the part of the British. Since there were many persons of such extraction in the American military and civilian forces stationed in Germany, ideal relations with the British could hardly be expected. Moreover, among the British there are those who look with resentment and disfavor on the United States, maintaining that American culture is inferior, American morals are shocking, American manners are vulgar, American pride is beyond tolerance, and Ameri-

---

[5] For detailed discussions of the Russian policy and actions, see J. P. Nettl, *The Eastern Zone and Soviet Policy in Germany, 1945-1950* (Oxford University Press, New York, 1951), and G. Klimov, *Terror Machine; The Inside Story of the Soviet Administration in Germany* (Praeger, New York, 1953).

[6] British attitudes and organization are discussed in W. Friedmann, *The Allied Military Government of Germany* (Stevens, London, 1947); H. Ingrams, "Rebuilding Democracy in Germany," *Quarterly Review* (London), April 1947; and M. Balfour and J. Mair, *Four-Power Control in Germany and Austria, 1945-1946* (Oxford University Press, London, 1956).

can expertness in handling delicate international problems is far from notable. This attitude, too, complicated British-American relations, though it is a striking tribute to the British that their treatment of the large numbers of American personnel stationed on their soil during and after the war was remarkably free from hostility or even discourtesy.

During the German Country Unit period, when plans were being drafted for the occupation of Germany, the contact between Americans and British was necessarily close. Shortage of available personnel on the part of the British resulted in a staff which was numerically weighted toward the Americans, but the British gave a good account of themselves. The deputy chief of the German Country Unit was a British colonel; two out of three officers on the board which had the responsibility of coordinating plans for the occupation of Germany were British; and the admirable efficiency of British noncommissioned officers who served in an administrative capacity was frequently commented on. Some Americans never condoned the British custom of taking time out for coffee and tea or the system of starting somewhat later in the day than is the tradition in the United States and working later. But after General Eisenhower had done some "knocking of heads" and threatened to dispense with those who could not work together on his staff, the situation became at least reasonably satisfactory.

Of course much depended on the personalities involved in particular positions. Thus a temperamental British chief of a section of the German Country Unit dealing with education and religious affairs did not win the respect accorded certain other Britishers. In the case of the group of officers engaged in the very arduous and time-consuming task of coordinating occupation plans in the various fields, relations between the British and American officers were very satisfactory; differences of opinion were not uncommon, but there was not a single instance in which the members split on purely national lines during the extended discussions.

With the dissolution of the Anglo-American German Country Unit in the late summer of 1944 and the establishment of British and American agencies, the situation naturally changed. No longer were Americans and British working side by side in the same organization. At one time both of the new national planning groups occupied nearby

111

quarters and maintained close contact in those areas where the personnel on both sides had respect for each other and were broad enough in background to realize the importance of Anglo-American collaboration in attacking the complex problem of the occupation of Germany. When the American group moved some miles outside of London, it was more difficult to maintain close liaison; nevertheless a considerable amount of exchanging of papers and information continued. The transfer of the U. S. Group, Control Council for Germany to France in early 1945, with the British group remaining in London, obviously reduced the opportunities for communication, but even so there was a certain amount of "commuting" on the part of both Americans and British. In the cases of education and religious affairs, local and regional government, and civil service, for example, reasonably close relations were continued.

With the surrender of Germany and the movement of both American and British groups into the country to effect the occupation plans, contact between the Americans and the British diminished, despite the importance of a common cause. To begin with, the U. S. Group, Control Council for Germany set up headquarters near Frankfurt, while the British Control Commission for Germany had its offices in and around Minden in the north. The distance and the poor transportation facilities between the two points made frequent meetings impractical. To offset this to some degree, a British liaison team was stationed at the American military government headquarters and vice versa, but this did not prove too successful in bringing about close working relations, though there was a certain amount of exchanging of papers. When the U. S. Group, Control Council for Germany moved to Berlin in the late summer of 1945, the British Control Commission, for the most part, remained in and around Minden. However, as time passed, more and more of the British Commission transferred to the site of the Allied Control Authority in Berlin.

After the occupation of Germany actually got underway, the problem of Anglo-American relations was accentuated by the apparent unwillingness on the part of General Clay to have his staff members keep in close touch with their British opposite numbers. He and his immediate associates saw the British top military government officials regularly in the meetings of the Coordinating Committee and at social functions, but it was understood that beyond the necessary official

112

Relations with the Russians, British, and French

associations American military government personnel should remain more or less aloof from their British colleagues. It is reported by a reliable source that General Clay, upon leaving Washington to take up his military government duties in Germany, was warned by officials of the Civil Affairs Division of the War Department to be on his guard in the case of the British. Be that as it may, the policy of General Clay during the early period of the occupation of Germany was such as to discourage, if not entirely break off, the earlier intimate working relations of his staff with the British. An effort was made to justify this course by the explanation that the Russians resented close Anglo-American relations and that, in order to get along with the Russians, American personnel must remain aloof.

With the enormously difficult problems to be faced and the impossibility of completely cutting off one zone from another, it seems in retrospect distinctly unfortunate that mutually advantageous working relations between the Americans and the British military government officials were permitted to lapse in some measure. The months passed and the efforts on the part of the U. S. Group, Control for Germany and its successor OMGUS proved insufficient to cope with the overwhelming problems of feeding the Germans and getting the German economy back to the point where Germany ceased to be supported by charity; and any prospect of working with the Russians became increasingly remote. It became apparent that something had to be done to rebuild Anglo-American collaboration. When the United States in 1946 called on the Allies to aid in tackling the paralyzed German economy, only the British responded favorably. Steps were then instituted to join the American and British Zones into Bizonia for a joint attack on the economic problem, with Americans and British military government officials forming a working team.[7]

But the separation which had taken place earlier could not be easily bridged. The pattern of collaboration had been broken; an air of distrust had taken the place of confidence. The first organization set up under Bizonia did not function well and in some respects the German economy seemed to deteriorate further rather than to improve. The location of most of the bipartite offices in the Minden

---

[7] For a British account of the setting up of Bizonia, see M. Balfour and J. Mair, *Four-Power Control in Germany and Austria, 1945-1946* (Oxford University Press, London, 1956), pp. 137ff.

area, which was neither readily accessible nor a center of important industrial concentration, was a weakness; but perhaps the main difficulty was the bringing together of divergent British and American views and the establishment of satisfactory working relations. A revision in the bizonal setup was made in 1947 which sought to bring about a better understanding between the American and British military governments. An Anglo-American Bipartite Board was created to supervise the five administrations charged with handling such things as transport, trade, food and agriculture, and finance and to exercise a veto over the Bizonal Economic Council. This step improved the situation and led to closer collaboration between the British and the Americans in Germany.

A third revision of the bizonal organization was undertaken in 1948. Frankfurt was made the headquarters of bizonal operations and an elaborate structure just short of a full-fledged government was set up under Anglo-American auspices to deal with the complicated problems arising out of the occupation of Germany. By this time former patterns of cooperation between the Americans and the British had been more or less re-established and, as the end came to any pretense of joint effort with the Russians, the main hope of putting the occupation of Germany on a firm basis lay in joining British and American energies.

The negotiation of the Trizonal Fusion Agreement in 1948-1949 made it possible to proceed with the establishment of a West German Federal Government under an Allied High Commission in which the United States, Britain, and France participated. This initiated the final stage in Anglo-American relations in the occupation of Germany. High Commissioners representing State Department and Foreign Offices supplanted Military Governors, and the relations consequently changed from primarily military to primarily civil. True, American military representatives were stationed with British military headquarters and vice versa and joint maneuvers on the part of the two military establishments were at times undertaken. But it was at the High Commission level that the most significant contacts were maintained during the period 1949-1955.

The American and British High Commissioners with their top advisers came together in the formal meetings of the Allied High Commission usually scheduled three times each month. In addition,

114

there were fairly frequent informal meetings for special purposes or for social intercourse. The location of the main Office of the U. S. High Commissioner at Frankfurt during the years 1949-1951 when the Office of the British High Commissioner was near Bonn interfered with the maintenance of close contacts to some extent, but in late 1951 the former moved to the Bonn area. The degree of personal intimacy on the part of the British and American High Commissioners and their chief associates naturally varied somewhat, depending upon the particular personalities involved. In general, there was a large measure of official agreement and collaboration, though on occasion the two governments did not see eye to eye.

Perhaps even more important than the good working relations which characterized the American and British High Commissioners and their chief associates was the spirit displayed by the various tripartite committees under the Allied High Commission. Here in weekly or even more frequent meetings, representatives of the British and the Americans (as well as the French) discussed in detail the main problems of the occupation and sought agreements as to what should be done.[8] The formal sessions of the High Commissioners might be on the dull side and largely routine in character, though this was by no means always the case, but the tripartite committees performed the basic work without which the Allied High Commission could not have functioned. In the sessions of these committees and in the discussion that went on between their members on the outside, relations between the American and British representatives were usually very good.

The United States maintained a liaison representative at the Office of the British *Land* commissioners and the British reciprocated. These officials maintained a continuous contact between the two occupying powers. Resident officers of the United States, particularly in border areas, contacted their British neighbors. During one period a program of official exchanges was inaugurated which permitted British resident officers to spend several days in a *Kreis* under American control to observe what was being attempted, and of course American resident officers had the same opportunity in the case of the British Zone.

It would be too much to say that there was complete agreement

---

[8] See Elmer Plischke, *History of the Allied High Commission for Germany*, in the Historical Series of the Office of the U. S. High Commissioner for Germany (1951), Chap. 4.

115

between the United States and Britain in matters relating to Germany and that there was full cooperation on the part of British and American occupying authorities, but the joint efforts of the two countries in German affairs were of real significance.

THE UNITED STATES AND FRANCE

The French participated in the occupation of Germany at a somewhat later date than was the case with the United States, Britain, and the Soviet Union. With no representatives at the Yalta and Potsdam conferences which canvassed the problems involved in the occupation of Germany, France was given a role in the occupation mainly because of British and American arguments that she deserved a place in postwar affairs.[9]

Although the attitude of the Americans and British might have been expected to elicit some appreciation from the French—and possibly it did in some quarters—the French came to Berlin to associate themselves with the other Allies in the Allied Control Authority in an unhappy frame of mind. Suffering from their accumulated hatred of the Germans, their apprehension of the future, their unimpressive record of repelling the German invasion, the French also were resentful that they had not been included in the Potsdam Conference. The result was an almost insuperable barrier to close collaboration with their American Allies. Because they had not been represented at Potsdam, they maintained that they were not bound by its decisions. During the early period of the occupation the French often seemed even less willing to cooperate with their Allies than did the Russians.[10]

Had American representatives fully realized the psychological basis of the French behavior, allowance would perhaps have been made and the situation might have adjusted itself in some measure, though the attitude of the French would have constituted a serious barrier in any event. But most of the American officials knew comparatively little about French psychology or French traditions, and

[9] For two French points of view relating to Germany under occupation, see C. Bourthoumieux, *La politique et le régime interalliés d'occupation de l'Allemagne de 1945-1949* (Paris, 1950), and A. Grosser, *Colossus Again: Western Germany from Defeat to Rearmament* (trans. from French, Praeger, New York, 1955).

[10] For a statement of French attitudes by a high government official, see Georges Bidault, "Agreement on Germany—Key to World Peace," *Foreign Affairs*, July 1946.

116

even the British seemed unable to appreciate fully the complex character of the situation. Under heavy pressure themselves, the American officials tended to take French stubbornness and feet dragging at face value. It is not surprising that this, together with the French disabilities, led to a most unsatisfactory situation. Americans sharply criticized their French colleagues, frequently blaming them more severely than the Russians for failure to get ahead with the work of the occupation.

At lower levels the relations between the American military government organization and the French military government personnel, it is true, were often relatively cordial. In the military government section of the Army Group Headquarters, located at Heidelberg immediately after the German surrender, there were both American and French representatives who apparently got along very well, with respect and liking on both sides. French liaison groups stationed with American military government headquarters elsewhere also often maintained quite agreeable relations with their hosts. But the influence of the misunderstanding and bitterness which characterized the highest level in Berlin was considerable, and it was by no means limited in its effect to Berlin.

Franco-American relationships in the occupation of Germany were complicated not only by the embittered reactions of the French and the failure on the part of the Americans to make due allowance for such an attitude, but by other major factors. The language barrier was without any question a serious obstacle. Few Americans could carry on even a minimum of conversation in French; possibly a larger proportion of Frenchmen understood English but their national pride was such that they were reluctant to admit this. Interpreters were in general not very expert and sometimes contributed to intensifying rather than ameliorating difficulties.

Then, too, French temperament is not easy for most Americans to comprehend, and doubtless the reverse is true. A pattern had already been established in France for many of the American military government personnel. These Americans recalled the difficulty of becoming acquainted with the French people, the chilling criticism on the part of the French of American behavior, the tricky efforts of certain Frenchmen to take advantage of Americans, and so forth. Having shaken the dust from their feet when they left France to enter

Germany, American military personnel often remarked that they preferred the Germans, despite their enemy status, to the French. Contacts with the French in Germany alleviated this unfortunate feeling somewhat, but it was an uphill grind. Even in the case of opposite numbers on the American and French sides, where the intellectual level may have been about the same and professional competence relatively equal, relations frequently remained distinctly formal, with little of the good fellowship which is important in promoting cooperation and understanding.

The French did a remarkable job in some aspects of their occupation of Germany, despite the great difficulties which confronted them. To recruit a competent staff for occupying a foreign territory after a country has itself been occupied for some years is no mean task. Add to this the problem of keeping that staff from being taken over by the French Communists for ulterior purposes and one has a heavy assignment indeed. But most Americans in Germany were not aware of these complicated problems, though they doubtless realized that the French suffered some disadvantages as a result of being a recently liberated people, occupying a relatively small and poor zone in Germany, and so forth. However, most Americans were conscious of what seemed a mean and almost despicable attitude on the part of certain French officials. The French Zone was for years an almost closed preserve for the French. American personnel desiring to visit that area were frequently treated in a manner that they regarded as insulting. Refusal to grant permission to enter the Zone might have aroused some ill feeling, but when French officials made personal remarks that seemed to indicate the deepest hatred and contempt for Americans in general, tempers naturally became incited. Even Americans traveling to the French Zone on official business sometimes encountered many barriers and not only had to spend a great deal of time working out what they regarded as purely French inventions to inconvenience Americans but often found themselves given the run-around in the form of incorrect information, evasions, and the like.

The French made no response to the initial appeal of the United States to join their zone to the American and British zones in an effort to attack the German economic problem more successfully, despite the sad level of the economy in their zone. When Marshall Aid was

118

Dr. James B. Conant, U. S. High Commissioner and Ambassador to Germany and Prof. Otto Hahn, (*left*) German Nobel-Prize winning chemist, at the U. S. Atoms for Peace Exhibition in front of a model of Prof. Hahn's experimenting table for the first atomic fission.

President Theodor Heuss, Federal Republic of Germany.

The Farben Building at Frankfurt. This large building constructed as general offices by the I. G. Farben-Industrie was scarcely damaged during the bombing which laid most of Frankfurt in waste. It was used as a headquarters by USFET during the early years of the occupation, then provided offices for various agencies of Bizonia, and during 1949 to 1951 served as headquarters building for HICOG.

One of the most successful programs of the United States in Germany revolved around America Houses. Here library facilities, film exhibitions, musical programs, classes in English and current events, lectures, and art exhibits along with many other activities were to be found. The photograph shows a typical America House at Stuttgart.

extended to Germany, the French reluctantly were forced to permit their zone to enjoy some of the benefits, but they displayed a lack of enthusiasm and at times even set up obstacles which made the way difficult. Gradually this suspicion, if not downright hostility, subsided, as it became apparent that the Marshall Aid organization desired to cooperate and had no anti-French objectives. The critical state of the economy in the French Zone persuaded the French to join in some of the financial and other programs set up by Bizonia, and by 1948 there was considerable cooperation between the French on one hand and the Americans and British on the other. Nevertheless, France was reluctant to approve trizonal fusion, and only long-drawn-out and patient negotiations attained that end.[11]

With the agreement to combine the three western zones in 1948 and 1949 and the actual establishment of an Allied High Commission and a West German Federal Government in 1949, Franco-American relations became more cordial and normal. No longer was the French Zone almost as inaccessible as the Russian to American personnel. French military forces occupied certain points in the American Zone and American military bases were set up in the French Zone. The French participated quite actively in the tripartite committees of the Allied High Commission and gave a good account of themselves, frequently gaining the respect and admiration of their American colleagues. The relations between French High Commissioner A. François-Poncet and the American High Commissioners were invariably courteous and correct, though perhaps rarely if ever very intimate. To this writer at least it appeared that it was not always easy for M. François-Poncet to approve of what he regarded as the inconsistent, shortsighted, opportunistic, and the sometimes bungling American efforts. To one who had had prewar experience as his country's representative in Berlin,[12] who knew at first-hand the evil character of Hitler's regime, who through his writings had become one of the world's leading authorities on German affairs, and who during his service as French High Commissioner received the high honor of being elected one of the forty immortals in the French Academy, the

---

[11] For General Clay's account of this, see his *Decision in Germany*, Chap. 21.

[12] For his account of these years, see *The Fateful Years, Memoirs of a French Ambassador in Berlin, 1931-1938* (Eng. trans., Harcourt, Brace, New York, 1949).

knowledge of German affairs on the part of the succession of American representatives may have seemed a good deal like that of a college freshman in comparison with a candidate for a Ph.D. Yet M. François-Poncet swallowed his doubts on many occasions and generally sought to cooperate with his American colleagues.

8

Civil-Military Relations

One of the frequently proclaimed traditions of the American political system has been the primacy of the civilian element and the subordinate position of the military. When military influence in the governments of other leading nations of the world has seemed (at least to the people of the United States) to be outstanding and often dominant, it has been a source of great pride to Americans that their own affairs were in the hands of civilians and that the military could be looked upon as a necessary and useful servant. To what extent the American analysis of the situation in other nations, as well as within its own borders, has been accurate may of course be subject to question. Military dominance in the affairs of some other nations during certain periods may have been less than was commonly assumed in the United States. Although civilian secretaries invariably headed the departments of War and the Navy in the United States, there was some evidence that in the last analysis professional military men on occasion either determined policies or managed to evade decisions which were not to their liking. Nevertheless, until World War II the separation of civilian political and administrative heads from military leaders in the government of the United States and the subordination of the latter seemed to be one of the principal foundation stones of the commonwealth.

During the years since 1940 there have been significant modifications in civil-military relationships in the United States. President Franklin D. Roosevelt perhaps unconsciously substituted the Joint Chiefs of Staff, whom he saw almost every day during the war years, for the Secretary of State in the formulating of far-reaching political policies for the United States. The appointment of one of the top military leaders, General George C. Marshall, to the office of Secretary of State at a critical period was another striking instance of a

121

change. But it was actually only one of a series involving the placing of military officers in positions of considerable influence in the civil departments of the government, climaxing in the election of General Eisenhower as President. General W. Bedell Smith as Undersecretary of State, General John H. Hilldring as an Assistant Secretary of State, Colonel Henry Byroade as head of German Affairs in the State Department and later as Assistant Secretary of State in charge of Near Eastern and African Affairs and ambassador to Egypt, and the appointment of a fairly sizable number of generals and admirals to represent the United States as ambassadors to the Soviet Union, China, the Philippines, and other countries may be cited as examples in one department, the State Department, where civil dominance has been supposed to be particularly important.

During the period prior to the capitulation of the Germans in May 1945 the position of the military in American forces in Europe was naturally not only dominant but almost exclusive. True, military commanders of a high order usually had political advisers representing the State Department to offer suggestions and furnish information relating to political matters, but there is little to indicate that the role of such advisers was very outstanding. A commonplace attitude toward these State Department Foreign Service Officers both during the war and immediately after was that expressed by General Hilldring and others: they might be useful but that they could never be given important responsibilities because it was impossible for them to reach decisions promptly and to carry heavy assignments involving the administering of concrete problems satisfactorily. There were also a few civilians in the Office of Strategic Services (OSS) and other agencies who had certain responsibilities overseas. But, by the very nature of the case, military personnel carried the basic responsibility in the field, subject of course to orders from the Joint Chiefs of Staff which might reflect civilian policies established by the President.

After the surrender of the Germans, the magnitude of the Allied forces in Europe and such tasks as the demobilizing of the German military organizations, the destruction of fortifications, and supplies of poison gas required a continuance of military dominance for some time. Millions of American soldiers could not be sent home at once and plans had to be implemented providing for a security force in the American Zone of Germany. At this stage many additional civilians

122

were brought from the United States to do work which the military either was not prepared to do or preferred to have done by civilians. However, even if these represented the State Department or some other civil agency in the United States, they were made a part of the military organization, were compelled to don uniforms (though without insignia), and were subject to the rules and regulations designated by military authorities. Moreover, they usually were placed far enough down in the scale so that they had little or no direct access to top military commanders. If they were given nominal recognition, as in the case of State Department representatives serving as political advisers and staffing Offices of Political Affairs, their role was frequently such as to be frustrating. Had the responsibility for dealing with the civilian population of Germany been entrusted to a non-military American agency, as has been the case in some instances elsewhere, a different pattern might have been established at a formative period, but under the existing circumstances there was little or no alternative to almost complete military dominance.

It was expected in certain quarters that the period of exclusive military control in Germany would come to an end within a few months after German surrender. On other occasions when the United States has occupied foreign territory, military dominance has lasted only as long as military necessity demanded. Thereafter civil agencies have taken over the responsibilities of occupation relating to the population, leaving the military to handle strictly military problems. The first representatives of the State Department to arrive in Europe fully expected such a development in Germany and were making preparations accordingly. But a combination of circumstances ordained otherwise. The death of President Roosevelt left a vacuum in Washington which, as has been pointed out in Chapter 6, for some months almost paralyzed action concerning the occupation of Germany. The State Department which expected to set up a civil administration in Germany within a few months of the end of fighting found itself unprepared to take the practical steps necessary. Having expanded from a comparatively small, closely knit department before the war to a large, sprawling, more or less uncoordinated agency, it faced administrative problems which were complicated and which more or less defied any immediate solution.

Although General Eisenhower and other top military leaders in

123

Germany indicated a desire to transfer responsibility for nonmilitary aspects of the occupation to a civil administration with a few months after the surrender,[1] important elements in the armed forces vigorously opposed any such arrangement. These elements felt competent to deal with all aspects of the occupation, denied that there was any satisfactory dividing line between military and nonmilitary aspects of the occupation, and in many instances apparently resented any effort to deprive the military of what were regarded as rewards for victory.

The elaborate plans that had been drafted for military government and the sizable organization that had been set up to deal with occupation problems other than strictly military perhaps contributed to the arguments against an early transfer to a civil agency, despite the fact that most of the military government specialists succeeded in returning to their personal responsibilities in the United States within a few months after the fighting came to an end. But even more important than the unpreparedness of the State Department and the reluctance on the part of many military men to give up their empire in Germany, there was, as noted in the previous chapter, the highly unsatisfactory and rapidly deteriorating relations with the Russians. Any hope which Americans may have had of satisfactory working relations with the Russians rapidly disappeared during the months following May 1945. With the Russian problem so acute, a normal occupation pattern seemed out of the question in Germany and a strictly military occupation was consequently maintained month after month until mid-1949.

On various occasions General Clay pointed out the steps taken to civilianize the Office of Military Government of the United States in Germany as 1946, 1947, and 1948 passed. Large numbers of civilian specialists were brought in from the United States to staff OMGUS. However, the numerical preponderance of civilians as the years passed did not actually bring civil administration. Not only did General Clay remain as Military Governor and later as Commander of American military forces in Germany, receiving his orders from the Department of the Army, but he was surrounded by a group of military officers who, to a considerable extent, isolated him from the numerous civilians serving in OMGUS. Relatively few civilians had immediate

[1] See Dwight D. Eisenhower, *Crusade in Europe* (Doubleday, New York, 1948).

124

access to General Clay. Most matters had to be handled through traditional military channels. The result was that OMGUS remained, at least until mid-1949 when Mr. McCloy took over as Military Governor, a distinctly military agency. Military dominance, which might under other circumstances have been terminated shortly after the German surrender, remained firmly entrenched until well into 1949. A pattern was consequently well established and it was hardly to be expected that civil-military relations following 1949 would be uncomplicated and smooth. The military had come to regard themselves as more or less exclusively responsible for American interests in Germany. The steps which resulted in the setting up of an Allied High Commission and HICOG came at too late a stage to make a change easy.

Because of the extraordinary talent which American High Commissioner McCloy displayed for working with competing and conflicting authorities and to some extent no doubt as a result of his long service as Assistant Secretary of the War Department, the relations between the military and the civil administration in Germany were kept under control during the period following 1949. Nevertheless, the strain and stress underlying such relations were often considerable and much effort was expended by HICOG in maintaining working relations with the American military establishments in Germany. Of course, the exact situation varied widely from place to place within the American area of Germany and the time factor was also important. Some military authorities made a serious attempt to cooperate with HICOG, perhaps recognizing the tradition of civilian dominance in United States history. Others seemed to resent the mere existence of an American civil agency in Germany. The attitude of one officer who characterized the staff of HICOG as "carpet baggers" was probably at least fairly widespread among military personnel. The remark of an Army wife overheard in a commissary, "We do not associate with civilians," may seem too absurd to be taken seriously, but it too reflected the relatively slight personal contacts between civilian and military representatives of the United States in Germany on other than formal occasions. Another very commonplace attitude was indicated by the not infrequent query put by military personnel to representatives of the civil agency, "What is the Office of the U. S. High Commissioner?"

125

Military persons frequently were reluctant to have facilities operated under the Army used by the staff of HICOG. There seemed to be a widespread feeling on the part of the military that the two American establishments were competitors rather than cooperating arms of the United States, that the military was the sole representative of the United States in Germany and that HICOG perforce must be the agency of some other government. Personnel of HICOG, on the other side, admitted the necessity of the security function of the military, but complained that too much of the time and energy which should have been devoted to German problems had to be given to correcting mistakes of their military colleagues, negotiating their demands on the German population, and maintaining at least fair working relations.

The problem here presented received formal and informal consideration both from HICOG and the military, but perhaps especially from the former. It was decided in the setting up of HICOG to give OMGUS personnel, both military and civilian, a preference, particularly where existing functions were being taken over. While some military employees were not successful in the interviews that were given by screening boards, many were taken over—indeed, as noted in another connection,* some thoughtful persons often maintained that a good deal of the weakness displayed by HICOG resulted from taking over too many military personnel. A joint committee, which met regularly in Heidelberg, the headquarters of the American military establishment in Germany, gave continuing attention to relations between the civil and the military organizations and at a high enough level to represent both sides quite adequately. The resident officers maintained by HICOG in the various *Kreise* of the American Zone until 1952 were instructed to promote good relations with any military agencies within their *Kreise*.

Special conferences at regular intervals were sponsored by HICOG at which a fairly large number of senior military personnel conferred with HICOG officials. On these occasions the U. S. High Commissioner and the Commanding General of U. S. forces in Germany addressed general meetings, and various panels considered specific aspects of military-civil relations. Efforts were made by HICOG to plan these meetings with more than ordinary care so that no feelings

* See Chap. 5.

would be hurt and maximum results might accrue from the exchanging of views. As a result of these conferences the military representatives agreed to carry on special programs intended to acquaint the rank and file of American military personnel in Germany with the purpose, policies, and activities of HICOG. The conferences and general programs doubtless served a useful purpose, breaking down some measure of distrust on the part of the military, though there always remained much basic ignorance of the purpose of the civil agency.

However, the gulf between the military and the civil administration was too wide to be bridged by such measures. One Commanding General of the U. S. forces in Germany perhaps unwittingly disclosed the basic concept of the military when he stated in an address to HICOG officials that it was the G.I.s in Germany who really counted. There is no reason to believe that this high ranking and long experienced officer had any desire to offend his listeners unnecessarily—he sincerely believed that the security forces of the United States in Germany outranked in importance the American political program of winning the Germans to the side of the West or any other program with which HICOG could conceivably be charged.

To sum up, the primary aspect of civil-military relations in Germany was that the two agencies were competing with each other rather than working in conjunction on a common problem. The firm belief on the part of the military in its own overriding mission and its relegation to a subordinate place of the political, economic, cultural, and other programs of HICOG involving the Germans was a manifestation of this.

SPECIFIC CIVIL-MILITARY ISSUES

Several specific civil-military issues must be dealt with if a true picture of American civil-military relations in Germany is to be achieved. First of all, though perhaps hardly perceptible to most observers, there was the basic question as to whether the American High Commissioner or the Commanding General of the U. S. military forces was the chief American representative in Germany. During normal conditions it was agreed on both sides that the High Commissioner had authority over HICOG and its activities and that the

Commander of the U. S. military forces in Germany was responsible for security matters. The executive order setting up the position of High Commissioner specifically provided that the High Commissioner should be the supreme United States authority in Germany.[2] But if the High Commissioner and the Commander found themselves in conflict as regards military matters, which would take precedence? The executive order stipulated that such disputes should be submitted to the State Department and the National Military Establishment in Washington for decision. But under the same executive order the Military Commander was given authority to take any action he considered essential to safeguard his troops if an emergency arose. The military seemed to take the position that in case of an emergency, which presumably they would define according to their own ideas, it would be the Military Commander who would decide the steps to be taken and his orders would apply to all American personnel, both civil and military in Germany. Such a position seemed to some to make the military rather than the civil agency actually paramount in Germany. Since no emergency arose during the occupation this remained an academic question.

A second specific problem involved the authority to decide what sums of money should be demanded from the German government for American occupation costs. The U. S. High Commissioner conducted American negotiations with the German authorities and his terms of appointment gave him the final authority in determining the exact amounts to be asked of the Germans as occupation costs. The military apparently accepted this in principle, but when it came to concrete items which they desired, it became difficult for them to give way. For example, as the West German Federal Government became more and more insistent that occupation costs be reduced, it was proposed by HICOG that items such as free maid service for the homes and billets of American personnel, both civil and military, and large numbers of German servants in clubs and other American installations be dispensed with. The military refused to accept such adjustments for a considerable time on the ground that American officers must live in a style to impress the Germans and that this involved household maids. When HICOG cut out maids from the homes of its own officials, suggesting that individuals requiring such

[2] Executive Order 10,062, June 9, 1949.

128

service pay for it themselves, the military declined to follow on the ground that morale would be jeopardized if officers were required to meet such costs out of their own pockets.

In the early days after the German surrender, American military establishments requisitioned buildings and land about as they pleased. But as the war receded into the past and huge influxes of refugees and expellees came to West Germany, the German government naturally brought pressure to have as many of the buildings and as much of the land as possible derequisitioned. HICOG realized the importance of meeting the German demands as far as reasonable and requested military cooperation. But the military, though agreeing in principle to derequisitioning where property was no longer essential to military activities, was reluctant in concrete cases to surrender hotels, residences, resort places, land, and many other properties which it had taken over. This resulted in a third issue involving civil-military relations. Even if such property was not presently in full use, it was often argued by the military that the future might bring such necessity and then there would be no facilities available. Moreover, the military felt that it would impair the morale of its personnel if the resort hotels of Garmisch in the Bavarian Alps, for example, were returned to their owners who were most anxious to resume business. A concomitant of this problem involved the sudden desire of a local American military commander to take over German land for a sports field, for a target range, and the like. With the German population already embittered by the requisitioning of great amounts of property, HICOG was anxious to avoid more hostile reactions and consequently urged the military to refrain from new requisitioning except under the most pressing circumstances. But it was frequently difficult for the local commanders to see why the American Army should not have anything that it wanted.

A fourth problem which, though rather minor in import, required more time from HICOG than more important matters involved hunting and fishing privileges for American military personnel. In the early days of the occupation American officials hunted and fished where they liked, since the German owners were in no position to make their objections heard. However, it was natural as conditions became more settled and denazification came to an end, that the German estate owners, the hunting and fishing clubs, and other own-

129

ers of such lands clamored for their property rights. In the meantime American military personnel had developed what at times seemed a voracious appetite for wild boar, deer, and other game and for fish—even if they were not successful in bagging much game or landing fish they found the sport much to their liking. One mighty nimrod of a colonel claimed that he provided all of the meat requirements of his house by his own gun. When HICOG brought the claims of the German owners to the attention of the military, an impasse often arose, with the military unwilling to curtail their privileges. Various arrangements were eventually made under which military and other American officials wishing to hunt or fish paid certain amounts which were given to the German owners, but for many months difficulties kept breaking out anew.

A fifth type of situation which complicated civil-military relations arose out of the insistence on the part of the military that all untreated water is unsafe for human consumption and domestic use. With American military installations located in almost every locality, military health officials felt that virtually all German water systems should be subject to American control and that the water, whether tests revealed contamination or not, should be chlorinated. Germans, apparently more allergic to chlorinated water than Americans, and particularly those in the wine-producing sections raised a great to-do about what they regarded as the ruinous effect of such water on wine. The representatives of HICOG in the field sometimes found their relations with German local officials strained by military policy in regard to water treatment. Appeals were made usually without success to the military authorities and then brought to HICOG for settlement. The military found it difficult to make any exceptions to its inflexible rule in regard to the treatment of water supplies. On the other hand, the civilian representatives of the United States, anxious to maintain cordial relations with the German officials, desired to free water supplies from chemical treatment unless tests indicated contamination.

It would have been unreasonable to expect military and civilian agencies of the United States to operate without a certain amount of friction in an environment as complex as that in postwar Germany. However, it can hardly be denied that the extent of the stress and strain actually manifest weakened the net impact of the United States'

130

efforts in Germany to some extent and that a considerable amount of HICOG energy had to be diverted to dealing with the general problem of keeping the Army satisfied. The unwillingness of the military to accept the role which long-established American tradition dictates may have resulted in part from the abnormally extended period of military government in Germany due to the Russian factor, but this does not appear to be the full explanation. While comparison in this field is hazardous, it is interesting to note the different experience of the British. The available information reveals a certain amount of friction between military and British Control Commission (civilian) personnel, but there is little evidence of the gulf that separated the military from the civil agencies of the United States in Germany. British military officials apparently were content to yield the overriding responsibility for handling British interests in Germany to the political representatives of the British Control Commission. The military accepted their role as that of supporting the civil agency by providing security, maintaining various supply services, and the like.

9

The Personal Impact of the Americans

It is not uncommon to hear it said that the most significant impact of the American occupation of Germany resulted from the presence of large numbers of individual Americans, both military and civilian, in Germany for more than a decade. The exact number of Americans who served in Germany in one capacity or another would be difficult to fix, since they came and departed in what sometimes seemed far too rapid a turnover. The total number of those who spent at least a short period on German soil as a result of military service or State Department employment must run into the millions, though, of course, the number at any one time was far less. Some of these Americans, such as visiting congressmen and Washington officials on special mission, spent only a few hours on German soil, whereas others remained during the entire occupation period. No doubt, most served in Germany no longer than a year or at most two years, but a fairly sizable number who started out with the Army later transferred to civilian status and held positions under HICOG.

A large proportion of the individual Americans serving in Germany had rather casual contacts with the German people. They were housed in military barracks or High Commission compounds, and their official duties did not involve intimate relationships with Germans. Studies have indicated that about eight out of ten young G.I.s dated German girls more or less frequently; but otherwise their contact with the Germans was more or less incidental through traveling about, making purchases, eating in German restaurants, and the like. However, many individual Americans had official assignments that necessitated regular association with the German people. The fact that large numbers of Germans were employed by American military government in various capacities, by the American military installations scattered throughout the American Zone and later beyond its borders, and by HICOG brought about contact in offices and depots.

132

The Personal Impact of the Americans

Americans frequently had German secretaries, German interpreters, German clerks, German messengers, German professional people, German laborers, and so forth, either directly under them or working alongside them. Some of the programs carried on by OMGUS and HICOG were aimed at the masses of the German people, and Americans assigned to these naturally had the opportunity of meeting large numbers of the German population.

It is obviously difficult to assess the results of the contacts of so many different American individuals with the German people. Certain Americans went to Germany with a consuming bitterness and hatred of the German people and in some instances it seemed that their main purpose was to treat individual Germans brutally and harshly.[1] At the other extreme were those Americans who dug themselves deeply into German life, perhaps marrying a German girl, seeking to penetrate as far as they could into German social and cultural life, and maintaining the most intimate relations with members of a German community. The great mass of Americans have fallen into varying positions between these two extremes. They exhibited no active sadism; but neither did they display any unusual interest in Germany, its culture, its institutions, and its people—at least beyond sex. They were there as part of their national military service. They had little or no background that would make them understand the German people and regarded a stay in Germany much as they would regard an assignment in Japan, Greenland, Italy, or any other place. They were often homesick and their main goal was to return to their families and homes in the United States at the earliest possible time. Nevertheless, it is probably true that Germany has been more popular as an assignment area than most others. Large numbers of Americans have taken advantage of visiting German art treasures, museums, historic centers, and the like, and attending cultural events.

THE EARLY NONFRATERNIZATION POLICY

Although the German people for the most part welcomed the American invaders as liberators and often warmed the hearts of in-

---

[1] Such books as Ernst von Salomon's *Fragebogen* (Putnam, New York, 1955), give the impression that there were large numbers of Americans who acted with great brutality, beating innocent Germans without provocation, etc. Undoubtedly there were too many who abused their positions, but the proportion seems comparatively small.

133

dividual Americans by such expressions of friendship, a strict policy of nonfraternization with Germans characterized the initial period of the occupation. Under orders issued by General Eisenhower carrying out JCS 1067, Americans were to treat the Germans humanely, but they were to avoid personal contacts with them beyond those necessary in the performance of their official duties. And in such dealings it was stipulated that there should be no fraternization. As an aftermath of war, it was not surprising that some such policy would be adopted for American forces in Germany, but only a very naive person expected that such a policy would prove effective.

Americans in general are a very friendly people and, with the fighting over, those in Germany were in no mood to treat the defeated Germans as outcasts and outlaws, unless they encountered Germans who for some reason or other struck them as unworthy of decent treatment.[2] After very little opportunity to have social relationships with members of the feminine sex during a period of months it was not strange that the G.I.s looked at the German *Fräulein* with pleasure and accelerated pulses. These girls seemed to them very like many girls they had left behind in the United States: they liked their appearance and they found their company agreeable. German youngsters are as appealing as children elsewhere, and during the early days of the occupation they were even more touching because many were hungry.

Nonfraternization orders or not, the G.I.s proceeded to associate with the Germans on friendly terms. Military police, pushed on by their superiors, sought to enforce the orders, but after charges had been filed against a large proportion of the personnel in various American units, it was apparent that nonfraternization would not work. No court-martial system could possibly try the thousands who refused to follow the nonfraternization orders. Hence the top command informed Washington that a modification had to be made and it proceeded to make such a change. To save face, the modification did not go all the way in repealing the directive, but for practical purposes nonfraternization had proved itself a failure.

If the nonfraternization policy proved more or less of a fiasco as far as the irrepressible G.I.s were concerned, it had its unfortunate aspect in the case of military government officials charged with han-

[2] See C. Dreher, "Close Up of Democracy," *Virginia Quarterly*, Winter 1947.

dling political affairs and certain other matters. The nonfraternization directive made no distinction between the worst and most vicious
of the Nazi leaders and the Germans who had rotted in concentration
camps and gone through hell because of their determined opposition
to Hitler and his regime. Under it all Germans were bad Germans
for the time being, though it was admitted that there might be a few
good Germans scattered among the bad ones. The defenders of the
directive held that in the beginning there was not time to sort out the
good from the bad and that until this could be done American military
and civilian personnel—for the directive applied to State Department
officials and other civilians as well as to members of the military—
could have only the bare minimum of relations with any Germans,
however deserving these latter might be.*

The result was that, when the anti-Hitler Germans came to offer
their services to American military government, as many did, they had
to be turned away, often even discourteously. Germans, as the world
knows, are fond of handshaking and they consider it exceedingly rude
if hands are not shaken before and after an interview. Yet under a
literal interpretation of the nonfraternization directive American officials could not so much as shake a German hand without rendering
themselves subject to a court-martial. Some Americans refused to
follow such an extreme policy, but the more conscientious did. And
even if they attempted to treat the anti-Hitler Germans who came to
offer their cooperation with common courtesy, they still could not
accept their assistance.

Since American military government obviously needed all of the
cooperation and assistance it could get from responsible and uncor-
rupted Germans, it was very unfortunate to have to turn these people
away. Most of them were unable to understand such irrational behavior and they never returned to repeat their offers. The United
States consequently not only lost valuable resources but, in some instances at least, made enemies.

Some leeway might well have been given to senior officers in
applying the rule, but a military system does not lend itself to such
flexibility. The argument that the situation in Germany was firmly

---

* One American official writes: "We could not take Germans out to eat, even when
we were doing business at our request; we could not share a cup of coffee with colleague
officials; and we could not offer a cigarette."

135

under American control, that under the provisions of the Allied proclamations the German people had lost all initiative and become merely the pawns of the Allies did not hold water. Washington officials could maintain that there was no hurry about distinguishing between the real enemies among the Germans and our friends and that in the meantime a nonfraternization policy must apply to all, but not even victorious military forces can defy natural laws except on paper. Human affairs do not remain suspended because top brass so decree. The failure to recognize this simple truth cost the United States dearly in Germany.

LOOTING, RAPING, AND THE BLACK MARKET

It was a shock to some Americans to observe the conduct of certain fellow Americans after the German surrender.[3] It has been commonplace in the United States to criticize looters as barbarians, as relics of the age of Attila and his Huns, and to imply at least that American military forces do not engage in such a practice. It would not be fair to conclude that looting was all-prevailing among American forces in Germany, but there was a good deal of it. One of the truly sensational cases involved the theft of the crown jewels of the Prince of Hesse from Kronberg castle. One commanding general of a division went so far as to justify looting on the part of his troops by stating that many of his men had lost their lives or been wounded by the Germans and now that victory had come it was quite proper that they should take what they wanted of German chattels. Certainly it could not be said that the majority of American senior officers endorsed such a point of view. Looting always remained a serious offense on the boards. Nevertheless, it must be admitted that looting was all too frequent and that the efforts to punish such conduct during the early period of the occupation were not as vigorous as they might have been. Had the Americans not sharply criticized the Germans for these very practices in Poland, the Ukraine, and elsewhere, the impression made on the German people as a result of looting would have been less important. As it was, many Germans early got the impression that Americans preach one thing and do another and are hypocrites of a high order.

[3] See, for example, W. H. Hale, "Our Failure in Germany," *Harper's Magazine*, Dec. 1945.

The Personal Impact of the Americans

Rape is one of the most serious offenses under American military law and the punishment for such an offense can be the death penalty. However, no American with even faint eyesight could ignore the widespread sexual relations between American males and German women. It has sometimes been stated that such relations were largely confined to the young G.I.s who were at an age where they were not responsible, but particularly during the early period of the occupation all ages and all ranks of Americans from generals down to privates and, including of course civilians, engaged in sexual relations with Germans. That is not to say that *all* Americans had German mistresses or carried on promiscuous sexual intercourse with Germans. As a matter of fact, a considerable number seem to have refrained from such conduct for one reason or another, perhaps because of family ties at home, perhaps because of a feeling that it was not appropriate for responsible officials of an occupying power to conduct themselves in such a fashion with the people of a vanquished country. But despite the sensational record of sexual activity on the part of Americans in Germany, the number of cases of rape was not large. In comparison with the Russians the American statistics as regards rape were very low indeed. It may be argued that the number of rape cases among American forces was very small because American authorities applied the law very loosely and interpreted rape very carelessly. This may be true to some extent, but the primary explanation was doubtless the general willingness on the part of the German women.

Since German women were willing and, during the early period of the occupation when the proportion of females was so high in relation to German males, even eager to engage in sexual relations with American males, there was little place for rape. To what extent the attitude of the German women was the result of their own desires and to what extent it grew out of the need for food, nylons, and other supplies at a time when these were very scarce in Germany, it is difficult to ascertain—there is little doubt that the proffers of food and luxury items did bring many German women to the point of consent.

It is not easy to evaluate the impact of the widespread sexual relations between Americans and Germans. Fairly large numbers of illegitimate children resulted, but probably not more than might have been reasonably expected. Justice Minister Fritz Neumayer in 1956

137

told the Bundestag that Allied soldiers had left at least 67,753 illegitimate children behind and that Americans were responsible for more than half of these—some 37,000.[4] It may be added that estimates made by others have been higher.[5] Some of these youngsters were accepted by the Germans, but a good many were not and had to be housed in institutions, where in some instances they were later adopted by Americans in Germany desiring children.[6] There is little question that many of the older Germans deeply resented this conduct on the part of the occupying personnel with their women. Religious leaders naturally deplored the situation. On the other hand, such relations brought about an acquaintance between the occupiers and the occupied that may have made the general problem of occupation easier. The sexual antics of some colonels and a larger number of lower officers who belonged to the age group over forty certainly must have served to reduce the respect of some Germans for the American military government personnel almost to the point of ridicule. This had a serious effect on the operations of military government. But as far as the conduct of the rank and file of G.I.s went, it seems probable that it was regarded by the majority of the German people as more or less to be expected. Perhaps some went so far as to feel that such activity revealed a warm humanity and animal vitality on the part of Americans which could be admired.

If looting and sexual activity on the part of the Americans shocked more conservative Americans, black-market practices left them even more disturbed. Looting was not infrequent, but it was certainly not indulged in by everyone. Sexual relations were prevalent, but rape was not frequent. However, in the case of black-marketing it almost seemed like the classical story of Diogenes going about with a lantern to seek out an honest man. Not every American engaged in black-market activities of one kind and another during his stay in Germany, but this sort of activity was so general that there was very little criticism of it and indeed those who did not take advantage were often regarded as "peculiar" or "freaks." Some of those who participated

---

[4] Reported in the *New York Times*, June 7, 1956.

[5] N. M. Lobsenz, quoting the West German Interior Ministry, places the number at 85,000. See *Readers Digest*, July 1956, p. 108.

[6] Children of Negro soldiers constituted a special problem. For the attitude of certain Germans, see K. H. Wolff, "German Attempts at Picturing Germany: Texts" (Ohio State University, Columbus, 1955), p. 32.

in black-marketing would be among the first to deny any such record, for their definition of black-marketing covered only large-scale operations involving tons of coffee, hundreds of cartons of cigarettes, the disposal of military vehicles for personal profit, and similar offenses. It would be unjustifiable to suggest that most Americans engaged in any such large-scale black-market operations in Germany. There were officers (like the military government colonel later sentenced to a state penitentiary in the United States in connection with misappropriation of state funds) who were reported to be active in rings which sold military vehicles and other army supplies to Germans, but these were quite exceptional cases. In the great majority of cases black-marketing involved the regular disposal of a carton or so of cigarettes, a pound or two of coffee, a small amount of chocolate, and so forth. To begin with, these items were in very short supply among the Germans; later the shops offered adequate supplies but prices were high because of the heavy excise tax imposed by the West German Federal Government—thus coffee retailed at the equivalent of four dollars a pound or so.

The ration of cigarettes and coffee to American personnel in Germany varied from time to time, but for the most part it was so generous that even chain smokers and the most enthusiastic coffee addicts could not consume their rations. During certain periods American personnel in Germany were permitted to supplement the generous rations available in Germany by importing from the United States under the cheap A.P.O. postal rates. German officials complained bitterly at American sales of these items, maintaining that they resulted in the loss of hundreds of millions of D-marks in taxes. Even a blind man could not have been unaware of the traffic going on in the offices and homes of American personnel; yet the Army officials who controlled the PXs and commissaries gave little or no heed. It almost seemed that these officials must themselves be so involved that they were unwilling to do anything about correcting the situation which made a black-market inevitable.

The existence of such activities was officially recognized during the early period of the occupation and shops were opened where Americans could take cigarettes and other black-market goods and exchange them for Meissen china, paintings, art objects, and other luxury items. General Clay finally saw the inappropriateness of such

139

official outlets and these were closed. However, the black-market went on and on and on, despite the continuing outcries on the part of the German officials.

It was figured that an ordinary American secretary or wife or official could add to his monthly income to the extent of about $50 if surplus cigarettes and coffee were sold to the black-market during the latter period of the occupation; earlier, when supplies were more limited and cigarettes particularly brought fabulous prices, rewards were much higher. An enterprising person who took advantage of every opportunity could of course do much better.

Fifty dollars per month may seem an infinitesimal sum to many wealthy men, and a traffic that would add only that sum to the monthly income of American employees in Germany might seem hardly worth consideration. But the widespread character of the activity resulted in an enormous black-market which deprived the German government of substantial amounts of revenue. Individuals indulging in such activity often denied any responsibility, maintaining that they were underpaid and hence deserved the added income. They also argued that the American government must intend them to have such benefits; otherwise it would have tightened up on the ration system which made such a practice possible.

It would be unduly harsh to blame the rank and file of Americans who were involved in black-market operations as severely as the military government colonel who allegedly bartered an honorary doctor's degree from a German university for a few cartons of cigarettes or the top brass who, at least according to report, accumulated fine wine cellars by disposing judiciously of coffee and cigarettes. But the very prevalence of the petty black-market activities contributed to a gigantic fraud which gave many Germans the impression that Americans are fundamentally dishonest and weak. This was not an enviable reputation and it detracted from the effectiveness of American efforts in Germany.

"LITTLE AMERICAS"

The French followed a general policy of billeting their military personnel with German families, though of course officers occupied requisitioned houses. This had the effect of throwing the French

The Personal Impact of the Americans

soldiers into such close and continuing contact with large numbers of German civilians that they became pretty well acquainted. In contrast, the United States policy during the entire period of the occupation was to keep its personnel, both military and civilian, in colonies apart from the Germans. American soldiers were lodged in barracks which had been constructed by Hitler for his *Wehrmacht* or, later, in camps specially built for American use. American officers and civilians were quartered in German houses which were surrounded by barbed-wire barriers. The barbed-wire was later removed, but the clusters of buildings remained as little islands among the German habitations, though at times there were German-occupied houses scattered among the American-occupied houses. Later a HICOG compound was constructed for High Commission personnel in Frankfurt and, when HICOG moved to the Bonn area, another "Little America" was built there to provide housing. The military also established "Little America" housing projects in the vicinity of the Rhine-Main Airport and elsewhere near its various headquarters in Germany.

The result was that Americans, both military and civilian, lived in Germany but were never a part of the German community. As noted above, the G.I.s had frequent social relations with the German girls, and other American personnel had continuing contact with German maids, barbers, waiters, clerks, caretakers, guards, etc., but beyond that the average American in Germany knew comparatively little about the German people who surrounded him. The top American representatives of course had official contacts with the German officials, including a certain amount of social intercourse, but the social relations of the great mass of Americans were limited to other Americans. There were some exceptions, of course, and individuals might have very intimate German friends and see a great deal of German social and family life.

It was recognized in some quarters that the isolation of Americans in Germany was unfortunate, and tributes were at times paid in high American quarters to the French policy, but little that was concrete was done to change the situation or perhaps could have been done. Various efforts to organize German-American clubs were launched, with the hope that Americans and Germans from similar social and professional levels might be brought together. A few were partially successful, but for the most part they did not flourish. The Germans seemed to display a greater interest than Americans and an attendance of 50 or so Germans and half a dozen Americans might make for such imbalance that little could be done. Attempts were made to organize clubs to bring together representatives of the British, French, American, and German communities, and again these achieved little—the French hardly participated, and the British even less than the Americans. As time went on and the occupation approached an end, German leaders were given opportunities to become members of American military and civilian clubs where dining and other facilities were available. In certain cases this may have served to bring the two groups into social contact, but this program was very limited and was instituted too late to accomplish a great deal.

American individuals therefore had comparatively little opportunity to make any distinct impression on German social groups on the basis of their intellectual vigor, their moral fervor, their professional attainments, and their cultural patterns. The impact, such as it was, was an indirect one difficult to measure.[7] Germans in large numbers saw the exteriors of the elaborate and expensive American housing projects and, according to official statement, were supposed to have been greatly impressed at the high level of American living standards. The HICOG compound at Frankfurt was built with the idea that it would be later turned over to the Germans as a model example of superior American housing, but so many mistakes were made in its planning that it seemed probable, to its occupants at least, that when the time came to turn it over to the Germans it could hardly be expected to have the intended impact. Much-vaunted American plumbing, for example, was represented in the largest three-bedroom apartments by a single wash basin, whereas any German apartment of consequence would have had at least two such appliances, quite likely individual basins in each bedroom, and perhaps two lavatory rooms. The hotels and resort places occupied by Americans were for the most part requisitioned from German owners, but in a few instances, such as the Godesberger Hof in the Bonn area, several million D-marks were spent in new construction or complete overhauling. While the Godesberger Hof was a most pleasant place to stay, with private baths for every bedroom, radiant heating, great

---

[7] For a valuable discussion of the impact during the early years, see H. Price and C. E. Schorske, *The Problem of Germany* (Council on Foreign Relations, New York, 1947).

142

picture windows and balconies overlooking the Rhine, and lovely gardens, the cost of carpets and other fittings which were charged to the German government occasioned sharp criticism in German quarters which went far to counteract any favorable impression.

CONCLUDING COMMENTS

How much of an impression the numerous chromium-trimmed high-power American automobiles made on the Germans, as they streaked by the smaller and less ornate German vehicles and buses on the highways and streets, who can say. Or who can measure the German reaction to the quality of the clothing worn by American soldiers and civilians? It was often argued that the fact that the American G.I. had a considerable amount of money to spend left a deep impression on the German public. The comparatively easy discipline to which American G.I.s were subjected and their fairly informal relations with their officers were cited as significant examples to the Germans. No one can question that Americans, being ubiquitous, were much in the German eye, but the net impression on the Germans will always be controversial.[8] It is probable that one impression was made on some classes of Germans and quite another on others. The situation seemed to vary somewhat from place to place—the stock of Americans was higher in Berlin, for example, than in Frankfurt or Munich or Heidelberg. There was also some variation from time to time. The early situation where Americans were received into virtually any type of German family circle, however exalted, deteriorated to a point where the better class families often brought pressure on their daughters to have as little as possible to do with Americans. At times German girls had their hair cut off if they were found in the company of Americans. Although these were extreme cases, at the low point of relations between the Americans and Germans, most of the German young women who were easily available as companions of young Americans belonged to the marginal social groups.

By the very nature of an occupation the relations between the

---

[8] Various impressions of individual Germans are recorded in K. H. Wolff, "German Attempts at Picturing Germany: Texts" (mimeographed, Department of Sociology and Anthropology, Ohio State University, Columbus, 1955), pp. 28 ff.

representatives of the occupying power and the local population are almost bound to be abnormal. Shortages of food and luxury items lead to a willingness on the part of many local inhabitants to acquiesce in the desires and importuning of the occupying personnel who tend to be made up of young males in large measure. As the occupation progresses and more normal social and economic conditions are re-established, there is almost bound to be a withdrawal of the local population, a resentment at the presence of the occupation forces, and numerous stresses and strains. Under the circumstances existing in Germany, with the Russian-American relations so unsatisfactory and the consequent American effort to woo the Germans, these strains did not reach a point which might normally have been expected during an occupation extending over a decade. Americans, despite all their idiosyncrasies and weaknesses, were regarded more as friends by the German people than as soldiers and policemen of a foreign power. Consequently there was much less of the sullen resentment which has typified certain occupations.

How permanent the impact left by the Americans may be depends in some measure upon future developments. If the occupation has ended, the presence of American troops on German soil continues and the role of the United States in European affairs remains important. Favorable developments leading to the unification of East and West Germany and a continued prosperous economy would probably tend to emphasize the pleasanter and more agreeable impressions made by individual Americans. Frustration in the desire for unification and economic depression would, on the other hand, perhaps underline the unfavorable impressions.

10

War Crimes Trials

The series of international and national trials of the top-flight Nazi leaders, German military personnel, Foreign Office officials, concentration camp directors, industrialists, and others have been much publicized and, not surprisingly, have occasioned a great deal of controversy. International trials were entrusted to an International Tribunal, and trials in the American Zone to special courts set up for the purpose. Military government was of course deeply interested in the trials, and its legal and public relations subdivisions were charged with certain responsibilities, particularly in connection with the trials in the American Zone. The Legal Division of OMGUS, for example, had the overall responsibility of preparing the charges against the accused in the American trials; and in both the international trials and the American tribunal proceedings, OMGUS took over the publicizing of the trials in Germany through newspaper stories, radio broadcasts, the medium of films and photographs, and the like.

The international trials at Nuremberg naturally have received the greatest publicity, the proceedings of which started in November 1945 and continued for almost a year until October 1, 1946. The United States contributed two judges to the bench responsible for hearing the charges against the accused and rendering judgment: Francis Biddle and John J. Parker. Mr. Justice Robert Jackson of the Supreme Court of the United States obtained leave from his Washington duties and represented the United States as a chief prosecutor, being assisted by General Telford Taylor, Dr. R. M. W. Kempner, and others. The 24 defendants included Field Marshal Goering, Rudolf Hess, Foreign Minister von Ribbentrop, Bormann, and other top-ranking Nazi leaders, Admiral Doenitz, Generals Keitel and Jodl, Ambassador von Papen, financial wizard Schacht, and others.

The proceedings in the International Tribunal were of consider-

145

able interest to both the outside world and the German people, though the latter particularly tired as the trials went on month after month. The reputations of the judges were such as to guarantee at least reasonable attention to due process of law. It would be difficult to argue that the trials were "railroaded" through, lasting as they did for almost a year and being conducted on a group, rather than an individual, basis. The charges varied from case to case, but in general the defendants were tried for the brutal and notorious atrocities committed by the Hitler regime both in connection with the war and otherwise. Most of the defendants finally received either a death sentence or life imprisonment—nine were sentenced to death and seven to life imprisonment. However, several fared better, and von Papen, Fritsche, and Schacht were vindicated.[1]

The protracted period required to complete the international trials and the conduct of the Russian representatives made further proceedings on an international basis unacceptable to the United States, Britain, and France. Therefore following, and in some instances concurrently with, the international trials, the United States, Britain, and France tried a much larger number of Germans under incarceration in their zones in purely national tribunals. In the American Zone the Dachau trials alone involved some 1,672 prisoners. Although the Nuremberg trials got the limelight, it was the tribunals in the four national zones that tried most of the Germans. General Telford Taylor took over the prosecution in the American trials and judges were brought from the United States to preside over the courts—they were all of the state level since Mr. Chief Justice Vinson of the Supreme Court of the United States did not regard it as appropriate to

[1] Much material is available relating to the Nuremberg trials. The official record was published in 37 volumes under the title *Trial of Major War Criminals Before the International Military Tribunal* (Nuremberg, 1948). A summary of the trials may be found in P. Calvocoressi, *Nuremberg: The Facts, the Law, and the Consequences* (Macmillan, New York, 1948). Mr. Justice Jackson recorded his version in *The Nuremberg Trial* (Knopf, New York, 1947), and Telford Taylor in *Nuremberg Trials, War Crimes, and International Law* (Carnegie Endowment, New York, 1949). The reaction of a defendant is to be found in F. von Papen, *Memoirs* (Dutton, New York, 1953). A German official viewpoint is to be found in H. Ehard, "The Nuremberg Trial Against the Major War Criminals and International Law," *American Journal of International Law*, April 1949. A political scientist has analyzed the proceedings in the same journal, F. B. Schick, "The Nuremberg Trial and International Law," Oct. 1947. Other valuable sources of additional material are: Sheldon Glueck, *The Nuremberg Trials and Aggressive War* (Knopf, New York, 1946), and V. H. Bernstein, *Final Judgment*, (Boni and Gaer, New York, 1947).

146

use federal judges in light of the sharp criticism directed at the role of Mr. Justice Jackson in the Nuremberg trials.

The offenses charged in the American tribunals varied widely. But some idea of their scope can be derived from the first twelve cases which were selected as sort of test cases. These involved military officers who had served Germany in connection with the occupation of Poland, Czechoslovakia, and other areas, heads of the great industrial concerns of Krupp, Farben, and Flick, Foreign Office officials who had worked with the Nazis in carrying out their program, Nazi S.S. leaders who allegedly had been responsible for mass murders, doctors who were charged with using prisoners for sensational experimental purposes, and officials of the Ministry of Justice who had cooperated with the Hitler regime, even if not Nazis themselves, in putting National Socialist laws into effect and approving mass murders. The Dachau trials, which went on at the same time as the Nuremberg proceedings, involved the murder of American airmen and soldiers, the almost incredible brutalities committed in connection with the concentration camps, and so forth. The Dachau trials, unlike the others, were under special military tribunals rather than courts staffed by civilian judges.

It is difficult to obtain a clear view of the trials in the American Zone. Those carried on by military tribunal at Dachau during the period prior to December 30, 1947, were in general rather different from those handled by the special courts. Much, though not all, of the criticism involving undue haste, denial of democratic legal processes, and the like, arose out of the special military tribunals, particularly the Malmedy case where feeling was deep as a result of the murder of American soldiers. The record of convictions in the Dachau trials was high: only 256 persons being acquitted out of 1,672 tried, and 426 receiving the death sentence. Actually, however, reviews of these cases by General Clay set aside 69 convictions, commuted 119 of the sentences, and reduced the penalties in 138 cases.[2] In the cases tried by the courts presided over by judges brought from the United States, the conviction record was particularly low in the trials of industrialists and businessmen, who were found guilty only, if at all, for using and abusing slave labor. Altogether there were 1,539 persons

[2] See L. D. Clay, *Decision in Germany*, p. 253.

147

convicted in the American Zone, of whom 444 were sentenced to death but only 250 actually executed.

Critics have noted that juries were not employed in trying these many German prisoners. Consequently it has been charged that the United States denied its own legal guarantees to the Germans. While this is the case it can hardly be denied that it would have been very difficult to make use of juries at this stage in Germany—moreover, juries are not required under judicial rulings in unincorporated territory of the United States, in military court martials, and so forth. More serious is the question as to whether evidence was improperly obtained through third-degree and other methods and whether due attention was given to the evidence in deciding cases. In the Malmedy case there were perhaps serious shortcomings in these respects and third-degree methods may have been employed to some extent in other cases, though the evidence is less strong. The atmosphere of the times was such, especially in the Malmedy and Ilse Koch cases, that it was somewhat difficult to maintain the fairness that is traditionally associated with American justice. However, when one takes into account the war which had recently ended and the deep resentment and bitterness generated by Nazi brutality and fiendishness, it is perhaps remarkable that there was not more inclination to rush proceedings through and to find defendants guilty on flimsy evidence. In comparing the record of the German war crimes trials with their counterparts in Japan, there seems to be little doubt that the former involved fewer failures to observe the established traditions of American justice.

The main basis for controversy in connection with the German war crimes trials has probably not been the denial of juries, the use of third-degree techniques, the far from calm atmosphere in which some of the trials were conducted, and the like, but the holding of Germans responsible for official acts arising out of their employment or military service. Military personnel in the United States and elsewhere regard with deep concern a new international law under which generals and other senior officers of defeated forces may be held responsible to the point of the death penalty for carrying out orders given to them by their military and political superiors. Diplomatic, justice, and other public officials share this feeling, though their positions are perhaps less vulnerable. It is maintained that under the new rule the military officers of a defeated country are likely to be severely punished, if not deprived of their lives, more or less automatically and that this places an undue and unfair onus on the shoulders of professional military men the world over. Supporters of the new rule reply that officials should not feel themselves bound by orders which by their very nature involve inhuman and brutal measures and that they should surrender their posts rather than be parties to such actions.

Anyone who followed the course of the Nazi regime either in Germany or elsewhere must have been shocked by the almost incredible lack of humanity, the sacrifice of hundreds of thousands and even millions of lives on such flimsy excuses as non-Nordic race, disagreement with programs, and the like, and the gross corruption which characterized the system from top to bottom. The new genocide law seeks to give some remedy in such a situation by forewarning future gangsters that they may be held responsible for their acts.

Some of those who regard the new rule as generally tenable express concern because of what they regard as the *ex post facto* character of the law in its application to Germans following World War II. These people, who are often unusually thoughtful persons, maintain that, however guilty the German leaders may have been, there was no international law when they committed the acts for which they were later tried and that no attempt should have been made to apply the new rule retroactively. While one may sympathize with the program intended to curtail brutality and notorious lawlessness, it is difficult to ignore the grave concern of some of the most reputable legal authorities in the Free World as to the injurious effects of the experience in the war crimes trials in Germany on western justice. One military government officer in legal affairs who had been dean of an American law school prior to entry upon military service became so apprehensive on the above grounds that his colleagues were convinced that his premature death was to a considerable extent the result of such forebodings and genuine shock.

11

The Denazification Purge

The denazification efforts of the United States in Germany have, from the beginning, occasioned controversy in large measure. The most zealous proponents have perhaps regarded this undertaking as the most significant, certainly the most necessary, of all American activities in Germany. To these people denazification represented an attempt to transform the entire population of a major country from a band of international outlaws, murderers, looters, and the like, through purges, prison sentences, confiscation of property, and fines to decent representatives of the human race and responsible citizens of the world. At the opposite extreme there are those who consider the American denazification program in Germany as completely without justification, as one of the worst travesties on justice in all history, as a "fiasco," and generally as an ineradicable blot on American reputation.[1] There are, of course, many varying points of view between these two extremes.

A record involving the violent emotions and divergent points of view characterizing the American denazification program in Germany cannot be readily evaluated even after a decade has passed. It is probable that honest men will for many years differ as to the justification and results of the denazification purge. By the very nature of the case there is no possibility of deriving a completely objective and clear-cut set of conclusions even after many years have elapsed and emotions have subsided. However, the picture was clearer in 1955, as the occupation ended, than it was in 1945, 1946, 1947, and 1948, and it may be profitable to examine the record as carefully as possible.

---

[1] For examples of various types of critical analysis, see J. H. Hertz, "The Fiasco of Denazification in Germany," *Political Science Quarterly*, Dec. 1948; C. E. Schorske, "The Dilemma in Germany," *Virginia Quarterly Review*, Winter 1948; R. Niebuhr, "Germany: Vengeance or Justice," *The Nation*, July 23, 1949.

The Denazification Purge

To some of those who have studied the American record of denazification in Germany it is absurd to speak of American policy on the subject—these observers regard such an activity as the result of extreme hatred, a desire for revenge, the outgrowth of a hurricane of mass emotion which swept politically influential groups in the United States off their feet and frightened political leaders into irresponsible action. It is true that the development of American plans in the denazification field did not proceed in an orderly fashion and that they were in large measure influenced, if not entirely controlled, by strong political pressures in the United States. Nevertheless, it is desirable to trace the events leading up to the full-blown American denazification program which, for a time in late 1945 and 1946, overshadowed all other American activities in Germany.

While there was doubtless some early official discussion in Washington of what would be done about the National Socialist party and the Nazi leaders after the successful conclusion of the war, this does not seem to have had any great significance in the actual chain of events in Germany. Washington eyes were fixed firmly on winning the war itself, and what would come after was naturally crowded into the background. Responsibility for planning for the nonmilitary aspects of the occupation of Germany was in large measure left to the Anglo-American German Country Unit of the Supreme Headquarters and to its American successor, the U. S. Group, Control Council for Germany as noted earlier.*

Although there were sizable staffs of American and British officers and enlisted men to draft plans relating to economic matters, local government, civil service, education, religious affairs, administrative courts, the legal system, labor organizations, and so forth, there was no special provision made for planners to deal with the National Socialist party. Of course it was generally agreed that the party must be liquidated and its leaders dealt with, but no specific machinery was set up to provide such plans. After considerable delay it was understood that since the German Country Unit had no political division, the planning for denazification would be farmed out to

* See Chap. 2.

OSS (Office of Strategic Services) and its British counterpart in Military Intelligence. But as the pressure increased to complete the *Handbook for Military Government in Germany* and other plans were in hand, little was forthcoming from these outside agencies. Inquiries revealed that they were working on the job, but that its complexity coupled with other responsibilities made delay inevitable. The time came when plans for dealing with the National Socialist party and its leaders had to be produced for inclusion in the general set of plans for the occupation of Germany. After some advice from OSS and discussion on the part of the staff of the German Country Unit, the task of preparing a section of the general plans to cover denazification was handed to the harassed members of the board which had the arduous responsibility for coordinating the plans drafted by the various subdivisions of the German Country Unit into a single handbook. The time factor was such that this emergency job had to be completed in a few days.

Under the hastily drafted denazifications plans of the German Country Unit, provision was made for the complete liquidation of the National Socialist party, the confiscation of its property and funds, and the seizure of its records.[2] There was little difficulty here. But when it came to deciding where the dividing line would be fixed between the Nazi leaders who were regarded as so dangerous that they must be arrested and imprisoned and the lesser fry, the situation was more complicated. Emphasis was placed on the danger involved in permitting National Socialist officials to remain at large rather than upon punishment as an end in itself in fixing such a dividing line, and in the last analysis reliance was placed on advice tendered by OSS.[3]

It was the accepted opinion among those responsible in the German Country Unit that it would be impractical to imprison the lower ranks of Nazi officials, not because they deserved any particular consideration but because facilities available and probable resources to deal with several hundred thousand such persons could not be expected. Pressure was too great at the moment to permit the German Country Unit staff to indulge in speculation as to whether

---

[2] See *Handbook for Military Government in Germany*, Part III, Chap. 2.
[3] For the categories to be interned, see *ibid.*, Part III, Chap. 2, Table "C."

The Denazification Purge

the denazification plans represented an "easy" attitude toward the Nazis, but the general philosophy motivating the staff of the German Country Unit emphasized the major interests of the United States and Britain and the desirability of handling the occupation of Germany in such a manner that these Allied interests would be protected and served to the fullest extent. Had individual staff members been polled, it is probable that they would have replied that their plans called for a distinctly "hard" treatment of the Germans rather than an "easy" one. Military events, including the bombing of German Country Unit headquarters in Princes Gardens in London and the narrow escape which certain planners had in other buzz-bomb incidents, while the planning was going on, were not such as to encourage any "easy" attitude toward the Germans. On the other hand, a highly emotional spirit of revenge did not play a leading role.

While there is little evidence of detailed attention to the problem of denazification in official circles in Washington, there was a great deal of interest on the part of certain individuals and private citizens. One such group was led by Harry Dexter White, who served as Assistant Secretary of the Treasury and came into notoriety when he suddenly died and was later charged by Attorney General Brownell as an important link in the Communist plot to infiltrate key public agencies in Washington, and Henry Morgenthau, Jr., the Secretary of the Treasury. The White-Morgenthau group felt, as noted earlier,* that the Germans had, by their outrageous treatment of the Jews, their international gangsterism, and their irresponsible aggression which involved the laying waste of Poland and other sections of Europe, forfeited any claim to ordinary humanity as defeated people. Since the National Socialist party and its leaders were regarded as the arch criminals, it was maintained that a gigantic program should be undertaken to purge the German people of such elements. Any fair-minded person has to give attention to the White-Morgenthau indictments and many will express sympathy for their strong feelings.[4] The German record was without question a very bad one and the National Socialist guilt very great. But the philosophy back of the

---

* See Chap. 6.

[4] The point of view of the White-Morgenthau group is presented in Henry Morgenthau, *Germany Is Our Problem* (Harper, New York, 1945).

153

White-Morgenthau proposals was one of revenge rather than one which placed the emphasis on practical considerations. No heed was given to the key role of Germany in Europe and the impossibility of getting European economy back on its feet while Germany remained prostrate. The fact that the United States had little in the way of facilities for administering such a purge of Nazism apparently received no attention at all. The influence of the White-Morgenthau combine and groups holding somewhat similar views became increasingly apparent in the United States.

As Secretary of the Treasury, Mr. Morgenthau found it desirable to maintain a personal representative in the German Country Unit in the person of Colonel Bernstein who headed the finance subdivision. The influence of Mr. Morgenthau is indicated by the unusual position occupied by Colonel Bernstein. Where other officials of the planning agency had few if any direct contacts with Washington and, only with considerable difficulty, could make trips to Washington for consultation, Colonel Bernstein had the most intimate contacts with Mr. Morgenthau, Mr. White, and others, could communicate the developments in planning directly to them, and could at any time demand transportation facilities for going to and from Washington.

When the third draft of the German Country Unit set of plans for the occupation of Germany, and the first to contain the hastily drafted plans for the liquidation of the National Socialist party and the imprisonment of Nazi leaders, came out in mimeographed form, Colonel Bernstein almost immediately took off by air for Washington, carrying a copy. The White-Morgenthau clique regarded these plans as much too "easy" on the Germans and particularly objected to the section dealing with the Nazi leaders. The influence of this group was such that Morgenthau had ready access to the President and shortly took the set of plans to President Roosevelt. It seems unlikely that Mr. Roosevelt looked at the plans themselves, but he must have listened to the Morgenthau interpretation and objections. At any rate he seems to have been persuaded that the plans for the occupation of Germany were too "easy" and therefore unsatisfactory. Arrangements which had been made to issue the plans in the European Theatre for use by military government personnel had to be

154

canceled despite the great need of the numerous military government teams headed for Germany.[5]

THE QUEBEC CONFERENCE AND JCS 1067

At the second Quebec Conference which met during the period September 11-16, 1944, shortly after President Roosevelt had received and rejected the plans drafted by the Anglo-American German Country Unit for the occupation of Germany, various matters were considered. Among these was the general treatment of Germany after the successful termination of military operations. The influence of the White-Morgenthau group on President Roosevelt led to the virtual ignoring of the Department of State and its Secretary, Cordell Hull—he was not even in attendance.[6] This was supposed to be justified by the military character of the Quebec Conference, but it is significant to keep in mind that the strong views of the Secretary of War, Henry Stimson, on the general policy of economic dismantling were also cast aside.[7] The British delegation led by Winston Churchill was apparently persuaded to accept the White-Morgenthau position, though they soon realized the folly of such a commitment and withdrew from the stand taken at Quebec.[8]

Even before the Quebec Conference the drafting of a directive to the American Commander relating to the occupation of Germany was in process—this became known as JCS 1067 and has been discussed elsewhere.* While this directive did not reach Germany until the spring of 1945 and President Roosevelt had already turned away from the White-Morgenthau Plan, at least in its extreme stipulations,[9] the provisions of JCS 1067 reflected in large measure the

---

[5] After some revision by the civil affairs section of SHAEF—the German Country Unit having been dissolved—the plans were published "unofficially" under the title *Handbook for Military Government in Germany* in late 1944.

[6] See *The Memoirs of Cordell Hull* (Macmillan, New York, 1948).

[7] See H. L. Stimson and G. M. Bundy, *On Active Service in Peace and War* (Harper, New York, 1948), pp. 568-82.

[8] The agreement initialed by Roosevelt and Churchill at Quebec is included in Stimson and Bundy, *op. cit.*, pp. 576-577. No mention is made of denazification, but emphasis is placed on "converting Germany into a country primarily agricultural and pastoral in its character."

* See Chap. 6.

[9] See Stimson and Bundy, *op. cit.*, p. 582.

thinking at Quebec. In commenting on JCS 1067 Secretary Stimson noted that reading it two years after its issuance he "found it a painfully negative document," admitting that in the spring of 1945 it "seemed so much less punitive and destructive" than the White-Morgenthau demands that his general reaction was one of relief.[10]

JCS 1067 appeared in a number of drafts, but all of them dealt with denazification. The draft which was made public on October 17, 1945, included detailed provisions relating to denazification.[11] Providing that a proclamation should be issued dissolving the National Socialist party and all of its associated, affiliated, and supervised organizations and prohibiting their reconstitution, that laws devised by the Nazi regime to further their own purposes should be abrogated, that National Socialist property should be confiscated and Nazi records taken over, the directive then stipulated as follows:

All members of the Nazi party who have been more than nominal participants in its activities, all active supporters of Nazism or militarism and all other persons hostile to Allied purposes will be removed and excluded from public office and from positions of importance in quasi-public and private enterprises such as (1) civic, economic, and labor organizations, (2) corporations and other organizations in which the German government or subdivisions have a major financial interest, (3) industry, commerce, agriculture, and finance, (4) education, and (5) the press, publishing houses, and other agencies disseminating news and propaganda. Persons are to be treated as more than nominal participants in Party activities and as active supporters of Nazism or militarism when they have (1) held office or otherwise been active at any level from local to national in the party and its subordinate organizations, or in organizations which further militaristic doctrines, (2) authorized or participated affirmatively in any Nazi crimes, racial persecutions or discriminations, (3) been avowed believers in Nazism or racial and militaristic creeds, or (4) voluntarily given substantial moral or material support or political assistance of any kind to the Nazi Party or Nazi officials and leaders. No such persons shall be retained in any of the categories of employment listed above because of administrative necessity, convenience or expediency.

[10] *Ibid.*, p. 582.

[11] For the full text, see State Department, *Germany, 1947-1949: The Story in Documents* (Washington, 1950), pp. 21-33.

The Denazification Purge

When the first version of JCS 1067 arrived in Germany in the spring of 1945, the military government organization was in more or less embryo form and the tactical military units occupied the scene. Consequently, instead of attempting to promulgate a uniform American order relating to denazification and other matters, the Joint Chiefs of Staff directive went from the headquarters of General Eisenhower as American Commander in Germany to the Army Group headquarters. Under the pattern which had been established during the war and which gave a considerable amount of autonomy to Army Groups, these headquarters did not consider it sufficient to transmit JCS 1067 to the Armies under it but rather framed their own directives based of course on the provisions of JCS 1067. The Armies, being also very proud of their own positions and self-sufficient to a marked degree, were not content to send the Army Group directive down to corps and division levels but formulated their own.

All of this not only occasioned delay in getting the orders to the operating units, in the case of denazification the military government teams, but it resulted in a considerable amount of variation in operating orders despite the common derivation from the Joint Chiefs of Staff directive.[12] One Army, finding the qualifying adjective "active" vague, ordered that "all" Nazis be summarily removed. In another case those who joined the party after 1936 were defined as "not active." Despite the express provision in JCS 1067 that "administrative necessity, convenience or expediency" should not be used to justify exceptions to the enforcement of the ban on Nazis, one Army actually more or less suspended denazification activities on the ground that there was a job to be done and that this superseded denazification. The net result was that in the summer of 1945 American military government was operating under at least four different denazification policies. Obviously this was highly unsatisfactory.

The deactivation of the Army Groups during the latter part of 1945 removed one link in the long chain of command and promoted

---

[12] Some idea of the complexity of directives in this field may be obtained from looking at the compilation made by the Bavarian Office of Military Government, published under the title *German Denazification Law and All Implementations and American Directives* in 1946 and in a revised edition in 1947. Supplements were issued in 1947 and 1948.

the achieving of uniformity in the denazification program of the United States. Perhaps even more the summary removal of General Patton from his command of the Third Army and his position as military governor of Bavaria because he had insisted on administering his own version of a denazification program, breaking into great notoriety when he expressed doubt as to the sound basis of the denazification policy and described members of the National Socialist party in Germany as the counterparts of members of the Republican or Democratic parties in the United States, served notice that a uniform denazification course was to be followed.

During the early days of the occupation denazification occasioned a certain amount of difficulty to military government, particularly after the newspapers in the United States, avid for news of what was going on in Germany, emblazoned their front pages with lurid tales about the use of Nazis in the emergency administration of Aachen.[13] However, denazification was only one of many matters which had to receive attention in the field and it perhaps may have been regarded as less pressing by many military government detachments than such emergency tasks as getting a supply of water available, procuring food for the hungry people, providing primitive means of transportation, and the like. As time passed, increasing emphasis was to be noted in giving priority to the denazification program in Germany. The Political Division (Office of Political Affairs) of the U. S. Group, Control Council for Germany started out with a single officer working on denazification. Before long it is probable that more of its sizable staff had to concentrate on that program than on any other.[14] The Public Safety and Legal Divisions became so immersed in denazification that it was sometimes difficult to find time and energy to handle other important assignments. When the U. S. Group, Control Council for Germany was merged into OMGUS, an even greater amount of pressure was exerted to give denazification priority. A special adviser on denazification, Dr. Walter L. Dorn, was appointed.

In the military government field organization there was more or

[13] See S. K. Padover, *Experiment in Germany* (Duell, Sloan & Pierce, New York, 1946).
[14] For a discussion of the problems arising at this period by one who participated in the headquarters administration, see E. Plischke, "Denazifying the Reich," *Review of Politics*, April 1947, and by the same author, "Denazification Law and Procedure," *American Journal of International Law*, Oct. 1947.

less the same build-up. To begin with, denazification was only one of many assignments to be handled by military government detachments and there was no special denazification personnel. Before long, "Special Branches" were set up in the military government field organizations which literally mushroomed in growth. More and more military and civilian personnel had to be assigned to the job of "vetting," as denazification came to be called. Millions of forms known as *Fragebogen* were printed and circulated among the German people in the American Zone. As these were filled out and returned, filing space became a major problem; and in many instances the forms were stacked in bundles, more or less as fire wood is stacked, in the hallways, in closets, in cellars, and indeed wherever vacant space could be found. Altogether some thirteen million completed questionnaires (*Fragebogen*) were returned by the Germans living in the American Zone.[15]

If the task of deciding what to include in the *Fragebogen* was complicated and the job of printing, distributing, and receiving the completed forms burdensome, the assignment of going over the thirteen million completed forms, investigating the validity of the data furnished, and deciding on the action to be taken in each individual case was positively overwhelming. More and more personnel were assigned to the Special Branches, but they made almost no noticeable progress in completing the work, despite assistance received from the Counter Intelligence Corps. Some of the persons assigned to the Special Branches had backgrounds which at least to some extent fitted them for the complicated task of review, investigation, and decision involved, but large numbers were largely "bodies" who could be drawn out of the military supply of personnel.

It would have required many thousands of trained American officials to administer in any reasonably adequate manner the denazification program in Germany. Sufficient numbers of such persons were probably not available in the military forces—at any rate if they were available their services could not be released for such a purpose. To make matters worse, as noted earlier,* great pressures were developing to return military personnel in Germany to their homes and responsibilities in the United States, and a large-scale

---

[15] See L. D. Clay, *Decision in Germany*, p. 259.
* See Chap. 2.

program of discharging military personnel was actually being carried out. Theoretically the political authorities in Washington could have appropriated many millions of dollars to recruit and train a special staff of investigators and evaluators in the United States for "vetting" in Germany. However, although the White-Morgenthau influence remained strong, it was not powerful enough to push through such an undertaking at a time when attention was focused on reducing the military expenditures and a return to normalcy in the United States. The inescapable result was that the United States was faced with an immensely involved task in Germany which offered almost no possibilities of even fairly satisfactory solution. To drop the denazification undertaking was politically out of the question at the time, though it is probable that many Americans in high military positions would have liked nothing better. On the other hand, experience in the field clearly indicated that it was utterly impossible to handle the job of "vetting" more than thirteen million Germans in the American Zone.

If the denazification program could not be cast aside, steps at least could be taken to impose limits on its scope. Thus in August 1946 the American Military Governor granted an amnesty to the younger generation, those born after January 1, 1919, unless they had held prominent places in the Hitler Youth. The argument that people who were in their teens could not have been contaminated by Nazi propaganda, as advanced by General Clay,[16] may seem somewhat naive to those who knew the Hitler *Jugend* in their full activity, but at any rate a large number of records could be cut from the more than thirteen million *Fragebogen* being processed. A second amnesty at Christmas in 1946 cleared the mass (some 800,000) of "little men" whose incomes had been low (less than RM 3,600 and with taxable property valued at less than RM 20,000) during the Nazi regime and who therefore were not regarded as the beneficiaries of the vast looting of German industry undertaken by Goering and other Nazi leaders. At the same time, the disabled received an amnesty. These two acts further cut the size of the denazification lists sharply. But even so some two million active cases remained to be resolved.

---

[16] See his *Decision in Germany*, p. 260.

The Denazification Purge

In mid-1946 one of the most controversial of all the debated steps taken by American military government was decided upon. Denazification had bogged down; the time being devoted to this single activity exceeded that available for any other program and consequently highly important responsibilities were being neglected. Prospects of carrying out the "vetting" to any satisfactory conclusion appeared remote. To relieve American military government of this impossible situation, the responsibility for denazification was transferred to the Germans, under American supervision of course. The Minister-Presidents of the *Länder* in the American Zone gave their approval to a "Law for the Liberation from National Socialism and Militarism" which, as of June 1, 1946, made the Germans primarily responsible for the denazification program.[17]

Defenders of this move have maintained that it was appropriate for the Germans to purge themselves and that the American policy involved the best democratic traditions since it let the German people themselves decide. Critics have derided such an argument, scoffing at the idea that there was any democracy or any other noble sentiment involved and maintaining that American military government found itself in an impossible situation and therefore, in a desperate effort to get "out from under," made the Germans the scapegoat. General Clay points out that, with some thirteen million Germans filling out *Fragebogen* and approximately three million chargeable in the various guilt categories, three fourths of the Germans were called on to decide the fate of one fourth.[18] This implies that the great majority of the Germans had kept themselves free from Nazi taint and evil relationships and therefore were in a position to judge their fellows who had succumbed to Nazi blandishments and corruption. But many of those at least familiar with the situation under National Socialism find it very difficult to accept such a specious argument. With more than 80 per cent of the teachers and approxi-

---

[17] This law together with supplementary regulations and numerous interpretations is to be found in E. Schullze, *Gesetz zur Befreiung von Nationalsozialismus und Militarismus* (3rd edition, Munich, 1948).

[18] See his *Decision in Germany*, p. 259.

mately proportionate numbers of other professional classes in National Socialist organizations of one kind or another, with virtually the entire German economy under Nazi control, and with German life almost completely geared to Nazi operations, even the most ardent defender of the German people cannot, with a straight face, maintain that the majority were anti-Hitler and opponents of the Nazi regime. The French doubtless went too far in holding that all Germans who survived the Nazi period were in one way or another responsible for what went on in Germany under Hitler, but their position would seem to be more tenable than that of those Americans who regarded three fourths of the German population in the American Zone as so innocent of dealings with the Nazis that they could fairly administer a denazification program.

Under the "Law for the Liberation from National Socialism and Militarism" 545 German tribunals, with staffs exceeding 22,000, were created to complete the process of denazification instituted by American military government. Five classes were set up under the law as follows: (1) major offenders, who might be subject to as many as ten years of imprisonment, permanent exclusion from holding public office, and property confiscation, (2) offenders, who could be imprisoned, fined, and/or excluded from public office but were subject to probation, (3) lesser offenders, who might be fined, (4) followers, and (5) nonoffenders and exonerated after trial. Denazification ministries which were of course subject to political and other pressures associated with governmental bodies were organized in the several states (*Länder*) in the American Zone to exercise general control over the program. Appellate tribunals were set up to hear cases appealed from the local denazification tribunals.

It is not surprising that there were numerous difficulties encountered in getting such an elaborate system of state ministries, local tribunals, appellate tribunals, and so forth, in operation. To find adequate judges, prosecutors, investigators, and other staff members for such a far-flung organization would have been far from easy in any country under any circumstances. In a country still suffering from the shock of war and with the economy and social structure almost prostrate, the difficulties were accentuated. To make the situation almost impossible, there was the Nazi record of almost all persons who would otherwise have qualifications for such positions.

162

The Denazification Purge

However, it had been decided that the Germans would carry on a denazification program and, whether there were qualified Germans or not to staff the machinery, strong pressure was exerted to proceed and proceed without delay. In five months the German tribunals had examined 583,985 cases, eliminating 530,907 without trial. General Clay made it clear that he was very dissatisfied with such a record and gave the Germans 60 days to mend their ways "or else."[19]

Reporting to the House of Representatives in February 1948, the Case Sub-committee of the House Select Committee on Foreign Aid unanimously recommended the winding up of denazification proceedings in Germany by May 8, 1948. It saw no objection to giving complete amnesty to the lesser offenders and followers, leaving only the two top categories, major offenders and offenders, to be penalized. General Clay opposed such a step on the ground that many of the leading Nazis still remained to be dealt with.[20] Consequently no formal end was decreed at this time. However, revenge sentiment in the United States was cooling rapidly, and the record of many of the German tribunals was so unsatisfactory and even scandalous that the denazification operations were brought to an end shortly.

The records show that the German denazification tribunals tried some 930,000 persons on various charges, though more than two million persons were reported as "chargeable" after the amnesties had reduced the numbers. Of these only 1,549 were found guilty as major offenders and approximately 21,000 as offenders! Some 104,000 were branded as lesser offenders and 475,000 as followers. Approximately 9,000 received some sort of prison sentence; 22,000 were excluded from public office; 25,000 had some or all of their property confiscated; and in excess of 500,000 were fined.[21] This on its surface may seem an impressive record, though the numbers in the major offender category were very small indeed, when one considers the size of the National Socialist organization and the vicious deeds of many of its leaders. It is true, as General Clay points out, that in viewing the prison sentences one must take into account the fact that most of the 74,000 persons turned over by American military government to the German denazification authorities had been in

---

[19] In a speech delivered to the *Länderrat* on Nov. 5, 1946.
[20] See his *Decision in Germany*, pp. 259-260.
[21] As reported by General Clay in *Decision in Germany*, p. 260.

prison for various periods up to three years when they were finally tried and sentenced.[22] Nevertheless, it seems very doubtful whether the record insofar as it relates to major offenders and offenders really indicates more severe punishment than would have been forthcoming under the less complicated and less time-consuming plans of the German Country Unit. When one contemplates the enormous amount of energy expended by American military government, the serious interference occasioned in other major programs, the loss of prestige and respect which the United States suffered among Germans in its own and other zones, and various other factors, the achievement seems small indeed.

The scandals arising out of the German administration of the denazification program were numerous and frequently sensational. The Munich Denazification Tribunal had to be thrown out and a new organization set up. It was commonplace for judges, prosecutors, and investigators to be charged by responsible persons with accepting bribes. Minor Nazis sometimes drew heavier penalties than the most active Nazi leaders. Influential Nazis managed in some instances to get their cases disposed of with little fuss. Local communities were frequently so badly split by bitterness arising out of cases that it will be many years before the scars disappear. Very few Germans have anything good to say about the denazification program as administered in the American Zone—perhaps this is not to be taken seriously, though the basic loss of respect for the United States which resulted in many instances must be regarded as a major matter.[23] Perhaps the worst aspect of the entire denazification program, both as carried out by American military government and the Germans, was that it permitted some of the most notorious Nazis to escape. The very fact that the net was so widely spread made it possible for certain shrewd and wily Nazi "big boys" to get through the mesh. Even General Clay admitted as early as 1950, when the record was less clear than in 1955, that it might have been wiser to concentrate on a small group of leading Nazis.[24]

---

[22] *Ibid.*, p. 261.

[23] The most widely circulated book setting forth the German view is probably E. von Salomon, *Fragebogen*, published in English translation in New York in 1955. Earlier views are to be found in K. H. Knappstein, "Die versäumte Revolution," *Die Wandlung*, Nov. 1947, and E. Kogon, "Das Recht auf des politischen Irrtum," *Frankfurter Hefte*, July 1947.

[24] See his *Decision in Germany*, p. 261.

The Denazification Purge

DENAZIFICATION IN THE OTHER ZONES

As General Clay points out, the denazification record in the British, French, and Russian Zones was very divergent from that in the American Zone.[25] Not every one would agree with his contention that no other occupying power carried on a vigorous search for Nazi leaders, for there is some evidence that by concentrating on the big fry the British, for example, actually handled the denazification problem more effectively than did the United States. However, the American Zone had many more trials than any other zone. Covering the period down to January 1, 1947, when the denazification program had not of course been completed, Professor W. Friedmann, a British scholar and staff member of the British Control Commission for Germany, compared the records of the several Allies.[26] In the case of persons tried as members of Nazi organizations under Control Council Directive No. 38, he found that the British had, as of the above date, tried 2,296 persons; the French, 17,353; the Russians, 18,328; and the Americans, 169,282. However, in administering Control Council Directive No. 24 which provided for the removal of Nazis from public or important private positions, Professor Friedmann found greater similarity: the British removed 186,692 and excluded 104,106; the French removed and excluded a total of 69,068; the Russians removed 307,370 and excluded 83,108; and the Americans removed 292,089 and excluded 81,673. The numbers of those interned as Nazi leaders or influential Nazi followers were also not too divergent except in the case of the French Zone. In the British Zone 27,477 such persons were interned as of January 1, 1947; in the French Zone the number was 4,018; in the Russian Zone, 50,565; and in the American Zone, 45,020.

The Potsdam Agreement stipulated as follows:[27]

Nazi leaders, influential Nazi supporters, and high officials of Nazi organizations and institutions and any other persons dangerous to the occupation or its objective shall be arrested and interned.

---

[25] See *ibid.*, p. 261.

[26] See his *The Allied Military Government of Germany* (Stevens, London, 1947), p. 332.

[27] See articles 5 and 6 of the section relating to "Political and Economic Principles to Govern the Treatment of Germany in the Initial Control Period."

All members of the Nazi Party who have been more than nominal participants in its activities and all other persons hostile to Allied purposes shall be removed from public and semi-public office, and from positions of responsibility in important private undertakings.

Under this general Allied policy, the Allied Control Council, despite its many difficulties, issued two important directives relating to denazification. Directive No. 24, approved on January 12, 1946, and Directive No. 38, approved on October 12, 1946, contained elaborate provisions which might have served as a basis for a widespread program of mass trials, such as the United States promoted in its zone. Here one finds the breakdown into major offenders, offenders, lesser offenders, followers, and exonerated persons already familiar in the denazification tribunals in the American Zone, together with detailed penalties to be applied. But for various reasons only in the American Zone was a serious effort made to implement these directives in full. Perhaps it is fair to state that there was never very strong sentiment on the part of the British, French, and Russians in favor of these directives and that their promulgation was largely the result of American pressure.

The Russians perhaps acted most decisively and at the same time followed the most expedient policy as regards denazification. They moved quickly to seize, imprison, and doubtless in numerous instances to liquidate Nazis whom they wanted to put out of the way. However, they did not hesitate to overlook a very black Nazi record if it seemed that they could use a former Nazi leader to their advantage. They apparently had very little interest in proceeding against the rank and file of little fellows.

The French perhaps held the most cynical views in regard to the Germans of any of the Allies. It was difficult for them to see much difference between Nazis and other Germans, all Germans being distrusted by them and regarded as inherently dangerous. To purge a single group out of the general body of German people seemed to the French impossible and a waste of time. They did, of course, seize Germans whom they particularly wanted and regarded as their enemies.

The British perhaps most nearly approached the American attitude toward Nazis, but being a realistic people they did not permit themselves to be drawn into the toils of an impossible denazification

166

program.[28] Though their people had suffered far more grievously than Americans as a result of the bombing of their cities, the submarine warfare, and so forth, there was never in Britain the wildfire of revenge which was kindled in the United States. Denazification never became the political issue in Britain that has been noted in the case of the United States. The British could never see the basis for President Franklin D. Roosevelt's denunciation of the plans drafted by the Anglo-American German Country Unit and consequently followed these in spirit if not in letter. They were persuaded for a brief period to go along with the United States at Quebec and to accept the American position at Potsdam and in the Allied Control Council. But they had little desire to set up a spectacular program of mass purges and trials and concentrated on seizing and punishing the Nazi leaders whom they held responsible for the worst evils of the Nazi regime.[29]

CONCLUDING COMMENTS

There is no yardstick which can be applied to the denazification efforts of the United States in Germany to produce exact measurements of positive and negative results. There will undoubtedly be controversy for many years as to the justification of the American policy and program and the concrete results in Germany, though most admit that some attention was required to this ugly problem. It may be significant that an increasing body of opinion, in looking back after the occupation has come to an end, seems to regard this particular aspect of American activity in Germany as more vulnerable than others. It is apparent that denazification was intimately tied to personal emotions on the part of many Americans and that it became a political issue of considerable strength in the domestic scene in the United States. Under the American system a red-hot political issue naturally had its impact on the President, cabinet

---

[28] For additional discussion of the British record in the denazification field, see W. Friedmann, *The Allied Military Government of Germany* (Stevens, London, 1947).

[29] This attitude was expressed by Nigel Birch in the House of Commons thus: "Extensive de-Nazification is only right if you assume that the great mass of the German people were not Nazis, but the history of the last 12 years is only explicable on the hypothesis that the vast mass of the German people were Nazis." Quoted from M. Balfour and J. Mair, *Four-Power Control in Germany and Austria, 1945-1946* (Oxford University Press, London, 1956), p. 183n.

members, members of Congress, and even the military departments. Denazification activities in Germany were influenced in large measure by the political heat emanating from the United States. Whether this is the rational way to deal with a highly complicated problem arising out of the occupation of foreign territory may be questionable. But anyone familiar with the way things are done under the American political system will not be surprised at what happened as regards denazification in Germany. Indeed the whole denazification episode is one of the most interesting examples in recent years of the American political process and its relationship to military and foreign policies.[30]

---

[30] The literature relating to denazification is fairly extensive. J. G. Kormann, "U. S. Denazification Policy in Germany, 1944-1950," originally prepared as a dissertation at Columbia University and issued in multilithed form by the Historical Division of the Office of the U. S. High Commissioner for Germany in 1952, emphasizes the policy aspect. G. Roth and K. H. Wolff, "The American Denazification of Germany: A Historical Survey and an Appraisal," issued in mimeographed form by the Department of Sociology and Anthropology of Ohio State University in 1954, deals with the problem from a sociological angle. E. von Salomon, *Fragebogen* (English translation, Putnam, New York. 1955), presents a widely held German point of view in the form of a satirical piece of autobiography. W. E. Griffith, "Denazification in the United States Zone of Germany," *Annals of the American Academy of Political and Social Science*, Jan. 1950, and in a dissertation prepared at Harvard University, stresses the administration of the program. Griffith writes from the background of a district Special Branch officer and chief of the Special (later Denazification) Branch in the Bavarian Office of Military Government.

12

Constructing a New German Government

There seems to be no record in modern history of the complete destruction of a governmental structure from the top to the bottom in a major country aside from Germany. In Japan the war had caused some disarrangement of the government apparatus, but the machine as a whole was intact and could be used as an instrument of control by the occupying forces. It was anticipated in the early Allied planning that there would be a German government to take over and that it would play a considerable role in administering the country. But the fanaticism of the Nazis, and particularly of Hitler personally, was such that a devilish plan was devised to pull down the government from top to bottom as the Allies advanced. To begin with, this policy appeared to be of the "scorched earth" variety as a defense measure. As the Allies penetrated farther and farther into Germany not everything was destroyed and left barren, but a vigorous effort was made to wreck the government apparatus by withdrawing public officials, moving or destroying records, and otherwise bringing about chaos. Detailed plans called for dividing the staffs and records of the great central ministries into two or more parts and transporting these to various scattered points throughout Germany, with instructions that the archives should be destroyed before Allied capture. These plans, it is true, were only partially completed during the dying days of the Nazi regime because of the faulty transport, the bombing raids, and other exigencies. But the fact remains that, when Germany surrendered in May 1945, there was virtually no government left intact, and the Doenitz "Government" which offered the capitulation was no more than a paper affair.

The job of getting a new governmental structure set up was one of the major tasks of the occupation. No one can possibly understand the military government record in Germany without taking this

169

enormous problem into account.[1] The responsibility was of course by no means limited to the United States, since all of the Allies faced the same situation and, to begin with, it was expected that the task would be shouldered jointly as far as a central government apparatus was concerned. However, because of the inability of the Allied Control Authority to agree and its eventual paralysis, the undertaking had to be tackled by the Allies individually, both within their zones and beyond. Since the United States had more energy to devote to this problem than Britain and France and since its solution was intimately tied up with getting the German economy back on its feet, thus relieving the American taxpayer and food producer of the terrific burden of supporting the Germans, the American role in pushing on to the establishment of the West German Federal Government was outstanding, though certainly dependent upon British and French assistance and cooperation. Of course, the Germans themselves also played an important part in the rebuilding of their government apparatus, and indeed the undertaking could not possibly have succeeded without their major contribution.

AT THE LOCAL LEVEL

Immediately after an area of Germany had been taken over by American tactical forces, a military government detachment came in to take charge. Perhaps the chief responsibility of this military government detachment was to get a skeletal German government established, since most of its activities—the maintenance of law and order, the provision for public health measures, emergency repairs of water supply systems, electric and gas works, transportation facilities, and the like—depended in greater or less degree on having a German government in operation. Even where American military government detachments themselves performed these tasks, they required

---

[1] For general discussions of this problem, see K. Loewenstein, "Political Reconstruction in Germany, Zonal and Interzonal," in J. K. Pollock, ed., *Change and Crisis in European Government* (Rinehart, New York, 1947); C. Menck, "The Problem of Reorientation," in G. A. Almond, ed., *The Struggle for Democracy in Germany* (University of North Carolina Press, Chapel Hill, 1949); S. Neumann, *Germany, Promise and Perils*, Foreign Policy Association Headline Series, July-Aug. 1950; A. Brecht, "Re-establishing German Government," *Annals of the American Academy of Political and Social Science*, Jan. 1950; J. K. Pollock, "Germany under Military Occupation," in *Change and Crisis in European Government;* "Postwar Reconstruction in Western Germany," entire issue of *Annals of American Academy of Political and Social Science*, Nov. 1948.

Constructing a New German Government

German assistance in the form of manpower and information, and if their orders were followed they refrained from direct activity as much as possible, pursuing the course of using the Germans to do the various jobs. While the American military government detachments were usually notable in their ingenuity and resourcefulness and did remarkable things to meet the emergency, they frequently knew so little about Germany, German institutions, and German psychology that they often fared rather poorly in organizing local government in their localities. City halls and county buildings were more often than not either totally destroyed or badly damaged, and records were frequently gone or buried under debris. Treasuries were usually empty or near the bare bottom. Local government employees were dead or scattered to the winds. All in all, it was very difficult to make a beginning in tackling this problem.

Military government instructions called for finding an anti-Nazi who was energetic, reliable, and experienced to head the new local government, whether it be a village, city, or a county, and then relying on him to recommend other promising Germans with anti-Nazi records to take over the major positions. With this start, military government was then supposed to work through these Germans, helping them to meet the many problems that confronted a devastated and defeated country and supporting them in their efforts to expand this skeletal government, which to begin with was invariably a weak affair, into a full-fledged government capable of performing the functions traditionally associated with local governments, along with many extra duties occasioned by the war. It was understood that "black, white, and gray" lists would be furnished by the OSS to guide the military government detachments in the selection of the key Germans to take charge and to enable them to evaluate other German officials.*

Although American military government detachments had supposedly spent a great deal of time studying the layout of the particular places they were to occupy in Germany, the confusion of war counteracted their efforts in large measure. To begin with, it proved difficult if not impossible to obtain adequate background material

---

* The black lists were to include the names of those definitely unacceptable; white lists were to give the names of those whose records were acceptable; and gray lists included the names of those regarded as doubtful.

171

relating to some of the German localities. If information was available, it was frequently not up-to-date, and in any event the devastation and dislocations caused by the war so changed the faces of most communities that it was often difficult to recognize them from the prewar descriptions. There had been large-scale movements of population during the fighting, and any information relating to the leaders in the community was likely to be obsolete. The assistance which was promised by OSS proved less than had been anticipated, though what there was served a useful purpose. OSS had various responsibilities and this made it difficult to carry out the commitment to provide the "black, white, and gray" lists indicating whether prominent Germans were to be avoided because of their black records, could be depended upon because of their reliable records, or were to be regarded with some suspicion because of doubtful records.

As a result, American military government detachments arrived at their destinations in Germany only to find that their preparations were inadequate and the information promised by OSS either not forthcoming or sketchy. Yet the situation confronting them was one demanding immediate action. They simply had to move ahead as effectively as they could and hope for the best. Unable to speak or understand German in most cases and therefore dependent on more or less unsatisfactory and often unreliable interpreters, they were even more at a loss. In their desperation they looked about and took the best material which they could find to start a new German government. Since the more substantial local citizens often sought to keep in the background at this time and had little desire to be associated with the occupation, the Germans who came under the eyes of American military government detachments tended to be the adventurers, opportunists, the schemers, and the less reliable element. Irrespective of their past Nazi records, they almost never let it be known that they had been anything but the most honorable and self-sacrificing of men. Considering this situation, it is not strange that American military government detachments encountered so much trouble and made so many errors—indeed the surprising thing is that the record was as good as it was.

The military government officials had been told by lecturers in the United States that churchmen, particularly of the Catholic variety, might be valuable sources of advice, because the Catholic

172

church especially had not fared well at the hands of Hitler. In many instances, therefore, American military government officials in the absence of OSS or other guiding information called on the local priest or bishop for counsel in selecting Germans to get a new local government going. On occasion this assistance proved reliable, but in many cases the local clergy were more anxious to help their parishioners and friends, even if erring, than to give dependable advice to the Americans. After following such advice the American military government officials often learned later that they had taken Germans with unsavory records. Consequently they were compelled to throw them out and start over.

Despite all of their mistakes, American military government detachments began the process of constructing German local governments within a few days of their arrival, and very shortly after the German surrender new local government structures were to be seen throughout the American Zone. It should be emphasized that these were not local governments in the sense in which such a term is employed in a stable country. There was a mayor (*Bürgermeister*) and a handful of other officials in the cities, a county manager (*Landrat*) in the counties, and some progress had usually also been made to get new officials in the many villages (*Gemeinde*). But the staffing of the governments with employees of one kind and another remained to be accomplished, and this obviously required many months of hard work. Records had to be dug out, carted from some remote place, or started anew. The tax machinery had to be modified. It was not then for many months or even several years that local governments in anything like the normal sense existed in Germany.[2]

After the prompt start which virtually all American military government detachments reported, there were many obstacles to progress. Doubtless the most serious was the denazification directive. Many mayors, county managers, department heads, and other officials and employees had to be fired, despite the good work which they seemed

---

[2] For a detailed treatment of the establishment of German local governments, see a monograph in the Historical Series of the Office of the U. S. High Commissioner for Germany prepared by J. F. J. Gillen under the title *State and Local Government in West Germany, 1945-1953, with Special Reference to the U. S. Zone and Bremen* (1953); Roger Wells, "Local Government," in E. H. Litchfield, ed., *Governing Postwar Germany*, Chap. 3; C. Glaser, *Land and Local Government in the U. S. Zone of Germany* (Berlin, 1947); and H. Puender, *Die deutschen Gemeinden: Gestern, Heute, und Morgen* (Cologne, 1948).

to be doing, because their Nazi records were regarded as disqualifying. Efforts to obtain replacements brought forth few who could meet the denazification tests and these tended to be too old, too infirm, or too embittered as a result of their sojourn in concentration camps to be very satisfactory in the arduous job of reconstructing a system of local government. Military government had to do the best it could under what it often regarded as unreasonable and almost impossible limitations.

Another serious obstacle in some localities was the American insistence on pushing ahead rapidly, even if it meant bypassing important items. Americans in general are known for their impatience with time factors, and in the American army there was even more than the usual pressure toward adhering to a schedule and getting the job done, even if superficially. With his experience in building dams and harbor facilities, General Clay did not see why a definite schedule could not be set for meeting the various aspects of reconstructing German government. The human element, the traditions of the Germans, and similar factors were at times more or less ignored in pushing ahead toward the goal. Despite the confusion which existed among the Germans, the war-shock, and the near-starvation level of the food supply, OMGUS ordered election codes to be rushed through in the autumn of 1945 so that local elections could be held early in 1946. The fact that there had been little or no opportunity for the people to discuss political matters or for political parties to get organized was more or less brushed aside. The goal was to hold elections, and they were held whether the people were ready for them or not.

This impatience led to the bypassing of a cardinal principle of military government, as laid down in the manuals and instructions, which was to the point that military government should supervise, control, and assist but *not*, except in emergencies, undertake the direct performance. Seeing the Germans unable to carry a program through, American military government in many instances took over the job itself, thus weakening the German system which it was attempting to organize. This inclination, together with the habit of giving orders to the German officials in regard to the smallest items rather than allowing them leeway and holding them responsible for the results, led to the abandoning of the military government detachments in the winter of 1945-1946. It was apparent by that time that no vigorous system of German government at the grassroots could be built up with Americans taking over, giving orders, and interfering with the local German officials. Hence the old military government detachments were liquidated and new liaison and security teams were substituted to report and maintain contact with German officials but with no authority to give orders or interfere.* With the pattern established, it was not, however, an easy matter for Americans, even under another name, to stand by and watch the easygoing and what often seemed inefficient ways of the German officials. Consequently, there were many cases of giving orders and interference despite the directive from OMGUS headquarters.

AT THE REGIONAL LEVEL

In planning for military government it was decided that some time would elapse between the setting up of city and county and village governments and the establishment of *Regierungsbezirke* (district governments in Bavaria) and *Land* (state) governments. But the planning was unrealistic and regional governmental structures were initiated in a skeletal form almost immediately after the German surrender. The military government detachments assigned to *Regierungsbezirke* and *Länder* had been "cooling their heels" so to speak for many months, and they were naturally anxious to arrive at the scene of their assignments and begin work. But more important was the pace with which problems within the German society and economy developed. It had been assumed that village, city, and county governments would handle all of the pressing problems for several months and that there would be little need to go ahead with district and state governments immediately. Actually it was apparent almost at once that village, county, and city governments could not cope with the food problem, with transportation reconstruction, with public finance, with banking necessities, and the like, and that larger units of government were required to give attention to such matters. Events therefore overtook the policy and plans and the latter were in large measure ignored. During the month of May 1945—the very month of the capitulation—German governments were started

* See Chap. 3.

at the district and state level in Bavaria. Since it was still uncertain what would be done in the remainder of the American Zone in joining together the bits and pieces remaining after the boundaries had been fixed to suit military demands based on maintaining satisfactory communication lines, progress was slower there.

The situation in the western part of the American Zone may be cited as an example of the serious weakness more or less inherent in planning for the occupation of a defeated country. An effective occupation requires careful attention to the economy of the country, its transportation network, its food resources, its cultural patterns, and other related items of major importance. The planners attached to the German Country Unit and to the U. S. Group, Control Council for Germany were at least reasonably conscious and aware of such basic considerations, but they did not have the last word. It was the politicians in Washington, Moscow, and London and the military leaders in those capitals and in the field who had the authority to make final decisions, and they were motivated by local political pressures, the desire to show the defeated Germans that the conquerors could do anything they liked, military conventions, and the like.

The argument that decisions based on any considerations which ignored the economy, food resources, transportation network, and cultural patterns would enormously complicate the difficulties of the occupation, require the additional expenditure of large amounts of money, and occasion misery to numerous Germans meant little under the conditions existing at the close of the war. Indeed, it was all to the good in some eyes that decisions striking at the very foundations of the German economy should be taken. As to food, it was supposed that the Germans were the best nourished people in Europe and could easily feed themselves better than they deserved—one of the Russian demands was that the German standard of living be cut back to a point where it would be more nearly that of the Russian millions. The argument that much additional misery would be occasioned also received little weight, since with the emphasis on punitive measures the more misery the Germans had to bear the better it would be for the Allies. As for the necessity of spending great amounts of American funds if such considerations were ignored, that was disputed—something for the future to bother about. In any event, the

176

taxpayer's money was not rated very high during a period when billions were being poured out, as they must obviously be during war.

Thus, despite all of the apprehensions of the German experts and the military government planners, the boundaries of the American Zone and the division into states within that zone were fixed in such a manner as to ignore many basic factors. It is true that Bavaria was brought almost intact into the American Zone, and, despite some effort to divide it up, remained the most important state of the American Zone. But the important cities of Frankfurt, Karlsruhe, Mannheim, and Stuttgart were deprived of their markets and sources of supply in large measure. The western part of the American Zone was made up of such an assortment of legs, arms, fingers, ears, and other stray pieces of a dismembered body that one could hardly believe one's eyesight. As if to cap the climax and make a bad situation worse, Frankfurt was for a time removed from the rest of Hesse and made into an enclave to salve the feeling of an American military commander.[3]

Out of this chaos there emerged two states in the western section of the American Zone: Hesse* and Württemberg-Baden, though for a time it seemed that there would be three, with the dismembered parts of Württemberg being divided among the Americans and French and the parts of little Baden similarly grouped into a weak American Baden and a French Baden. The American sections of Württemberg and Baden were finally combined to make one fairly viable state, but the French maintained two weak states in the form of Württemberg-Hohenzollern and South Baden. This was remedied under the West German Federal Republic, when a Southwest State was formed from the fragments of two states in the French Zone and one in the American Zone.

Until something could be done to reduce the confusion, it was impossible to proceed very far with the organization of regional government in the western part of the American Zone. But, as it was decided during the late summer of 1945 to do the best possible with the two curious creations of Hesse and Württemberg-Baden,

---

[3] See Harold Zink, *American Military Government in Germany* (Macmillan, New York, 1947), pp. 97-98.
* The formation of Hesse as a state was not announced until September 19, 1945.

progress was made in laying the foundation stones for state governments in those *Länder*.[4]

The early efforts of the military government detachments at the regional level resembled those at the local level in many respects. There was not the pressure to deal with emergencies, such as water supply, sanitation, and public utilities; but there was the rapidly increasing threat of mass starvation and other immensely complicated problems to demand attention. The detachments of military government at the regional level were larger and in general more specialized, with officers specially designated as government affairs specialists. Also the data furnished by OSS were naturally more adequate at this level; but, even so, the military government detachments had to find their own way by groping a good deal of the time. Instead of searching for a mayor or county manager, the regional military government detachments looked for someone suitable to head a district (*Regierungsbezirke*) in Bavaria or a state (*Land*). This task was even more complicated than that of finding an anti-Nazi with other acceptable qualifications for mayor or county manager. The Germans who would be at all likely to succeed as Minister-Presidents or heads of states had usually been prominent enough in German life to make them prime targets of Nazi persecution or puppets to further the Nazi cause. In the former cases, they were usually so mutilated either in body or mind, or both, by concentration camp and *Gestapo* brutality that they were hardly fit for the arduous task of organizing a state government. In the latter cases, they could not of course be used because of their Nazi pasts. Nevertheless, the military government detachments were reasonably fortunate in finding Minister-Presidents for all three states, though, in the case of Bavaria, the first incumbent, Dr. F. Schaeffer, was later thrown out because of what some regarded as his unsatisfactory past record (it may be added that he later became the able finance minister of the West German Federal Republic).

Having selected Minister-Presidents and various other ministers in such fields as economic affairs, finance, educational and cultural affairs, and denazification for the state governments, the military

---

[4] For discussions of later developments in setting up these two state governments, see André Lewin's and Horst Locher's contributions to A. Grosser, ed., *Administration et Politique en Allemagne Occidentale* (Paris, 1954).

government detachments were shortly displaced by the offices of *Land* military government. Unlike the local military government offices, these *Land* offices continued to supervise and to give orders to the German state governments and through them to the district, county, and city governments throughout the military government period. The process of building up a body of civil servants to staff these state governments and of public officials to serve in state legislatures, courts, and the like, was long and drawn out, as might be expected.

Having made a start in organizing the state governments, American military government bent its energies to seeing that state constitutions were drafted, election codes enacted, and elections held to choose members of the *Landtage* (state legislatures). Although the German industrial system remained almost paralyzed—its production was approximately 10 per cent of the prewar period at the end of 1945—and the German people faced starvation as a result of serious food shortages, General Clay felt that it was desirable to push on with constitution-drafting and elections. The British delayed constitution-drafting in the states of their zone for several years and finally came forth with constitutions after the military government phase of the occupation was over, maintaining that there was no great hurry about getting new constitutions and that it was preferable to wait until the Germans could give careful attention to the contents of the state constitutions. But the American attitude was quite in contrast and there seemed to be the feeling that no breath could be taken until state constitutions had been disposed of. Perhaps the frustrations in the economic field led to a concentration on constitution-drafting and elections so that some progress could be reported by the Military Governor at an early date. General Clay, as the chapter heading in his *Decision in Germany* suggests,[5] apparently regarded such activities as drafting of constitutions, preparing election laws, and the holding of elections as synonymous with preparation for German democracy, irrespective of how little time was allowed or how superficial the work might be. At any rate, election codes

[5] Chap. 5 is entitled "The Way to Democracy: Rebuilding Government in the American Zone." General Clay wrote to John J. McCloy as follows: "If the Germans are to learn democratic methods, I think the best way is to start them off quickly at the local levels." Quoted from J. F. J. Gillen, *State and Local Government in West Germany, 1945-1953*, p. 8.

were prepared and the first elections held in January 1946, at which towns and villages of fewer than 20,000 inhabitants chose councillors.

Other elections were scheduled in the counties and larger villages on April 28, 1946, and more than 70 per cent of those eligible turned out to vote, in contrast to some 86 per cent in the January elections. City elections were held in May 1946 and brought out more than 80 per cent of the eligible voters. State advisory legislative assemblies were inaugurated in January 1946, with members selected by political parties and various other groups. Constitutional assemblies were elected on June 30, 1946, and completed their work during the summer or autumn. After being reviewed by military government, the constitutions were submitted to the voters in the respective states in late 1946 and early 1947 and approved by respectable majorities. Thus by 1947 the states were able to elect members to *Landtage* (legislatures) and to function more or less on their own, subject of course to military government approval.[6]

The constitutions of Bavaria, Hesse, and Württemberg-Baden have been widely circulated in printed collections prepared by OMGUS and consequently are generally familiar to students of government. In general, they make a favorable impression, despite the close schedule under which they were drafted and ratified. Even a casual reader will note that they are not like "peas in a pod," as was the case with the ill-fated constitutions of the states in the Russian Zone.[*] Staff members of OMGUS kept close touch with the work in the various states and made various facilities available. Yet it cannot be fairly stated that the constitutions were their brain children, as was the case with the Japanese constitution usually known as the "MacArthur constitution." The members of the German constituent assemblies took their assignments seriously and discussed at length the proposals made by the Minister-Presidents and other Germans. Many of the provisions were copied from the state constitutions under the Weimar Republic, and some were lifted from the Weimar Constitution itself.[7] All included proportional repre-

---

[6] For further details of the state legislatures, see J. H. Kaiser, *Der Landtag* (Munich, 1951).

[*] The states in the Russian Zone were abolished before the end of the occupation in Western Germany and their almost identic constitutions came to an end.

[7] For further discussion of the state constitutions, see Harold O. Lewis, *New Constitutions in Occupied Germany* (Foundation for Foreign Affairs, Washington, 1948), and R. G. Neumann, "New Constitutions in Germany," *American Political Science Review*, July 1948.

sentation as a device for choosing some, at least, of the members of the *Landtage.* Rather than following the pattern of state government in the United States, the German constitutions provided for a setup under which the executive would be closely related to, and generally responsible to, the legislative branch. In Hesse, where the Social Democratic strength was greater than in the rest of the American Zone, the constituent assembly insisted on inserting a provision under which the state government could take over and operate certain industrial enterprises. This was hardly welcome to General Clay and most of the OMGUS staff, to say nothing of public opinion in the United States, but after due consideration it was concluded that it would be improper for American military government to order the clause deleted. Therefore, it was determined to hold a special referendum in Hesse on this clause. After the voters sustained it, General Clay decided that, while it would remain in the constitution, its operation would be suspended for the time being.

In looking back at the haste with which election codes, elections, and constitutions were rushed through in the American Zone, it is difficult to perceive that any great damage was done or that distinct advantage accrued. The Germans were hardly ready for elections in 1946. Nevertheless, a much larger proportion of voters turned out than can normally be attracted in the United States. The constitutions might have been somewhat more meticulously prepared had more time been allowed, but they are certainly not striking examples of careless drafting. Perhaps the British were wiser and more mature in handling the situation, but there is little to indicate that any major advantage was derived from their more leisurely schedule.[8]

THE COUNCIL OF STATES

In order to coordinate the efforts of the states in the American Zone in certain fields where it was regarded desirable and, as time went on, to handle overwhelming problems such as supplying food to the German people, a Council of States (*Länderrat*) was set up in

---

[8] For a more detailed discussion of state reconstruction, see J. F. J. Gillen, *State and Local Government in West Germany, 1945-1953, with Special Reference to the U. S. Zone and Bremen,* a monograph in the Historical Series of the Office of the U. S. High Commissioner for Germany (1953); and Roger Wells, "State Government," in E. H. Litchfield, ed., *Governing Postwar Germany,* Chap. 4.

October 1945 and a secretariat was established at Stuttgart. At the top of this Council were the Minister-Presidents of the several states who met regularly to discuss pressing problems but did not have the authority to act—their recommendations had to be approved by military government and then could be implemented in each state. In connection with the secretariat there was a Commission for Food and Agriculture to deal with what was probably the most critical problem confronting the Council and indeed American military government at the time: the onerous job of setting up a uniform system of food rationing throughout the American Zone. Some 14 committees and 46 subcommittees operated within the Council to consider all sorts of matters, such as housing, labor supply, welfare, education, and the like. Dr. James K. Pollock, as coordinator of regional government, provided liaison between the *Länderrat* and OMGUS and exercised considerable influence on the working of the Stuttgart center. The Council of States could not, of course, supply the deficiency created by the lack of a central German government, but it did serve a useful purpose in dealing with situations which could not easily be handled by the states.[9]

BIZONAL ORGANIZATION

It has been noted elsewhere that the economic situation in the American Zone became so critical during the early months of the occupation that a bizonal merger of the British and American Zones was proposed in 1946. Secretary of State Byrnes extended such an invitation to the Allies in the spring of 1946, and the British accepted the invitation on July 30, 1946. It should be borne in mind that the first steps in the bizonal organization were not political in character; that is, no effort was made to establish a governmental structure. On the other hand, it is fair to conclude that Bizonia came into being largely because the Allied Control Authority failed in the objective set at the Potsdam Conference looking toward the organization of central German agencies to deal with such matters as eco-

---

[9] For a discussion of this agency, see Heinz Guradze, "The *Länderrat*, Landmark in German Reconstruction," *Western Political Quarterly*, June 1950. The acts of this body are to be found in R. Picht-Hempken, ed., *Sammlung der Länderratsgesetze* (Düsseldorf, 1950).

nomic reconstruction, transportation, posts, telegraph, and telephone, and fiscal affairs.[10]

Experience under the bizonal organization during 1946 and 1947 indicated the difficulty of drawing a line between economic and political matters. The first two agreements relating to a bizonal organization had not proved effective. In the third step taken to strengthen Bizonia, a political-governmental organization in everything but name was actually authorized. The Germans were reluctant to admit that a central government for all of Germany would not soon materialize, and they therefore were touchy about proceeding in the American and British Zones along lines that would result in a government for the West. Nevertheless, the Economic Council, with an elective membership of 104, and the *Länderrat* (upper house), made up of two representatives from each state government, constituted a political structure in almost every sense. These bodies could not pass general legislation, it is true; but the economic and fiscal areas in which they were active covered most of the field. The fact that the actions of this "legislature" were subject to military government approval does not vitiate the argument in favor of its governmental status, since any government at the time would have been subject to the same limitations. The reorganization of Bizonia in 1948 even went so far as to include the establishment of a High Court and a central banking system—the former to interpret and enforce legislation passed by the Economic Council and *Länderrat*. All that was needed to have a full-fledged government in the merged British and American Zones was a change in terminology and a slight extension of the scope of the bizonal organization.

THE WEST GERMAN FEDERAL GOVERNMENT

The Potsdam Conference had looked upon the immediate reestablishment of a central German government as undesirable, but it did authorize the organization of German central agencies to deal with problems, such as transportation and communications, fiscal affairs, and foreign trade and industry, which could not be handled

---

[10] For further discussion of bizonal organization and operations, see E. H. Litchfield's "Emergence of German Governments," in *Governing Postwar Germany*, Chap. 2.

adequately on a zonal basis.[11] By stating that "for the time being, no central German government shall be established," the Potsdam Conference implied that such a government would be required within a reasonable period of time. But the exigencies of the Allied Control Authority were such as to make the establishment of central German administrative agencies impossible, to say nothing of proceeding to the consideration of the next step, the authorization of a central German government. However, if the Allied Control Authority more or less stood still or at least did not get beyond marking time, developments in Germany were by no means at a standstill. The four zones simply could not cope with many of the most complex problems confronting them; therefore, the American and British Zones were joined under a bizonal organization.

As the years passed, it became increasingly apparent that, Allied Control Authority or not, something had to be done about proceeding with the organization of a German central government. The bizonal setup in the West was valuable, but, despite its political character beginning with 1948, it could not be considered an effective substitute for a central German government. By 1948 it had become pretty obvious that nothing could be done toward providing a government which would cover all of Germany unless on the Russian terms, which would have made any such government merely a Russian puppet. The Russian position at the London meeting of Foreign Ministers late in 1947 made this clear. The United States became increasingly concerned about the situation and beginning in 1948 discussed the problem with the British and French. A conference held in London early in 1948, with representatives of the United States, the United Kingdom, France, and the three Benelux countries participating, canvassed the possibility of going ahead without the Russians. The Russians angrily protested at such a meeting and the French had many apprehensions, insisting that agreements be reached on security and economic problems before a German government be set up in the West. The United States strongly supported the principle of a government for West Germany, though it recognized the seriousness of a split between East and West Germany.

[11] II, 9, iv of the Potsdam Agreement reads: "certain essential central German administrative departments, headed by State Secretaries, shall be established, particularly in the fields of finance, transport, communications, foreign trade and industry. Such departments will act under the direction of the Control Council."

Constructing a New German Government

After the London conference had considered the problem and had recessed for a time, the American, British, and French Military Governors set up a tripartite working party to give attention to the form of a political organization for West Germany and they themselves met to discuss the general question of a government for West Germany. Neither the working party nor the Military Governors themselves achieved a meeting of minds—the former got bogged down in a mass of details rather than concentrating on the items which needed clarification at this stage.[12] It was apparent from these military government exploratory conversations that the positions of the British and Americans were not far apart and could be brought together fairly easily, but that the French stood some distance away. The sensational episode mentioned elsewhere, when the Russians walked out of the meeting of the Allied Control Council in Berlin, took place during the discussions carried on by the military government representatives, and this seemed to change the French point of view to some extent at least—the French for the first time recognized the almost complete lack of hope of achieving an agreement with the Russians on this matter.

When the London conference of Foreign Ministers resumed its sessions later in the spring of 1948, basic agreement was finally reached, after long discussion, on the necessity of going ahead without the Russians in organizing a government for West Germany.[13] The French insisted on having an International Authority of the Ruhr to supervise the coal and steel industries of West Germany and expressed definite opposition to giving a West German government authority over police or taxes. The agreement of the London conference was approved by the governments involved; and the American, British, and French Military Governors were instructed to take further steps looking toward a government for western Germany. One section of the agreement directed the Military Governors to hold a meeting of the German Minister-Presidents not later than June 15, 1948,* at which authorization would be given to convene a constituent assembly not later than September 1, 1948, to draft a "democratic constitution" for a "governmental structure of federal

---

[12] See L. D. Clay, *Decision in Germany*, p. 397.

[13] For the text of this important agreement, see Department of State, *Germany, 1947-1949; The Story in Documents*, pp. 76-83.

* The French delay in ratification held up the meeting until July 1.

type." Another laid down certain principles which were to guide the Military Governors in their role as general overseers and in reviewing the draft prepared by the Germans. A third listed the basic considerations which must be kept in mind in preparing an Occupation Statute that would define the relations between the western Allies and a West German Federal Government.

The meeting of the Minister-Presidents of the states in the western zones of Germany was characterized by long-drawn-out discussion, as might have been expected; and during the course of this it appeared that they were reluctant to employ the terms "constituent assembly" or "constitution," though they were generally agreeable to going ahead. These terms seemed to them to imply too irrevocable a separation of eastern and western Germany, and they were most anxious to leave the way open to unification. The Military Governors agreed to the substitution of "parliamentary council" and "basic law," and the German state legislatures (*Landtage*) elected delegates to a Parliamentary Council to meet in Bonn on September 1.

In contrast to the preparation of a constitution for Japan by American drafters under General MacArthur, the Basic Law which constitutes the foundation of the West German Federal Republic is definitely a German product. That is not to say that the Germans had a completely free hand, for they were instructed by the Allies as a result of American and French desires (the British had less strong ideas on the matter) to follow the federal rather than the unitary pattern. Individuals went further and in some instances prepared models which might be followed by the German drafters.[14] OMGUS appointed Dr. Hans Simons, who, after a career in Germany as director of the Berlin Institute of Political Science and a district governor of Lower Silesia, had migrated to the United States and joined the New School for Social Research, as its chief liaison officer with the Parliamentary Council—he was at the time serving as the head of the governmental structures branch of its Civil Affairs Division.[15] Dr. Simons collected several hundred books and reports

---

[14] See C. J. Friedrich, "Rebuilding the German Constitution," *American Political Science Review*, June and Sept. (1949). Also see C. J. Friedrich and H. J. Spero, "The Constitution of the German Federal Republic," in E. H. Litchfield, ed., *Governing Postwar Germany*, Chap. 5.

[15] For his observations on this assignment, see "The Bonn Constitution and Its Government," in H. J. Morgenthau, ed., *Germany and the Future of Europe* (University of Chicago Press, Chicago, 1951).

186

dealing with constitutions and constitution-making that might be of use to the German drafters of the new Basic Law, but, as he himself reported, virtually no use was made of these by the members of the Parliamentary Council. They apparently felt quite able to proceed without outside assistance, though the personal influence of Dr. Simons and others may have been significant.

The deliberations of the Parliamentary Council were lengthy, even when judged by German standards, and at times it seemed that the differences were such as to preclude agreement. In general, the Weimar Constitution, despite the many aspersions which had been cast at it earlier, was used as a model. Even a casual reading of the Bonn Basic Law will reveal a striking similarity to many parts of the Weimar Constitution. In January 1949 a draft of the Basic Law was forthcoming from the committee designated by the full Council to give attention to detailed provisions and this was considered by the Military Governors in February 1949. While the Military Governors regarded the work as a whole favorably, the American and French representatives objected to what they regarded as undue concentration of authority in the central government and a vague division of power between the central government and the states. The French and American Military Governors supported by their British colleague took exception to provisions which seemed to support the traditional German concept of a civil service and gave a status to Berlin as a member state of the West German Federal Republic.[16] The draft was therefore returned to the committee of the Parliamentary Council with the objections noted and the request that the draft not be considered by the entire Parliamentary Council until revised. The objections of the Military Governors were communicated to the Parliamentary Council early in March and a revised draft was produced which did little or nothing to satisfy the American and French representatives. The Germans still regarded a strongly centralized government as desirable and had little appreciation of the federalism so cherished by Americans—indeed in this revised draft they inserted a provision under which the central government could have shifted revenues from the wealthier states to the poorer ones, which in American eyes at least would have destroyed the states as viable units of authority.[17]

[16] See L. D. Clay, *Decision in Germany*, p. 422.
[17] See Clay, *op. cit.*, p. 424.

At the meeting of the Military Governors on April 25, 1949, the British and French Military Governors had apparently more or less given up hope of prevailing against the insistence of the Germans on a strongly centralized government. The position of General Clay was a difficult one, since he continued to feel strongly about the threat to federalism, though he had been advised by Political Adviser Murphy on his return from Washington that the main desire of the United States was to proceed with the setting up of a German government, making the best bargain possible.[18] He restated his apprehensions to the Germans and after withdrawing for an hour and half the German delegation agreed to a compromise under which the federal legislature would be given power to levy taxes for education, health, and welfare and to assist the poorer states in the form of grants from these funds. The Parliamentary Council then proceeded to approve the Basic Law on May 8, 1949, by a quite unexpected majority—there were only 11 dissenting or abstaining votes. It was then formally approved by the Military Governors and submitted to the states which all ratified except Bavaria. It became effective in September 1949.[19]

In the meantime the drafting of an Occupation Statute proceeded. Representatives of the Allied powers meeting in London experienced almost as much difficulty in completing their assignment as has been noted in the case of the Basic Law. After lengthy discussion covering some months they produced such an involved and detailed draft that it could not be employed. In a spectacular move the Foreign Ministers discarded this rather botchy job and substituted a brief draft covering some two and a half pages in April 1949. This Occupation Statute provided that the West German Government should have more or less full power over domestic matters other than military.[20] However, in the international field its authority was curtailed for the time being and it had to yield to the occupying powers in respect to the coal and steel industries of the Ruhr, displaced persons, foreign exchange, war prisoners, and protection, prestige, and security of the Allied forces in West Germany. A revision was later under-

---

[18] See *ibid.*, pp. 432-435.

[19] For additional discussion of its contents, see Arnold Brecht, "The New German Constitution," *Social Research*, Dec. 1949.

[20] For its text, see State Department, *Germany, 1947-1949; The Story in Documents*, pp. 89-91.

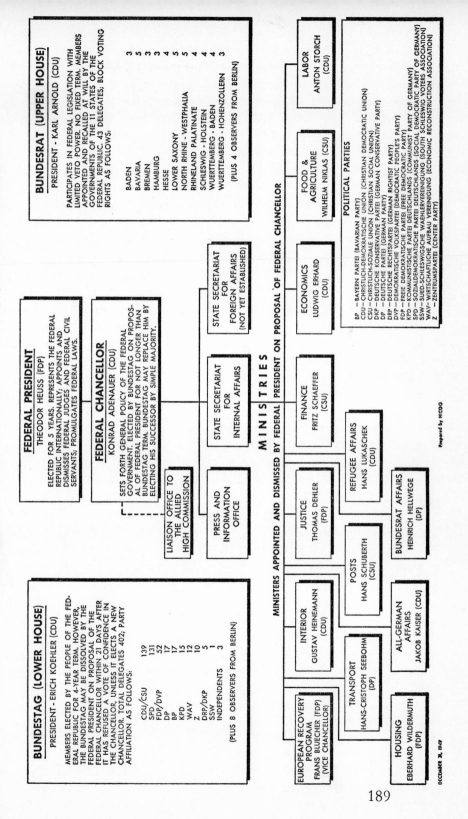

BUNDESTAG (LOWER HOUSE)

PRESIDENT - ERICH KOEHLER (CDU)

MEMBERS ELECTED BY THE PEOPLE OF THE FEDERAL REPUBLIC FOR 4-YEAR TERM. HOWEVER, THE BUNDESTAG MAY BE DISSOLVED BY THE FEDERAL PRESIDENT ON PROPOSAL OF THE FEDERAL CHANCELLOR WITHIN 21 DAYS AFTER IT HAS REFUSED A VOTE OF CONFIDENCE IN THE CHANCELLOR, UNLESS IT ELECTS A NEW CHANCELLOR. TOTAL DELEGATES 402; PARTY AFFILIATION AS FOLLOWS:

CDU/CSU	139
SPD	131
FDP/DVP	52
DP	17
BP	17
KPD	15
WAV	12
Z	10
DRP/DKP	5
SSW	1
INDEPENDENTS	3

(PLUS 8 OBSERVERS FROM BERLIN)

BUNDESRAT (UPPER HOUSE)

PRESIDENT - KARL ARNOLD (CDU)

PARTICIPATES IN FEDERAL LEGISLATION WITH LIMITED VETO POWER. NO FIXED TERM. MEMBERS APPOINTED AND RECALLED AT WILL BY THE GOVERNMENTS OF THE 11 STATES OF THE FEDERAL REPUBLIC. 43 DELEGATES; BLOCK VOTING RIGHTS AS FOLLOWS:

BADEN	3
BAVARIA	5
BREMEN	3
HAMBURG	3
HESSE	4
LOWER SAXONY	5
NORTH RHINE - WESTPHALIA	5
RHINELAND PALATINATE	4
SCHLESWIG - HOLSTEIN	4
WUERTTEMBERG - BADEN	4
WUERTTEMBERG - HOHENZOLLERN	3

(PLUS 4 OBSERVERS FROM BERLIN)

FEDERAL PRESIDENT

THEODOR HEUSS (FDP)

ELECTED FOR 5 YEARS. REPRESENTS THE FEDERAL REPUBLIC INTERNATIONALLY; APPOINTS AND DISMISSES FEDERAL JUDGES AND FEDERAL CIVIL SERVANTS; PROMULGATES FEDERAL LAWS.

FEDERAL CHANCELLOR

KONRAD ADENAUER (CDU)

SETS FORTH GENERAL POLICY OF THE FEDERAL GOVERNMENT. ELECTED BY BUNDESTAG ON PROPOSAL OF FEDERAL PRESIDENT FOR NOT LONGER THAN BUNDESTAG TERM. BUNDESTAG MAY REPLACE HIM BY ELECTING HIS SUCCESSOR BY SIMPLE MAJORITY.

LIAISON OFFICE TO THE ALLIED HIGH COMMISSION

PRESS AND INFORMATION OFFICE

STATE SECRETARIAT FOR INTERNAL AFFAIRS

STATE SECRETARIAT FOR FOREIGN AFFAIRS (NOT YET ESTABLISHED)

MINISTRIES

MINISTERS APPOINTED AND DISMISSED BY FEDERAL PRESIDENT ON PROPOSAL OF FEDERAL CHANCELLOR

EUROPEAN RECOVERY PROGRAM
FRANS BLUECHER (FDP) (VICE CHANCELLOR)

HOUSING
EBERHARD WILDERMUTH (FDP)

TRANSPORT
HANS-CRISTOPH SEEBOHM (DP)

INTERIOR
GUSTAV HEINEMANN (CDU)

POSTS
HANS SCHUBERTH (CSU)

ALL-GERMAN AFFAIRS
JAKOB KAISER (CDU)

JUSTICE
THOMAS DEHLER (FDP)

REFUGEE AFFAIRS
HANS LUKASCHEK (CDU)

BUNDESRAT AFFAIRS
HEINRICH HELLWEGE (DP)

FINANCE
FRITZ SCHAEFFER (CSU)

ECONOMICS
LUDWIG ERHARD (CDU)

FOOD & AGRICULTURE
WILHELM NIKLAS (CSU)

LABOR
ANTON STORCH (CDU)

POLITICAL PARTIES

BP — BAYERN PARTEI (BAVARIAN PARTY)
CDU — CHRISTLICH-DEMOKRATISCHE UNION (CHRISTIAN DEMOCRATIC UNION)
CSU — CHRISTLICH-SOZIALE UNION (CHRISTIAN SOCIAL UNION)
DKP — DEUTSCHE KONSERVATIVE PARTEI (GERMAN CONSERVATIVE PARTY)
DP — DEUTSCHE PARTEI (GERMAN PARTY)
DRP — DEUTSCHE RECHTSPARTEI (GERMAN RIGHTIST PARTY)
DVP — DEMOKRATISCHE VOLKSPARTEI (DEMOCRATIC PEOPLES PARTY)
FDP — FREIE DEMOKRATISCHE PARTEI (FREE DEMOCRATIC PARTY)
KPD — KOMMUNISTISCHE PARTEI DEUTSCHLANDS (COMMUNIST PARTY OF GERMANY)
SPD — SOZIALDEMOKRATISCHE PARTEI DEUTSCHLANDS (SOCIAL DEMOCRATIC PARTY OF GERMANY)
SSW — SUED-SCHLESWIGSCHE WAEHLERVEREINIGUNG (SOUTH SCHLESWIG VOTERS ASSOCIATION)
WAV — WIRTSCHAFTLICHE AUFBAU VEREINIGUNG (ECONOMIC RECONSTRUCTION ASSOCIATION)
Z — ZENTRUMSPARTEI (CENTER PARTY)

Prepared by NICOD

DECEMBER 31, 1949

189

taken which clarified some of the language and further increased the scope of German actions.[21] In general, the Occupation Statute could be regarded as liberal under the existing circumstances.

The West German Federal Government started operations on a modest scale in September of 1949. However, during the relatively short period of 1949-1955 it developed a strength and an expertness which have impressed many observers. Although the United States had expected the capital to be located in Frankfurt, and indeed a building was constructed in Frankfurt for that purpose, Bonn was chosen as the seat of government. Since there was some evidence that this choice was made to get away from American influence so prevailing in Frankfurt, a certain amount of embarrassment on the part of American military government and HICOG officials was to be noticed. But the United States took this in good grace and in late 1951 moved its headquarters to the Bonn area, where it had spent some months in constructing office and residential buildings. The choice of a rather small university city which had been seriously damaged during the war as a capital for the new German government may have proved a handicap to begin with because of its poor transportation facilities and lack of housing, but the Germans soon overcame such an obstacle and managed to construct offices for their burgeoning administrative agencies.[22] Bonn was well located from a security point of view. One of the most modern legislative buildings to be found anywhere was constructed by remodeling and adding to a normal school building on the banks of the Rhine. A visitor to the capital in the latter years of the occupation was almost always favorably impressed by what he saw; the entire governmental structure seemed to operate in a manner suggestive of a much older government.

Such an achievement was the result of various forces. Certainly the leadership of Dr. Konrad Adenauer as chancellor played a considerable role. A second force which has not perhaps been sufficiently

---

[21] A detailed treatment of the development of the Occupation Statute through its formal revision on March 7, 1951, is presented by Elmer Plischke, *Revision of the Occupation Statute for Germany*, in a monograph in the Historical Series of the Office of the U. S. High Commissioner for Germany (1952) (Restricted).

[22] For additional discussion of the selection of a federal capital, see E. Plischke, *The West German Federal Government*, a monograph in the Historical Series of the Office of the U. S. High Commissioner for Germany (1952), Chap. 7.

190

recognized is to be noted in the constructive attitude of the three western powers as expressed in the Allied High Commission and in HICOG toward the West German Federal Government. Once having agreed upon the establishment of such a government, the three western Allies and especially the United States followed a course—which might not have been adopted under other circumstances or by other powers—of attempting to assist rather than hinder. The United States did not always agree with the wisdom of the actions taken by the West German Federal Government, and on occasion the conferences between the Allied High Commissioners and the West German leaders and between the U. S. High Commissioner and these leaders were marked by high tension. Yet throughout the period 1949-1955 the general attitude of the western Allies and of the United States in particular was a benevolent one. Instead of trying to push the reserved powers under the Occupation Statute to the limit, the western Allies interpreted the Occupation Statute through the Petersberg Protocol and in their actions to the advantage of the Germans, until charges have even been made that the Allies had no backbone and permitted the Germans to get away with anything they pleased. The latter charge does not seem well substantiated since the actions of the western Allies were not the result of lack of force and courage on their part but rather of a studied policy to help build up and strengthen the West German Federal Government. Anyone who followed the work of the tripartite committees of the Allied High Commission or who was familiar with the actions of the Allied High Commission itself could not ignore such a constructive attitude toward the West German Federal Government. The contribution of the American High Commissioner, Mr. McCloy, was particularly outstanding in this respect. His frequent and lengthy conferences with Dr. Adenauer and his associates and to a lesser extent with opposition leaders, such as Dr. Schumacher of the Social Democratic party, went far beyond what would be ordinarily encountered in administering an occupied area.

The strength and effectiveness displayed by the West German Federal Government have been diversely regarded. Some have been favorably impressed and have seen in such development promise for the future. Others who distrust German reliability and attachment for democratic principles feel that this vigor constitutes a serious threat to the western Allies and that the time will come when these powers will rue the day when they permitted such a build-up to take place. Much of course depends upon what the future brings forth. If the policy of the western Allies, and especially of the United States, which must bear a heavier share of responsibility than the French, for example, who remained more or less uncertain, looking toward the integration of West Germany into the European community and the western defense alliance proves to be a sound one, then one can only express admiration for the accomplishments of the West German Federal Government.[23]

---

[23] For additional discussion of the West German Federal Government, see E. Plischke, *The West German Federal Government*, a monograph in the Historical Series of the Office of the U. S. High Commissioner for Germany (1952). It includes a useful bibliography listing other sources of information.

13

American Activities in the Education Field

The education program of the United States in Germany has been the occasion of a great deal of interest as well as widespread controversy from the very early stages of the occupation. To begin with, there has been a wide divergence of views as to what might appropriately be included. Some of the idealists have conceived of a program which would not only totally reconstruct German educational organization and curriculum but transform German thinking, standards of values, and cultural patterns. To these visionaries education is a marvelous touchstone which can be used to correct all defects and bring about the millennium. At the other extreme are those like Professor Emeritus William E. Hocking of Harvard who regard German educational standards as perhaps superior to any others in the world and maintain that it would have been more fitting for the representatives of the United States to sing paeans of praise at the doors of the German educational institutions than to engage in the sacrilegious act of reconstruction. Indeed Professor Hocking would apparently go so far as to argue that the United States should modify its own educational system to incorporate various German practices.[1] Between these two extremes there are almost innumerable points of view, some favoring an elaborate program of reconstruction, others maintaining that, irrespective of the merits of the case, the re-education of a country is beyond the realm of possibility, and still others arguing that the chief emphasis should have been placed on the rather modest task of bringing current educational literature

---

[1] See his book entitled *Experiment in Education; What We Can Learn from Teaching Germany* (Regnery, Chicago, 1954), for his views.

from other countries to the teachers of Germany.[2] Considering such divergent points of view, it is not strange that the educational program was incohesive.

Few divisions of either OMGUS or HICOG had a larger turn-over in personnel than that handling education, and during the years there were representatives of most if not all of the points of view noted above. Certainly there was a good sprinkling of those who saw in Germany the opportunity which comes only once in several lifetimes to experiment in a vast laboratory and who sincerely believed that it was not only feasible but that it was a primary responsibility of the United States to re-educate the Germans. But it would be a mistake to conclude, as some have done, that all, or perhaps even a majority, of those staffing the Education Division were so dewy-eyed and filled with the emotions of modern Crusaders. A fair number were unusually thoughtful persons who doubted whether a program of basic re-education could be successfully carried on in an occupied country, but at the same time felt that the needs of German education were such that every effort should be made by the United States to do whatever was possible, maintaining that even a slight impact would justify many failures and the expenditure of substantial amounts of money. A number of those holding positions on the Education staffs of both OMGUS and HICOG apparently had no fixed ideas of any kind as to what might or should be attempted.

Not only were there great differences of opinion among the staff members of the Education subdivision as to what should be attempted in Germany, but the attitude of Washington and those at the top in OMGUS and HICOG varied perhaps more than in most other fields from time to time. The fact that education was given a third- or fourth-level position in the early planning of the U. S. Group, Control Council for Germany and during the initial stage of OMGUS

---

[2] For various points of view, see F. N. Pitt, "Education Mission to Germany," *America*, Jan. 18, 1947; T. V. Smith, "Personal Impressions of Current Education in Italy, Germany, and Japan," *The Educational Record*, Jan. 1947; Agnes Snyder, "Elementary Education in Occupied Germany," *National Elementary Principal*, June 1947; G. A. Ziemer, "Our Educational Failure in Germany," *American Mercury*, June 1946; G. F. Zook, "Japan and Germany: Problems in Re-education," *International Conciliation*, Jan. 1947; F. H. Cramer, "Re-education of Germany," *Forum*, Oct. 1945; J. Stonborough, "Can Germany Be Re-educated?" *National Review* (London), Feb. 1947; F. Evans, "The Re-education of Germany," *Political Quarterly* (London), March 1945; H. Liddell, *Education in Occupied Germany* (Columbia University Press, New York, 1949).

indicates the relatively minor importance attached to such a function in Washington and by the top echelon in the field at one stage. Education during the early period not only failed to receive status such as was accorded economic affairs, political affairs, public relations, legal affairs, and other major areas, but it was at times not even a major subdivision of one of these primary divisions, being given a place as part of a subdivision. The result of such a comparatively low level was reflected in the small staff authorized to give attention to education.

Perhaps mainly as a result of widespread criticism in education circles in the United States a drastic change took place in 1947, under which education became a major division of OMGUS. Its staff underwent a notable expansion, and its director was able to get the ear of the Military Governor with greater ease.

Through the reorganizations of OMGUS which took place at intervals during the years 1947-1949, education managed to retain major status, but the Occupation Statute which came into effect with the setting up of the Allied High Commission in the autumn of 1949 did not list education among the powers reserved by the Allies. When this came to the attention of professional educators both in OMGUS and in the United States, there was a great outcry which led to formal protests being lodged with the State Department in Washington. The State Department finally drafted a letter in which it interpreted a general clause in the Occupation Statute which protected the interests of the occupying powers in such a manner as to include education.[3] But such an interpretation was not accepted by the Allied High Commission or by the other occupying powers. Education was accorded a place as a subdivision of one of the major divisions of HICOG and hence not dropped entirely, but its staff was cut and its subordinate position made access to the High Commissioner somewhat more difficult, though it seems probable that as a matter of practice High Commissioner McCloy at least opened his doors to the Education Chief as freely as General Clay had done to the more highly placed Director of Education. Nevertheless, the loss of staff, the cut in funds, and the general position of the other Allies that education was something to be left

[3] See H. P. Pilgert, *The West German Educational System* in the Historical Series of the Office of the U. S. High Commissioner of Germany (1953), p. 11.

largely, if not entirely, in the hands of the German authorities seriously curtailed American education activities in Germany after 1949.

THE PRE-1947 PERIOD

In early 1944 provision was made for an education planning subdivision in the German Country Unit of SHAEF. Its position was a distinctly modest one and its staff consisted of a handful of officers and enlisted men headed by Captains John Taylor and Marshall Knappen. Taylor, who had been trained at, and later served on, the staff of Teachers College, Columbia University, brought to his job a considerable familiarity with German education as well as an expert knowledge of education in the United States. Knappen had been a Rhodes scholar and a professor of modern European history at Chicago and Michigan State Universities.[4] At the dissolution of the German Country Unit in the autumn of 1944, Taylor, Knappen, and most of the American personnel in the education unit of that organization were moved to a small and subordinate subdivision of the newly established U. S. Group, Control Council for Germany. Here they continued their planning and, after the surrender of the Germans in May of 1945, found themselves in charge of the educational activities in the American Zone. Some additions were made to the staff and promotions raised the rank of the top officers in the subdivision to that of major and eventually to that of lieutenant colonel; but the Education subdivision, even after the U. S. Group, Control Council for Germany had been incorporated into the Office of Military Government of the U. S. in Germany (OMGUS), remained a small and closely knit group. Although seriously handicapped in theory by its low level, it is probable that Education actually enjoyed some advantage over larger and more prominent agencies. With a ranking position, its head would have been a general or a V. I. P. civilian, neither of whom, as the world is run, would have had expert knowledge of German educational systems and problems. This would have necessitated a sizable staff fitting to a general or V. I. P. and at the same time would probably have meant

[4] Knappen who was also in charge of religious affairs has given an account of his experiences in his book *And Call It Peace* (University of Chicago Press, Chicago, 1947).

the assignment of many persons with little or no professional background for their job. As it was, the Education Branch, despite its humble position and small size, could pride itself on a high professional competence, an extraordinary degree of cooperativeness, and unusual freedom to go ahead without undue interference—the latter because it was too far down the scale to attract the envy or jealousy of the "top brass."

Being intellectually superior and professionally competent and with a considerable knowledge of German institutions and history, the Education staff during this period did not make the mistake of wasting its time on elaborate paper plans which had little if any chance of being put into effect. Its general thesis was that a conquering power or group of powers could not, under a democratic system at least, re-educate a nation which had been brought to its knees by defeat in war. It recognized the weaknesses in the German education system, particularly those growing out of the Nazi infiltration of the schools and universities. It conceived of its task as that of performing emergency services which would make it possible for the German school system to re-open in a manner reasonably satisfactory to American responsibilities. It recognized the hard necessity of concentrating on policing measures of a more or less negative character during the months immediately following surrender, but it also placed some emphasis on assisting the German educators by furnishing information, counsel, and leadership.

The most pressing problem confronting the Education staff during the early days of the occupation was to get the German elementary and then the secondary schools open. The available information revealed that over 80 per cent of the German school staff had been Nazified to the extent of belonging to the National Socialist Teachers' League and that many were active members of the party itself. Obviously a responsible occupying authority could not simply authorize the opening of the schools. Steps had to be taken to eliminate the worst Nazis from the schools. This not only involved the heavy task of screening all teachers, but it necessitated drawing an exceedingly tenuous line between those so badly contaminated by the Nazis as to be dangerous and those who, though somewhat contaminated, could still be used. Ideally perhaps all German educators with Nazi

197

affiliations might have been discarded; but, with more than 80 per cent in such a category, schools could not have operated under such a course.

The American education authorities followed what seemed a moderate policy of throwing out something like half of the German teaching staff. There was some criticism that the screening was not sufficiently drastic. More recently it has been fashionable in certain quarters to blame the officials for discarding so large a number on the ground that a good many of those refused clearance were not really Nazis at heart but had been forced into membership in the National Socialist Teachers' League against their wills and that, by eliminating so many teachers, the schools were extremely understaffed. Mistakes were doubtless made in screening the teachers, but by and large the task was done as well as could have been expected under the confused conditions and far better than some other programs carried on at the same time. To supplement the screening, vigorous efforts had to be made to set up emergency training facilities for supplying additional teachers. This did not receive as much publicity as the denazification activity, but it was constructive in character, highly essential, and in general well done.

If more than 80 per cent of the German teachers had been involved in National Socialism, the textbooks and teaching materials were virtually 100 per cent National Socialist in character. The Education Branch saw little or no purpose in reopening the German schools until reasonably satisfactory textbooks could be provided. As early as 1944 the planners had recognized this problem and efforts had been directed at finding pre-Nazi German textbooks. The library of Teachers College at Columbia seemed to offer the best collection, and a program of photographing these books was undertaken. Unfortunately when an examination of these pre-Nazi texts was made, it was evident that the extreme nationalism of some of them made them hardly more satisfactory than the Nazi texts. Hence efforts had to be made to revise these so as to eliminate the most objectionable parts—a far from easy undertaking. A second problem involved obtaining authorization, funds, and paper for printing enough of these texts to supply the German school children. With paper shortages critical throughout the world and printing establishments with heavy backlogs, this was extremely difficult. When the time came to

198

reopen the German schools, the printing was behind schedule, but some 5,328,616 copies of textbooks were available to the some 1,849,206 children enrolled during the first year.

With a large proportion of the German school buildings either completely destroyed or badly damaged by bombing and fighting, places to house the schools was a major problem and one to be faced by the Education Branch. By the time the schools reopened on October 1, 1945, cold weather was in the offing, and with fuel supplies very low it was often impossible to furnish heat.

There was some feeling that the schools in the American Zone should have reopened more promptly—children were roaming the rubble-filled streets, playing in dangerous places, and getting into trouble with the police. The Russians did re-open the schools in their zone during the summer. The American education officials resisted the pressure to re-open prematurely, maintaining that the disadvantages were greater than the admitted advantages. They were not, however, able to withstand the pressure to re-open certain university facilities. The original plan had been to get the elementary and secondary schools going and then give attention to the universities. As it turned out, limited university facilities opened in November 1945, despite the slight opportunity on the part of the American education officials to give attention to them. Evidence reveals that it was a mistake to yield to such pressure, since it established a pattern of permitting universities to reopen before meeting satisfactorily basic requirements of ridding themselves of the worst sort of Nazism—there probably never was a real chance to get rid of all Nazi influence.

As one reviews the work of the small band of hard-working, underranked education officials during this early period, it is difficult to refrain from admiration and high praise. That so able a performance was given under extreme difficulties is remarkable.

THE PERIOD 1947-1950

As the Office of Military Government of the United States in Germany became more familiar to the American public and especially to the teaching profession, the question arose as to why education should have such a minor place in comparison with certain other areas. Enough pressure developed to influence Washington and, indirectly, OMGUS in the direction of setting up education as a major activity of the United States in Germany and to give it a second-level position in OMGUS. This decision necessitated officials of higher rank, thus more or less eliminating the little group of valiant workers led by John Taylor and later by Thomas Alexander who had done the pioneering—it is only fair to note that many of these felt that their ties at home required a return to the United States. At any rate, emphasis was placed on finding a "big name" in the United States to head this new major division of OMGUS. It may be added that this was the period when it was popular in Washington circles to stress the need for "big names" for service in Germany. Perhaps the craving for added prestige and publicity largely explained this attitude—comparatively little attention seemed to be given to pertinent professional experience and the consequent ability to perform a difficult service well; it was enough if someone could be found who had what the Army regarded as a prominent place in some field. One can understand this desire to some extent, for there is obviously a relationship between personal distinction and successful administration. The unfortunate aspect of the situation was that the exact relationship did not seem to be clear to the Army personnel people and, instead of seeking an authority on elementary and secondary education with expert knowledge of the systems both at home and in Germany, the emphasis was placed simply on a "big name." Granted, the supply of leading educationists with a sound professional knowledge of both American and German educational systems was not large, but there is little evidence that any serious effort was made to secure the services of such a person at this time.

An announcement was eventually made that President H. B. Wells of Indiana University had been selected to head the new Education subdivision of OMGUS and that he had been released by his university temporarily to perform such a public service. An unusually energetic, expansive, and popular man in his forties, Dr. Wells had transformed Indiana University on the physical side from a somewhat run-down and distinctly modest institution in the hills of southern Indiana to one of the most modern and impressive campuses in the country, largely through smart use of PWA funds. Few university or any other executives knew Hoosier politics and Hoosier traditions and psychology as well as President Wells. He had been

200

an able head of the state banking department and an intimate associate of Governor Paul V. McNutt before taking over the deanship of the College of Business Administration at Indiana University and subsequently the university presidency. Having had little to do with education below the university level, Dr. Wells' interest at the university level seemed to be primarily in relations between the university and the state legislature. He had had little professional experience outside of Indiana, and his previous acquaintance with Germany or any other foreign country was slight.* He certainly could not be expected to bring to his task in Germany any considerable knowledge of German history, German political, economic, and social institutions, or German education. But he did have what appeared a genuine interest in his new assignment, and remarkable energy and ability to make a favorable impression.

President Wells started his new job as head of the Education and Cultural Affairs Division of OMGUS and as Education Advisor to General Clay with characteristic decisiveness and aggressiveness. The division under his direction expanded rapidly to a point where it numbered its staff by the score rather than as individuals—it may not have reached the size of the Economic Affairs Division, but it became one of the largest and most active major segments of OMGUS. Dr. Wells became a familiar figure in American circles in Germany and undoubtedly brought valuable publicity to military government. He was immediately faced with the difficult problem of constructing a sizable staff supposedly of experts in a short period. How well he succeeded in this task is a controversial topic. It can hardly be doubted that there were numerous staff members who had very little formal background for their work in Germany—their sole experience and knowledge related to education in the United States. The attitudes and adaptability of many of the newly appointed staff members struck some observers as being far from promising in a situation such as had to be faced in Germany. Nevertheless, Dr. Wells displayed not a little acumen in selecting such associates as Milton Muelder, more recently dean of the Arts College of Michigan State University. A professor of History who had done graduate work in a German

---

* However, he had served as special adviser on liberated areas to the State Department, acted as consultant to the U. S. delegation at the San Francisco Conference, and been a member of the Allied Mission to observe Greek elections.

university and who had served from an early date with distinction on the staffs of the German Country Unit and the U. S. Group, Control Council for Germany, Muelder knew a great deal about German institutions and psychology as well as about the development of American military government in Germany.

It was unfortunate that Dr. Wells was faced with the problem of building a large organization from the ground up in a very short period. There was neither adequate time for carefully weighing qualifications of candidates nor for meticulous planning of an educational program. An Aladdin with a golden lamp and genii at his command might have achieved the task of selecting a sizable professional staff and putting it in a high-gear program almost immediately with ease; but mere humans, even if able and energetic, rarely can emulate such an example. In the limited time at his disposal Dr. Wells probably did as well as could be expected, but the much-heralded *new* education effort of the United States in Germany occasioned great disappointment in informed circles. Despite the great increase in the number of "bodies" and the larger funds available, there is grave doubt as to whether the achievements were as notable as those of the handful of men who had shouldered the responsibility during the initial period.

Too many of the new education staff members were "empire builders" who knew very little about German problems and cared less, but saw in the Education Division an opportunity to gain recognition, build up personal power, and the like. Because of the time factor and the lack of detailed knowledge of German institutions, many ill-conceived programs were set up which had no chance of succeeding and squandered large amounts of public funds. There was duplication of effort, conflict, and an immense amount of sheer waste of effort. *

Perhaps the chief weakness of the education program during the Wells' regime arose out of the general inclination to see German educational problems in terms of American patterns. The early tasks of getting the schools reopened, screening teachers, providing emergency textbooks, and so forth, were either completed or had

---

* The situation was such that one observer remarked: "The 32 Education officers at Bad Nauheim have now created so much red tape that they are kept busy 100 per cent of the time administering each other."

settled down to a routine. With a big new Education Division which operated to some degree in the limelight, ambitious plans had to be drafted for action. The very size of the new staff and the emphasis placed on spectacular action served to divert the American policy from its goal—that of handling emergency problems and giving such advice and counsel as might be desired by the Germans—to the point of undertaking a major work of reconstructing the German educational system.

Under any circumstances such a drastic change in basic concept would have involved grave dangers. With the time factor so important and the staff mainly familiar only with the American educational system, the new education effort was almost bound to be directed toward setting up an "American" education system in the American Zone of Germany. At least this is what happened. Elaborate paper plans were devised calling for the reorganization of the German school system along American lines. Education below the university level was to be mainly public education rather than religious. No longer would the undemocratic route to the university through the gymnasium be countenanced—secondary schools which would train all types, whether destined for the university, business, or a trade would be set up. The curriculum would be reconstructed in such a fashion that it would be basically similar to that used in American schools, with proper emphasis on social studies, citizenship, and the like. An elaborate program of turning out textbooks and other teaching materials which would be used in the reorganized schools with their new curricula was undertaken. The German universities alone escaped from such drastic paper reconstruction, and their time perhaps would have come later.

Such progress had been made in making plans for the reforming of German education in the American pattern that President Wells could report to the press when he returned to Indiana University in 1948 that the problems incident to a complete reorganization of German education along American lines had been surmounted. Actually most of the plans, probably fortunately for both Germans and Americans, remained on paper and were never executed.

When Dr. Wells returned to his university duties, a search was carried on for another "big name" to head the Education and Cultural Affairs Division of OMGUS. This time a more permanent arrangement was contemplated, and Dr. Alonzo G. Grace, who had been Commissioner of Education of the State of Connecticut for a decade following 1938, was appointed. Dr. Grace had received a musical education in France and had served for several years on the education staff of the University of Minnesota. During his commissionership in Connecticut he had lectured for several years at Yale University. Like Dr. Wells, his main professional experience had been in the United States and his expertness lay in American educational administration.

Dr. Grace brought to his task in Germany a good deal of energy and strong ideas. In his contribution entitled "Education" in *Governing Postwar Germany*, Dr. Grace characterized the first three years of the American occupation as "more or less devoid of an educational and cultural relations effort."[5] He apparently dismissed the work done by his predecessor, Dr. Wells, as worthless. Like many others who came to work in both OMGUS and HICOG, Dr. Grace perhaps did not bother to inform himself of what had gone on before his arrival and hence possibly was completely unaware of the very valuable work done in the education field during 1945 and 1946. He could hardly have been unaware of the Wells' regime however.

Under the direction of Dr. Grace, the Education and Cultural Affairs Division remained a large section of OMGUS, though during the transition period leading to HICOG and during the rather short time that Dr. Grace served with HICOG, reductions in force took place. Numerous changes of personnel however were effected, and many of those serving under Dr. Wells returned to the United States or took other posts in OMGUS, being replaced by those selected by Dr. Grace.

Dr. Grace has stated that under his direction: "The emphasis was removed from structural change in education and placed on the aim and spirit of education, the equalization of opportunity, the importance of the human element in educational systems, the importance of cooperation."[6] At a conference held at Berchtesgaden in 1948 shortly after the arrival of Dr. Grace, the following basic education policies were adopted:

1. The true reform of the German people will come from within. It will be spiritual and moral. The types of school organization, or structure,

[5] *Governing Postwar Germany*, p. 458.
[6] *Ibid.*, p. 458.

for example, are of less importance to the future of Germany and the world than what is taught, how it is taught, and by whom it is taught.

2. The solution to the so-called 'German problem' will be more readily attained when we recognize that it is a part of the entire European problem. We will not enlist the support of the German people in the struggle of ideologies or prevent them from arising again by superimposing an educational structure, or program, which ignores the history of this and other European countries.

3. It will not be the purpose of Military Government to superimpose an American system of education on the German people. It is our purpose to indicate to the German people that the education of children and youth should be so organized and developed:
   a. That each individual, irrespective of race, class, creed, or economic status, shall have equal access to education.
   b. That each individual shall be allowed to pursue that form or type of educational opportunity for which it is endowed.
   c. That each individual shall, as a result of his schooling, be able to make the maximum contribution toward the maintenance of world peace, and international understanding, the maintenance of law and order, and the development of social justice.

4. The most effective method of establishing a society based on the democratic ideal is to abandon the use of the term as such and, by practice and precept, lead the German people to accept this ideal.

5. The provision for a corps of educated teachers and leaders in Germany is a primary necessity. We must observe that schooling does not necessarily guarantee education; that the acquisition of knowledge does not indicate the possession of wisdom; that instruction does not necessarily mean learning; that schooling, instruction, and knowledge without moral responsibility, spiritual enlightenment, and intellectual integrity will fail to produce the character necessary to resist the effort of those who would destroy the dignity of the individual.

6. We must not be guilty of attempting to develop in Germany the ideal, which may not have been accomplished elsewhere, in the midst of an environment fraught with confusion and uncertainty.

7. The redirection of the goals, programs, or policies of social institutions must grow from the people. Wide citizen participation in community planning, in the discussion of community problems, and in the aiding in the formulation of public policy is one guarantee that no one individual can dominate the thinking and living habits of the people. Power *through* people must supplant power *over* people.

8. No army of occupation has or possibly ever will successfully superimpose an educational and cultural pattern on a conquered people. Military government will be regarded as military government, irrespective of the high motives of those who would 're-educate or re-orient' a defeated, conquered, occupied Germany. It will be the purpose of Military Government, therefore:

    a. To bring into co-operation with the German people the voluntary nongovernmental organizations that are able to contribute toward the attainment of the common goals.

    b. To encourage an effective German program by UNESCO.

    c. To identify and encourage known democratic elements in the German population.

    d. To support the development or re-establishment of institutions and organizations in Germany which will contribute toward the accomplishment of the purposes of this mission.

9. The more rapid the material reconstruction and economic recovery, the more difficult becomes the problem of intellectual, moral, and spiritual redemption. The United States will have failed in Germany if materialism is allowed to supersede moral values. A concurrent program of educational and cultural reconstruction on a long-term basis is required.[7]

This rather amazing statement which combined shrewdness, idealism, admission of the impossible character of the task, and an appeal for the long life of the Education and Cultural Affairs Division of OMGUS together with various platitudes, according to Dr. Grace, became "the basis of policy, and a systematic program of education and cultural relations was inaugurated."[8] How such an inconsistent and contradictory set of basic principles could serve as a foundation of a "systematic program" it is difficult to perceive. In part a return was made to the original point of view of the Education Branch of the United States in Germany, though Dr. Grace does not so much as indicate an awareness of this fact, devoting himself mainly to the throwing into the ash can of the program of his immediate predecessor, Dr. Wells. The emphasis on "redemption" indicates a very low view of the German people as late as 1948; the statement that German economic recovery would render an education and cultural relations program difficult if not impossible smacks of the era of the camp meeting and "old-time gospel" in the United States. After analyzing the basic principles one cannot help wondering what there was left for a sizable Education staff to do. Certainly one could hardly justify the expenditure of large sums of American funds to "encourage an effective German program by UNESCO." All of this is not to say that there was no valuable work performed by the Education and

---

[7] A. G. Grace, *Basic Principles of Educational Reconstruction in Germany*, Education and Cultural Relations Division, OMGUS, 1948.

[8] E. H. Litchfield, ed., *op. cit.*, p. 458.

206

American Activities in the Education Field

Cultural Relations Division of OMGUS under Dr. Grace, but it can hardly be denied that there was a great deal of fuzziness of reasoning and too much rather pompous talk. Those, for example, who were giving themselves energetically to the program of citizen participation in community life—and some excellent work was being done in the field along these lines—often felt utterly neglected by the experts at OMGUS headquarters, maintaining that they received little more than empty words by way of support.

THE PERIOD 1950-1955

With the winding up of OMGUS and the establishment of HICOG, education came in for a drastic shake-up, though Dr. Grace remained for some months. The Occupation Statute which listed powers to be reserved to the occupying powers and thus indicated those to be handed over to the West German Federal Government placed education in the latter category. An interpretation by the State Department elicited under pressure from educational forces in the United States, referred to previously, saved education from entire extinction; but the major position given education and cultural affairs in the organization charts of OMGUS since 1947 was lost, and education resumed its place as a secondary subdivision. Its staff was cut and its funds reduced. Some of the old hands remained, but most of the Grace staff returned home.

In this final period of the occupation, efforts to reorganize the structure of the German school system were dropped, though some attention was given to the long-drawn-out struggle to strengthen the public as against the religious schools, to provide for free tuition at all levels up to the university, and the like. Some of the projects involving the preparation of textbooks were not wound up until this period. The chief emphasis after 1949 was placed on sending German teachers to the United States and, to a limited extent, to other democratic countries for purposes of observation, bringing educational leaders from the United States to confer with German school personnel, and making available books, periodicals, and other educational material from the United States and elsewhere to German school staffs. Financial grants in D-marks available from counterpart funds were made in various amounts to assist German

207

education in carrying on research, to conduct surveys, to hold conferences, to carry on experiments of a variety of types, and the like.[9] Teacher unions and parent-teacher associations were encouraged.

Although less noise was made about the education and cultural affairs activities of the United States in Germany during this period and the staff and budget were more modest than during the preceding period, it seems probable that some of the most effective work was done. More could have been accomplished, it is true, had there been less deadwood among the American staff. Some observers felt that there was a notable lack of dynamism. The running feud which went on for many months between the Educational and Cultural Relations and the Exchanges Divisions absorbed a good deal of the energy of both and reached almost the proportions of a scandal. One could hardly have called the program "systematic," as Dr. Grace had grandiloquently advertised under his regime; it was more a piecemeal affair involving doing a bit here and a bit there which seemed to promise results. This approach probably accounted in large measure for the achievements which, though not spectacular, nevertheless frequently deserved commendation.

CONCLUDING COMMENTS

It is not uncommon to encounter the categorical assertion that sufficient time has passed to justify a definitive evaluation of the education efforts of the United States in Germany. Indeed Professor Hocking felt able to pronounce a final judgment several years ago.[10] However, some of those who are familiar with the occupation, including this author, believe that it is too early to obtain a clear picture of positive results. Another decade or so would seem to be necessary before an objective conclusion can be reached; even then, because of the intangibles involved, definitive conclusions may be difficult. It is, of course, obvious that numerous failures were encountered, that there were serious shortcomings in both the Education staff and the programs, that a good deal of money and effort may have been expended fruitlessly. It was also more or less clear at the

---

[9] For a more detailed treatment of the program during this period, see Henry Pilgert, *The West German Educational System*, a monograph in the Historical Series of the Office of the U. S. High Commissioner for Germany, particularly Chap. 2.

[10] See his book *Experiment in Education*. He wrote in 1954: "It is now for the first time possible to estimate fairly the degree of our success or want of success" (p. xiii).

end of the occupation that some of the efforts in this field were at least reasonably successful. But whether these positive influences were temporary or whether they may prove lasting, and whether they are mainly surface or whether they go beneath the surface and, if so, how deep, are questions which cannot at present be answered with any certainty.

One of the greatest disappointments to those who have observed the American education record in Germany has been in connection with the personnel given the responsibility of carrying on the job. The obstacles to any meaningful educational effort on the part of the United States in Germany have been almost overwhelming. A fundamental question in the minds of thoughtful persons has always been whether it is within the realm of the possible for an occupying power which claims to be democratic in character to do anything worthwhile in the field of education among a people bowed down by defeat, suffering the humiliation of being occupied by foreign military forces, and facing the basic problems of family adjustment, economic reconstruction, and the like. It is by no means certain that it is possible to do anything significant, let alone re-educate such a people. At any rate, the success of such an undertaking depends in large measure on the people who are selected or drafted to direct and administer the program. The education officials in such a bold attempt should rank with the very best persons in the education field in the United States. They should have first-rate intellectual capacity to begin with, they should have had superior professional training, and they should have demonstrated their professional competence in outstanding manner in the United States. But this is not enough for such a task as that which confronted the United States in Germany. In addition, such persons need an expert knowledge of foreign education systems and of the history, institutions, and psychology of the occupied country, in this case of course Germany. It may well be said that it is unreasonable to set up such standards as already listed. But there are others to be added. Such persons should have something of the finest qualities of the missionary: the desire to help, willingness to sacrifice professional advancement at home, patience, imagination, a love for humanity even in degradation, modesty, ability to work under appalling difficulties without undue discouragement, and the like.

Some of the staff selected by the United States for service in the education field in Germany would rate pretty high on such a basis, but their number was small. A somewhat larger group would make a fair showing. But the sad aspect was the large number of those who had virtually none of the above qualities. They had distinctly limited intelligence, inferior professional training, unimpressive professional records in the United States, little or no knowledge of anything outside of the United States, and instead of possessing the missionary spirit were frequently selfish, pompous, impatient, intolerant, lazy, and the like. Under any personnel system it is to be expected that serious mistakes will be made; but it is difficult to explain how so many persons, lacking proper qualifications, received jobs in education. The official explanation is that good people were not available and that appointing officers therefore had to take the ones who offered themselves. The supply of adequate persons in the education or any other field in the United States is not enormous, but it is this author's belief that it is larger than is sometimes assumed. The evidence is not convincing that the personnel officials in OMGUS and in Washington ever made a serious effort to find properly qualified people and to persuade them that they were needed for a most important work in Germany. Instead, people were selected who sought the jobs because they offered more salary than these people could command in the United States; or deserving surplus military personnel needing jobs were appointed; or friends of officials were picked out.

It is not difficult to perceive that many of the ambitious paper programs sponsored by some of the staff in the education field have definitely failed—indeed they often never really got started. German school systems have been modified somewhat since the war, but these changes have probably resulted from German initiative in large measure. In general, the organizational pattern remains much as it was prior to the occupation from the beginning level through the university. However, Berlin and Bremen and, to a lesser extent, Württemberg and Hesse have made some progress in setting up public school systems in contrast to the confessional schools of Bavaria.

The revision of the curriculum envisaged by some Americans has been hardly more successful than the revamping of the educational structure. National Socialist indoctrination has of course been eliminated in large measure, but the United States can claim only incidental credit here. Perhaps the policing of American education authorities has had some effect in getting rid of the super-nationalistic character of some of the textbooks. The large amounts expended on the textbook program do not seem to have produced the results anticipated. There have been some outright scandals in this connection; but probably more serious is the indifferent work that was submitted. Out of 1,366 projects, 392 had to be discarded entirely.[11] The American program looking to a larger place in the curriculum for the social studies may have had some practical influence, particularly at the university level, but the achievements have been far less than was expected. Political science, sociology, and related fields still occupy a very small place in the German universities, despite the generous grant of the Ford Foundation to the Free University of Berlin, the establishment of social science research institutes under American sponsorship, the provision for chairs of political science in several universities, and so forth.

Financial assistance for the establishment of student centers, student unions, and similar facilities in the German universities was forthcoming from the Special Projects program of HICOG and from other American sources. There is little question that such facilities were needed and that they serve a useful purpose in bringing students together, thus contributing to the development of university-wide consciousness among the student body. These are likely to prove permanent, but what their exact role may be it is difficult to predict.*

The large-scale program of providing school meals from the elementary school level through the university and technical schools financed by American funds has not received much publicity, but it made it possible for large numbers of German children and youth to pursue their studies at a time when proper food was lacking in many homes. To measure with any degree of exactitude the concrete results of this undertaking is obviously impossible and it may not be remembered by the Germans, but it deserves commendation.

Gifts of books and other educational equipment to schools and universities were fairly commonplace. In some instances collections

---

[11] See L. D. Clay, *Decision in Germany*, p. 300.

* However, in at least one instance it is reported that the student center has been diverted to another purpose.

of several thousand volumes were presented to special libraries, such as those of law schools.* The contribution of the Ford Foundation made possible the building of a much-needed library building at the Free University in Berlin. An even larger American contribution, not directly a part of the education program but nevertheless related to it, financed the construction of one of the most modern public libraries in the world for West Berlin. It can hardly be doubted that these and other American gifts have done something to strengthen the German education program.

It is probable that the most significant American contribution to German education was in the field of making it possible for fairly large numbers of German education staff members to establish contact with the outside world. During the years of World War II German teachers had almost no opportunities to keep abreast of world developments in the education field. Prior to that time the situation was little if any better, due to the Nazi regimentation of the schools and universities. During the Weimar Republic there was some contact with the outside world, but the catastrophic inflation, the economic collapse, and other emergencies set up many barriers. It is not too much to say that prior to the occupation German education personnel had had little direct or indirect contact with educational activities in other countries for a generation or more. The American education program made it possible for many German teachers and administrators to visit the United States and other democratic countries to observe educational operations.† The selection of those to be sent abroad was not always wise, and some of those who had the opportunity did not take full advantage of it. Visits to schools and universities in the United States were all too frequently poorly planned, and the German educators derived less profit than might have been possible. Too much emphasis was placed on bringing the German teachers to the United States and too little on sending them to nearby European democratic countries where problems are more similar to those in Germany. This incidentally would have cost far less and perhaps made it possible to send considerably larger numbers for a refresher journey. Nevertheless, it is

---

* These books were usually in English and that made them limited in usefulness to begin with, but an increasing knowledge of English among Germans has brightened the picture recently.

† In 1951, 344 were sent to the United States and 228 to other European countries.

212

justifiable to conclude that considerable benefit accrued and that, despite the impossibility of exact measurement, a useful purpose was served.

To supplement the program of sending German teachers abroad, professional education personnel from the United States and other democratic countries were dispatched to Germany.* Although far less influential than the French arrangement of placing a young Frenchman or French woman in every German secondary school to instruct in French literature and culture, to associate with the young Germans and German teachers, and to live as a part of a German community, this American plan cannot be dismissed lightly. Too many pompous mediocrities came to Germany to patronize and condescendingly relate the marvels of American education and too many regarded their weeks or months in Germany as an opportunity to see Europe at the expense of the government. But nevertheless some excellent representatives of American education went to Germany and expended effort generously to discuss mutual problems with their German colleagues. Who can say what the impact of this personal association may be? It seems fair to assume that in certain instances at least it was and may continue to be significant.

Possibly the most effective arrangement for bringing visiting American teachers into useful contact with their German colleagues was through workshops. Various workshops were organized at which American and at times other European teachers and groups of German teachers discussed major problems in their fields over a period of several weeks. Foreign teachers were not always very adequate representatives, frequently being too limited in background and unduly nationalistic. The German teachers who participated may have been carelessly chosen in certain instances. The arrangement under which American teachers sometimes received more adequate lodging and food than the Germans militated against the establishment of the best atmosphere for exchange of ideas. The arrogance and condescension on the part of one of the mediocre HICOG officials in charge of this program was deeply resented by the foreigners and Germans alike who participated in the social science workshop held at Heidelberg during the summer of 1950. But despite these

---

* In the fiscal year of 1951, 112 such persons were brought to Germany.

limitations, worthwhile results were achieved which may have an influence over many years.

Another technique employed to acquaint German educators with experience in their field in other countries was that of providing books, periodicals, and other literature. Education Service Centers were sent up at Augsburg, Berlin, Bremen, Bremerhaven, Bruchsal, Essen, Freiburg, Hamburg, Hanover, Heidelberg, Jugenheim-Bergstrasse, Kaiserslautern, Karlsruhe, Kassel, Kiel, Koblenz, Mannheim, Munich, Nuremberg, Regensburg, Stuttgart, Weilburg, and Wiesbaden. In these centers there were education libraries, materials in audio-visual aids, educational and psychological testing materials, and vocational guidance files. Not only could German teachers come to these centers for information, but during certain periods they could find specialists of various sorts to confer with. Discussion groups were at times organized to bring teachers together with others, including parents.[12] Eventually these facilities were transferred to the Germans.

It is difficult to measure the effectiveness of such facilities. The rank and file of German teachers were probably too driven by the huge enrollments in their classes and their other work and too harassed by the problems arising out of everyday living to find time for Education Service Centers. The minority who did avail themselves of the facilities offered were sometimes disappointed: books and periodicals were usually in a foreign language which they could not use with any ease; the problems dealt with sometimes seemed far removed from those encountered in German schools and the treatment of those problems which were familiar too often struck the German reader as utterly unrealistic. But this is not an experience unique in Germany, for in the United States and elsewhere the rank and file of teachers do not keep their heads sufficiently above water to interest themselves in educational literature. The main questions are: How many of the German teachers, who do have a professional consciousness and who regard education as a personal responsibility of great magnitude requiring efforts beyond the routine tasks, made use of the Education Service Centers? To what extent did they find useful materials therein? What was and will be the lasting influence of information and ideas derived from such sources?

[12] For further information relating to these centers, see H. P. Pilgert, *The West German Educational System*, pp. 23-25.

214

Free University in West Berlin. Henry Ford Building.

Mr. John J. McCloy, U. S. High Commissioner for Germany, strikes the cornerstone of th
American Memorial Library at Berlin.

General Sir Brian H. Robertson of the United Kingdom, M. André François-Poncet of France, and Mr. John J. McCloy of the United States, the Allied High Commissioners, signing the Occupation Statute which authorized the functioning of the West German Federal Government.

The signing of the first major agreement between the United States and the West German Federal Republic in the Chancellery at Bonn. Under this agreement West Germany was made a full member in the European Recovery Program. Left to right are: High Commissioner McCloy, Chancellor Adenauer, and R. M. Hanes, head of the Office of Economic Affairs of HICOG and ECA Special Mission representative.

14

The Exchanges Program

During the early period of the occupation Germany was almost completely quarantined. Consequently Germans could not leave Germany and foreign nationals, except on official business and under official auspices, could not enter Germany. Looking back it may seem somewhat strange that such a policy should have been acceptable to the United States, even if the other Allies found such a course desirable. The Germans had been more or less out of touch with world developments since 1933, due to the Hitler regime and the war, and this constituted a great handicap to certain of the Allied programs, particularly in such fields as education. The re-establishment of normal travel would have brought information and ideas from the outside world to Germany and provided a background which would have been distinctly valuable. But military organizations are conservative in many respects, justifying such a policy on security and other grounds, and they are reluctant to move ahead rapidly except in purely military undertakings. Considering the thinking prevalent in the United States during the early days of the occupation, the general policy of quarantining a people who had established an unenviable record in international relations and who, it was alleged, might contaminate other peoples if permitted to leave home was probably a natural one. The apprehension in American circles lest communism might prove a mighty force in postwar Germany doubtless had some bearing on keeping the borders closed to other than official travelers. The difficult food situation and the critical shortages in housing also were advanced as telling arguments against permitting ordinary visitors to come to Germany.

Although the exchanges program belonged mainly to the Allied High Commission period of the occupation, it is only fair to note that OMGUS had given thought to the matter at an early stage and that the foundations on which the ambitious program which char-

215

acterized the latter years of the occupation were laid were put in under military government. A specialist program under which carefully screened civilians could act as visiting experts from the United States to assist in certain aspects of the occupation got under way in late 1946 and early 1947. It can hardly be said that these visiting specialists came in a private, unofficial capacity, since they were given military transportation, provided billets in military installations, permitted to use military messes and so forth, and paid a per diem salary for their services; but they were not quite in the same position as the regular staff of military government and perhaps may properly be regarded as part of an exchanges program. Plans were started in 1946 and an Exchanges Section was set up in the Education Branch of OMGUS in 1947. But time was needed to complete the necessary budgetary work and other arrangements, and it was not until the fall of 1948, a year before OMGUS came to an end, that the first Germans, in this case students, were actually sent to the United States. A little later the program was expanded, and German leaders in various fields visited the United States for periods of 30 to 120 days. Prior to this some Germans had been sent to Switzerland, Denmark, the United Kingdom, and other democratic countries in Europe to observe educational techniques and other special activities, but if a date has to be set as the significant start of the exchanges program it would be late 1948.[1]

THE FORMAL BASIS OF THE EXCHANGES PROGRAM

Although JCS 1067 proved so inadequate for the direction of military government and expectations of a new directive were apparently widely held during 1946, it was not, as noted earlier, until July 11, 1947, that such a directive actually reached Germany. This directive contained the following clause relating to an exchanges program:

In furtherance of the program of the reorientation of the German people and the revival of international cultural relations, you will permit and assist

---

[1] This historical summary as well as much of the remainder of this chapter is based on H. P. Pilgert, *The Exchange of Persons Program in Western Germany*, a volume in the Historical Series of the Office of the U. S. High Commissioner for Germany (1951).

the travel into and out of Germany of persons useful for this program within the availability of your facilities.[2]

Even more important as a basis of the exchanges program which attained such sizable proportions under HICOG, though not applying to the limited program carried on by military government prior to 1949, was Public Law 402 entitled "An Act to promote the better understanding of the United States among the peoples of the world and to strengthen cooperative educational exchanges" which was passed by Congress early in 1948. This act authorized the establishment of "an educational exchange service to cooperate with other nations in (a) the interchange of persons, knowledge, and skills; (b) the rendering of technical and other services; (c) the interchange of developments in the field of education, the arts, and the sciences."

MACHINERY FOR ADMINISTERING THE PROGRAM

It has been noted previously that an Exchanges Section was organized in the Education Branch of OMGUS during 1947. As budgetary preparations and program-planning progressed, this organization expanded at a fairly rapid pace. With the giving of major status to education and cultural relations as a first-line division of OMGUS, the Exchanges subdivision naturally improved its position. Planning for the exchanges programs of fiscal years 1949 and 1950 was handled by this military government agency and in general there was no serious break in continuity when OMGUS came to an end and HICOG assumed responsibility. Some of the same people who had operated the exchanges program under OMGUS continued to exercise responsibility under HICOG.

Naturally there were changes in the organization as military government gave way to the High Commission phase. Education and cultural relations lost its place as a major subdivision under HICOG, and the exchanges program was transferred from education and cultural relations to a coordinate place as a division of the Office of Public Affairs. Such a modification was recommended by an Information and Exchanges Survey Mission, made up of eleven

---

[2] Paragraph 27.

State Department officials, sent out from Washington in June 1949 to look at the situation. Although this might appear to reduce the general importance of the exchanges program, the result was otherwise. Education probably did suffer somewhat as a result of this reorganization; but the Exchanges subdivision remained in about the same secondary-level position as before and, because of the expansion of the exchanges program, actually assumed greater, rather than less, importance as a division of the HICOG Office of Public Affairs. Two subdivisions of the Exchanges Division were set up a: Personnel Exchange Branch and a Material Exchange Branch. The former more or less overshadowed the latter.

According to a policy statement drawn up in Washington, the Exchanges Division in Germany would be guided by the following:[3]

1. That the Exchanges Division in the Office of Public Affairs have exclusive responsibility for the control and administration of all exchange of persons projects, including responsibility for all stateside contacts relative to the program.
2. That the Public Affairs Officer call upon professional personnel in other interested divisions and offices for assistance in those aspects of the program requiring specialized knowledge and contacts in certain professional or civic fields.
3. That the emphasis in the program be increasingly placed upon younger people: that provision be made for a reasonable number of tuition and maintenance grants to German students for a year of study at institutions of higher education in the United States.
4. That, in general, the duration of the visits of German leaders and experts to the U.S. and of American expert consultants to Germany be set at a minimum of six months.
5. That the possibility be maintained of including selected and approved projects involving exchanges with democratic European countries within the framework of the approved program.
6. That projects not be included in the program which are calculated to serve the exclusive interests of particular religious denominational groups or political parties.
7. That adequate provision be made for the visits of outstanding American creative and performing artists to Germany.
8. That projects be considered for inclusion in the program on the basis of their contribution to democratization and reorientation objectives

---

[3] See Pilgert, *op. cit.*, pp. 14-15.

rather than the increase of German scientific and technical competence.

9. That special attention be given to the inclusion in the program of groups or individuals in Germany who have demonstrated their devotion to democratic ideals, who are actual or potential leaders, or who are particularly susceptible to anti-democratic influences.
10. That a vigorous publicity campaign be undertaken in Germany concerning the reception and activities of German exchanges in the United States.

The State Department in Washington would have responsibilities in connection with the exchanges program as follows:[4]

1. General policy guidance, program proposals, and suggestion of projects.
2. Consideration and final approval of total annual exchange of persons program proposal, and of adjustments or additions thereto which may be proposed in the course of the year, as recommended by the Exchanges Division and endorsed by the Policy Board.
3. Contact and correspondence with all public and private agencies, institutions, and individuals in the United States cooperating in the program on a contractual or voluntary basis.
4. Negotiation of contracts and control and supervision of contractual services performed by the Institute of International Education in relation to the German students program, including solicitation of scholarship and placement opportunities for German students and matching of approved candidates with such opportunities.
5. Arrangement of sponsorship of German leaders, experts, specialists, and trainees by suitable public and private agencies, organizations, and institutions in the United States, review and final approval of programs of observation, study, or training arranged by such sponsoring agencies for German participants in particular projects.
6. Recruiting and preliminary briefing of U.S. visiting experts to go to Germany under the program.
7. Security clearance of all German and U.S. citizens participating in projects under the program.
8. Reception and orientation of German exchangees arriving in the United States.
9. Issuance and transmittal of travel orders to all American and German exchangees; arrangements of U.S. travel, and disbursement of funds to all American exchangees and all Germans except those whose projects are administered by other federal agencies under contract.

---

[4] See Pilgert, *op. cit.*, pp. 15-16.

10. Arrangement of press interviews and other suitable publicity coverage of German exchangees in the United States; collection, screening, and transmission to the field of publicity material concerning German exchangees suitable for use in Germany.

These policy statements are included because otherwise it might be assumed that little or no detailed attention had been given to working out the necessary arrangements for a program which, unlike most of the activities of the United States in Germany, involved operations both in Germany and in the United States. A program operating in two widely separated parts of the world—at home and abroad—by its very nature would present difficulties and one would expect a certain amount of stress and strain, misunderstanding, working at cross purposes, and the like. However, during many months of the most crucial period of the exchanges program in Germany, the relations between the Exchanges Division of HICOG and the section of the State Department responsible for the Washington end were about as unsatisfactory as could be imagined. A large part of the time and energy that should have been expended in perfecting a program was directed to the "cold" and not infrequently it seemed "hot" war between Washington and the field and to a lesser degree between the Exchanges Division of HICOG and other field agencies.

In looking over the division of responsibility noted above, one is not aware of any very major defects. The provision giving the Exchanges Division of HICOG "exclusive responsibility for the control and administration of all exchange of persons projects, *including responsibility for all stateside contacts* relative to the program,"* is somewhat vague, it is true, and would seem to be inconsistent with authority reserved by the State Department. The reserving of security clearance to Washington also might be regarded as questionable as far as effective administration was concerned, but, considering the prevailing public opinion in the United States, one could hardly have expected anything else.

Some of the trouble was doubtless the result of the almost inevitable conflict which seems to develop between central and field agencies. This is to be noted in administrative organizations which operate

---

* The *underlining* has been inserted by the author to indicate words which might occasion conflict.

only in the United States, and it seems to be intensified when the field agency is in a foreign country, particularly when under a military occupation. Few of the subdivisions of OMGUS or HICOG enjoyed the most amicable and cooperative relations with their Washington counterparts. The fact that the exchanges program was dual in nature and necessitated fairly complex activities both in Germany and in the United States certainly added to the strains and stresses and misunderstandings.

But these factors do not seem to account fully for the bitterness of the conflict which was waged between the Exchanges Division of HICOG and Washington. The fact that the exchanges program seemed to be enveloped in a sort of "holy" atmosphere probably intensified the difficulties. To the exchanges staff in Germany and at least to some degree to the State Department staff responsible for this program this particular activity of the United States seemed to take on a sort of religious significance which one did not find in most other undertakings. The very nature of the exchanges program was fundamentally noble, it was said, and anything done in the name of promoting exchanges was tinged with infallibility. The slightest criticism was resented. As a result the field staff in Germany felt outraged when Washington tried to raise questions—such queries were not regarded as part of the ordinary process of administration but rather as unreasonable interference.

Finally, there were personal and other more ordinary factors involved in this difficult situation. The Washington officials often seemed condescending and patronizing in their attitude, as perhaps usually is the case in the eyes of field staffs. They seemed to have little understanding of the actual problems confronting the staff in Germany, being content to exercise their authority from offices in Washington. Their attitude often seemed to be rigid rather than flexible. They did not do a particularly good job of communicating their ideas and motives to the staff in Germany. Some of them seemed to have comparatively little background which fitted them for work in the exchanges field—they were simply bodies employed to hold a position on the government payroll. Some of these weaknesses resulted from a situation described by the *New York Times* as follows: "While everyone from the President down seems to believe that educational exchange is wonderful, the agency under which it is administered is treated something like a stepchild in the State Department, with no top-ranking official showing really vital interest in it."[5]

From the Washington vantage point, the exchanges staff in Germany lacked proper respect for the State Department and its representatives and appeared to consider themselves more or less independent. They seemed so out of touch with current developments in the United States that they failed to appreciate political and other pressures. They exhibited a touchiness which made it impossible to carry on normal relations. They took pride in ignoring and, on occasion, even defying Washington, seeming to feel that they were the only ones who counted in the exchanges program. At times they gave the impression of lacking imagination, perception, and even professional qualifications.

It seems clear that neither the State Department officials nor the field staff had understanding, mutual respect, and willingness to adjust in sufficient measure. Dr. Ralph A. Burns, a professor of education at Dartmouth College and the chief of the Exchanges Division of HICOG for several years following 1949 when the exchanges program was in a particularly formative stage, had been taken over from OMGUS. He and his chief associates gave themselves wholeheartedly to their task, but they tolerated no criticisms and tended to regard the exchanges field as their own empire. They not only breathed fire at the mere mention of their opposite numbers in Washington, but managed the extra energy for waging a feud with the Education Division of HICOG.

Although an interdivisional committee was maintained at HICOG to coordinate the plans of the various offices and divisions relating to exchanges with the work of the Exchanges Division, a rather acute situation developed. The Education Division, for example, considered itself primarily responsible for planning the exchanges program involving teachers and educational personnel; the Office of Political Affairs had more or less the same attitude in regard to the exchange of German officials from the *Länder* and the West German Federal Government; the Office of Legal Affairs did not take kindly to any invasion of its prerogative to select the judges, lawyers, and others

---

[5] *New York Times*, June 20, 1956. Though written after the occupation had ended in Germany, these words seem to fit the earlier situation.

from the legal field to be sent to the United States to observe judicial administration. But the Exchanges Division, as noted above, conceived of itself as the infallible instrument in the entire exchanges program.[6] Conflict was inevitable under such circumstances, though it fell short of that characterizing the Exchanges Division and Washington.

TYPES OF EXCHANGE PROGRAMS

Various types of exchange programs were developed to meet the needs of the operating subdivisions of OMGUS and HICOG. Modifications, of course, took place from time to time, and the emphasis on the individual programs varied widely from period to period. The most ambitious exchange of persons programs were as follows: (1) German leaders and experts to visit the United States, (2) German students to visit the United States, (3) American specialists to visit Germany, (4) German teen-agers to live with American families for a year, and (5) the Economic Cooperation Administration scheme involving industrial personnel.

There would probably be a large measure of agreement that the program aimed at bringing German leaders and experts to the United States has received the greatest amount of support. When other programs were allowed to wane, this one continued to flourish and it was apparently destined to operate at least on a curtailed scale after the occupation had ended. This program involved the selection of mature Germans who had established themselves in places of responsibility in German political life, in the professions, and in other significant fields. Although originally limited to the American Zone, this program after 1949 was extended to all parts of Western Germany. More than a thousand of these leaders were brought in a single year to the United States for periods ordinarily ranging from 30 to 120 days.

A breakdown for a single year (1951) when the program was operating at a high level may be of interest:[7]

---

[6] On occasion it appeared to ignore completely outside considerations. Thus in Project F-5023-E, "Development of Research, Administrative Methods and Procedures in Home Economics" which called for nine German women specialists, it submitted the names of five men to Washington. See Pilgert, *op. cit.*, pp. 62-63.

[7] See Pilgert, *op. cit.*, p. 43.

223

Educational personnel...................... 169
Community leaders......................... 156
Information specialists...................... 20
Religious leaders.......................... 30
Women leaders............................ 62
Public health and welfare specialists........... 101
Political leaders........................... 228
Labor leaders............................. 166
Legal experts............................. 30
Food and agriculture....................... 83
Journalists, radio-broadcasters, publishers, etc.... 85

The German students program, though supported by some advocates as one of the most promising, received less support than the leaders program. It was argued that students were a more uncertain proposition to begin with because they had not as yet reached the point where they have demonstrated their worth to society. Being immature they are presumably more adaptable, it is true, but their impressions are perhaps less enduring. Moreover, they presented a problem because many became enamored of American life and opportunities and, marrying American girls, wanted to live permanently in the United States. Also, it was not ordinarily feasible to send students to the United States for less than a year and this involved heavy expense if they were entirely dependent on public funds. An effort was made to secure financial grants for many of these from colleges and universities in the United States, and public funds paid only transportation charges. As many as a thousand German students were brought to the United States in a single year to study teacher-training methods, community activities, social work, farm methods, law, labor affairs, government, and journalism.

The greatest concentration of American specialists to Germany was during the military government and early High Commission periods of the occupation. As the High Commission period progressed, this program tapered off and, before the occupation ended, it had almost disappeared. As many as 192 visiting experts from the United States went to Germany in a single year to consult, to lecture, to advise, and all too frequently, it must be admitted, to twiddle their thumbs. Education personnel outnumbered all other categories, with more than one fourth of the visiting experts belonging to this group. But fairly large numbers of community activity specialists,

224

public health and welfare leaders, and political affairs experts were brought to Germany. Their transportation was paid, they were given a per diem salary of from $5-$35, and they received a living allowance of $6 per day. They usually remained for periods of from three to nine months, though special dispensations were sometimes made.

The teen-age program brought several hundred German youth between the ages of 16 and 19 annually to spend a year in the United States as a member of an American family, usually a farm family, and to attend an American high school. The Grange served as an agent for arranging many of these placements and the host families provided board and lodging. The transportation and other incidental costs were met out of public funds.

Finally, there was the program administered by the Economic Cooperation Administration. Productivity teams, business leaders, and others were sent to the United States to study industrial techniques and methods. In general, this program was well administered and proved valuable. It virtually disappeared when the International Cooperation Administration was incorporated into the State Department.

SELECTION OF GERMAN EXCHANGEES

To begin with, there was no formal system for selecting Germans to visit the United States, and the fact that there was abuse is not surprising. In certain cases, for example, American officials took advantage of an excellent opportunity to send their German mistresses on an excursion to the United States. In others, selection was regarded as a reward for faithful service rendered by Germans to various American offices and agencies. These weaknesses were quickly eliminated by providing that relatives, employees in American installations, etc., were not eligible. Actually, in an effort to avoid abuse, probably too many safeguards were stipulated—the disqualification of those Germans who worked for American agencies eliminated some very promising and worthwhile candidates.

As the program progressed, efforts were made to bring the exchanges opportunities to the attention of large numbers of Germans. Press releases were sent to the German newspapers and posters announcing the offerings were placed in *Amerika Häuser*, the OMGUS and HICOG offices in the field, and elsewhere. Notices were sent by mail to various German educational institutions, professional groups, and other agencies, calling attention to the exchange programs in the several categories. As a result of such publicity, considerable interest was generated and numerous applications were forthcoming, particularly in the student and teen-age programs.

Applications were processed in various ways, dependent upon the time and the type of program. At first, *Kreis* resident officers in the local areas of the American Zone handled most of the applications for mass programs, but after the local offices were closed other arrangements obviously had to be made. In the French and British Zones, applications were received through *Land* offices. In Bremen and Berlin, applications were processed even during the period of resident officers by an exchanges officer. In the cases of specialized programs involving teachers, journalists, lawyers, and others, the functional divisions of OMGUS and HICOG often had a leading role in securing applications and, even when these were lodged with resident officers and exchanges officers, these divisions received the applications for processing. The leader program, by way of contrast, was noncompetitive and functional divisions made nominations on their own intiative, usually after consulting with Germans.

In the general programs, panels of Germans canvassed records, interviewed candidates, and made recommendations. There were also such German panels for more specialized programs, though labor unions recommended candidates for labor exchanges and special arrangements were sometimes made in other limited programs. Recommendations of these panels were sent to a *Land* selection committee, composed of representative German leaders without respect to specialization under the chairmanship of an American representative of the Exchanges Division. These committees were larger in size than the lower panels, often including as many as fifteen Germans drawn from *Land* ministries of Education, universities, labor unions, public administrators, lawyers, doctors, journalists, welfare workers, etc. The selection committees interviewed candidates individually or in groups and evaluated them on an "A," "B," or "C" point basis on such matters as technical qualifications, leadership and initiative, influence and contact with other Germans, educability and alertness

226

to new ideas, maturity and stability, education and general knowledge, and proficiency in English.[8]

Reports and recommendations of the selection committees went to the Exchanges Division and ordinarily recommendations were followed by that agency, though occasional rejections might be made. The nominations of the functional divisions in the leader program also were similarly processed by the Exchanges Division and this, as noted above, resulted in clashes, because the functional divisions had ideas that did not always coincide with those tenaciously held by the Exchanges Division. The Exchanges Division communicated with the American consul in the district where a candidate resided in order to start security clearance, but final action in this matter had to be referred to the State Department and the Office of the Attorney General in Washington under the Internal Security Act of 1950. The last step before final appointment was the sending of the papers of those selected in Germany to the State Department.

EVALUATING COMMENTS

A program such as the exchanges program in Germany is bound to be controversial and there will be an honest difference of opinion as to its worth among those who attempt to be fair-minded. Consequently, it is not surprising that one finds those who regard the program as without flaw or blemish and one of the most successful undertakings ever launched by the United States. At the other extreme are those who are highly critical, maintaining that so many weaknesses entered in that the evils outweighed the achievements. Most of those who have observed the program in action and try to be objective probably fall somewhere between these extremes. Many honestly see in the exchanges program an undertaking which, though not perfect, has accomplished extremely valuable results. A fairly sizable group of others do not dispute the concrete results of a constructive character, but they are so aware of the serious shortcomings arising out of the strife between the field and Washington and among the Exchanges Division and the functional divisions in Germany

---

[8] For a sample rating sheet, see Pilgert, *op. cit.*, p. 26.

that they regard the record as disappointing and less impressive than the American people had a right to expect.

Although a definitive evaluation cannot be made at this time, it does seem justifiable to make various comments at the end of the occupation period. Some thousands of Germans, young and old, male and female, experienced and inexperienced, established in their professions and yet to start their professional activities, were brought to the United States under the exchanges program. Some remained only a few weeks; others stayed for many months. Many millions of dollars were expended—a single year's program has cost in excess of six million dollars.

It is clear that many Germans now know more about the surface of life in the United States than was earlier the case. Having seen American cities, American legislatures at work, American industrial establishments, American schools and universities, American retail outlets, American railroads, air lines, and steamships at first hand, they have gained a familiarity with the structure of the United States that could not possibly result from reading, seeing films, and the like. Almost all of the German exchanges have met Americans of varying status, and they therefore have certain impressions to supplement those derived from the Americans stationed in Germany.[9]

It is probable that most of the German exchangees have enjoyed their visits to the United States. Some have complained at the inadequate allowances made to them for meeting expenses; others have not found American food to their liking. Many have said that they were exhausted at the end of their visits. A number have encountered treatment, particularly in the earlier years on the troop ships, which marred their pleasure to a considerable degree. A fair number have found it impossible to do what they wanted or hoped to do. Students have frequently been disappointed because they could not be assigned to the universities which they regarded as the ones with the greatest prestige. Some of the German leaders have found Americans whom they expected to see absent from their offices or perhaps too busy to give them more than a brief appointment.

[9] For reactions of returned exchangees, see Pilgert, *op. cit.*, pp. 68-74, summarizing the results of a survey conducted by a German member of the staff of the Historical Division of HICOG. Also see "German Youth View of the American Program," Office of Public Affairs, Office of the U. S. High Commissioner for Germany, Report No. 44, Series No. 2, Oct. 30, 1950.

The Exchanges Program

A few have been utterly disappointed and disillusioned as a result of their visits to the United States. Certain public officials have found in the spoils system of the United States something which they at least regard as more evil than anything to be encountered in German government. After being severely criticized for their treatment of the Jews, some German exchangees have been unprepared to find anti-semitism in the United States in some quarters. In contrast to the democratic sentiments expressed by visiting lecturers in Germany, some of the Germans have witnessed treatment accorded to Negroes, Mexicans, and other minority racial groups in the United States which has shocked them. Standards in certain American educational institutions have sometimes seemed inferior to those familiar in Germany.[10]

Perhaps the most serious failure to be noted is that the exchanges program has not succeeded in bringing most of the German visitors into intimate contact with American home life or with American life beneath the surface. The teen-agers constitute a glaring exception, since they have become integral parts of American families for a year and have acquired an intimate knowledge of the standards that characterize such a social unit, the relationships between husband and wife, parents and children, brothers and sisters, etc. Moreover, attending a rural school in the United States for a year, they have come to know a great deal about social patterns in the rural areas of the United States. But the leaders have frequently had little opportunity to penetrate beneath the surface. They have rarely been entertained in an American home more than once or twice, if at all, and then only briefly. The contacts of the German students in the universities have often been very superficial, though in the smaller colleges it has been possible to bring them into reasonably close contact with fellow-students. It may be argued that it is not feasible to achieve such personal relationships between exchangees and Americans and it is certainly not easy. However, an exchanges program which is aimed not so much at increasing professional and technical knowledge as acquainting the visitors with the spirit and

---

[10] The attitudes of a small number of Germans are presented in a monograph by the Institute of Social Research of the University of Michigan entitled *Learning Across Cultures, A Study of Germans Visiting America* (University of Michigan Press, Ann Arbor, 1955).

basic foundations of the American way of life must inevitably fail unless more than a surface understanding can be offered.

Possibly because the State Department and others responsible have desired to avoid the evils of the Russian pattern under which visitors have usually been carefully guided and had little leeway, it seems probable that too little careful planning has gone into the exchanges program.[11] German leaders have often not used their time to the greatest advantage because of the lack of detailed arrangements. They have not always seen the Americans who could offer them the most. Much of their time has been spent in more or less routine sightseeing. They have not observed how the American political system actually operates through committees, discussions in lobbies, conversations in offices, and the like. It is of course not a simple matter to see behind the scenes in American politics and government.

All too often the officials in charge of the exchanges program have not themselves had sufficient background to know what can be done to the greatest advantage. They have frequently been comparatively low-level employees who just happen to be working in the exchanges section of the government because they need jobs. Thus it is inevitable that the arrangements that they make will be more or less conventional, if not ineffective. Private agencies under contract to administer some of the programs may have had more capable staffs in certain instances, but the amounts which they were paid were not sufficiently large to cover the cost of adequate planning, detailed arranging, and careful evaluation. Students have been sent to universities to pursue special programs, but too little effort has been made to ascertain that the universities would agree to waive their rigid requirements to the extent necessary to enable the German exchangee to derive maximum advantage. It has not been uncommon for German students to arrive at an American university, with of course only a single year in which to complete their special program, only to find that the administrative officials subjected them to the regular requirements of American candidates for degrees. Thus they were required to meet the mathematics requirement, the science re-

---

[11] However, some good schedules have been worked out. For an article by one who did some of this scheduling, see Paul Van Riper, "The Cultural Exchange Program," *Annals of the American Academy of Political and Social Science*, Jan. 1950.

quirement, the language requirement, the fine arts requirement, the philosophy requirement, and so forth, as well as have the prerequisites for the special courses they had been sent to take. By the time they had taken the various required courses there was little if any time to take the courses for which they had come and then they might well find that they could not be admitted to these courses because they lacked the prerequisites. The net result has been that the year has been largely wasted professionally and there has been only the nebulous advantage of having spent a year on an American campus.*

No mention has been made thus far of the weaknesses which have characterized the selection process. One cannot overlook the more or less complicated machinery which has been set up, but there is some reason to believe that so much emphasis may have been put on the machinery that sight has been lost of the main goal. At any rate, those who have had much contact with the German exchangees in the United States have frequently felt that the job of selection has been poor. Of course, some very able Germans have been brought, but too many have seemed to lack the personal qualities and the professional background to profit more than minutely from a visit to the United States financed by public funds.[12] The term "leader" must be very loosely defined by some of those who administer the leader program, since some of those selected have had little in their records to suggest that they occupy positions of more than slight influence in Germany. Indeed, the entire program has suffered as a result of the feeling on the part of some American participants that more than a minimum of time devoted to exchangees was not worth the effort. In fairness it must be pointed out that many of the top leaders have been unable to get away or possibly have been uninterested, but does this justify sending nonentities?

If the old adage that one enemy can counteract the good work of twenty-five friends has any foundation, the United States in administering the exchanges program has built up a considerable amount

---

* It is only fair to note that some universities have established a more satisfactory record. Foreign student advisers on some campuses have accomplished a good deal, particularly during the final years of the occupation.

[12] Certain observers have maintained that first-rate candidates would not subject themselves to the "tortuous procedure" of selection, leaving second- and third-raters to receive the awards. See Pilgert, *op. cit.*, p. 65.

of enmity among the Germans which may prove a serious liability. Obviously not all applicants can be given appointments, but if seemingly well-qualified candidates feel that they have been dealt with unfairly, a serious situation may develop which will in large measure counteract the good affects. The security aspect of the exchanges program has been a most difficult one and exchanges officials themselves have been more or less powerless to do anything about its shortcomings. Nevertheless, something is seriously wrong when German candidates in considerable numbers feel that they have been badly treated. It has been fairly commonplace for Germans to be informed that they had been selected under some exchange program and that they should make the necessary arrangements to leave home on a given date, only to have such a notice withdrawn later. After making the arrangements, bidding their families and friends farewell, putting their business affairs in shape, being honored guests at farewell parties, etc., they have been informed a day or even a few hours before the time for departure that their appointments have been canceled. The humiliation and even rage which results can well be understood.

If there have been serious weaknesses in the exchanges program designed to bring Germans to the United States, the record is not much if any better in the case of the effort to take American specialists to Germany. This program has not operated to any large extent since 1951, but while it did have funds it convinced many observers of its serious shortcomings. Some excellent appointments were made and valuable contributions were certainly given by various able men. But there were too many cases of Americans who seemed to have little or nothing to offer Germans, regarded the exchanges program as merely an opportunity to see Europe at the taxpayers' expense, did virtually nothing in Germany to justify their visits, and, if they did make any effort, disgusted the Germans by their patronizing manners and unwillingness to see anything of any value outside the United States. Even able visitors sometimes found themselves twiddling their thumbs because of the defects in scheduling. Perhaps by the time they had been cleared and transportation arranged, the program under which they were requested had come to an end. University professors from the United States arrived to lecture at German universities after the academic year had ended and were unable to await a new year. Obviously their visits were a complete waste of public funds. The defense may well be that in a sizable program there are bound to be errors, but one may reasonably inquire whether it was necessary to have so many errors even under the limiting conditions which surrounded the American exchanges program in Germany.[13]

---

[13] A USIE Survey Mission made the following report in 1949: "The performance of United States experts who have come to Germany has been extremely uneven. Some have done excellent work with German groups. . . . Other United States experts have been poorly selected and briefed. Some have come with no clear conception of what they were expected to do. In many instances they have stayed only long enough to become acquainted with the situation or to come to grips with a problem and have returned to the United States about the time when their real usefulness would have commenced." See Pilgert, *op. cit.*, p. 66.

15

Bringing Information to the Germans

From an early date in the occupation it was realized by at least some of the officials of the United States that one of the most constructive services to the German people would be an information program of various sorts.[1] Having been cut off from the world during the war and deprived of international contacts in large measure under the Hitler regime, the rank and file of the Germans knew little of what had been going on without their borders for a long time. During the days when the ration was at a near-starvation level and the war shock was severe, no doubt few of the German people were interested in anything beyond their own survival, the fate of their relatives, and such matters. It is true that many of those most severely hit by the war had scant energy in their personal misery to devote to bringing themselves up-to-date in matters of the outside world. But even at this time many Germans were starved for news of what was happening in other countries; and particularly in the rural areas, where the brunt of the war had been perhaps less heavy, there was a keen interest in looking at films.

As the occupation proceeded, more interest naturally developed, and a more ambitious information program was organized by the United States which eventually covered not only the American Zone but most of West Germany. With RIAS, the powerful radio broadcasting station in Berlin, the information program actually extended into East Germany. The success of the program is attested by the petitions signed by large numbers of Germans to keep information centers open when a movement was under way to close them and by the willingness of the Germans to take over many of the facilities when it was no longer possible for the United States to continue them as the

---

[1] For a discussion of the early attitude and activities, see J. Dunner, "Information Control in the American Zone of Germany, 1945-1946," in C. J. Friedrich and others, *American Experiences in Military Government in World War II* (Rinehart, New York, 1948).

occupation came to an end. The favorable reaction of the Germans was doubtless due not only to their interest in the program itself but also, during the early period, to the constructive character of the information program at a time when most of the American efforts seemed to be directed at negative objectives of one kind or another: denazification, war crimes trials, dismantling, demilitarization, decartelization, and the like.

THE PRESS

The Allies occupying Germany thought that any German newspapers still being published should be closed because of the system of control which the Nazis had established over the press. No German newspaper of any independence had appeared for some years: editors and owners who resisted the Nazi control were sent to concentration camps and their papers taken over by the party. In order to fill this gap temporarily, American military government decided to publish its own newspapers for the Germans, and ten papers with a combined circulation of some 3,785,000 copies appeared during the first few months of the occupation.[2] However, it was recognized that American newspapers were no permanent answer to the problem and that, except as an emergency measure, there should be a "German press run by Germans." A system of licensing was initiated and German-operated newspapers gradually made their appearance. As the German papers became available, the military government publications were terminated; six ended in October 1945 and three in November, leaving only *Die Neue Zeitung*, which was really not a good example of an "overt" publication, since it was started as late as October 18, 1945, to represent American military government directly.

As early as July 31, 1945, a German newspaper was given a license in Frankfurt under the name *Frankfurter Rundschau*, but the process of granting licenses was slow in the beginning. In September, October, and November more speed was developed and 19 newspapers were given licenses, thus providing a newspaper for every sizable city in the American Zone. By the end of the licensing period in mid-1949, 59

---

[2] The information on which this section is based is taken in large measure from Henry P. Pilgert, *Press, Radio, and Film in West Germany*, a monograph in the Historical Series of the Office of the U. S. High Commissioner for Germany (1953).

newspapers were being published in the American Zone. If the progress in the American Zone seems slow, it may be noted that the British granted no licenses to newspapers until January 1946.

Under the American licensing system an effort was made to encourage a free German press without close ties with political parties or other special interest groups. In granting licenses newspapers were encouraged to have editorial staffs made up of representatives of several political parties—even Communists were included to begin with. Press officers were provided by the United States in OMGUS, in the *Land* offices of military government, and in the field on the basis of a single press officer for each two or three *Kreise* (counties). But these officers permitted the German editors considerable leeway, exercising more of a post-publication censorship than the direct control which the French saw fit to institute over newspapers in their zone. Since newsprint was very limited in supply during the early period of the occupation, American military government allocated supplies on a quarterly basis. Through this as well as by reprimands, and in extreme cases the revocation of licenses, the American officials were able to control the German newspapers quite effectively without making them mere instruments of American military government.

It was sometimes charged that the United States paid more attention to its own ends in granting licenses than to recognizing outstanding journalistic talent. In a sense this was true, since major emphasis was placed on licensing only those with anti-Nazi records. Many of the most active journalists found it difficult to get re-established in their professions after the war. Many of those who edited newspapers were far from skilled and in some instances had had little recent experience in newspaper publishing. The fact that the Nazis had obliterated most of the qualities which make for great journalism undoubtedly contributed substantially to the slow progress in retrieving the superior position enjoyed by some German newspapers before 1933. The limited supply of newsprint and the willingness of the Germans to buy almost any paper, however bad, during the early years of the occupation, were also influential. Nevertheless, by the end of the occupation certain newspapers appearing in Frankfurt, Munich, Stuttgart, and Bremen had established very good journalistic reputations, comparing favorably with the better newspapers in the United States.

236

Bringing Information to the Germans

In September 1948 the United States decided to put an end to licensing as soon as the German *Länder* could provide satisfactory legislation for guaranteeing freedom of the press. No licensing was to be permitted by the Germans, and the only censorship was to be through legislation dealing with libel, defamation, breach of the peace, and the like. Strangely enough, this announcement brought considerable criticism from the Germans rather than relief, as might have been expected. The licensed press was apprehensive of the cut-throat competition which some of the wealthy Nazi publishers threatened. The German *Länder* wanted to continue licensing on their own and did not look favorably on the safeguards to a free press which American military government demanded. It was therefore May 1949 before licensing by military government actually came to an end. At this time there were 113 newspapers being published under license in the three states of Hesse, Bavaria, and Württemberg-Baden in the American Zone.

Having ended licensing the United States by no means lost its interest in the German press. When it appeared that the presses used by the licensed newspapers were in large part owned by the former Nazi publishers and that after licensing came to an end these facilities might not be available to the newspapers started under military government, the United States devised an ingenious scheme by which money collected under a 20 per cent license fee on newspaper gross receipts beginning in 1945 and ECA counterpart funds were loaned to German publishers to enable them to purchase modern press equipment and otherwise strengthen their positions. The sum of 36,210,000 Reichsmarks from the 48,000,000 RM collected in fees had been turned over by OMGUS early in 1948 to furnish capital for a press cooperative bank to assist publishers in purchasing presses and supplies, but this was drastically reduced under currency reform to DM 2,350,000. Also as a result of currency reform, the private capital of the newspapers licensed by the United States was frequently not adequate to meet the basic needs. After the West German Federal Government had declined to appropriate DM 15,000,000 for a press aid fund, HICOG arranged for this amount to be made available in ECA counterpart funds. This money was loaned to newspapers that could meet the requirements and was to be repaid during the period 1955-1960. As a result, the former Nazis found it much more difficult to

237

get their publications launched after the licensing period ended than would otherwise have been the case, and the section of the German press which had already demonstrated its loyalty to the objectives of a free press was not crowded to the wall.*

In order to give the German people an example of American journalism, *Die Neue Zeitung* was published from the autumn of 1945 until almost the end of the occupation. Starting out as a newspaper published twice a week in Munich, *Die Neue Zeitung* became a daily paper in September 1947 and appeared eventually in three editions from Munich, Frankfurt, and Berlin. At the end the Munich and Frankfurt editions were closed down and only a Berlin edition was published to meet the special needs of that city. *Die Neue Zeitung* announced itself on its masthead as an American newspaper in Germany and not only gave special attention to reporting American news but supposedly embodied American journalistic traditions. Perhaps it succeeded in the former to a greater extent than in the latter—at least its columns gave much attention to items which OMGUS and HICOG desired to bring to the attention of the German people. An American newspaper reader in Germany would probably have found difficulty in recognizing *Die Neue Zeitung* as a sample of American journalism because of the slight space devoted to advertising (no advertising was permitted prior to October 1949), the inclusion of literary contributions, and the tendency toward dullness rather than sensationalism. Some of this resulted from the predominantly German character of the staff; the necessity of providing the Germans with at least some of the features which they associated with a newspaper also controlled the contents to some extent presumably. Its top circulation ran to some two million copies, but this dropped rapidly after licensing came to an end and German readers had more choice—it was less than half a million in the autumn of 1949. As the pressure became greater and greater to reduce American occupation costs in Germany, proposals were made to end the publication of *Die Neue Zeitung* and it was felt in many quarters by 1952 that its usefulness no longer justified its heavy cost. However, publication was continued despite falling circulation until nearly the end of the occupation

---

* Indeed some of these publishers became wealthy as a result of the advantages enjoyed and this occasioned some bitterness in certain circles. One German editor who had so benefited drove to a HICOG-sponsored meeting in a new Mercedes Benz car driven by a chauffeur; he himself being in afternoon dress wearing a high silk hat.

(January, 1955), though the Munich and Frankfurt editions were dropped.*

In order to provide a news service for the German press American military government set up the *Deutsche Allgemeine Nachrichten Agentur* (DANA) in June 1945. In October 1946, this news service was turned over to the publishers of the licensed newspapers in the American Zone under the name of DENA. In September 1949, as military government came to an end and the High Commission period started, the news service in the American Zone was combined with similar agencies in the British and French Zones. Somewhat earlier (August 1948) the U. S. Feature Service, known in Germany as "*Amerika Dienst*" began its operations in Germany as a representative of the Information Service of the United States. Since the material supplied by this agency was free and much of it was well designed to attract the attention of the readers of German newspapers and periodicals, it enjoyed a wide usage. A survey made in 1951 indicated that *Amerika Dienst* furnished some 10 per cent of all foreign news dispatches and 90 per cent of the American news sent out by DPA, the general German news service.[3] Approximately 1,200 German publications received the feature material of *Amerika Dienst*, and a teletype service supplied the large German newspapers and radio stations directly with the latest news items.[4]

OTHER PUBLISHING PROGRAMS

In addition to licensing newspapers, American military government saw fit to license publishers of books and periodicals during the early period of the occupation. Book dealers were also required to register. As in the case of newspaper licensing, this system came to an end in May 1949.

In order to provide at least a minimum of periodical material in a country which had been accustomed to a great array of periodicals and which following the surrender found itself almost completely bereft of such reading material, the United States military government

---

* The Munich edition was discontinued Sept. 30, 1951.

[3] See Pilgert, *op. cit.*, p. 60.

[4] For an account of OMGUS press activities by one who was a first-hand observer, see Albert Norman, *Our German Policy: Propaganda and Culture* (Vantage, New York, 1951), Chap. 3.

alone or in cooperation with Allies brought out several publications other than newspapers. *Heute,* which reminded Americans somewhat of *Life* in the United States, started publication in the autumn of 1945, first as a monthly and later as a biweekly, and was published until 1951. As a pictorial magazine it is not surprising that it was well received by the Germans, reaching a top circulation of some 750,000 copies. *Amerikanische Rundschau,* a magazine which attempted to combine literary, scientific, and other features, was issued every two months and had a much more limited appeal to the Germans. It was discontinued in 1950. *Neue Auslese,* somewhat similar to *Reader's Digest* in the United States, was a joint British-American enterprise until 1948, when financial losses led the British to withdraw. With a top circulation of 260,000 in March 1948, its circulation fell to some 20,000 in 1950 and it was discontinued. *Der Monat,* a publication of the *Atlantic Monthly* or *Harper's* type, was inaugurated as late as October 1948 and, though it had a group of discriminating readers who were enthusiastic, its circulation remained small—it was estimated that some 30,000 persons saw it.[5] This publication was later transferred to private auspices and in such a guise has succeeded not only in surviving the occupation but establishing a position of leadership in German literary circles.

OMGUS-HICOG undertook the translation of various American books into German and contracted with German publishers to bring them out. This program was started at Bad Homburg as early as 1945. In order to spur the interest of German publishers, arrangements were made to procure paper stock from the scarce paper supply. Several hundred American books were translated into German and published for German readers under this program.[6] In addition, a good many American books were translated into German under private auspices and brought out by German publishing firms. A pamphlet program, inaugurated in 1947, was given much greater support under HICOG in 1950. Copy was supplied by the State Department, by Germans who were employed by HICOG, and by the HICOG publications staff itself. More than 70 pamphlets were printed in

---

[5] See Pilgert, *op. cit.,* p. 57.

[6] 341 books had been translated and published down to March 1, 1953. See Pilgert, *op. cit.,* p. 61.

editions averaging about 200,000 copies. These were distributed widely to labor organizations, schools and educational institutions, libraries, public officials, and German leaders.

RADIO

American military government to start out used the radio broadcasting facilities within its zone to make announcements to the Germans and to some extent at least to present an information program. Stations were operated at Munich, Frankfurt, Bremen, and Stuttgart. As in the case of the other information facilities, the American policy looked toward turning over the radio broadcasting stations to the Germans, when it appeared that they would be able to operate them in a satisfactory manner. The *Länder* in the American Zone were called upon to enact legislation under which broadcasting facilities would be placed under a council made up of representatives of the public interest, the *Land* government, and educational, economic, and cultural groups. It was required that news must be broadcast without editorial comment. The radio broadcasting stations were turned over to the Germans in 1949.

Throughout the occupation the American Forces Network (AFN) operated as a broadcasting agency to bring programs to the American military forces stationed in Germany. Its programs were listened to by numerous Germans, but they were primarily of an entertainment variety rather than informational in character, though newscasts might fall under the latter.

When the American forces entered Berlin in 1945, it was assumed that Radio Berlin, located in the western sectors, would be available for Allied broadcasts. However, it shortly became apparent that the Russians had no intention of sharing the facilities of this station and that they were even using it to spread their propaganda among the Germans, often to the detriment of the United States. Hence the United States decided to set up its own radio station in Berlin. This was done first on a very modest scale in February 1946 through wired radio using the telephone system. The damaged character of the municipal telephone system and the fact that many people had no access to telephones led the United States to abandon this system after

241

a few months. In September 1946 a radio station using the conventional system was set up under American auspices in Berlin under the name of RIAS. And after the stations in the American Zone were returned to German control, RIAS remained the chief broadcasting facility of the United States in Germany, being operated throughout the occupation. Intended originally for the people of Berlin and operating with a 1,000-watt transmitter, it was later employed in large measure as a means of communicating with the people of East Germany. The Russians started out by more or less laughing off American efforts in this field, but they soon realized that American RIAS had to be taken seriously and consequently started their program of jamming and other interference. Various devices including increasing the power of RIAS were resorted to in order to meet the Russian interference. A re-broadcast station at Hof in Bavaria transmitted the RIAS broadcasts to areas behind the Iron Curtain where the Russian interference was particularly effective.

There can be little doubt that RIAS deserves a position as one of the most important information devices of the United States in Germany. Large numbers of Germans in Berlin and in East Germany regularly listened to its broadcasts and indeed depended upon it as their main contact with the free world. While RIAS displayed considerable ingenuity in planning its programs, it faced the difficult problem of deciding how to divide the time between entertainment and serious informational broadcasts. The American pattern of regarding the radio as primarily a medium of entertainment naturally influenced RIAS and its programs included a considerable amount of popular music and other light features. The West Berliners apparently liked this mixture of entertainment and information, though, as time passed and the German stations became more active, they could rely on the latter for entertainment. The people behind the Iron Curtain who listened to RIAS were sometimes critical of the entertainment features of the broadcasts, maintaining that it was intolerable that they should be expected to run the risk of tuning in on RIAS only to hear dance tunes.[7]

---

[7] For additional discussion of the radio activities of the United States, see Pilgert, *op. cit.*, Chap. 6.

THE FILM PROGRAM

The Nazis had so taken over the German movie industry that the victorious Allies considered it necessary to ban the production and showing of films until a system of control had been worked out. The Nazi holding company, UFA, which had enjoyed a monopoly over film production and distribution and also owned the big theatres, was taken over and its assets broken up, but this required several years.[8] An effort was made to license film producers, and some 150 German firms received recognition. But the financial and other problems were such that the progress was very slow. By mid-1952 only some 36 of these concerns had produced any films at all. The United States also controlled the entry of foreign films into its zone in Germany during the early years of the occupation, and the inferior and antiquated character of many of these importations led to widespread criticism.*

From an information standpoint, the direct activities of the United States in connection with the movie field were perhaps most important, though a great deal of effort was expended in liquidating UFA and licensing new film producers. In cooperation with the British, American military government produced a newsreel under the title "*Welt im Film*" which until 1949 had to be shown in all German movie houses. It is estimated that some twenty million Germans saw this feature every month during the winter and fourteen million during the summer. In 1950 this project was taken over by HICOG as an exclusive venture, and in 1952 it was dropped because the German newsreel producers seemed to be competent to cover the field. Whether they liked it or not, the millions of Germans who attended the movies had to look at the "*Welt im Film*" unless they covered their eyes during its showing. Actually this feature enjoyed considerable popularity among the German movie-goers because of its good technical and interest-holding qualities.

Possibly the most important single American information activity

---

[8] On activities in the movie field, see Pilgert, *op. cit.*, Chap. 7.

* Royalties from these foreign films could not be converted into foreign currencies and hence there was little incentive to bring in new films of good quality. The large DM balances resulting were later used by American, Italian, French, and British companies to make films in Germany. This further weakened the German film industry and caused not a little bitterness.

243

in the film field, at least during the first years of the occupation and in rural areas, was the showing of documentary films. With almost all types of group activities except church services banned during the early days of the occupation and with living conditions miserable, the Germans were understandably eager to attend any sort of gathering from which they could extract a little relief from the boredom of everyday living. The showing of documentary films in the villages, schools, and elsewhere under American military government auspices attracted large audiences. The military government units located in the *Kreise* all were furnished projectors and German operators, together with an assortment of short documentary films. Under regular schedules, these films were shown at schools during the day and to groups of adults in various halls and even out-of-doors during the summer in the evening. Originally, the films were collected from any possible sources in the United States and often had little or no bearing on the program of the occupation in Germany. They were prepared for American audiences and, though German titles might be added, their script was in English. But irrespective of their strange character and frequently mediocre quality, they served as an acceptable, if not always a very palatable, diet to the film-hungry Germans. Many of these documentary films were based on travel in the national parks and other scenic spots in the United States; others were prepared by American industrial concerns to advertise their products; still others were of the public health and educational variety. As time passed, some use was made of documentary films obtained from Britain and other democratic countries. Special films prepared under American military government auspices were also made available.

In the rural areas it was not uncommon to encounter persons in the group looking at the documentary films who confessed that they had never seen any kind of a motion picture previously. What sort of a notion the Germans got from this fantastic mixture of odds and ends of films, it is difficult to say. Certainly here was no organized course of indoctrination or propaganda, though, after the special documentaries prepared under military government were circulated, there was at least some semblance of central theme perhaps. It is probable that the main ideas which many Germans living in the rural areas have of the United States and of the American way of life have been derived from the documentary films which they turned out to see in such numbers. So great indeed was the demand that it was difficult to keep the projectors in repair, to provide transportation for the operators and their equipment, and to give the German operators time to breathe. Admission to these showings was free, and some two and half million persons attended them each month. As the German movies got back on their feet, the need for this program was reduced and in urban areas the documentaries were then shown only in the America Houses.[9]

AMERICA HOUSES

The U. S. Information Center or America House program got a fairly late start in Germany, but it eventually came to a point where it occupied a large role in the American information program.[10] Shortly after the German surrender, the Psychological Warfare Branch of the Army experimented with a reading room for Germans at Bad Homburg, near Frankfurt. This modest venture seemed to indicate the need for a center where Germans could go to obtain American and Allied publications. In 1947 the Bad Homburg library was moved to the city of Wiesbaden and opened as a U. S. Information Center and soon other centers were inaugurated in about a dozen of the cities of the American Zone. This number was later increased to 20 and finally 26, and the 26 Information Centers operated 137 reading rooms in smaller places located in their vicinity. Under OMGUS these centers were confined to the American Zone, but after the establishment of HICOG an effort was made to extend the program to various key places in West Germany and centers were opened in Hamburg, Hannover, and Essen. There was an information center in West Berlin and in the following cities in the American Zone: Munich, Frankfurt, Stuttgart, Bremen, Wiesbaden, Marburg, Würzburg, Erlangen, Heidelberg, Bamberg, Fulda, Augsburg, Nuremberg, Giessen, Darmstadt, Kassel, Mannheim, Heilbronn, Ulm, Coburg, Regensburg, Karlsruhe, and Bremerhaven. The name "*Amerika Haus*" was applied to the information centers as a result of a contest

---

[9] On the documentary film program, see H. P. Pilgert, *The History of the Development of Information Services Through Information Centers and Documentary Films*, a monograph in the Historical Series of the Office of the U. S. High Commissioner of Germany (1951), Chap. 4.

[10] The material for this section is drawn mainly from Pilgert, *op. cit.*, Chap. 2.

in which German users of the facilities were asked to suggest appropriate names.

The America Houses carried on programs which varied somewhat from time to time and from place to place, depending upon the ingenuity and energy of their directors. However, in general, the program was a fairly homogeneous one which emphasized open-shelf reading rooms, exhibitions of art, showing of films, and evening lectures, concerts, and the like. Of these the library, reading rooms and related bookmobile program probably occupied first place. An average America House had a library of some 16,000 volumes, together with a fairly large number of periodicals, pamphlets, and so forth, whereas a branch reading room consisted of about 2,400 books. About one fourth of the books were in German and the remainder were for the most part in English, though there might be a few in French. Books were arranged on open shelves so that visitors could browse around to see what was available. Tables and chairs were provided for those who wanted to use the materials on the premises, but many of the patrons borrowed the books to read at home. A cheerful and informal atmosphere was intended, in contrast to the traditional German library which was distinctly formal and likely to be not too well lighted. Sections were provided for children. Bookmobiles took books to the Germans living in outlying areas.

The America Houses maintained film collections, an average of some 159 in each center, and also had film strips, slides, and the like. Under certain conditions these could be borrowed for the use of schools and groups. There were also programs at which Germans could view some of these on the premises of the America Houses.

Many Germans were found to have the curious notion that Americans have no artistic interests. In order to correct this to some extent various exhibits of painting and sculpture from the United States were circulated among the America Houses. Visiting singers and other musicians from the United States put on programs during the evening hours and were frequently not only welcomed by numerous Germans but given considerable favorable publicity in the press. Apparently many Germans could hardly believe that the United States produced singers and other musicians, and some of those who attended came more out of curiosity than anything else. The evening programs also featured lectures on various subjects by visiting Americans.

The historic Brandenburg Gate in Berlin on the famous *Unter den Linden*. Decorative parts damaged during the war have been removed. This gate stands almost on the dividing line between the West Sectors of Berlin and the Russian-controlled East Sector.

The devastated old city of Nuremberg shortly after the surrender in 1945.

A typical street in Berlin during the early period of the occupation, showing the almost complete devastation caused by the war. The rubble has been cleared from the surface of the street to allow traffic to pass.

Esso oil refineries at Hamburg. Striking industrial reconstruction has occurred in West Germany since 1948.

Hamburg University Hospital, destroyed during the war.

Hamburg University Hospital after reconstruction.

Bringing Information to the Germans

Other programs arranged by the America Houses drew large numbers of Germans. English classes catered to those desiring to learn English. Groups were organized to discuss current topics of interest. Children came for special children's hours. There were programs for mothers and for parents, for those interested in the theatre, and so forth. A collection of phonograph records drew those who wanted to listen to recordings.

Despite these elaborate programs, the America Houses for some reason never drew the financial support which might have been expected. Enthusiastic comments often were showered on the America Houses by top American authorities in Germany and by visitors from the United States, but, like libraries and educational institutions in the United States, words were more generously given than money. While the libraries were fairly well off and could purchase many of the obvious books and periodicals, funds for providing staffs were not adequate. America Houses often seemed to visitors more "German" in their administration than American, since, except for one or two Americans to direct, the entire staff was made up of Germans—on occasion there was not a single American attached to a center. Not only was the niggardly financial support evidenced by the small American staff but by the relatively low rating given these American employees. Persons doing less specialized and less important work in OMGUS and HICOG received higher salaries because their jobs were classified at a higher level. This made it difficult to recruit the sort of Americans who were needed for the direction of the program. Most of the buildings occupied by America Houses had been taken over on requisition from the Germans. They might be well suited for their new use or they might be poorly adapted, but there were almost always serious limitations. There was little or no money to bring visiting lecturers and artists from the United States and use had to be made mainly of those who were passing through Germany.

One of the chief problems confronting the America Houses was the inability of most Germans to read English sufficiently well to make use of professional books or journals in English. Even those Germans who professed a knowledge of English could rarely do more than read novels, detective fiction, and other light books. Thus the main purpose of the libraries often seemed lost, since the books and periodicals of chief consequence to an information program remained more or less

247

unused on the shelves. The German translation program mentioned earlier helped to some extent, but it was obviously not feasible to translate, and arrange for publication in German of, any considerable proportion of the great number of professional works produced in the United States.

It is difficult to evaluate the significance of the attendance and use made by Germans of America House facilities. When the America Houses were operated at perhaps their maximum effectiveness during the period 1949-1951—after this period a curtailment took place which involved the closing of various centers—attendance varied from somewhat over 600,000 per month to 1,500,000 or so, with the average being over one million. Book circulation was much smaller, running from under 200,000 per month to over 300,000.[11] It was sometimes alleged by detractors of the programs that many of those involved in the above numbers used the America Houses not because of any interest in information about the United States and other democratic countries but as hangouts, much as the down-and-outer may use libraries in the United States to keep warm. America Houses provided no dormitory facilities for the homeless, but their doors were usually open from morning until perhaps ten in the evening and they were well heated, even when it was unpleasantly cold outside. Their cheerful atmospheres and fairly comfortable chairs made it pleasant to spend some hours there if one had nothing to do and perhaps no place to go. A good many of the displaced persons and expellees from the East made use of the America Houses as places of warmth and shelter. It is to the credit of the America House directors that they recognized the misery of these unfortunates and ordinarily permitted them to remain in the centers even when they slept and snored during lectures.

A survey made in March 1948 served to shock American military government personnel and particularly America House staff—it revealed that more than nine Germans out of ten in the American Zone did not know that there were America Houses and U. S. Information Centers. As a result of this, efforts were made to publicize the work of these centers, and later surveys showed that a much larger proportion of Germans were aware of the centers, whether they made use of them or not. A survey in September 1948 in Berlin, Bremen,

---

[11] For a table showing the varying attendance and circulation, see Pilgert, *op. cit.*, between pp. 24-25.

Frankfurt, Nuremberg, and Stuttgart revealed majorities of from 52 per cent to 74 per cent familiar with America Houses. A later study made in May 1950 indicated that 62 per cent of the Germans in the American Zone as a whole were aware of the existence of the U. S. Information Centers.[12] While the attendance figures, not allowing for duplications, show that a million or so Germans were using the Information Centers every month during the years 1949-1950, there is no way of estimating how many different Germans were reached during the course of a year. It is apparent that a fairly small minority of the German people used these information facilities—possibly something like 10 per cent of the population of the American Zone.[13] However, there is reason to believe that many of the users came from the ranks of those somewhat above the average in influence—this despite the many refugees and expellees who frequented them—and that the impact of the program was greater than the numbers attending would suggest. Studies of those availing themselves of the America Houses seem to indicate that twice as large a proportion of young people visited these centers as of the older age groups. In the university towns of Marburg, Heidelberg, Würzburg, and Erlangen it was not surprising that university students and faculty constituted a large proportion of those using the Information Center libraries. Teachers and professional people in general drew more heavily on the resources of the America Houses than public officials and businessmen, and again this is hardly surprising, considering the interests and reading habits of Americans in corresponding classes.[14]

As the occupation neared an end, the reduced funds available and the general retraction of American activities in Germany naturally brought about a drastic curtailment in the Information Center program. The center in Berlin was kept open, and information centers including libraries were operated by American consulates in key cities. But other America Houses had to be closed or arrangements made to turn them over to the Germans. The fact that the Germans indicated a regret that some of the centers were being closed by circulating

---

[12] For a more detailed summary of these surveys, see Pilgert, *op. cit.*, pp. 25-28.

[13] An official estimate as of January 1951 fixed the proportion at 11 per cent. See Pilgert, *op. cit.*, p. 28.

[14] For additional analysis of those using Information Centers, see Pilgert, *op. cit.*, pp. 27-28.

petitions and the willingness of German groups to take over the facilities of certain America Houses that could not be continued under direct American operation suggests an acceptance that cannot be associated with certain other programs of the United States in Germany.

16

American Participation in Economic Reconstruction

The United States gave a great deal of attention to economic matters from the beginning to the end of the occupation of Germany. Even before the occupation started, groups were set up by the German County Unit of SHAEF and the U. S. Group, Control Council for Germany to make preparations for handling the many problems arising out of economic reconstruction. When other subdivisions of American military government and HICOG found it difficult to obtain what they regarded as adequate recognition and staffs, the Economic Affairs subdivision almost invariably fared well.

Despite a prominent formal position and a large staff, the Economic Affairs subdivision perhaps encountered more obstacles and greater frustration during the early period of the occupation than any other agency.[1] It would be difficult to name any other field where so little was accomplished during the early days and where such spectacular achievements were reported before the occupation came to an end. For a considerable time after the occupation started, economic reconstruction was hardly more than a phrase—German economy in the American Zone remained almost prostrate. Indeed, the situation was such that many of the staff members of the Economic Affairs Division found themselves twiddling their thumbs with little or nothing to do. The drastic transformation which brought German industry from this state of collapse to a point where it was booming and producing something like twice as much as it had produced before the war will doubtless long remain one of the most dramatic aspects of the occupation.

---

[1] For a discussion of some of these difficulties, see B. U. Ratchford and W. D. Ross, *Berlin Reparations Assignment* (University of North Carolina Press, Chapel Hill, 1947).

251

The United States in Germany, 1944-1955

In the early planning which was carried on looking toward the occupation of Germany, the basic consideration was twofold: to close down the military and paramilitary plants so as to disarm Germany and to reconstruct the German economy to the point where a reasonable support could be provided for the German people. It was recognized that the German economy was among the most highly industrialized in the world and that it had been long before Hitler was ever heard of in Germany. Therefore, plans were drafted for the ultimate restoration of industrial facilities to the degree essential to make the German people self-supporting and with a standard of living in keeping with modern concepts of an adequate, but not by any means generous, food allowance.[2] There was some vagueness in specifying the exact level of production, since not all factors were clear prior to the German surrender.

The widespread feeling among both the American people and officials as the war came to an end that postwar Germany should be reconstructed on an agricultural-pastoral basis, with industry drastically curtailed, has been mentioned in various connections in this study. In no field was this influence more serious than in the economic. The provisions relating to economic matters of the Potsdam Agreement were in large measure a reflection of such a point of view. The basic Joint Chiefs of Staff directive to the American Commander which served as the foundation of American military government during the critical period from the spring of 1945 to well along in 1947 was even more solidly based on the same philosophy. The result was that the Economic Affairs Division found its hands more or less tied. Even the driving energy of General Draper, the wisdom of Dean Calvin Hoover who had been borrowed from Duke University to advise on economic matters, and the efforts of such men as Laird Bell, James Boyd, and Arthur Barrows were not sufficient to overcome the negative influence of JCS 1067.[3]

The German economy had been badly damaged by the war.[4] But the damage in many cases was surface damage which seemed worse

---

[2] *Handbook for Military Government in Germany*, Chaps. 11-13.

[3] For discussions of the economic policy at this period, see J. F. Byrnes, "U. S. Economic Policy Toward Germany," *Commercial and Financial Chronicle*, Dec. 20, 1945; Department of State, *United States Economic Policy Toward Germany* (1946); E. S. Mason, "Has Our Policy in Germany Failed," *Foreign Affairs*, July 1946.

[4] General Clay concluded that it had "collapsed." See his *Decision in Germany*, p. 202.

than it actually was. A survey conducted by the Foreign Economic Administration of the United States estimated that only some 20 per cent of German industry had been destroyed by the bombing and fighting, leaving approximately 80 per cent intact, even if covered by debris. At the time such an estimate seemed almost fantastically high to those who cast their eyes about the American Zone of Germany. On the basis of impressions gathered from visiting large numbers of industrial areas one might have accepted a figure of 80 per cent covering the destruction and 20 per cent the remaining assets, but certainly not the other way around. However, the FEA estimate was less exaggerated than seemed to be the case—the huge amount of debris resulted in an impression of far greater damage than the facts bore out. Many of the industrial plants could be rather easily cleared out and many machines were in usable condition after the rubbish had been removed.

Not only was the German industrial machine in better shape than appeared on the surface, but the supplies of raw materials and fuel were larger than had been anticipated. Despite the heavy mortality rate occasioned by the bombing and fighting, German manpower remained strong. There had been a great deal of dislocation, it is true, and many of the plants had been manned to a large extent by the slave laborers imported by the Germans from countries which their *Wehrmacht* had overrun and who at once after the defeat refused to work any longer. Nevertheless, manpower was available in sufficient numbers, allowing for the loss of the foreign labor, to operate many of the vital plants. Moreover, the labor force was generally in good physical condition immediately after the surrender. Imported food stocks from the conquered countries had been available to maintain a high calorie food ration in Germany until the final days of the war; adequate clothing was in the possession of most of the workers.

Had American military government been free to proceed immediately with economic reconstruction, how different the story might have been—at least during the period 1945-1948. American expertness in industrial management is known the world over and the Economics Division had on its staff men who could have done a skilled job in getting German industry back into production. But JCS 1067 forbade "steps (a) looking toward the economic rehabilitation of Germany or (b) designed to maintain or strengthen the German economy." [5] According to military government statistics, industrial production in the American Zone was no more than 10 per cent at the end of 1945—more than seven months after the occupation started. And the rate of production during the period from May through December 1945 was estimated at a mere 5 per cent. During the first half of 1946 the rate in the American Zone increased from 10 per cent to some 29 per cent, with an average for the period of something like 20 per cent. Yet the Russians, with less know-how and a much greater amount of dismantling, had managed, at least according to their own claim, to push the production rate in their zone to approximately 33 1/3 per cent.[6]

Although JCS 1067 remained the primary directive to OMGUS during all of 1946 and authorized little or nothing in the way of economic reconstruction, General Clay discovered in the Potsdam Agreement a basis for some leeway in this field.[7] Consequently, he saw his way clear after a time to authorize some action in meeting the critical economic situation. Certainly few situations confronting American military government or HICOG were more desperate than the economic collapse which characterized Germany during this period. The German people were brought as near the door of actual starvation as could easily be imagined short of mass starvation itself.

But by the time the Economic Affairs people found it possible to go ahead, the general situation had deteriorated to such an alarming extent that it was difficult to know where to begin, how to proceed, and what to concentrate on. Moreover, it was often not easy to see any concrete results from the steps taken. The German working force which had been well nourished in mid-1945 was, by 1946, so weak from a food ration of approximately half of the 2,000 calorie standard set as a minimum by food experts for inactive persons that they could not run industrial plants at all effectively, even if they were willing to try. Fuel to run the plants was very scarce and, despite vigorous efforts on the part of OMGUS, remained in short supply because of the debility of the coal miners. The fuel supplies that had been available in many plants immediately after the surrender had disappeared, despite the guards set to protect them. Likewise there were few or no

---

[5] Paragraph 16.
[6] See the *New York Times*, August 12, 1946.
[7] L. D. Clay, *Decision in Germany*, p. 202.

254

raw materials to feed into the industrial plants. The stores of such materials which were found when the occupation began, like the fuel stocks, had been pilfered or at least carried away in spite of precautionary steps for guarding the plants. The artificial division of Germany into zones had shut off even the German-produced raw materials in large measure. Foreign sources were not available for various reasons including world shortages. In any case there was no foreign exchange available in Germany to pay for them.

After some months of very discouraging efforts the United States called on her Allies to join their zones with the American Zone in order to cope with what otherwise seemed an almost hopeless problem. As noted earlier, the Russians gave no consideration to such a bid and the French held back, but the British complied because of their own desperate plight. The fusion of the British and American Zones for economic purposes was agreed upon late in 1946, but it was not until 1947 that they were actually joined. And then the relations between the British and American military governments were such, as noted in Chapter 7, that considerable time and effort were required to bring about a workable system. Bizonia, it may be added, got started at a time when the gloom was particularly great among the Economic Affairs staff of OMGUS—they had managed to get industrial production up to 44 per cent in November of 1946, only to have it fall back to 39 per cent in December.

The establishment of Bizonia made it possible to send raw materials produced in the American Zone to the Ruhr and to bring manufactured goods and coal from the Ruhr to the American Zone. It did not restore the strength of the German working force by making an adequate supply of food available, but it did better the food situation by putting food rationing on a bizonal basis. The efforts to improve the effectiveness of Bizonia have been detailed in Chapter 12, but it should be borne in mind that three revisions had to be made and not until 1948 was the situation well in hand.

THE JOINT EXPORT-IMPORT AGENCY

As early as 1945, General Clay recognized the key role of imported raw materials in Germany. Moreover, he saw that in order to obtain such materials foreign exchange was essential. Consequently he inaugurated a system under which German exports from the American Zone would be sold to other countries only in return for dollars which could in turn be used to purchase raw materials on the world markets. Other European countries which wanted to trade their fruits, vegetables, dairy products, and so forth—all of which were much needed of course in Germany—for German coal and other exports deeply resented such a system; but OMGUS resisted their pressure, believing that such a dollar source, though far from ideal, was about the only possible hope for future achievements of a substantial character. With the fusion of the American and British Zones for economic purposes, a Joint Export-Import Agency (JEIA) was organized with branches in each of the *Länder*. This agency, with a capital of $121,000,000, of which some $90,000,000 was paid in at once, played an important role in financing foreign trade and consequently furnishing the funds with which raw materials could be purchased for German industry. The United States put up $43,800,000 of this; the British furnished the same amount in goods or sterling convertible into dollars; and the remainder was realized from payments which Sweden made to extinguish claims to German assets within her borders. Under JEIA, as it was commonly known, exports of some $225,000,000 were made in 1947 and $600,000,000 in 1948. Exports during 1946 had been only $21,000,000 from the American Zone, though the British Zone had a much larger export business of $139,000,000, mainly in coal which was badly needed in Germany itself.

DISMANTLING

The Russians had suffered grievously as a result of German invasion and not unnaturally were anxious to be compensated for such damage as far as possible. One of their most vigorously presented demands at the Yalta Conference was that involving reparations from the Germans which would amount to the equivalent of some ten billion dollars. The American delegation recognized the justice of the Russian demands, but at the same time knew that reparations cannot be drawn out of the air. Hence they attempted to placate the Russians but without assenting to the specific Russian demands for reparations. The Russians apparently believed what they wanted to believe and interpreted the American position as agreeing to their demands. This later became apparent at the Potsdam Conference, if it had not been apparent before, and one of the most controversial questions confronting that conference was the Russian insistence on reparations from the Germans to cover their war losses. The United States did not feel able to agree to an arrangement under which it would in all probability have been left to foot the bill. Being the only Allied country coming out of the war with any considerable financial resources, it would probably have had to replace the funds taken out of Germany by way of reparations. But it did reluctantly agree to a program of dismantling under which numerous German industrial plants would be torn down and distributed among the Russians, British, French, Dutch, and other claimants against Germany—it did not desire itself to participate.[8]

The Russians lost no time in starting a large-scale program of dismantling in their zone, and whole trains were to be seen moving from the Russian Zone eastward carrying the machines and other equipment of German industrial plants. Pressure was soon brought on the United States to commence the dismantling program in the American Zone, though the relatively unimportant position of industry in that area made the problem far less serious than in the British Zone for example. Some plants were dismantled in the American Zone and turned over to various claimant countries, and a larger number were earmarked for dismantling. The deteriorating relations with the Russians slowed up the program involving the plants intended for them, and indeed General Clay halted the program as it related to Russia as early as March 1946. But the Moscow Conference held in early 1947 agreed on a new plan calling for the dismantling of 682 plants in Bizonia and 172 in the French Zone.

Public opinion in the United States as the war receded into the past increasingly regarded dismantling in Germany as a foolish and unwarranted action. American businessmen, congressmen, and others visiting Germany on official missions became more and more critical of dismantling, until the program finally came to an end with the Petersberg Protocol in 1950. A committee headed by George M. Humphrey in 1948 recommended that 167 plants slated for dismantling should be retained in *status quo;* an earlier committee, headed

---

[8] For a severe criticism of this program, see F. Utley, *The High Cost of Vengeance* (Regnery, Chicago, 1949).

by N. H. Collisson thought that 332 plants scheduled for dismantling should be kept intact. Reports from Russia and elsewhere revealed the unwisdom of dismantling. Plants could not be easily reassembled and, when this was successful, often could not be effectively operated because of lack of trained workers. Even the Russians came to realize the waste involved in such a program and concentrated on taking reparations out of their zone in the form of manufactured products rather than dismantled plants. Dismantling never was the big undertaking in the American Zone that it was in the British and Russian Zones and probably had comparatively little negative effect on economic reconstruction in the United States Zone. Its psychological impact on the Germans was, however, at least fairly important, and in that sense it may have weakened American efforts.

LEVEL-OF-INDUSTRY DISCUSSIONS

During the early period of the occupation the feebleness of German industry was such that there was little basis for discussing the maximum limits of German production. The Potsdam Agreement had fixed 55 per cent as the maximum amount of German production to be permitted by 1949 in terms of 1938 production after deducting for war output. Certain industries were prohibited completely; among these were the aircraft, ball bearings, arms and ammunition, seagoing vessels, synthetic ammonia, synthetic gasoline and oil, and synthetic rubber. Other industries were to be cut back sharply. Steel, for example, was to be limited to approximately 30 per cent of prewar production. Machine tools were to be cut to just over 10 per cent. Chemicals were to be manufactured at not over some 40 per cent of the 1938 rate. Textiles, on the other hand, could be turned out at 75 per cent of the prewar rate; farm machinery and tractors at 75 per cent; and boots and shoes at 70 per cent. Even by 1946 there were indications that the United States would support higher limits for German industrial production.

A study such as this is hardly the place for a detailed treatment of the long-drawn-out discussions looking toward a revision of the level-of-industry provisions of the Potsdam Agreement. However, it is important to note that a year did not pass without some liberalization. In 1947 a general liberalization was undertaken which provided for

258

an industrial output approximately equal to that of 1936—this year being selected because it was supposed to be the last year before the elaborate Nazi preparations for war were started. Under this the steel level went up from 5,800,000 tons to 10,700,000 tons and a capacity of 13,000,000 tons. The Occupation Statute provided a considerable measure of economic authority for the West German Federal Government and after 1949 level-of-industry controls came for the most part to an end. However, severe limitations on ship building remained in force and were only gradually relaxed by the Allied High Commission. Certain prohibitions remained in effect relating to airplane production, munitions, and the like, under the inspection of the Military Security Board and, while there was some movement in the direction of eliminating these, various items remained on such a list until the end of the occupation. However, as far as ordinary industrial production went, the West German Federal Government had an almost completely free hand during the latter years of the occupation.

CURRENCY REFORM

If one were to draft a list of the half a dozen most notable events associated with the Allied occupation of Germany, currency reform would without much doubt receive a place. The details of this action are dealt with in Chapter 17, since currency reform technically belongs to fiscal activities of the occupation. However, its impact on economic reconstruction was so outstanding that some attention must be given to it at this point. Even before the German surrender it was apparent that the reckless expenditures of Hitler for arms, for public works, and for various other projects had brought Germany very near to bankruptcy. The currency which circulated in Germany when the capitulation came was hardly backed by any assets at all and was indeed worth little more than the paper it was printed on. However, since currency was required for the few business transactions which took place during the early days of the occupation, this more or less worthless stuff was depended on by the Germans, though special occupation marks were used by the Allied forces. There might well have been a currency reform during the early months of the occupations, but the weakness of the German economy was such that it seemed risky to attempt such an operation at the time. The strained relations with the Russians made any agreement on this subject virtually out of the question. The net result was that it was not until April 1948, almost three years after the occupation had started, that the three western Allies finally undertook the reform of the currency in the three zones of the West. Up until the last there was a considerable amount of uneasiness about this step both on the part of the western Allies and the Germans. Economic recovery was still far from complete and there were those who were fearful lest currency reform would result in a serious setback.

Actually currency reform was apparently the specific treatment which the German economy was waiting for before throwing off its invalid status, for the effects of this action were almost immediate and positive. Indeed, so great a boost was given to the German economy by currency reform that it is commonplace to date the final spectacular development in this area from currency reform. The old currency had depreciated very drastically, and almost no one had any confidence in it because it was generally recognized that far-reaching reform was inevitable. This, of course, had a depressing influence on many transactions. Although currency reform was a shock to many persons and groups—it almost wiped out the resources of the newspapers licensed by the occupation, for example—after it was over there was a confidence which had been notably lacking before. Numerous business transactions which had been delayed were now consummated. Stores, which had had empty shelves, almost overnight displayed a rather wide selection of goods for sale. German industry, which had moved ahead slowly and with great hesitation and at times seemed to stagnate, now started the striking advance which brought it by 1950 to a point on a level with the prewar period and by the end of the occupation to a position something like twice as high on the index as the prewar level.

DIRECT AMERICAN AID TO GERMAN ECONOMY

Although it would not be fair to state that American action in the economic field was completely negative during the early part of the occupation, it can hardly be denied that under JCS 1067, which remained formally in effect until 1947, relatively little constructive assistance was possible. One of the earliest instances of direct aid to

260

the German economy took place in the fall of 1946 when the Commodity Credit Corporation of the United States government extended a credit of $33,000,000 for the purchase of American cotton to be used by German textile plants. But the price exacted was so high, the interest and service rates so steep, and the general quality of the cotton so poor that there may be some doubt as to whether this was an example of assistance to the Germans or vice versa.[9] At any rate, the raw cotton did make it possible to start certain textile plants and in some measure at least was a psychological boost to German morale.

During the military government phase of the occupation the Army of the United States rendered assistance to the German economy which cannot be easily assessed. Army finance has always resisted ordinary breakdowns, and an analysis of expenditures is sometimes virtually out of the question. There is a widespread feeling that indirect Army assistance was substantial and that any estimate of American aid to German economy which leaves out such assistance falls short of the true picture. Some of this Army aid, such as the surplus materials program, falls into a category which can be readily envisioned. Hundreds of thousands of tons of surplus American military supplies in Germany, together with some 40,000 tons of used but serviceable clothing from the United States, were turned over to a German public corporation late in 1947 for sale to German firms and individuals. Unlike the cotton deal where the price was high, the basic price and credit terms in this transaction were the same as those offered to other European countries. This program made available to large numbers of Germans vehicles, tools, clothing, and a vast array of other material which in a country as bare as postwar Germany served a very useful purpose.

The address delivered by Secretary of State Marshall at Harvard in June 1947 was widely publicized in Germany and many Germans apparently hoped, or perhaps expected, to be included under the benefits of the Marshall Plan.[10] This indicates something of the shift that had taken place in the American attitude which during 1945 and much of 1946 had been so punitive in emphasis. However, to begin with, Germany was not dealt with on the same basis as other European

[9] See L. D. Clay, *Decision in Germany*, p. 199.

[10] The recognition of Germany as an integral part of Europe was expressed even earlier by A. W. Dulles in an article entitled "Alternatives for Germany" in *Foreign Affairs*, April 1947.

261

nations, and assistance which it received was given by ECA through the Military Governors. An agreement was signed in mid-1948 which made the British and American Zones combined into Bizonia eligible for ECA aid, and a special bizonal agency was organized to handle the European Recovery Program as it related to Germany. Bizonia and the French Zone were represented in the Organization for European Economic Cooperation in the spring of 1948—the first postwar instance of German participation in an international organization—and became a member of EPU, the European Payments Union.

The British and American Military Governors discovered that under the Marshall Aid provisions for Germany no outright grants were contemplated, as in other European countries, but only loans. Thus while Germany was to be given a place under the foreign-aid program of the United States her place was, for the time being, to be less advantageous than that of countries which had not been enemies during World War II. This has been referred to in certain quarters as an example of the unfair treatment accorded Germany by the United States, and it does certainly indicate some measure of lack of confidence. But, in view of the early position as embodied in JCS 1067, the remarkable fact about the 1948 ECA terms is not the inferior position of Germany but the inclusion of Germany at all. That within the short period of three years the United States should have progressed from the punitive position reflected in JCS 1067, dismantling, denazification, war crimes trials, and the like, to a position where it would consider including Germany under any conditions whatsoever in the ECA program is truly extraordinary. Certainly there can be few instances in history where a defeated nation in a bitterly fought war involving the loss of many lives and the expenditure of astronomical sums of money has been made the recipient of large amounts of financial aid within a short time after the surrender.

There were many details to be worked out before ECA aid came to West Germany in any quantity. The initial request of the Military Governors of the British and American Zones for $500,000,000 was turned down and a tentative allocation of $364,000,000 made—a lesser amount than the small countries of Europe received. After much discussion this was increased to $414,000,000 in September 1948. It was December 1948 before arrangements had been completed to make the money available. Once started, the program of financial assistance moved ahead more smoothly, and Germany received more adequate amounts and under more advantageous arrangements. The break with the Russians and the ensuing cold war and the desire on the part of the United States to bring the West German Federal Government into the western alliance had their effect on financial aid.

During the years 1945 through the end of the occupation in 1955 West Germany received a total of somewhat more than three and a half billion dollars in economic assistance from the United States. Almost half of this was in the form of GARIOA or occupied area funds made available prior to July 1, 1950—$1,416,300,000. A slightly smaller amount—$1,359,000,000—was provided by ECA/MSA during the period 1948-1955. The remainder, $803,300,000, took the form of miscellaneous grants, including $276,200,000 for supplies furnished before and outside of the GARIOA program, $120,300,000 of Inter-European aid, and $172,400,000 of GARIOA funds administered by ECA/MSA.[11] Some Germans, including those in official positions, have complained at these amounts, pointing out that Germany has fared less well than France. For obvious reasons it is not feasible to compare the assistance rendered by the United States to two countries as diverse as West Germany and France, but the sum of $3,578,900,000 received by Germany during the years 1945-1955 is a sizable amount under any circumstances. This does not, of course, include the large expenditures of American personnel stationed in Germany, contributions made by American religious and relief organizations, and other significant indirect assistance.

It may never be possible to determine the exact influence of American contributions in money, matériel, and technical assistance in the reconstruction of the German economy which rose from an industrial production rate of some 2 per cent in May 1945 to 173 per cent ten years later,[12] but it certainly was substantial. This does not imply that a fair-minded person ignores the important role of German hard work, thrift, managerial skill, and the like, in such a remarkable recovery and expansion. But it seems improbable that German efforts alone could have achieved anything like the spectacular results to be

---

[11] American Embassy, *Handbook of Economic Statistics, Federal Republic of Germany and Western Sectors of Berlin* (Bonn-Bad Godesberg, 1955), p. 2.

[12] *Ibid.*, p. 12.

observed. Many Germans, it must be admitted, remember all too well the earlier period of American military government when it seemed to them at least that the United States had a heavy burden of blame for the delayed start and consequent critical weakness of the German economy. The very real misery resulting from the shortages of food, clothing, housing, and so forth during 1945-1947 was the result of many factors, but the Nazi misdeeds and the disastrous defeat in war bulk large as causes. The American economic policy of revenge, punishment, quarantine, and inaction intensified the shortages and consequent suffering, it is true, but were not the primary factors.

DECARTELIZATION AND DECONCENTRATION EFFORTS

From the early days of the occupation American military government was charged with the responsibility of attempting to destroy the hold of the great cartels over German economy and to break up certain of the industrial giants into smaller units.[13] This task was more related to the Legal Affairs Division and, under HICOG, to the Office of General Counsel than to the Economic Affairs agencies, but it will be dealt with here since it has its main bearing on economic reconstruction.

Both the decartelization and deconcentration efforts of the United States in Germany probably grew out of the desire to denazify rather than from any primary interest in these complex and controversial problems. Some of the concentration in the banking and industrial fields had been pushed forward under National Socialism, whether innately related to National Socialist philosophy or not. More important, Hitler had made considerable use of such giant concerns as the I. G. Farben Industrie in preparing for war and in exploiting occupied areas. Decartelization and deconcentration, therefore, appeared to the United States to be demanded or at least justified as part of the job of demilitarizing and denazifying Germany.

At the same time it should be noted that neither decartelization nor deconcentration had any great appeal to American business interests or indeed to American public opinion in general. The United

---

[13] JCS 1067, paragraphs 36-37.

States has its great corporations which are not infrequently charged with being trusts, the American counterpart of cartels. While some Americans may not regard General Motors, General Electric, du Pont, and various other concentrations of industry as assets, their role in the United States is important and their general reputations at least reasonably good. With such a background at home, it seemed of doubtful wisdom and positively evil to many Americans serving the occupation in Germany to proceed with a program of tearing down some of the best known industrial setups in Germany. Even if such action might be justifiable at a later date, it was argued in some quarters that the critical state of the German economy during the early years of the occupation made such steps most risky. The situation was complicated by the varying attitudes of the British and French and by the disagreements between General Clay and the OMGUS decartelization staff which included some very ardent supporters of a far-reaching breaking up of German industrial organizations.[14]

The paper achievements in this field were impressive. Early in the occupation OMGUS submitted the draft of a law to the Allied Control Council which provided for the deconcentration of any German enterprise employing more than 3,000 persons or covering more than 25 per cent of the production in any field or with an annual business exceeding RM 25,000,000. The British refused to accept this proposal, indicating opposition to any arrangement which did not apply the rule of reason. After the fusion of the American and British Zones for economic purposes in 1947, an agreement was reached with the British and military laws were issued in the two zones which were similar though not identical. Law No. 56 of the American military government made cartels, trusts, syndicates, combines, and similar setups illegal in the American Zone. It stipulated that all industrial enterprises in the American Zone employing more than 10,000 persons should be broken up unless military government decided otherwise, prohibited participation in international cartels, and so forth. Under the Occupation Statute decartelization and deconcentration were listed as powers reserved and consequently the American activity

---

[14] For the Clay version of this controversy, see *Decision in Germany*, pp. 325-334. For the other side, see James S. Martin, *All Honorable Men* (Little, Brown, Boston, 1950).

in this field continued under HICOG. Since the steel and coal industries had been taken over and administered by an Allied commission because of their great importance, no attempt had been made under military government to decartelize and deconcentrate these industries. The main attention during the Allied High Commission period was in these areas and in assisting the West German Federal Government in drafting and enacting legislation in this field.[15]

The properties of the I. G. Farben concern in the American Zone had been taken over by the United States in July 1945, and it perhaps represents the most interesting case of the application of deconcentration and decartelization laws. This industrial octopus, which had been heavily relied on by Hitler, owned 48 manufacturing plants and more than 100 other units in the American Zone alone, though only some 15 per cent of its properties were located within that zone. An action of the Allied Control Council in November 1945 placed all Farben properties under Allied administration and stipulated the break up and disposal of the assets of this concern which engaged in the pharmaceutical, photographic, chemical, and numerous other businesses. When the break between the western Allies and the Russians took place, a commission made up of British, French, and American representatives took over the Farben assets in the West and proceeded to deal with them in such a manner that they could be disposed of in various units. The early idea of breaking the properties in the American Zone into 52 separate units was later dropped as impractical. Any disposal of properties before currency reform was considered unwise because of the problems involving payment. When the situation seemed to justify disposal after the Allied High Commission phase started, there were legal difficulties and the problem of finding any one with sufficient capital to purchase. Eventually it was decided to divide the Farben properties in the western zones into three groups. The process had, however, not been completed at the end of the occupation and the West German Federal Government took over.[16] Legal problems arising in 1955 seemed to indicate that

---

[15] See J. F. J. Gillen, *Deconcentration and Decartelization in West Germany, 1945-1953*, in the Historical Series of the Office of the U. S. High Commissioner for Germany (1953).

[16] The early activities of American military government relating to the Farben concern are critically dealt with in H. W. Ambruster, *Treason's Peace* (Beechhurst, New York, 1947).

additional years might pass before the affairs of Farben were wound up.

Another important case of deconcentration involved the so-called Big Six Banks which held some 55 per cent of the assets of all German commercial banks.* They, like the Farben concern, had had intimate dealings with the Nazis. There were fewer complications here than in the case of the Farben concern and a number of smaller banking establishments were created out of the Big Six. However, even before the occupation ended some mergers were deemed necessary in order to make the banking facilities more adequate.

Deconcentration and decartelization in the steel and coal industries came at a comparatively late date after the western Allies had turned these properties back to the Germans. By this time the German owners were far better organized and in a much stronger position than had been the case during the military government phase of the occupation. They resisted the general idea of being broken up and only reluctantly agreed to a compromise arrangement after Mr. McCloy had personally intervened. The principal provisions of the compromise provided that the powerful sales agency of the coal industry should be broken up and that the steel companies should dispose of some of their coal properties.[17]

The legislation of the West German Federal Government relating to deconcentration and decartelization came also at a time when organized opposition was powerful. The provisions of the legislation represented considerably less than the American officials in the Office of General Counsel of HICOG regarded as desirable, but, with the leeway given the West German Federal Government even in reserved fields, it was accepted as the best that could be obtained at the time.

A full evaluation of the efforts of the United States in deconcentrating and decartelizing German industry cannot be made at this writing and possibly can never be made. It was apparent as the occupation ended that the results were much less than the strong sup-

---

* For details, see Chap. 17.

[17] For an important collection of source material relating to Allied activities involving the iron, coal, and steel industries, see H. G. Schmidt, ed., *Documents on the Reorganization of the West German Coal and Iron and Steel Industries under the Allied High Commission of Germany, 1949-1952*, in the Historical Series of the Office of the U. S. High Commissioner for Germany (mimeographed, 1952).

porters of such action had hoped for. Reports coming from Germany indicate that the steel and coal owners are not satisfied with the compromise which they agreed to and may shortly push to have such rather modest limitations dropped. German public opinion in 1955 did not seem to favor any stringent action in either breaking up large concerns or prohibiting cartels.

17

Public Finance, Currency, and Banking

The initial venture of the United States in the fiscal field in Germany did not augur well for the future, but fortunately it did not prove indicative of events to come. Prior to the end of the war American officials in Washington had entered into an agreement with the other Allies under which military mark notes would be printed and used for various purposes in connection with the occupation, though not as a general currency by the German people. Plates for printing such military marks were turned over by American Treasury officials to the Russians who apparently proceeded to run printing presses day and night. Large quantities of these notes were paid to the American soldiers by Russians who desired to purchase wrist watches and a varied assortment of items available to Americans in the PXs and through packages from home. Since there was comparatively little use for such notes in Germany on the part of American personnel, with the shop shelves almost, if not entirely, bare, the proceeds of these black and gray market sales were converted into dollars. Long lines of G.I.s formed in almost every military post office in Germany to purchase dollar money orders with their surplus military marks. At one time when the pressure became especially great, they sometimes remained all night waiting to proffer their paper military marks when the post offices opened.

In July 1945 regulations were issued that only amounts of military marks equal to military pay could be converted into dollars, but there were various means of evading such limitations. Many G.I.s waited, for example, until they were deployed to another theatre or to the United States and then they could, at least in some instances, change all of their military marks into dollars or another currency. It was not uncommon during the latter months of 1945 to encounter American soldiers on their way out of the European theatre with rolls of bills amounting to more than $1,000. At last in December 1946, a year and half after the occupation started, arrangements were made to substitute dollar military scrip for the military marks, but in the meantime American military personnel had exchanged some $300,000,000 worth of the military marks obtained from the Russians, which of course had no dollar backing, for American dollars. The American Treasury, which had been responsible in large measure for the original idea and had permitted the plates to be turned over to the Russians, refused to accept liability. American military government consequently found itself saddled with the debt of $300,000,000 which had to be paid off through profits from the PX system in Germany and by using the military marks to compensate German employees not coming under the occupation costs category and the like.[1] Needless to say, the experience was a bitter one.

The general situation confronting American military government in Germany in the fiscal field immediately after the German surrender was a most difficult one. The Hitler regime had perhaps been even more indifferent to established monetary conventions than most dictatorial governments. It would have taken more of a financial wizard than the famous Dr. Schacht to perceive anything but bankruptcy in the postwar picture. The machinery of the banking system had largely ceased to operate as a result of the confusion arising out of wide-scale bombing, the destruction of banking and public buildings and records, the carrying away of the remaining assets by fleeing officials, and the like.

In such a chaotic situation military government could do little more than take a few emergency steps to begin with, leaving the complicated jobs of re-establishing a system of public finance, currency reform, the reorganization of the banks, and so forth, until later. And these latter undertakings were to be seriously hindered by the failure of the Allied Control Authority to establish a central German finance agency, as stipulated by the Potsdam Agreement. The main initial task of the American military government detachments was to block bank accounts so that Nazis and other Hitler beneficiaries could not benefit, forbid changes in ownership of large properties, and seize any remaining public funds. The next step was to get the rudiments of a tax system operating so that the German governments

---

[1] For an account of this by General Clay, see his *Decision in Germany*, p. 63.

would have funds to meet their expenses and to permit the German banks to operate on a very limited scale in order to provide basic credit facilities essential for carrying on even an attenuated business structure. Some 1,300 banks were doing business in the American Zone within a short time after the surrender.

PUBLIC FINANCE

It may come as a surprise to many Americans that comparatively little was attempted by either American military government or HICOG in the way of far-reaching reforms in the public finance field. Professor Rodney Mott of Colgate University, who served as Chief of Finance of OMGUS at one period, notes that "The general character of the German tax structure has not been substantially changed since the Weimar period." [2] Perhaps the fact that the Nazis had not completely made over the tax system, in contrast to their general record, convinced American officials that no great changes were required, despite the considerable differences characterizing the public finance systems in the United States and Germany.

There had been approximately 500 tax collection offices in Germany under the National Socialist regime, together with some 200 chief customs offices supervising 1,300 customs houses. While the national Ministry of Finance had been broken up by the removal of its subdivisions to places outside of Berlin, the central treasury remained in Berlin. After the surrender, however, tax collections from the American Zone were no longer sent to the central treasury. Most of the local tax collection offices remained active, even if they had to move from building to building as a result of war damage. The instructions which the Nazis had issued involving the destruction of the tax records were not carried out. Under the orders issued by American military government detachments, these local tax collection offices were able to gather substantial amounts of revenues even during the first weeks of the occupation, but there was no machinery to distribute such funds to the newly established German governments which of course needed money to meet payrolls and other expenses. The British military government organized a system under which the

---

[2] See his article entitled "Public Finance," in E. H. Litchfield, ed., *Governing Postwar Germany*, p. 343.

271

local tax collection offices sent their funds to a new central office in Hamburg, but American military government looked with disfavor upon this as a step in the direction of centralization. Consequently it provided in June 1945 that the local tax collection offices in its zone should transmit their funds to the ministries of finance of the *Länder* (states) in which they were located. The state ministries of finance in turn were responsible for distributing the revenues to the counties, cities, districts, and the state governments.

Although Hitler had saddled a heavy burden on the German people in many respects, he was careful to keep the tax load relatively light. Tax collections paid only approximately 26 per cent of the public expenditures in Germany during the war years, in contrast to 61 per cent in the United Kingdom and 40 per cent in the United States.[3] Certain war exactions were made, it is true, in Germany, but in general the huge costs were met by borrowing and by exploiting the occupied territories. Despite its prevailing inability to agree, the Allied Control Authority took steps to bring about a change in the tax situation through a Control Council Law promulgated in 1946. Under this law the maximum income tax rate rose from 67 per cent to 95 per cent, while the basic rate was increased from 12 per cent to 17 per cent. The turnover tax, the most important single source of German revenue, was increased by 50 per cent, from 2 per cent to 3 per cent; the property tax from .5 per cent to a sliding scale ranging from 1 per cent to 2.5 per cent; the alcohol tax from 475 RM to 11,470 RM, and so forth. However, though rates were changed, the tax system itself was retained more or less intact.

These new taxes were regarded by the Germans as grossly excessive, and it is interesting to note that the West German Federal Government in 1950 reduced them sharply, though not to their former levels. Under the 1950 law the top income tax rate was lowered from 95 per cent to 70 per cent and the basic rate was cut from 17 per cent to 10 per cent, or 2 per cent below the 1945 level. The property tax was reduced to .75 per cent; the alcohol tax brought from 11,470 RM to 1,000 DM; the beer tax from 35-118 RM to 2-15 DM. The 3 per cent turnover tax was, however, retained and a new coffee tax of 10-13 DM was imposed. In 1951 the West German Federal Government proceeded to increase the turnover tax to 4 per cent, but the

[3] See Mott, *op. cit.*, p. 343.

proportion of national income required for taxes seems to have dropped since 1946, when the rather drastic Allied Control Council law took effect. The new rearmament program of the West German Federal Government may reverse the trend of course, but its impact was not felt during the occupation years, though the item of occupation costs, the amount required by the Allies from the Germans to meet various expenses arising out of the use of Allied forces in Germany, may be regarded in the same category.

CURRENCY REFORM

Currency reform in a defeated country which had been financed largely through borrowing and where inflation had progressed to a critical point was not a question of whether but of when. As early as 1946 American military government had given serious attention to the problem and had laid a detailed proposal based on the recommendations of the Colm-Dodge-Goldsmith report before the Allied Control Authority. This would have involved the exchange of a new currency at the rate of one for ten for the old Reich marks, a capital levy with a progressive scale rising from 10 per cent to 90 per cent imposed after currency reform, an equalization of war and currency burdens by mortgages on real estate, inventories, industrial equipment, and so forth, a reorganization of the banking and insurance businesses, adjustments in the price and wage structure, and an overhauling of the public finance setup.[4] The Allied Control Authority devoted a great deal of time to this general problem and it seemed at times that some agreement might be reached which would have embodied part of the American recommendations. However, the Russians must have eventually regarded currency reform as not to their advantage and, when it seemed that the really difficult obstacles had been overcome, they ended the negotiations by insisting that the new currency be printed in a poorly equipped printing establishment in Leipsig in their zone rather than under four-power supervision in a well-equipped printing plant in Berlin.

With the quadripartite efforts at a standstill and the Russians obviously unwilling to move ahead, the currency reform problem was

---

[4] For the details of this report, see Special Report: *A Plan for the Liquidation of War Finance and the Financial Rehabilitation of Germany*, OMGUS (1946).

tackled by the three western Allies. The Military Governors of the American, British, and French Zones agreed to issue a series of laws simultaneously in their respective zones during the period of June 18-20, 1948.[5] June 20-26, 1948, was set as the time for the actual reform to take place. It was estimated that outstanding currency and bank deposits in the three western zones amounted to 130,000,000,000 RM prior to this reform, and it was proposed to reduce these to between twelve and thirteen billion of the new currency known as DM. Each German was given 40 of the new marks to meet expenses during the week of conversion; the old money was not valid after June 21; and all old notes had to be turned in for conversion by the end of the period.

It was planned originally that one new mark would be traded for every ten of the old either in currency or bank deposits, but, as it turned out, only about .65 of a mark was given for every ten of the old marks. Under a system of blocking half of the new amounts it was discovered that there was already sufficient money in circulation on the basis of the increase of prices after the unblocked half had been distributed. Therefore, instead of proceeding with the issuing of the remaining half, 3.5 billion marks were canceled, an additional billion marks were made available for consumption purposes, and 500 million marks were set aside for capital investment.

At the same time indebtedness was generally reduced by 90 per cent, with a moratorium on debts fixed for one week. The internal debt of the Reich which amounted to some 400,000,000,000 RM was invalidated; but to keep certain institutions, such as banks and insurance companies, from disaster, new public securities were issued to provide assets. Other provisions of the currency reform stipulated the balancing of all government budgets, severe limitations on public borrowing, and a reduction in tax rates.[6] The striking effect of this reform on the German economy has been discussed in Chapter 16 in connection with the reconstruction of the German economy and consequently does not require treatment here. However, it has generally been concluded that the entire operation was the most extensive and

---

[5] For the titles of these laws, see Howard P. Jones, "Currency, Banking, Domestic and Foreign Debt," in E. H. Litchfield, ed., *Governing Postwar Germany*, p. 423.

[6] For a more detailed treatment of the provisions of currency reform, see Jones, *op. cit.*, pp. 420-427; and Jack Bennett, "The German Currency Reform," *Annals of the American Academy of Political and Social Science*, Jan. 1950.

far-reaching financial program ever undertaken to save something from what otherwise would have ended in complete collapse and bankruptcy.

BANKING REORGANIZATION

While the United States made few or no demands for the modification of the German system of public finance beyond insistence on a certain degree of decentralized administration, American interest in a reorganized banking structure was more intense. To start out, it is true that American military government recognized the old *Reichsbank* and even made use of its branches in the American Zone as agents. But even from an early date there was a strong feeling in American circles that far-reaching reforms were necessary in the German banking structure. American military government proposed that the Allied Control Authority liquidate the *Reichskreditgesellschaft* and the *Bank der Deutschen Arbeit* which had been established by the Hitler regime and that it break up the remaining three gigantic private banking chains by limiting the banking operations of a single banking concern to one *Land* (state). However, the Allied Control Authority was unable to agree on comprehensive action in this field, though it did set up an arrangement for clearing bank balances in the four zones as early as December 1945 and later issued two minor regulations in the field.

In December 1945 American military government issued a directive which required each *Land* in the American Zone to set up a central state bank.[7] However, there was such a divergence of opinion among Americans and Germans as to the status of such banks and particularly the extent of the authority which the state governments should exercise over their operations that it required a full year to obtain the necessary legislation in Bavaria, Hesse, and Württemberg-Baden.

These state banks were given the assets of the *Reichsbank* in their respective states as well as certain of the liabilities; but they were not authorized to issue currency. They could and did act as the fiscal

---

[7] The most comprehensive treatment of the banking reorganization is to be found in Rodney C. Loehr, *The West German Banking System*, a monograph of the Historical Series of the Office of the U. S. High Commissioner for Germany (1952) (Restricted).

agents of their state governments and they were empowered to regulate credit facilities, clear transfers, act as transfer agents in the exchange of securities, engage in open-market operations, and the like. They became the key to the American policy in the banking field since the United States was vigorously opposed to a strong central bank of the *Reichsbank* type in postwar Germany. Originally, the *Land* central banks were owned by the state governments, but this was an emergency measure accounted for by the inability of the commercial banks to take on additional financial burdens at the time. Within a period of two years it was stipulated that the state governments should dispose of their stock to member banks. However, this wish on the part of the United States was easier expressed than carried out in practice and at the end of two years an extension had to be made. When the West German Federal Government took over the primary responsibility for banking regulation in 1949, there was opposition to the provision requiring the states to dispose of their stock to member banks and legislation was introduced to repeal this stipulation. State central banks were later organized in Bremen and in West Berlin.

With the establishment of Bizonia, it was essential to extend the banking system, though the state central banks remained the keystone. A bizonal bank, known as the *Bank deutscher Länder*, was organized on March 1, 1948, and this was extended within a month to include the three western zones, since the French saw the need of a central banking organization, even if they were reluctant to join their zone with Bizonia. The *Bank deutscher Länder* continued its existence after 1949 and became the central bank of the West German Federal Republic. But whether it would continue to be the sort of central bank which the United States felt desirable for Germany remained to be seen.

From the beginning there was considerable controversy over the ideas of the United States in the banking field. Even among the Allies there was disparity of opinion, with the French generally favoring the American emphasis on decentralization and the British regarding the American position as not too tenable. German attitudes also varied widely and there was, from the early days, considerable support for a central bank of the variety familiar before the war in Germany. The fact that the state central banks had had an opportunity to gain experience before the establishment of the *Bank deutscher Länder* militated in their favor and, in general, they were supported as the keystone of the new banking system by the states. But after the setting up of the West German Federal Government with a Ministry of Finance, counter pressures became increasingly apparent. Few saw in the future any likelihood of a further trend toward decentralization in German banking and many predicted a considerable move in the direction of centralization.[8]

The *Bank deutscher Länder* was given the quarters of the old *Reichsbank* in Frankfurt and started out in a lively fashion to exercise its authority. It had the power to issue paper currency and before the West German Federal Government took over such a function it even provided metal coins. It had general responsibility for formulating the basic policies for banking and currency in West Germany, regulating credit, fixing interest and discount rates, stipulating minimum reserve requirements, handling clearing and transfer functions which involve crossing state lines, and regulating foreign exchange transactions. It acted originally as the fiscal agent of Bizonia and then assumed such a function for the West German Federal Government. The fact that the *Bank deutscher Länder* was owned by the state central banks as members is significant, though federal legislation later prescribed that most of its profits should go to the federal government rather than to the member banks. This bank did not engage in commercial banking activities and had no branches or subsidiaries; its exclusive business was with the state central banks, the central banks of foreign countries, the West German Federal Government, and the central bank of East Germany.

In October 1948 the Bizonal Economic Council, with the approval of the western Allies, authorized the creation of a Reconstruction Loan Corporation to provide long-term credit facilities which were badly needed in West Germany. Its function was to provide credit where other credit agencies were unable to do so. It was felt desirable to bring into its board of directors representatives of the *Länder*, the various banks, industry, labor unions, agriculture, and the like. Much

---

[8] The Bonn Basic Law provides that parliament shall "establish a Bank of currency and Issue as a Bundesbank." As early as 1953 the Free Democrats introduced a bill providing for a highly centralized system of banking. In 1956 the Government drafted a bill looking toward greater centralization though making certain concessions to those favoring a continuation of a decentralized system. See "Battle of the Bundesbank," *Economist* (London), Nov. 17, 1956.

of the money loaned by this corporation came from counterpart funds controlled by the United States. Its loans were ordinarily made through another credit agency rather than directly to borrowers.

In 1949 the United States had a part, though not the exclusive role, in the organization of two central banking institutions, known as *Landwirtschaftliche Rentenbank* and *Deutsche Genossenschaftskasse*, intended to provide credit for farmers and the food industry and the cooperative movement. Another central agency, the *Kassenvereine*, was set up to serve as a central depository for limited liability companies, cooperatives financing installment buying, and labor union banks.

American military government and HICOG displayed considerable interest in the breaking down of the great banking chains which remained from the prewar period. The record of the so-called "Big Six" during the Hitler era was anything but savory and this, together with the emphasis of the United States on decentralization in German banking, naturally made the *Grossbanken* targets. Since two of the big banking combines had no branches in West Germany and a third, the *Bank der deutschen Arbeit* founded by the Nazis, had been liquidated under a quadripartite agreement, only three were actually involved in the protracted efforts of the United States: the Dresdner Bank, the *Commerzbank*, and the Deutsche Bank.

The long-drawn-out negotiations among the occupying powers, the discussions with the Germans, the changes in position on the part of Washington and London, the complex legal questions presented, and other factors made this one of the most involved of the many complex operations of the occupation. It would require far more space than is available here to trace the many steps in this record. But to make a long story short, it may be noted that action taken by the western Allies resulted in the breakdown of the Big Three into 30 banks. The record of these banks at least to begin with was not impressive: they frequently lacked good management and they were economically unsound in certain instances.

With the establishment of the West German Federal Government and the transfer of the basic reponsibility for banking to German auspices, German legislation to supplant Allied regulations had to be enacted. The law which finally went into effect on March 31, 1952, was the result of numerous compromises and many conflicting attitudes. Under Allied pressure the West German Federal Government agreed to keep such legislation without changes for three years, but very few observers believed that its provisions would prove permanent. Some American officials felt that enough had been gained to justify the immense amount of effort that was expended on this project, but it is probable that a larger number were distinctly pessimistic, regarding the record as a failure in large measure.

18

Manpower and Organized Labor

Germany had had powerful labor organizations prior to the Hitler regime. It is true that labor organizations were somewhat slow in developing during the Empire because of the anti-socialist laws enacted under Bismarck, but with the repeal of these at the end of the century labor groups of one kind and another grew rapidly. The General German Federation of Labor Unions, the largest of the pre-Hitler labor organizations, claimed 7,890,000 members in 1920 and held a position as one of the most important labor organizations in the world at the time.* This organization was ideologically related to the powerful Social Democratic party, though formal ties had been severed in 1892. A much less powerful labor organization, the so-called "Hirsch-Dunker" unions, was closely related to the Progressive party. The Christian labor unions, deriving their appellation from their ties with the churches, claimed a membership exceeding half a million in the closing days of the Weimar Republic.† But with the coming of the Hitler regime, a drastic change took place. Under a decree of May 2, 1933, all labor unions were abolished and their treasuries, records, and property were declared confiscated. Their place was shortly taken by one of the most important Nazi-controlled organizations: the German Labor Front, created by Hitler early in 1934 under the Law for the Organization of National Labor. This Nazi organization included in its membership both employers and workers and, as a result of strong pressure, a total membership of some 26,000,000 was reached by the outbreak of World War II. It need hardly be stated that the German Labor Front was not a genuine labor organization and as such was not recognized by labor groups in the United States and other free countries. Hitler had no intention

---

* Its membership had declined to 4,418,000 in 1931.
† The total membership was reported as 578,000 in 1931.

of permitting labor or any other organized group to dispute his absolute power—instead his cunning devised a way under which labor regimented in the Labor Front would be a powerful tool which he could use to his advantage.

In dissolving the National Socialist party and taking over its multitude of controlled organizations and their assets, the Allies had to give a good deal of attention to the gigantic Labor Front. This very necessity perhaps brought the field of organized labor to the fore. And the fact that Hitler had seen fit to take over organized labor to suit his own purposes placed a premium on proceeding with the establishment of labor organizations which could be regarded as democratic in character.

The Potsdam Agreement stipulated the immediate re-establishment of labor unions in Germany,[1] and one of the early actions of the ill-fated Allied Control Council took the form of Law No. 22, dated April 10, 1946, which related to the position of labor organizations in Germany. It is doubtful whether either of the above resulted from American initiative, however. The early attitude of American military government as regards the re-establishment of German labor organizations was, in general, a rather cautious one. So many pressing items of an emergency character confronted military government that there was a disposition to regard such fields as organized labor as suitable for later attention. That is not to say that the attitude of the United States toward organized labor was a negative one, as has sometimes been concluded; rather it felt that labor unions were the sort of thing that required careful attention and that under the conditions facing American military government during the early months of the occupation it was not feasible to give such attention.[2]

The fact that American military government did not place labor higher on its list of priorities may be criticized, but it is easier to do this in the period after the occupation had ended than would have been the case during the early occupation. Conditions were critical in Germany during the first years of the occupation and, with denazification requiring so much time and energy and the problem of food so critical, it was not easy to find the time to give to such matters

---

[1] II, A, 10.
[2] The early activities are dealt with in S. Liss, "Revival of Free Labor Organizations in the United States Occupation Zone in Germany," *Southern Economic Journal,* Jan. 1947

as labor. Nevertheless, the fact that there was a major subdivision of OMGUS charged with dealing with manpower indicates that this field fared better in some respects than other important fields, such as education. Also, the appointment by General Clay of Joe Keenan of the A.F. of L. as his personal adviser on labor questions reveals a recognition of the important role of organized labor.

Part of the seeming delay in connection with labor organizations undoubtedly stemmed from the concern which was displayed in many American quarters lest the Communists take advantage of the situation by gaining control of such organizations as labor unions, political parties, and the like. Hindsight indicates that the Communists were less prepared to move ahead vigorously than was supposed, but this was not clear at the time. The argument was that by going slowly in re-establishing labor organizations in Germany, the considerable risk of having such organizations captured by the Communists might be substantially reduced if not eliminated entirely. Again there are those who interpret this as a failure to recognize the primary importance of organized labor. Actually it was probably more a shortcoming in breadth of view than a desire on the part of American military government to disregard labor.

THE MILITARY GOVERNMENT PERIOD

Labor, like virtually all other fields, was a direct responsibility of the United States in its own zone in Germany during the military government phase of the occupation.[3] Since no groups except those of a religious character were permitted to carry on activities or even to assemble without the express consent of military government, labor was more or less completely dependent on the latter. The United States' policy in the case of various groups was to proceed from the grass roots, so to speak, rather than from the top down—this was supposed to promote the democratic process and incidentally simplify the control problem. The French agreed with such a policy, but the Russians began with a program under which a central labor organization was set up to direct all labor activities within their zone. The German labor leaders in the British Zone apparently regarded a cen-

---

[3] For an authoritative discussion of American labor activities during the military government period, see Taylor Cole, "Labor Relations," in E. H. Litchfield, ed., *Governing Postwar Germany*, Chap. 14.

tral approach as advantageous, and the British military government permitted this arrangement, whether they felt any particular enthusiasm for it or not.

The weakness of the American position was that it did not fit easily into the German pattern. Unlike American labor organizations, German trade unions have never had local branches or units —the individual members of a union are banded together in a works council based on a given industrial plant, mine, or other establishment. Almost immediately after the German surrender these works councils sprang up at various points in the American Zone, but they were not recognized by American military government. Works councils were authorized by Allied Control Council Law No. 22, dated April 10, 1946, and of course the United States was bound to accept its provisions.[4]

General Clay states that, though it was the aim of American military government to build labor organizations from the ground up, state- and zone-wide organizations were not prohibited.[5] What actually happened in the American Zone was the establishment of *Land* (state) labor organizations which then proceeded to join together on a zonal basis. When Bizonia was formed out of the American and British Zones, it was agreed that the labor organizations could extend their boundaries beyond the American and British zonal boundaries to take in all of Bizonia, and this was shortly done in late 1947 and early 1948. Although this step was essential, it did not arouse great enthusiasm in OMGUS because it started the train of events that brought the German labor organizations in large measure under the influence and control of the labor leaders in the British Zone.

American G.I.s were fond of the saying that in the division of the German territory into zones: "The Russians got the agricultural lands; the British received the industrial areas; and the United States found itself left with the scenery." Like most other popular summaries, this represented considerably less than the truth, but it did have some basis. The Russians did receive some of the most important food-producing sections of Germany and the British did get the Ruhr. During the closing days of the military government phase of

---

[4] This and other sections of this chapter are based largely on J. C. F. Gillen, *Labor Problems in West Germany*, a monograph in the Historical Series of the Office of the U. S. High Commissioner for Germany (1952).

[5] *Decision in Germany*, p. 289.

the occupation (on June 30, 1949) there were 2,885,036 members of the German Federation of Labor Unions (British Zone) in contrast to 1,667,074 in the American Zone. But since the unions in the British Zone constituted a single united front, their strength was even greater than this comparison shows—the 1,677,074 members in the American Zone were split into a Bavarian Federation of Labor Unions reporting 815,161 members, a Württemberg-Baden Federation of Labor Unions with 464,905 members, and a Hesse Federation of Labor Unions with 397,008 members.

It is perhaps not surprising that the gigantic industrial plants of the Ruhr should have produced able leaders to a greater extent than the less highly industrialized American Zone. The history of German labor since 1948 has in large measure been identified with the names of Hans Boeckler, August Schmidt, Walter Freitag, Hans vom Hoff, all of whom came from the industrialized British Zone. It would not be correct to conclude that this situation precluded the Manpower Division of OMGUS from exerting influence on the German labor movement, but it is probably fair to say that the extent of the influence was significantly reduced, though the exact degree would be difficult to estimate.

The failure of the United States to recognize the importance of the works councils in German labor organization was undoubtedly one of the chief weaknesses of OMGUS in the labor field. To what extent this was the result of plain ignorance and to what extent it was the result of a stubborn belief that the United States had so much power in Germany that it could more or less ignore the past and create its own pattern, it is difficult to ascertain. The fact that shop stewards were authorized—elections being scheduled for their selection as early as October 1945 in some 3,000 plants—may indicate that the OMGUS course was not so much the result of ignorance as a studied policy of attempting to impose a foreign pattern on German labor. At any rate, the works-council arrangement prevailed even in the American Zone and the leading argument advanced as the foundation of the American labor policy in Germany—that is, the desirability of establishing truly democratic labor organizations based on the grass roots—to a large extent proved ineffective.

General Clay maintains that OMGUS was greatly handicapped in the conduct of its labor relations in comparison with the British

284

military government because Britain, during the military government phase of the occupation, had a Labor Government in power at home.[6] There may be some basis for this assumption, though it would seem that the less industrialized character of the American Zone was much more significant. If a Labor Government was in power in Britain, a "New Deal"-"Fair Deal" Democratic regime was in power in the United States and the Democrats have long prided themselves on their intimate relations with organized labor and the support which they have received from the labor unions. Moreover, there is a considerable question as to whether domestic politics in Britain were reflected in the British Control Commission for Germany any more than the Democratic administration in Washington was reflected in OMGUS.

Had the United States been more realistic in recognizing the place of the works councils, it is possible, indeed probable, that there would have been less Communist influence in these councils during the early years of the occupation. In the highly important mining industry, no less than 71 per cent of the members of the works councils during the years 1946-1948 were Communists. Under the Allied Commission phase of the occupation, when the Office of Labor Affairs of HICOG followed a course of non-interference with basic desires of German labor unions but displayed keen interest in minimizing Communist influence in works councils, the percentage was cut to 32 per cent in 1949 and 25 per cent in 1950.

Wages were more or less frozen in the American Zone until May 1948.[7] Consequently collective bargaining and strikes were of small consequence during the early years of the occupation. In May 1948 it was specified by OMGUS that wage increases up to 15 per cent might be permitted under collective bargaining between employees and employers. Despite the slight use of collective bargaining during most of the military government phase, the Manpower Division of OMGUS stressed the importance of this device in the development of labor organizations, maintaining that the greatest promise for labor advance lay in this instrument. To a considerable extent the predilection of OMGUS for a labor organization of decentralized character based on a grass-roots foundation was the result of a strong feeling

---

[6] See his *Decision in Germany*, p. 293.

[7] For a discussion of the early policy on wages, see M. A. Kelly, "Allied Policy on Wages in Occupied Europe," *International Labour Review*, May 1947.

that a democratic system of collective bargaining was most likely to grow out of such a system. But even at this early stage it was increasingly apparent that the German labor leaders were not too impressed by the advantages of collective bargaining. Many of them, though of course not all, were doctrinaire Marxian socialists of a rather mild variety and, as such, were more interested in ideology than in the practical results in hours and wages to be gained from collective bargaining. In their eyes, state ownership of certain industries was more important than improving the conditions of the individual workers. When, for various reasons, including the socialization program of the Russians in their zone, this did not seem likely to be widely supported, more and more attention was given to another goal that could be fitted into a doctrinaire system: co-determination or the representation of labor on the boards of directors of industrial concerns.

Under the pre-Hitler regime labor had had special labor courts to handle labor disputes and other matters. OMGUS recognized the justification for such tribunals, and the Manpower Division played an important role in the re-establishment of labor courts. By July 1946, slightly more than a year after the occupation started, the system of labor courts was again functioning in the American Zone. Late in the same year unemployment compensation was reinstituted in the *Länder* (states) of the American Zone, thus completing the full restoration of social insurance. Earlier in 1946 social insurance covering industrial accidents, old-age pensions, sickness benefits, and the like had been set up, but the critical condition of industry had prevented the payment of benefits for unemployment.

One of the incidents which has been severely criticized in some quarters took place on October 30, 1948, at Stuttgart. At a labor rally, a German labor leader made a vigorous verbal attack on American military government, especially on the basis of inflationary prices but covering other items as well. After the meeting had adjourned, certain of those who had attended the rally and perhaps outsiders started hooligan activities, breaking store windows, stoning American automobiles, and going so far as to turn one car over. Military police intervened to assist the German police in quelling the disorder and apprehending the ringleaders. In the eyes of many military government officials, including the able district military governor of Württemberg-Baden, Charles LaFollette, a former member of Congress, this ended

286

the matter, but General Clay took a more serious view of the incident. In his *Decision in Germany* he explains that to him this was not a labor outbreak, though labor was incidentally involved, but a case of intolerable disrespect for American military government.[8] General Clay therefore intervened and directed Mr. LaFollette to put the entire population of the large city of Stuttgart under a curfew as a warning of prompt action which American authorities would take in any future cases. The people of Stuttgart naturally did not like the curfew and maintained that the punishment was grossly unfair in that it penalized a whole city for the acts of a few unruly people. German labor leaders were critical in certain instances because they maintained that General Clay's action really violated the sort of democratic principles which had been so frequently preached to them by OMGUS.

Unemployment was not a serious problem during the years 1946-1948, despite the paralysis of industry, because the output of the individual worker was so small as to require enormous labor forces. OMGUS did not therefore find it necessary to give much attention to this problem. The Manpower Division did display an interest in improving food rations for workers so that it would be possible to increase coal production and otherwise get German industry back on its feet. Although it had no direct responsibility for housing, this division also took an interest in the problem of supplying housing facilities for workers, especially for those in the critical coal industry.[9]

During the military government phase a number of labor leaders from the United States were brought to the American Zone to confer with German labor leaders. Among these were David Dubinsky, W. C. Doherty, and George M. Harrison of the American Federation of Labor, and James B. Carey, Sidney Hillman, and Michail Ross of the CIO. Irving Brown, the AF of L representative in Europe, spent a good deal of time in Germany. These visits served a useful purpose, though the divergent patterns and views of German labor made a common meeting ground somewhat difficult and there is little evidence that the German labor leaders were persuaded that American labor ways were superior to their own.[10]

---

[8] *Decision in Germany*, pp. 296-297.

[9] See A. E. Brauer, "The German Housing Program and U. S. Aid," in the Historical Series of the Office of the U. S. High Commissioner for Germany (mimeographed) (1953).

[10] For further discussion of labor developments under OMGUS, see M. A. Kelly, "The Reconstitution of the German Trade Union Movement," *Political Science Quarterly*, March 1949.

THE HIGH COMMISSION PERIOD

With the passing of military government and the establishment of a West German Federal Government, the labor situation underwent a considerable change. Labor was not included among the fields reserved for Allied action under the Occupation Statute except as foreign affairs, refugees, and displaced persons and respect for the federal and state constitutions were involved. Consequently it became primarily a responsibility of the West German Federal Government. The trizonal fusion made it possible to organize German labor on a single basis throughout West Germany; therefore the zones no longer played any great role in labor affairs. Various labor meetings during September and October of 1949 resulted in the establishment of 16 industrial unions covering all of West Germany and a German Federation of Labor Unions. These embraced a total membership of some five million, or about 40 per cent of all workers in West Germany. Since neither the closed shop nor the check-off system was used in West Germany—the labor leaders themselves looked upon them askance because of the similar practices of the National Socialist Labor Front—this was an impressive record.

Despite the emphasis placed on keeping the number of major subdivisions relatively small, HICOG maintained a separate Office of Labor Affairs from its inception until the spring of 1952. However, since HICOG had little or no direct authority over labor affairs in Germany and German labor had passed the early formative stage, this office had a status quite different from that of the Manpower Division of OMGUS. Starting with a staff of only 12 Americans, the Office of Labor Affairs grew only slightly to the point where it could claim approximately 20 American staff members—consequently it always occupied a position as the baby of HICOG. As steps were taken to reorganize HICOG into a normal mission or embassy of the United States in late 1951 and early 1952, it was felt desirable to abolish such an office and to follow the normal procedure in an American Embassy by providing for a labor attache in the Office of Political Affairs.

Although a small office and without direct authority, it is probably fair to say that the Office of Labor Affairs, while it existed, was one

288

of the most active subdivisions of HICOG. When certain other HICOG officials sat most of the time in their offices pushing papers, the staff members of the Office of Labor Affairs devoted a great deal of their time to work in the field. No other HICOG official, whether a director of a subdivision or not, appeared to be more eager to talk about his subject than H. W. Brown of Labor Affairs. At meetings intended to canvass the general situation in West Germany HICOG officials often had little or nothing to report, but Mr. Brown could always be counted on to present the current developments in the labor field.

If OMGUS sometimes displayed a lack of wisdom and foresight in handling German labor affairs in such a fashion as to occasion charges of undue interference and lack of sympathy for labor objectives, HICOG followed a more consistent course of constructive character. It is only fair to note that OMGUS bore heavier responsibilities in the labor field and operated during a more difficult period. Under HICOG the point was stressed so frequently that it sometimes seemed unnecessary that the policy of the United States as regards labor was to furnish information, offer assistance, and otherwise help but never to attempt to force or indeed seek to persuade the German labor leaders to follow American ideas. The staff of the Office of Labor Affairs frequently confessed apprehension over developments in the field of German labor, but it at least professed never to bring pressure or even to offer detailed advice and urged other officials of HICOG to follow a similar course.

Perhaps the greatest single concern of the Office of Labor Affairs grew out of the unemployment situation in West Germany. As German industry got back on its feet, rebuilt plants, and installed modern machinery, German workers found adequate food to regain their former vitality, and a flow of expellees and refugees continued from the East, unemployment became a problem, despite the spectacular rise in production. In some fields there were actually shortages of labor while some hundreds of thousands of workers sought jobs in other areas, but the situation during the winter months of 1950 and 1951 was a source of great concern to the Office of Labor Affairs and indeed to the U. S. High Commissioner and other officials of HICOG. Efforts were made to channel the ECA program in such a fashion that maximum results might be achieved in the unemployment problem; special assistance was given to Berlin; but otherwise the main activity in this field was to keep as closely in touch with developments as possible and to pray for the best. Actually unemployment never reached the acute stage and, as the industrial revival progressed, it became increasingly less important. The time came when proposals were made looking toward the bringing in of workers from outside Germany.

Another matter of great concern to the Office of Labor Affairs of HICOG was the slow rise in wages and salaries in relation to the cost of living. Neither HICOG nor the West German Federal Government had absolutely reliable statistical data at hand, but the data available to the Office of Labor Affairs indicated that, as industry moved ahead to new highs and production advanced far beyond the prewar level, the workers were receiving less and less proportionately of the national income. It may be added that the West German Federal Government professed to have statistical data which controverted this and proved that the workers were at least holding their own. To the Office of Labor Affairs and others in HICOG a smaller and smaller share of the national income for labor not only indicated a basic weakness in German economic recovery but forewarned of a day in the future when there would be a reckoning which might well overthrow any government which had been built. The Office of Labor Affairs attributed such a situation to various factors, but maintained that the absorption of the German labor leaders in doctrinaire schemes such as co-determination and the lack of interest in collective bargaining constituted a major cause. The concern of the director of the Office of Labor Affairs became so great that it was alleged that he disregarded his own oft-repeated preachment that HICOG must neither interfere nor try to tell German labor what to do by scarcely disguising his own strong feeling that at one critical stage labor should stage a strike.

There had been no legal controls over wages in West Germany since 1948, and during the latter years of the occupation labor was free to engage in collective bargaining to improve its position. During 1950 and 1951 there were various strikes and these usually resulted in some improvement in the wage scale—the usual raise seemed to be in the neighborhood of 15 per cent. However, the German labor unions gave far less of their energy to collective bargaining than to attempts to have laws passed that would put the government in the role of attending to their interests.

At a time when HICOG was primarily concerned with unemployment and low wage scales, the German labor organizations were concentrating on co-determination[11] (*Mitbestimmungsrecht*) or the right of labor to participate in management through representation on boards of directors. The works councils acts passed by Hesse and Württemberg-Baden under military government had contained such clauses, but these had been suspended by General Clay.* German labor pushed vigorously for co-determination first in the great coal and steel industries and, having been successful there in 1951, to all sizable industries in West Germany.[12] Having obtained the passage of a federal law giving such representation in larger industrial establishments, labor announced that it would proceed to demand a similar right throughout the German economy. To HICOG officials it seemed a mistake to put all eggs in a single basket, even if that basket seemed a promising one.

But the Office of Labor Affairs was not fully convinced that co-determination would be a great boon for German labor. Persuaded that the great advances made by American labor are largely the result of collective bargaining carried on by the labor unions with the employers, it was natural that considerable doubt was attached to co-determination as a device for improving the conditions of the German workers. Co-determination would doubtless give influential positions on the boards of directors to labor representatives, but there was the grave question as to whether such influence would then be used to promote the welfare of the workers or if it would be enjoyed by a few labor leaders to their own advantage. This attitude of the Office of Labor Affairs of HICOG was made known informally to the German labor organizations, but if any influence was exerted by such views, it is not evident. German labor steadfastly adhered to its position of giving co-determination the first place on its list.[13]

It might seem from the above paragraphs that the Office of Labor

---

[11] For a discussion of this movement, see W. H. McPherson, "Codetermination: Germany's Move toward a New Economy," *Industrial and Labor Relations Review*, Oct. 1951.

* These suspensions were removed by High Commissioner McCloy on April 7, 1950.

[12] For the text of the co-determination law relating to mining and iron and steel industries, see Gillen, *op. cit.*, Appendix 3.

[13] For a detailed treatment of co-determination, see Gillen, *op. cit.*, Chap. 4.

Affairs of HICOG served no useful purpose, since its opinions received so little support from German labor. While it would be a mistake to assert that American influence of a direct character on German labor was notable during the High Commission period, it is equally unjustifiable to ignore the various American programs. An exchanges program which brought hundreds of German labor leaders to observe labor organizations in the United States served a useful purpose. The publication of a weekly journal, entitled *Internationale Arbeitsmitteilungen*, with a circulation of some 4,000, brought news in regard to labor activities throughout the world to German labor unions, labor schools, management, and other interested groups. A training-within-industry program, inaugurated under OMGUS in 1948, was continued under HICOG. A publication *Soziale Beziehungen in der Industrie* was started in 1951 to give German labor and management information dealing with personnel problems, training methods, supervision, worker morale, handling of grievances, and the like.

A circulating library of some 60,000 copies of approximately 700 titles supplied labor groups, labor schools, union headquarters, and so forth, with a great deal of material relating to labor throughout the world. Various pamphlets, books, and reports were translated into German and circulated more or less widely in labor circles. Films dealing with labor problems were made available to German labor groups. A productivity course based on American experience was offered for German labor leaders, though to what extent they were impressed by the record of American workers in producing more in a 35 hour week than German garment workers produced in 54 hours, it is impossible to determine. The Office of Labor Affairs conducted various research projects at Darmstadt and Frankfurt. It continued the interest displayed by OMGUS in the housing problem relating to workers.

Finally, it is appropriate to mention the personal interest of American High Commissioners and other officials outside of the Office of Labor Affairs in the labor field. Mr. McCloy and certain of his top staff, for example, maintained contact with various German labor leaders through conferences and other personal associations. At the very least this served a useful purpose.

19

Food and Agriculture

The provisions for food production and distribution in the early planning for the occupation of Germany indicate how exceedingly difficult it is to anticipate actual conditions in a war-devastated country. The plans of the German Country Unit of the Supreme Headquarters, which were largely duplicated by the U. S. Group, Control Council for Germany and G-5 of USFET, were based on the assumption that the German food production would suffice to maintain the population, with some scarcities, it is true, but nevertheless without too great hardships. The *Handbook for Military Government in Germany* stipulated that there should be no food imports into Germany "except in extreme emergencies, and then only to the extent necessary to prevent disease and such disorder as might endanger or impede military operations or occupation." [1] The Germans had produced approximately 85 per cent of the food which they consumed during the period before the Hitler regime took over, and it was generally recognized that their standard of living was the highest in Europe. Consequently after allowing for the effects of war and the 15 per cent of food which had normally been imported, it seemed to the Allied occupation planners that food would not constitute one of the major problems under an arrangement which would reduce consumption to an average of some 2,000 calories per person per day. Fats would be particularly lacking, it was realized, since Germany had traditionally depended on imports for large quantities of lard and other cooking fats; but it was maintained that it would not be unreasonable to expect the defeated Germans to tighten their belts for a time.

The planning in the food area apparently took little or no account of various major factors which changed the basic situation quite drastically. For example, sufficient recognition was not given to the

---

[1] See paragraphs 895 and 930.

fact that there had been significant changes in the food economy of Germany under Hitler. With the intense Nazi concentration on military production, many agricultural workers were moved from the farms to munitions factories. Their places were partly taken by laborers imported from other European countries who, in many instances, were virtually employed on a slave basis and who, immediately after the German collapse, left their jobs and either sought to return to their homes or congregated in cities and elsewhere. But these foreign workers did not completely fill the void left by the German agriculturalists and a considerably larger proportion of food than was normal was imported from eastern Europe. These imports were of course cut off by the German collapse. The net result was that German agriculture was far less intact at the end of the war than had been expected. Insufficient attention was also given by the military government planners to the fertilizer situation. It seemed to be taken for granted that fertilizer supplies would be fairly normal; but actually, except for natural fertilizers produced by farm animals, little fertilizer was available after the German surrender and a great deal of effort was required to get the plants running again. This would have been a serious matter in any country; it was almost catastrophic in a country where the soil has been cultivated for centuries and where crops depend almost entirely on what fertilizer is applied.

The food planners, along with their colleagues in other fields, originally assumed that Germany would remain a single economic unit, and even after the division into four zones was decided upon they were perhaps not completely aware of the full significance of such a step. Eastern Germany has been the section where agricultural production has traditionally excelled and where food surpluses have been available for movement to the industrial areas of the West. But the food produced in the eastern part of postwar Germany went to the Russians, insofar as it was not required for the miserable rations of the Germans themselves in the Russian Zone.

Finally, it should be noted that neither food experts nor any other military government officials were fully prepared for the vast influx of displaced persons, refugees, and expellees from Poland, Roumania, Hungary, Czechoslovakia, the Russian Zone of Germany, and elsewhere, into western Germany. A total of more than eleven million of these unfortunates came to West Germany, and nine million or more were present at one time. This was enough to upset any calculations as to food requirements.

Even after military government started its task of administering defeated Germany, it was not at once apparent how serious the food problem would be. To begin with, the general impression on the part of American and presumably other Allied personnel was of a people remarkably well nourished. Indeed, after coming from France, Britain, and other countries in western Europe immediately after the capitulation, it was striking to observe how much better fed the German population appeared to be than the other Europeans. And in the case of military police raids on German houses, it was common knowledge that fine hams, a good selection of wines and liquors, and other delicacies were often found. That the Germans as a whole had been well fed during the war, there can be little doubt; but much of the food had been gouged from the Poles and other unfortunate people under the German heel, and of course these supplies had ceased to flow even before the surrender. The stores of delicacies noted above gave an impression of plenty, when as a matter of fact the German larder was already down almost to bareness when the war came to an end. The wrecked transportation system complicated the situation by making it difficult, if not impossible, to move surpluses of potatoes and other commodities from the farms to the cities where they were so badly needed.

The military forces of the United States started out with a distinctly hardhearted attitude about food for the German people. To hear many of the tactical officers talk in May and June of 1945, it was almost inconceivable that any support whatsoever could be expected from them in connection with any food program aimed at assisting the Germans. Indeed, military government frequently found it very hard during the early days of the occupation to persuade tactical officers to provide military vehicles to move German supplies of food from one place to another where they were critically needed. Yet the situation became so desperate during the summer of 1945 before the harvest that the tactical officers in the military forces of the United States were advising their superiors both in the field and in Washington that they could not be responsible for maintaining order among

295

the German people unless food could be supplied to satisfy their emergency needs.[2] The result was that some 630,000 tons of military wheat were turned over by the Army to prevent mass starvation among the German population in the American, British, and French Zones during the autumn and winter of 1945.*

One of the first tasks of American military government in Germany was to set up a system of food rationing that would use the available food to greatest advantage. It soon became apparent that the problem was one which could not be handled satisfactorily on a local or indeed on a *Land* basis. The establishment of the *Länderrat* (Council of States) in October 1945 was to a considerable extent the result of the recognition of the need for an agency that could deal with food supply throughout the American Zone. A Commission for Food and Agriculture was one of the most active subdivisions of this council and organized a uniform system of food rationing throughout the American Zone. But the American Zone was really not an adequate unit for handling the problem of a food supply and the difficulties were many. A daily ration of 950-1150 calories of food was set up in the summer of 1945, but only 950 calories could be provided—less than half the minimum regarded as necessary for subsistence for persons not engaged in active work. Ordinarily some improvement in the general situation should have been expected after the harvest, and plans were drafted in August 1945 fixing the ration at 1550 per day for the normal person, with a goal of 2,000 calories, or exactly that which had been set by the German Country Unit.

The 2,000-calorie ration would have required supplementing German stocks with 4,000,000 tons of stuffs from outside, and General Clay made a trip to Washington to urge American officials to make such quantities available out of the granaries of the United States. However, the food supply of the world was in unusually short supply at this time, and the needs of the European countries other than Germany were desperate; consequently such amounts of foodstuffs were not available. The new ration of 1550 calories was honored for a brief period during the winter of 1945-1946, but by February 1946

---

[2] This and other material in this chapter is drawn from H. G. Schmidt, *Food and Agricultural Programs in West Germany*, a monograph in the Historical Series of the Office of the U. S. High Commissioner for Germany (1952).

* Some 300,000 tons were given to the Germans in the American Zone and the remainder used in the British and French Zones.

supplies had fallen to the point where it had to be lowered, and during May-June 1946 it went down to 1180 calories per day in the American Zone.

Appeals to Washington resulted in a visit of former President Herbert Hoover to Germany to look over the food situation. He recommended increased support, noting that the shortages in Germany were worse than anywhere else in Europe where he and his associates had investigated.[3] The increased support from Washington resulting from this recommendation and the 1946 harvest in Germany made it possible to increase the ration to 1550 again. But the fusion of the American and British Zones in January 1947, with the consequent necessity of pooling food supplies, brought about another crisis due to the heavy food requirements and very small agricultural production of the British Zone.[4] In April 1947 the normal food ration dropped to 1040—hardly more than the ration which had caused thousands in the Nazi concentration camps to die from starvation. Mr. Hoover made another trip to survey the food situation in Bizonia and gave vigorous support to a drive for more adequate assistance from the United States. He also succeeded in obtaining the release of some 40,000 tons of high-energy Army foods for a child-feeding program, under which 3,500,000 children in school received a noon meal of about 350 calories to supplement their normal ration. During the summer of 1947 the ordinary ration was upped to 1550 calories again as a result of the increased shipments from the United States.

It was anticipated that the food situation would be much improved after the harvest of 1947. The farm situation in West Germany had become more stabilized: the labor supply was more nearly normal, increased supplies of fertilizer were available, and good quality seeds were in more or less adequate supply. The provisions agreed to by Washington and the organization set up in Bizonia and the American Zone should have contributed substantially to this end. But the very severe winter of 1946-1947, followed by one of the worst summer droughts in history, reduced the German crop by about 20 per cent, thus bringing back again the threat of widespread malnutrition. In-

---

[3] See L. D. Clay, *Decision in Germany*, p. 267.

[4] During the period to December 31, 1946 relief shipments of food from American sources to be used in the American Zone totaled 1,318,341 metric tons. See Schmidt, *op. cit.*, p. 4.

creased food imports were arranged and by April 1948 the official ration was back to 1550.

An unusually good harvest in 1948 not only greatly helped Germany but eliminated the serious world food shortages which had complicated the military government efforts so seriously. The ration was increased to 1990 in July 1948. Thereafter the food situation steadily improved, until by 1949 it had ceased to be a source of anxiety. By 1950 the rationing system in West Germany could be dropped entirely because of the food supplies available, though in East Germany drastic rationing continued in force.

There can be no doubt that the years 1945-1948 were very difficult ones as far as food went for the rank and file of the German people. An active black-market made it possible for some Germans to have all they wanted to eat, but these were the exception rather than the rule. Even when the supply was at its top, the normal ration was only approximately 1,500 calories per day, or well below the sustaining level for those engaged in no active work. When the ration dropped below 1,000 calories, it brought the spectre of starvation very near to the masses of the German population. How great the aftereffects induced by such serious food shortages over a period of three years, it is difficult to say. During the worst part of the period there seemed to be less evidence of serious malnutrition than could be reasonably expected, but after 1948, when the situation had been much improved, a weighing program and nutrition teams found rather more evidence of serious undernourishment than had been anticipated. However, by 1949 these activities were abandoned because the need for them apparently no longer existed.

Some observers have maintained that the food shortages in Germany never were as bad as the official figures would show, alleging that most Germans managed to supplement their ration allowance with substantial quantities of other food. There was undoubtedly a great deal of foraging and scrounging on the part of Germans, particularly when the weather was favorable. Many garden plots were cultivated and provided their owners with a considerable amount of vegetables during the summer and autumn. Relief agencies in the United States and elsewhere sent large quantities of food into Germany during these years. Yet General Clay and his associates did not believe that the average supplementary food, including black-market supplies, exceeded 200 calories per day per person.[5] Diseases related to malnutrition increased, but less rapidly than had been predicted. Perhaps the most serious long-term impact in the way of disease was in the tuberculosis field.

Critics of the United States have sometimes made violent charges on the basis of the food shortages in Germany during 1945-1948. Some have gone so far as to attribute the widespread misery among the Germans to American inhumanity and a desire for revenge. Without minimizing the punitive character of the JCS 1067 directive, it seems unjustifiable to place major responsibility for the food situation on the United States. The root of the difficulty lay in the Hitler program of aggression which brought Germany to the point reached in 1945. The Hitler priority of weapons over fertilizer, the substitution of slave labor on the farms for regular domestic agricultural workers, the dependence on imports of food from the conquered territories in the East, the evil influence of the Nazi agricultural organization: all of these were the main causes of the starvation which confronted the German people. If the United States had not turned military stores over for civilian uses and if vast quantities of food, fertilizer, seeds, and agricultural equipment—during the two years and a half following January 1, 1947, approximately 14,000,000 metric tons of such supplies went into Bizonia—had not been furnished, there would without question have been mass starvation in Germany. As it was, not even the vigorous efforts of the United States staved off a serious food shortage and much suffering. However, in the absence of the most extensive food relief program ever undertaken, it is almost impossible to imagine what might have happened.

The United States may have to assume some blame for entering into an agreement with the Russians, under which the territory of Germany was divided into zones and the eastern bread basket of Germany was placed under Russian control. But it is difficult to believe that under a different arrangement the Russians would have permitted East Germany to remain free from Russian forces. At any rate the American food sent to West Germany exceeded any supplies which could under any system have been obtained from East Germany.

There was considerable resentment in some German quarters that the United States would not permit imports of food supplies from

---

[5] See L. D. Clay, *Decision in Germany*, p. 266.

other European countries into Germany during the early years of the occupation. The quantity of food available in such countries was not such as to permit any substantial export at the time—indeed these countries were themselves receiving food from the United States. Such imports into Germany were not permitted, as noted in Chapter 16, because of the lack of foreign exchange to pay for them and the great need of husbanding what foreign exchange there was to buy raw materials so that German industries could function.

AGRICULTURAL ASSISTANCE

The food-rationing system was set up by American military government as part of its operations to meet the emergencies arising out of the German defeat. The food-import program was devised to meet another emergency presented by the threat of mass starvation. Neither program was continued beyond the early years of the occupation and neither one was intended to have a permanent impact on German life, unless one could regard the saving of human lives as of some permanent consequence. The agricultural program falls into a somewhat different category. Some aspects were intended to help meet the emergency created by food shortages, but other elements had a long-term objective. Thus while rationing and food relief were discontinued when the need no longer existed, some phases of the agricultural program remained throughout the life of both OMGUS and HICOG.

One of the most pressing problems in the field of agriculture was that of providing sufficient high-grade fertilizers to support maximum production.[6] The Nazis had not only used fertilizer plants for other purposes and diverted raw materials to the making of munitions but such fertilizer as was turned out was often of a very inferior quality. American military government recognized the high priority of fertilizer almost immediately after starting operations in Germany, and the large plant at Trostberg in Bavaria was reopened in 1945. But the need was so great as a result of several years of neglect of adequate fertilizing that arrangements could not easily be made to deal with the situation at once. Efforts were made to get other plants in opera-

---

[6] For a discussion of the early program in the agricultural field, see H. Levy, "Pattern for German Agriculture," *Fortnightly*, April 1947.

tion and to supply the required raw materials. In addition, quantities of fertilizer were brought in from other countries.

The farm-equipment situation was another critical one. The Nazi concentration on war apparatus had left little industrial output for farm machinery, and at the end of the war the farmers were in a bad way. In order to produce crops, proper machinery and other equipment had to be made available. In 1945 American military government started reopening farm machinery plants and locating raw materials to operate them. In addition, equipment was imported from the United States. The long-term impact of this program lies in the emphasis on greater mechanization of German agriculture. The German farmer has been very conservative in using modern farm equipment, often seeming to prefer his oxen, wagons, and hand implements, when he could afford more modern equipment. It would be incorrect to say that German agriculture was completely mechanized under the American occupation, but it is proper to point out the progress made in this field during the period of 1945-1955. Particularly where the size of land holdings permitted the economic use of tractors and other mechanical equipment, quite noticeable increased use of these implements was to be observed.

Unlike its action in Japan, the United States undertook no land reform during its occupation of Germany. The character of the American Zone was such that land reform was not a major problem. Any such undertaking would have covered only a small area. The drastic action of the Russians in dividing up the land in eastern Germany probably would have discouraged a land-reform program in the American Zone under any circumstances. At any rate, this was not a matter to which either OMGUS or HICOG had to devote attention.

The most constructive and probably enduring efforts in connection with agriculture were made possible by the ECA program. A specialist staff attached to OMGUS and later HICOG as part of the Economic Affairs Office conducted an extensive and apparently quite successful program to show the German farmers how to increase crop yields, how to improve livestock strains, how to up the quantity and improve the quality of milk and dairy products, the practical advantages of mechanization, and so forth. This involved much the same sort of work as has been carried out over many years by county extension agents in the United States under the U. S. Department of Agriculture and the land-grant colleges. Since credit has been a serious problem in German agriculture for many years, ECA funds were made available for farm purposes and an attempt was made to establish cooperative credit facilities for farmers. A research program was inaugurated to test German soils, develop superior seeds and plants, and investigate other agricultural problems. An attempt was made to disseminate available information more widely among German farmers who often have followed the methods used by their ancestors a century or more ago. A program was organized to tackle the problem of better living conditions for rural inhabitants, with emphasis on such matters of diet, clothing, farm buildings, and the like. Attention was given to strengthening German educational facilities in the agricultural field. Finally, many German farmers were sent to the United States to observe farm management and methods under the exchanges program.

In carrying out such activities, the agricultural experts of OMGUS and HICOG prepared many pamphlets and reports which were translated into German and published in large quantities for circulation among the German farmers. Books and periodicals were brought in from the United States and elsewhere and made available to the Germans. Films were exhibited to show various techniques and their advantages. Many conferences were held at which German farmers met with American agricultural experts to discuss various problems confronting German agriculture.

OMGUS farm specialists made an effort to go to the agricultural areas to see what was going on and to contact the German farmers. With the establishment of the West German Federal Government which maintains a Ministry of Food, Agriculture, and Forestry, there was less of this field work on the part of the agricultural specialists of HICOG, though they too by no means regarded themselves as desk men. It was their policy to maintain close contact with the Federal Ministry of Food, Agriculture, and Forestry and with the agencies in the various *Länder* responsible for such activities, and to work through them as far as possible in strengthening German agriculture. It was realized that, with the occupation over, the chief hope for the future lay in the programs carried on by these German agencies. Attention

302

therefore was concentrated on assisting them to establish themselves as strongly as possible.

What the future will reveal as regards the agricultural efforts of the American military government and HICOG, only time will tell. German agricultural patterns are grounded in centuries of tradition and not easily changed. Nevertheless, there is some reason to believe that beginnings have been made which may have a long-term influence. Perhaps here are activities and techniques which are not associated in the German mind as aspects of the American occupation but rather as elements of a new agricultural economy.

20

Public Safety, Law, and the Courts

During the military government period, American public safety officers played an important role in supervising the rebuilding of German police forces and, in numerous instances, actually participated in the organizing of police forces on a basis which they regarded as satisfactory.[1] With the passing of military government, HICOG retained a few public safety specialists; but as this activity became less important, it was left increasingly in German hands.

The police under Hitler had not only been thoroughly nazified but centralized to almost the nth degree. American military government regarded both denazification and decentralization as requisites of a reorganized German police force. Neither was easy. The early days of the occupation saw public safety one of the most pressing problems of American military government. There were, of course, the American military police and later an American constabulary; but these could not take the place of German police despite their vigorous activities.[2] The fact that such a large proportion of the pre-surrender police had been active Nazis made the job of reorganizing a new German police force very difficult. Even after precautions had been taken to see that the worst Nazis were not taken into the new police forces, it was not uncommon to discover, as at Munich, that the reorganized police included numerous members with unsavory records. Had not some of the ablest American public safety officers been sent to work personally with some of these police reconstructions, the situation might have developed into a quite critical one.

Instead of having a national German police force, it was the opin-

---

[1] For further discussion of American activity in this field, see an article by R. M. W. Kempner entitled, "Police Administration," in E. H. Litchfield, ed., *Governing Postwar Germany.*

[2] On the U. S. Constabulary, see Oliver J. Fredriksen, *The American Military Occupation of Germany 1945-1953* (Hqts., U. S. Army, Europe, 1953), p. 65.

ion of American military government that the emphasis should be placed on local police administration and that the *Länder* (states) should be the highest level for control of public safety. Every urban place of 5,000 or more inhabitants was required to maintain its own police force, while in rural areas and smaller towns and villages state police forces were responsible. No such organizations as the *Sicherheitspolizei* or security police with its *Gestapo* (secret police) and *Kriminalpolizei* (criminal police) were permitted. In order to handle the special problem of protecting the borders from illegal entries, a border patrol of some 2,500 members was organized in the American Zone in February 1946, but even before this the ordinary police had been re-established, with 22,000 or so members in the American Zone by October 1945.

American emphasis continued to be particularly strong in the direction of keeping the German police decentralized. This encountered serious opposition from certain German elements. The *Länder* (states) at times seemed to feel it desirable to bring all police within their borders under their control, thus jeopardizing the status of the local police. Even more serious for the future was the inclination of the West German Federal Government after its establishment in 1949 to interest itself in the public safety field. In 1950 the Allied High Commission yielded to the pressure in favor of centralizing police forces as far as the *Land* level by issuing a letter dated November 14, 1950, which authorized the states through proper legislation to centralize their police forces but required them at the same time to permit local governments to maintain their own police forces. The Bonn Basic Law provided that the federal government should have under it a finance administration, the federal railways, and the federal waterways. This brought the border police, the railway police, and the water-protection police under the West German Federal Government. Since no military forces were permitted to the federal government during the years 1949-1955 and the difficulties with the Russians required some sort of force that could be used by the West German Federal Government to deal with emergencies, the western Allies finally decided to authorize the recruitment of limited numbers of special police to be controlled by the federal government. The New York meeting of the foreign ministers in September 1950 authorized the lifting of the suspension of Art. 91 of the Bonn Basic Law which

305

gave the federal government emergency powers over all police forces of West Germany; this step was taken by the Allied High Commission in February 1951.

It is too early to judge whether the decentralization imposed by the occupying powers will remain a permanent basis of German police organization. As noted above, there are strong pressures pushing in the direction of greater centralization, and it will not be surprising if at least some degree of federal centralization supersedes the system under the occupation. Nevertheless, the *Länder* have the advantage of an effective system of police control perfected before the establishment of the West German Federal Government, and they resist federal encroachments in this field. Beginning in 1949 fairly sizable numbers of German police officials were sent to observe police administration in the United States. They were usually impressed by at least some of the things they saw during these journeys, and they brought back to Germany many ideas for new equipment, modifications in organization, and the like. There can be little doubt that this influence has been reflected in the actual operations of German police forces, though its exact extent or how lasting it may be cannot be determined with any degree of certainty.

LAW

The Hitler regime had made a great effort to reconstitute German law to incorporate its own ideas. It had actually not been able to get along without some of the laws which had been built up during the years prior to 1933, but it had left a very definite mark on many if not all of the major laws. The task of American military government in eliminating this Nazi influence was one of the most weighty of the occupation.[3] It was assumed to begin with that this task would be handled in large measure by the Allied Control Authority, but the difficulties which have been pointed out in this body actually made it necessary for the United States to do a great amount of work alone.

---

[3] For authoritative analyses of the problem by one who participated in OMGUS, see Karl Loewenstein, "Reconstruction of the Administration of Justice in American-Occupied Germany," *Harvard Law Review*, 1948, and "Law and the Legislative Process in Occupied Germany," *Yale Law Journal*, 1948. Also see P. L. Weiden, "Impact of the Occupation on German Law," *Wisconsin Law Review*, May 1947.

Public Safety, Law, and the Courts

The general policy of suspending Nazi laws was of course not self-executing; law books had to be scrutinized, the acceptable had to be sifted from the bad, and old laws or new provisions had to be substituted for the sections thrown out. Thus the job was both negative and positive in character: negative in eliminating the vicious legal dictates of the Nazis, and positive in drafting and promulgating as Allied Control Authority, Allied High Commission, and the American military government laws, ordinances, regulations, directives, and so forth. Much of this work was performed by German legal experts employed by OMGUS and HICOG. Some of it, for example the revision of the Administrative Code, was turned over to groups of German legal and juridical authorities who had been carefully screened for the purpose.

As the legislatures of the *Länder* in the American Zone became established, they naturally relieved American military government of much of the burden of making laws for the Germans.[4] The *Länder* constitutions of the American Zone had conferred on the legislatures (*Landtage*) responsibility somewhat similar to that exercised by an American state legislature. The scope of their law-making authority was therefore broad in local and regional matters. American military government still issued some laws in the form of military government promulgations, but its chief job became that of reviewing the acts of the German legislative bodies. And this latter function required a great deal of effort and careful consideration during the latter years of military government and well into the High Commission period. The German legislatures were under many pressures,[5] as American legislatures are, and they passed a good many statutes which for one reason or another were not regarded favorably by American military government. In some instances a veto was consequently imposed by American military government either on a measure in its entirety or on certain provisions. Modifications frequently made it feasible to remove the veto and approve.

A West German Federal Government organized under an Occu-

---

[4] For discussions of the state legislatures, see H. M. Dorr and H. L. Bretton, "Legislation," in E. H. Litchfield, ed., *Governing Postwar Germany*, and J. H. Kaiser, *Der Landtag* (Munich, 1951).

[5] For a detailed treatment of these pressures, see J. H. Kaiser, *Die Repraesentation organisierter Interessen* (Berlin, 1956).

pation Statute reduced the American review task substantially. The fact that considerable authority was given to the West German Federal Government necessarily reduced the review scope, though a clause permitted the western Allies to intervene when their prestige was threatened. During the High Commission period review also was curtailed as a result of the emphasis on assisting the federal government rather than striking it down. Acts of the West German parliament were studied carefully, it is true; but there was less disposition to throw out and much more effort to persuade the Germans of the desirability of revision. Consequently, the review usually resulted in a temporary suspension or delay rather than final rejection.

Some idea of the great amount of labor involved in reviewing German legislation may be gained from the fact that, in a period of less than a year and a half before it was terminated, the Review Committee of the Allied High Commission convened 71 times and considered 1,682 pieces of German legislation, including 295 federal laws and implementing regulations, and 1,387 state laws and regulations. Of this body of legislation, only 30 adverse actions were taken by the Review Committee and of these only four involved federal legislation.[6] It may be added that during the period prior to the revision of the Occupation Statute in early 1951, the Review Committee had to complete consideration of acts within 15 days and that, unless the Allied High Commission interposed an objection within 21 days, the German legislation became effective. In March 1951 the Review Committee was ended and its remaining functions were turned over to the Political Affairs and Law Committees, but the role of review from 1951 to the end of the occupation was greatly decreased.

THE COURTS

At the beginning of the occupation there were no German courts in operation, and military government courts had to handle the many cases involving Germans as well as members of the occupation forces.[7] Some 343 summary, intermediate, and general military government

---

[6] See Elmer Plischke, *The Allied High Commission for Germany* in the Historical Series of the Office of the U. S. High Commissioner for Germany (1953), p. 120.

[7] For a more detailed treatment of American activities relating to the reconstruction of the German court system, see Karl Loewenstein, "Justice," in E. H. Litchfield, ed., *Governing Postwar Germany*.

courts were organized in the American Zone.[8] These courts disposed of approximately 385,000 cases during the period prior to August 1948, when a new system of military government courts was inaugurated, which handled only cases involving occupation personnel and cases directly relating to the occupation authority. Most of the early cases involved comparatively trifling matters of course, but the burden imposed on American military government was enormous. In many instances it was not feasible to assign legal affairs specialists to preside over the summary courts and, in general, these early military government courts involved a good many weaknesses. In order to relieve what otherwise might have become an intolerable situation, German courts were established at an early date—local courts actually starting to administer justice in August 1945. By early fall, German district courts were in operation in most places, and in October 1945 courts of appeal were authorized in the several states of the American Zone. German labor courts started to function in the American Zone in March 1946, and administrative courts were reopened in the autumn of 1946 after the Administrative Code had been revised. Federal courts were authorized by the Bonn Basic Law, but some of them, notably the Constitutional Tribunal, were delayed in getting started for various reasons.

In addition to dispensing justice directly through military government courts, American military government naturally took considerable interest in the reconstruction of German courts. Since most of the judges of the courts under Hitler had been associated with the National Socialist party, they were not very suitable for judicial service under the occupation. Finding possible judicial personnel was a major problem; and this extended to prosecutors and other court officials. Actually it has been estimated that as many as 85 per cent of those staffing courts under the occupation had Nazi records of one kind or another, but most of them were cleared as followers or as minor Nazis.[9] In general, the German courts were organized on the basis of earlier German experience rather than patterned on American

---

[8] For a discussion of these courts, see E. E. Nobleman, "American Military Government Courts in Germany," *Annals of the American Academy of Political and Social Science*, Jan. 1950, and by the same author, "American Military Government Courts in Germany," *American Journal of International Law*, Oct. 1946.

[9] See Karl Loewenstein, "Justice," in E. H. Litchfield, ed., *Governing Postwar Germany*, p. 249.

judicial organization. It has sometimes been assumed that the provisions for a Constitutional Tribunal at the federal level and constitutional courts in the *Länder* were the result of American influence, but there is not too much evidence to support such a thesis. The composition, organization, and procedure of the constitutional courts are so different from their counterparts in the United States that it is not easy to find much resemblance.

21

Youth and Women's Activities

The collapse of the Hitler regime created a special vacuum for the youth of Germany. The older people had numerous difficulties, but they also had experiences and resources which gave them something to fall back on—in any case most of them had to face the grim necessity of finding a place to live, scrounging for a bit of extra food, searching for fuel to provide some heat during the bitter weather of the winter, and the like. The youth frequently knew very little other than the Hitler regime and the Nazi youth organizations, which had required so much of their time and played such an important role in their daily existence. Not only were their adjustments serious because of the collapse of their Hitler *Jugend* and its elaborate program of sports, but they were often badly disillusioned as a result of the ignominious disintegration of the system which had proudly proclaimed its thousand-year domination over Europe. To make matters worse, there was ordinarily little or nothing for them to do and time hung heavily on their hands.

Both OMGUS and HICOG recognized the special problem presented by German youth.[1] During the early days there was concern occasioned by the delinquency on the part of large numbers of unhappy and idle youth. But perhaps even more serious in the eyes of both OMGUS and HICOG was the spectacle being made by the Russians to persuade the German youth that their hope for the future lay in the Free German Youth and its affiliated organizations for younger children—a setup with Communist foundations largely patterned after the *Komsomol*, Pioneers, and Little Octobrists in the Soviet Union. Very large sums of money were made available by the Russians to finance such a youth program in Germany, and activities of a sort designed to appeal to youth were freely offered. Not only were

---

[1] For a discussion of some of the early activities in the youth field, see P. M. Lambert, "Youth Activities in Germany," *Educational Record*, Jan. 1947.

there uniforms, catchy marching songs, and a sports program, but also some of the most spectacular youth conferences and festivals which have ever been put on, climaxing in the gigantic Berlin gatherings which brought together youth not only from Germany but from the Far East, and indeed all parts of the world.[2] Here there were reviews and addresses by high East German and Russian officials, colorful parades, many contests in the field of sports, gay folk dancing, and other pastimes devised to impress youth. As if this were not enough, the Russians made an all-out effort to convince German youth of their friendship and interest by appointing Free German Youth leaders to various coveted posts which would ordinarily be open only to middle-aged leaders. German youths in their early twenties were selected as heads of the school systems of populous cities, as superintendents of important railroad divisions, as managers of industrial plants which employed many workers, and so forth. And such appointments were of course publicized to the skies, though they were in reality of the window-dressing category.

Members of the American occupying forces naturally felt sorry for the plight of the German youth and, despite the early policy of nonfraternization, frequently gave candy, chewing gum, chocolate, and so forth, to the children if not to the older youth. Since many of the American soldiers were hardly beyond the youth stage themselves, there was a considerable amount of social contact with German youth, particularly of the feminine sex.

Sergeant P. J. Moriarity of the American Army and others started youth organizations intended to provide recreational opportunities for German youth shortly after the occupation started. In 1946 General McNarney announced an Army program for the American Zone which would extend such facilities to large numbers of German young people. GYA (German Youth Assistance) centers were opened in many of the towns and cities where American military forces were stationed, and members of the occupation on a volunteer basis sponsored baseball games, various other sports, and social activities. More than 600,000 German youth were members of the GYA clubs at one

---

[2] B. R. McClaskey, *The Free German Youth and the Deutschlandtreffen* a monograph in the Historical Series of the Office of the U. S. High Commission for Germany (1951), deals in detail with these activities. At the time of this writing it remained under a "Restricted" classification.

312

period. This program continued not only throughout the military government period but was carried into the High Commission phase of the occupation. Club houses and playing fields were requisitioned by the Army for the use of the GYA groups, and a sizable budget was maintained to finance the program.

The success of the youth centers naturally varied a good deal not only from place to place but from time to time in a single center. The oversight of the GYA was largely voluntary and, with American forces moving about so frequently, a dynamic leader often no sooner got a program well underway than he was moved on to another place. This rapid shifting of leaders and the consequent lack of continuity constituted a serious weakness in the program. Not only were talented members of the American military forces discouraged from volunteering their services for GYA work by the probability of a short stay in a place but, even more important, the German youth found it disheartening to see popular leaders go. In certain places it was alleged that American military personnel in charge of the German youth centers took advantage of their positions to engage in homosexual practices. This caused a great deal of criticism of the entire program among German parents, though it seems probable that there was comparatively little basis for such charges except in a few instances. The GYA program undoubtedly served a useful purpose. It was not, however, a very effective counterforce to the Communist-sponsored Free German Youth because of its more limited scope, volunteer leadership, and primary emphasis on entertainment.

By the time HICOG was established, the effect of the Communist youth program had become more and more apparent.[3] A Russian color film of the first Berlin Youth Rally in 1950, seized when the Communist party headquarters at Düsseldorf was raided, revealed much more of the ingenious and menacing character of the Free German Youth activities than had been generally realized. It also made more evident the extent of the influence being exerted on large numbers of German youth. HICOG maintained a section in its Office of Public Affairs to give attention to youth problems and a consider-

---

[3] The material in this section is largely derived from H. P. Pilgert, *Community and Group Life in West Germany*, a monograph in the Historical Series of the Office of the U. S. High Commissioner for Germany (1952), Chaps. 2 and 3.

able concern was evident at the highest levels, even on the part of the U. S. High Commissioner himself, over the general problem of youth in West Germany.

HICOG, although recognizing the far-reaching significance of the German youth problem, found it a difficult problem. To begin with, a monolithic youth organization of the Free German Youth type was considered not in keeping with American democratic ideals. This was doubtless a sound conclusion, but it made any concentrated approach to the problem more or less out of the question. By assisting various existing youth organizations based on religious and other lines, HICOG did something in the youth field, it is true; but these organizations were all weak when compared with the Free German Youth in East Germany. Moreover, they frequently competed rather than cooperated. Their appeal to German youth was not negligible, but fell below the requirement to effectively counteract the Russian efforts in this field. While HICOG had fairly substantial funds for supporting a youth program and probably could have obtained more if it had been demonstrated that additional funds could be used to good purpose, the amounts were hardly more than a drop in a bucket alongside the large amounts expended by the Russians. In its eagerness to strengthen a non-Communist youth program, HICOG on occasion found itself in an embarrassing relationship with nationalistic organizations which could hardly be identified with democratic principles.

In order to meet the charge that West German youth were receiving nothing like the official attention accorded East German youth, HICOG conferred on various occasions with high representatives of the West German Federal Government about the situation. While the latter naturally were reluctant to admit the accuracy of the charge that the West German Federal Government was an "old men's" government, made up largely of men well past fifty and including few representatives of youth, promises were made to do what could be done to give greater recognition to youth. However, little or nothing concrete seemed to materialize from these promises for a considerable time—one informed official of HICOG characterized "the apathy of the leading German statesmen" as "a matter of amazement." At the end of the occupation some change had taken place and the Bonn officials in charge of youth activities seemed to be more conscious of the need for a vigorous program in this field.

314

Youth and Women's Activities

The HICOG youth section was always a disappointment to many who desired a strong youth program under American auspices. Its chief had seen service with OMGUS and had been considered so able that he was made a member of the board to review the records of the field staff of OMGUS who desired to be taken over by HICOG. The initial impression which he made was an excellent one, for he was well fortified by an array of impressive charts and other exhibitions and could reel off a well organized summary of the general problem of German youth on the spur of the moment. And he was most generous in showing his charts and making his presentation. The charts and remarks were less impressive the second time than the first. After one had gone through the same performance on several occasions, it seemed too pat and too much of the canned variety to meet the needs.

Like certain other American officials both in Germany and Washington, the officials of the HICOG youth section were primarily desk men and found it either unpalatable or impractical to get out into the field where the actual work was needed. Consequently their knowledge of the situation tended to be out-of-date or secondhand. In their defense it should be said that the very nature of the assignment was such that active supervision in the field was by no means a simple matter. The frustrated and often almost distraught people working in the field on the youth problem had many questions for which there appeared to be no satisfactory answers. Those who took their assignments seriously—and some of them were almost pathetically eager to do an effective job—felt the crying need of support from above or at least some encouragement; yet they maintained that when they asked for bread from the youth section of HICOG, they usually got stones. Despite their discouragement which sometimes almost seemed to reach the point of desperation, some of the local resident officers and their wives and the few youth specialists assigned on a full-time basis to the field carried on some excellent work with German youth. If their number could have been multiplied a thousandfold—which was obviously impossible for various reasons, including finding competent and enthusiastic youth leaders in such numbers —a strong impact might have been made in this field.

The net results of the youth program carried on under American auspices can hardly be given a high rating, despite the good intentions and the really serious concern on the part of many individual Americans. Many of the projects for which money was spent, including bringing certain so-called youth leaders from the United States to circulate among the youth of Germany, were largely, if not entirely, a waste of public funds. In the case of the visits of youth from the United States, the language barrier was usually such as to make a common meeting ground almost impossible. Some of these young Americans gave the impression of having little genuine interest in German youth—they were enjoying a trip to Europe at public expense. Individuals among the German youth may remember for many years the cordial reception accorded by Mr. and Mrs. McCloy, Dr. and Mrs. Shepard Stone—the Stones entertained an average of some 500 per month—and other American officials in their respective homes and especially in Berlin during the gigantic youth rallies held by the Communists in that city. Others will long recall their associations with GYA or with HICOG resident officers and youth specialists with appreciation. Undoubtedly some students may pause during future years to recognize the permanent student-union facilities provided by American funds in German universities. Perhaps a good many will recall with appreciation the school meals provided through American aid during the military government and well into the HICOG stage.

Criticism of the achievement in the youth field should not perhaps be aimed primarily at either OMGUS or HICOG. The chief obstacle to an aggressive youth program that would compare with that of the Communists was the democratic character of the American occupation. How a democratic country can set up a youth program which will compete on equal terms with a youth program devised by a Nazi regime or a Communist police state is a thorny problem. Nevertheless, the impression should not be given that the Communist-dominated Free German Youth triumphed in West Germany. In East Germany its achievements have been spectacular and it may be able to make an indelible impress on the youth there if it can continue its efforts for a decade, though the revolt of Hungarian youth in 1956 casts doubt on any permanent enslavement of youth. In West Germany the repute of East Germany under Communist control was so low that even gullible youth were not taken in too completely by the Free German Youth. That is not to say that the impact of the Free

316

Youth and Women's Activities

German Youth has been negligible in West Germany, but it has been indirect rather than direct and, in general, far less than the Communists had hoped for. The evidence available seems to indicate a more international attitude on the part of West German youth than elsewhere in Europe. Dr. Shepard Stone feels that at least some credit for this belongs to the United States.*

WOMEN'S ACTIVITIES

Germany has produced some of the outstanding women scientists, professional leaders, and artists in the world and one cannot ignore their high achievements. Nevertheless, the place of women in Germany under Hitler was, at least in American eyes, a very inferior one. Universities were more or less closed to them, and emphasis was placed on keeping women in the home as breeding animals and domestic servants. But even under the Hitler regime some members of the feminine sex demonstrated their irrepressible energy by occupying important positions. It may indeed be noted that some of the most fanatical Nazi leaders were women. But it was the opinion of American women that some sort of program would be appropriate under occupation auspices to encourage German women to take their rightful place, and particularly to bring them in touch with women in other countries where women have had less difficult obstacles to surmount.

Some efforts were made in this field under OMGUS, but pressures occasioned by various emergency problems, such as food, made it somewhat difficult to give attention to a program for women.[4] A Women's Affairs Section of OMGUS was not established until January 1948, though as early as 1946 informal contacts between American and German women had been instituted. Under OMGUS the Women's Affairs Section was directed to serve as a channel of communications between German women and women in the United States and other countries, to bring to the attention of American military government problems relating to women in Germany, to furnish information and assistance to organizations for women in Ger-

---

* Expressed in correspondence and conversation with the author.
[4] The material in this section is largely derived from H. P. Pilgert, *Women in West Germany,* a monograph in the Historical Series of the Office of the U. S. High Commissioner for Germany (1952).

317

many, and to stimulate women to take active roles in political and community affairs in Germany.[5]

Under HICOG an Adviser on Women's Affairs was authorized in the Education and Cultural Relations Division of the Office of Public Affairs, but this was transformed shortly after HICOG got underway into a Women's Affairs Branch. Its responsibilities were similar to those noted in the case of OMGUS, but it was able to bring more resources to bear on executing such a program. Much of the credit for this doubtless belongs to Mrs. McCloy, the wife of the first U. S. High Commissioner, who found time amid her many other responsibilities not only to encourage the professional staff of the Women's Affairs Branch, but to go out herself to address numerous groups of German women. Combining charm and intelligence with a genuine sympathy for, and appreciation of, German women, Mrs. McCloy, with her fluent knowledge of German, was able to make a favorable impression on her listeners as few can hope to do. Her many contacts with German women of various backgrounds served a most valuable purpose and probably will be remembered after many other activities of HICOG have been forgotten.

Another important asset of HICOG in the program for women was the some 150 wives of the *Kreis* resident officers. Until 1952 when these officials were withdrawn, these American women constituted living examples of American feminine influence and interests in many German communities. It was their job to organize the groups of women to discuss current political and social problems which were intended to bring German women more actively to the front in political and community life, particularly at the local level. While their efforts were interrupted early in 1952 before they had had anything like the time needed to bring complete fruition, their activities were frequently quite valuable.

In the activities of the Women's Branch of HICOG the exchanges program occupied a high place. In 1952, for example, 73 German women were sent to the United States for periods varying from 60 to 270 days to study citizenship training, public administration, journalism, and the role of women in public affairs. Eight American women were brought in the same year to Germany to advise and

---

[5] For the text of the directive, see Pilgert, *op. cit.*, p. 7.

assist German women in their leadership training program, in improving their legal status, and to lecture on various subjects.

A fairly elaborate schedule of courses, seminars, and conferences was prepared for the women of all West Germany. During 1950 and 1951, for example, 14 courses were organized at Haus Schwalbach in Hesse lasting for the greater part of a week in each case to discuss topics such as "Women Representatives in Hesse Local Councils" and "Urban and Rural Women." Seminars on citizenship training were held at various centers. In 1951 an ambitious joint leadership training program for women was organized by the American, British, and French chiefs of Women's Affairs.

Finally, mention should be made of the information activities of the Women's Branch. Reports of various types were circulated by a Reference Service Bureau maintained on a trizonal basis. Encouragement was given to several publications intended for women readers put out under German sponsorship. Films were exhibited and various other information made available to organizations of German women.[6]

How many German women were touched by all of these activities and how deeply they were influenced, it is impossible to tell. Most of the courses and conferences were limited to rather small numbers of participants, but these were primarily of the leader category, and it was expected that they in turn would carry the message to other German women.

---

[6] Among other publications a *Handbuch deutscher Frauenorganisationen* was issued in order to furnish detailed information about the many organizations for women in West Germany and Berlin. This listed the names of the organizations, their addresses, and the names of their officers. It also indicated when the organization was founded, its membership, its publications, and its purpose as well as any international affiliations. A section gave the names of women in the Bundestag, in higher civil service positions, and in the women's committees of political parties.

22

Religious Affairs

Religious affairs constituted one of the comparatively few fields in which American military government did not deem it essential to undertake large-scale direct action in Germany. Yet the role of the churches has traditionally been so important in Germany that, from the beginning to the end of the occupation, American military government and HICOG displayed considerable interest in the various religious organizations, their activities, and their problems.

As early as 1944 the American planning staff in the field of religious affairs had drafted a general policy toward the churches of postwar Germany which emphasized freedom of worship, fair treatment of all religious groups, and respect for the various churches and other religious institutions. This was one of the statements of policy which were acceptable to the European Advisory Commission. Consequently the United States started out with the advantage of being on surer ground here than in most other areas. In April 1945 General Eisenhower issued a proclamation in which he announced to the German people this constructive policy relating to religious affairs. Despite their generally punitive character, both JCS 1067 and the Potsdam Agreement took a fairly liberal attitude toward the churches. Churches were singled out as the only groups which were permitted to hold meetings during the early days of the occupation without special permission of the military government authorities. In general, they were given freedom in handling their own affairs without undue interference on the part of the occupying forces. The German churches were therefore one of the few continuing elements to be found in the defeated land. They never ceased holding services. Indeed such crowds attended their services that standing room was at a premium.[1]

---

[1] The treatment in this chapter is based to a considerable extent on Beryl R. McClaskey, *The History of U. S. Policy and Program in the Field of Religious Affairs under the Office of the U. S. High Commissioner for Germany*, a monograph in the Historical Series of the Office of the U. S. High Commissioner for Germany (1951).

Religious Affairs

As the occupation continued, the same general policy of noninterference was maintained. There were those who looked upon the established position of German churches and their consequent public subsidies and right to collect church taxes as undesirable. Advocates of a system of public schools often regarded the German practice of recognizing the churches as controlling factors in elementary education as unsatisfactory—in 1931, before the Nazis had launched their attack on religious schools, approximately four fifths of the elementary schools of Germany had been denominational in character. But in drafting a statement on church-state relations in 1946 the Religious Affairs Section of OMGUS took the position that, as far as possible, decisions in such matters should be left to the Germans on the basis that "It is believed that any attempt to upset established German practice in such a controversial field not covered by our announced war aims would needlessly antagonize religious interests both in Germany and the United States." [2] This was approved both by OMGUS and in Washington. Thus the churches continued to depend upon state support and entered vigorously into the re-establishment of denominational schools. They were permitted at an early date to resume the issuing of pastoral letters, even when some criticism of the occupation was involved. They shortly began holding national conferences of their leaders, though such meetings of other groups were not allowed. This American attitude remained with very few modifications throughout the period of the occupation. Perhaps in no other area was there as great consistency in American policy as here.

The American staff in the religious affairs field was never a very sizable one, but it had a reputation which was enviable. Starting out under the leadership of Marshall Knappen, whose sound judgment and shrewd wisdom largely influenced the original planning, the Religious Affairs staff had less turnover and fewer serious disagreements than most other groups of OMGUS or HICOG. [3] Considering the differences of opinion which frequently characterize those professionally active in religious fields, this was a remarkable record. Representatives of both Protestant and Catholic denominations were always included on the staff, and they worked together amicably and

---

[2] For the full text of this statement of policy, see McClaskey, *op. cit.*, pp. 98-100.
[3] See his book *And Call It Peace* (University of Chicago Press, Chicago, 1947), for an excellent discussion of religious affairs policy and activities.

effectively. Under the U. S. Group, Control Council for Germany there had been only a handful of persons devoting themselves to religious affairs, and some of these doubled in the education organization. OMGUS authorized a modest increase in size and there were eight professional persons in the headquarters office and six in the field at one period, though by September 1949 this had shrunk to a headquarters staff of three professionals and a field staff of four professional persons. The entire professional staff of OMGUS in the religious affairs field was taken over by HICOG. Throughout the occupation the position of religious affairs on the organization charts remained modest—it was ordinarily given only status as a section, though, when education and cultural relations received its boost in 1947 to a place as a major subdivision of OMGUS, religious affairs was elevated to branch status.

Although the basic American policy in the religious affairs field was that of noninterference, careful attention had to be given to specific items.[4] To start out, there was the problem of denazification. The German churches had been less subservient to the Nazis than had most other social groups; nevertheless National Socialist contamination was by no means absent. Hitler had attempted to bring the churches under Nazi control along with the schools, the labor unions, the courts, the arts, and everything else. To this end he had established the post of Reich Minister for Ecclesiastical Affairs.

The Catholic Church found itself in conflict with the National Socialist regime almost from the beginning, and in general refused to bow down to the Hitler will. The Lutheran Church was split into factions and presented a less united front. Some of the Lutheran clergy allowed themselves to be influenced by Nazi blandishments and, if not active Nazis, at least were badly smeared by National Socialist associations. Others displayed great courage in withstanding the Nazi demands and bribes, even though it meant going to concentration camps. The record of the independent denominations, Baptists, Methodists, and so forth, varied somewhat. Hitler had sought to use some of them by dispensing favors to their leaders and he succeeded in this endeavor in certain instances. Altogether it was estimated that approximately 15 per cent of the German clergy had

---

[4] For a discussion of the early activities, see S. W. Herman, *The Rebirth of the German Church* (Harper, New York, 1946).

Nazi records which made them unacceptable to the United States. When one recalls that more than 80 per cent of the teachers, judges, and other professional groups were enrolled in National Socialist organizations of one kind and another, it is evident how relatively independent the churches had been.

Nevertheless, some of these 15 per cent were in strongly entrenched positions, even bishoprics, and they were often most reluctant to resign their places. American military government in general left the task of ousting the clergy with notorious Nazi associations to the churches themselves. However, it found itself in a position where it had to watch rather carefully what was done. Pressures of one sort and another arose to hinder the process of removing certain of the Nazi clergy and the churches moved ahead slowly. The Religious Affairs staff of OMGUS consequently had to let the church officials know that removals must be carried out, despite the influence exerted by powerful individuals and their friends.

One of the earliest moves on the part of the Religious Affairs Branch of OMGUS was to re-establish contacts between German churches and religious bodies in the United States and other democratic countries. Before representatives of other groups were permitted to visit Germany, the Federal Council of the Churches of Christ in the United States was invited to send its president, Bishop G. Bromley Oxnam, to Germany to confer on a plan for establishing liaison representatives of Protestants, Catholics, and Jews in Germany. Three liaison representatives from the United States, one for each of the three groups noted above, came to Germany in 1946 and served a useful purpose in counseling with the German churches on their many problems. These representatives naturally worked in close conjunction with the Religious Affairs staff of OMGUS, though they were not an integral part of the latter. They were permitted by the British and French military governments to carry on their work of establishing contacts with religious bodies in the United States in the British and French Zones and thus were not limited to the American Zone.

The Religious Affairs staff also realized the importance of establishing relations with European church leaders, whose problems were in many respects similar to those facing the German churches, as well as with American religious groups. Consequently from an early stage more attention was given in the religious affairs area than in perhaps

323

any other to building up relations with European countries. The Protestant churches of Germany were admitted to the World Council of Churches in 1947 and took an active part in the first meeting of that organization held at Amsterdam in 1948. Representatives of the Catholic Church in Germany also were encouraged to attend various international Catholic assemblages. Beginning in 1947 conferences were held annually in Germany to which representatives of European and American churches were invited to confer with German pastors. These were arranged by the German churches themselves, but the Religious Affairs Branch rendered considerable assistance. In 1950 four such international conferences were held in the form of summer institutes in Germany by the Lutherans. Representatives from various European countries and the United States spent many hours discussing significant problems with some 650 German religious leaders at these conferences.

The Religious Affairs subdivisions of OMGUS and HICOG actively participated in the exchanges program. During the single year of 1950, for example, 39 foreign religious leaders were sent to Germany to consult and 152 German church leaders were brought to the United States to observe various religious activities. Approximately one fourth of the German church leaders going to the United States were primarily interested in religious education, and nearly half had projects involving the teaching of religion as part of the regular school curriculum.

Under the sponsorship of the Religious Affairs subdivision, various surveys were carried on in Germany by foreign religious experts. Dr. R. P. Barnes of the Federal Council of the Churches of Christ and Dr. Paul C. Empie of the National Lutheran Council were sent from the United States to survey the activities of the West German Protestant churches in 1949, particularly those receiving financial grants from the United States. In reporting, these American leaders pointed out certain fields, especially of a social character, in which German Protestantism had been backward and in which greater efforts should be made if the support of the masses of the people were to be expected in the future. Similar work was done by Fathers E. E. Quinn, G. C. Higgins, and W. E. McManus of the Catholic Church in the United States for the Catholic group in Germany. Both Protestant and Catholic reports interestingly enough agreed on a number of points which required greater attention by German Christians.[5]

The Religious Affairs subdivision naturally displayed much interest in Jewish religious activities in Germany, hoping to assist in meeting the very great problems of the comparatively small number of Jews remaining in Germany after the war. Attention was given to the organizing of Councils of Christians and Jews in Germany.

With the problem of German youth so acute following the war and the collapse of the Hitler Youth, attention was given to religious youth groups in Germany by the Religious Affairs staff. Grants from the Special Projects Fund of HICOG were made available to buy equipment for some of these youth groups. International work camps, at which youth from various countries gathered to live and work together on some constructive project for several weeks during the summer, were assisted. There were 30 such camps in the American Zone in 1950 alone.

Sharp criticism was leveled at American military government by German religious leaders on the score of making paper and publishing facilities available to the secular press before the religious press received such assistance. It was noted that there were 23 secular daily newspapers published in the American Zone before the first religious daily was licensed in August 1948. Perhaps no item in the religious area stirred up as much feeling as the delay in re-establishing the religious press. Paper shortages were very serious, so much so that it was impossible to print the school books needed in the required numbers. American policy gave priority to the information and news type of publication over the religious during the early years of the occupation, acknowledging at the same time the importance of the religious press in principle. As paper supplies became more adequate, the religious press in Germany fared better, and by the end of 1949 it was flourishing. By July 1949 the Reid survey reported no less than 280 religious publications in Germany, with a total circulation reaching almost ten million.[6]

[5] For summaries of these reports, see McClaskey, *op. cit.*, pp. 33-35.
[6] For a breakdown of this number, see McClaskey, *op. cit.*, pp. 70-71.

23

The Problem of Democracy for Germany

There is little convincing evidence that democracy can be imposed by one country or a group of countries on another, though the democratic example set by a given country may have influence outside of its own borders. If democracy can be transplanted at all, it will presumably be only under favorable conditions, and these do not exist in a defeated country where war shock is prevalent, living conditions are precarious, and the psychology of the people is abnormal.[1] Yet both the Joint Chiefs of Staff directive to the American Commander in Germany and the Potsdam Conference Agreement stated that a basic purpose in Germany was "To prepare for the eventual reconstruction of German political life on a democratic basis."[2]

The fact that the United States, the Soviet Union, and Great Britain all subscribed to the Potsdam Agreement perhaps is sufficient to indicate the vague or perhaps meaningless character of this objective. Obviously a brand of democracy acceptable to the United States and Britain would have little recognition in the Soviet Union and vice versa. Since the language in the April 1945 draft of the Joint Chiefs of Staff directive is almost identical with that contained in the later Potsdam Agreement, it would seem probable that America had considerable influence on the inclusion of such a provision in the latter.

There is of course no public record indicating what the Joint Chiefs of Staff were thinking about when they included "the preparation for an eventual reconstruction of German political life on a demo-

---

[1] For a realistic discussion of this problem, see T. V. Smith, "American Democracy: Expendable and Exportable," *Virginia Quarterly Review*, Spring 1947. Also see Ian Colvin, "Exporting Democracy to Germany," *National Review*, Aug. 1947. Dr. Theodor Heuss, president of the West German Federal Republic, is quoted as saying: "Occupation is not and cannot be simultaneously instruction in the democratic way of life." See M. Balfour and J. Mair, *Four-Power Control in Germany and Austria 1945-1946* (Oxford University Press, London, 1956), p. 64n.

[2] See JCS 1067, Pt. I, Sec. 4, paragraph 3, and the Protocol of the Proceedings of the Potsdam Conference, Pt. II, A, Sec. iv.

cratic basis" as one of the "basic objectives of military government in Germany." It may be inferred that this statement received comparatively slight critical consideration, being included because it sounded well. On the basis of the "making the world safe for democracy" experience of World War I, it would seem that any serious discussion on the part of the Joint Chiefs of Staff in the drafting of such a provision would have led to the conclusion that the imposition of democratic forms on a defeated nation is a futile proposition. It is particularly difficult to suppose that the Joint Chiefs of Staff gave very careful attention to this provision when it was more or less smothered by punitive stipulations of one kind and another. The transplanting of democratic political institutions to Germany would be most uncertain at best, but when such a goal was coupled with a vengeful program emphasizing denazification, the imposition of a low living standard on the German people, nonfraternization, the destruction of German industry, and the like, it would seem to have little or no concrete significance.[3]

It should be noted that the Joint Chiefs of Staff directive did not order the democratization of Germany, as wide publicity has led some to assume, but the more nebulous "preparation" for an "eventual reconstruction" of German political life on "a democratic basis." But how the generally negative provisions of the directive could be regarded as any real "preparation" for such democratic reconstruction it is difficult to perceive. Of course, hindsight is clearer than foresight, and it is easy to forget the war psychology and pressures under which the Joint Chiefs of Staff operated. Perhaps it was too much to expect even simple logic in the basic American directive relating to the occupation of Germany.

At various periods during the occupation of Germany there was talk of democratization and of a program to bring democracy to the Germans. Much of this talk was ambiguous, disregarding reality and motivated in large measure, if not completely, by emotionalism and wishful thinking. Some maintained that the democratization of the Germans was the chief purpose of the United States and that such an undertaking took on the guise of a great modern crusade. A certain amount of discussion centered around the provision of JCS 1067

---

[3] See A. R. L. Gurland, "Why Democracy Is Losing in Germany," *Commentary*, Sept. 1949.

relating to democratic reconstruction, but no agreement was reached as to a specific "program." Some of the military government officials did not believe that democracy could be brought to Germany and consequently did not favor a program. Others were less skeptical and felt that the occupation following World War II offered a great opportunity to determine whether or not the Germans could be started on the path leading to democracy. Because other immediate emergencies presented heavy pressures, the tendency was to leave the problem of democratic reconstruction in abeyance.

Yet the official speeches and pronouncements never dropped the democratic objective. The Stuttgart address of Secretary of State Byrnes in September 1946 made various references to such a purpose. In discussing the Potsdam provision that there should be no central German government, Byrnes declared that "this only meant that no central government should be established until *some sort of democracy was rooted in the soil of Germany*." [4] Again he said: "All that the Allied governments can and should do is to lay down the rules under which German democracy can govern itself." [5] In advocating the establishment of a provisional government, Secretary Byrnes noted that "The German National Council should also be charged with the preparation of a draft of a federal constitution for Germany which, among other things, should insure the democratic character of the new Germany. . . ." [6] Perhaps the common characteristic of all of these utterances was their vagueness as to specific avenues leading to a democratic Germany. It was never suggested that there could be other than a democratic regime in Germany, but no concrete proposals were made that could lead to such a transformation. The general tendency was to ignore the undemocratic record of the past and the lack of any considerable sentiment on the part of the German people favoring democracy.

Although there was never a single, overall, organized effort to carry out the basic objective of democratic reconstruction, various programs were launched which at least indirectly had some bearing on the subject. Some of these were negative in character and actually achieved little or nothing in the way of constructive results: the denazification purge, the war crimes trials, the ban on student fraterni-

[4] See Department of State, *Germany, 1947-1949; The Story in Documents*, p. 6.
[5] *Ibid.*, p. 6.
[6] *Ibid.*, p. 7.

ties, and so forth.* Others, such as the exchanges program, the information program, and the encouragement given to organized labor made a contribution to such an end.** In the remaining pages of this chapter, attention will be given to the abolition of Prussia, the attempt to curtail the influence of the guilds by giving the German people an opportunity to select their own occupations, the attempted reform of the German civil service, community programs aimed at increased participation on the part of citizens in their local governments, and political parties, all of which bore some relationship to preparing the way for democracy in Germany. But perhaps the most significant contribution toward building democratic foundations in West Germany resulted from no specific program or programs, but rather from the constructive attitude of the western Allies and particularly of the United States during the High Commission period. The emphasis by the United States and its allies on assisting the West German Federal Government to develop effective institutions of a progressive type rather than on exercising a veto may not have been without its dangers, but it perhaps made the chief impact in the direction of democracy.† The personal example of American G.I.s was often cited by high American military officials as the most important factor in promoting democracy in Germany, but it seems probable that this estimate represented considerable exaggeration, though such a factor certainly had some significance.‡

THE ABOLITION OF PRUSSIA

The role of Prussia in German political history of the eighteenth, nineteenth, and twentieth centuries was spectacular. Even after the unification and the establishment of the German Empire in the latter part of the nineteenth century, the influence of Prussia remained great if not paramount. Thus the Prussian King automatically held the position of German Emperor, and the Prussian voice in the powerful Bundesrat was sufficient to veto if not achieve action. With more than half of the population of Germany within its borders and with more territory than all of the other states combined, Prussia inevitably loomed large. There is considerable controversy as to the exact charac-

* See Chaps. 10, 11.
** See Chaps. 15, 16, 19.
† See Chaps. 4 and 12 for further discussion of this attitude.
‡ See Chap. 9 for additional discussion.

ter of the Prussian influence in German political affairs: some regard it as distinctly evil and others defend it warmly. Supporters of a democratic system have usually concluded that Prussia exerted far from a salutary influence. Many have expressed the opinion that one of the most serious weaknesses of the Weimar Republic was represented by the Prussian dominance, maintaining that the Allies made a grave error in not insisting on the abolition of Prussia following World War I.

The United States was of course in no position to force single-handed the liquidation of Prussia following World War II, but its influence was exerted in this direction in the Allied Control Council. Despite its record of disagreement and deadlocks, the Allied Control Council did manage to take action which legally put an end to Prussia. Control Council Law No. 46, dated February 25, 1947, was entitled "Abolition of the State of Prussia." The division of the territory remaining to Germany after World War II surrender into four Allied zones did not follow the lines of the prewar German states. Small states, particularly in the British Zone, were thrown together to make a single administrative unit. Prussian territory was included in all four of the zones, and in order to give legality to the new states set up within these zones it was necessary to take legal action dissolving the old Prussia.

Many will agree with General Clay in characterizing this action of the Allied Control Council as one of the most important, if not the most important, undertaken by that ill-fated body.[7] While Prussia has been brought to an end under the four-zone arrangement, there still remains of course the threat of emergence in the future. It is not at all uncommon to encounter Germans who hold the opinion that Prussia will again arise to take her old position of pre-eminence; only time will determine the permanence of the action taken by the Allied Control Council.

FREEDOM TO CHOOSE AN OCCUPATION

Long after the medieval guilds controlling the various occupations had disappeared from most of the rest of western Europe, they retained a position of great influence in Germany. In their earlier days

---

[7] See his *Decision in Germany*, p. 144.

330

the guilds had accomplished good by establishing standards and furnishing protection to their members, but in the twentieth century their general influence seemed to be primarily negative. Recognized by the law and authorized to control entrance into their fields, they had a near stranglehold on certain segments of economic life in Germany, especially on the trades and in the retail selling fields. It was literally impossible for young men in Germany to exercise much free choice in determining an occupation because of the control exercised by the powerful guilds.

It is not surprising that such a system seemed an evil one to American military government. Steps were consequently taken to set up systems in the states of the American Zone under which Germans could, within reason, engage in any occupation they might choose. Of course, various qualifications had to be offered for the professions and for positions where the public welfare necessitated certain types of experience and training. But otherwise a German could engage in the electric appliance business, in the dispensing of pharmaceuticals, or whatever else attracted him if he could find the capital, a building to house his enterprise, and the like.

The opposition on the part of the old guilds and of many vested interests to such freedom in engaging in occupations was naturally bitter. As the occupation proceeded, this opposition became more and more organized and entrenched. No *Landtag* (state legislature) ever met in the American Zone without finding itself faced with various proposals to re-establish the old system in some measure. Many of the proposals were so ingeniously worded that they seemed at first sight to be aboveboard and without objection. In defense of a return to the old system, arguments were presented that the new arrangement was very wasteful in that it permitted the establishment of more business enterprises than the demand would justify, thus leading to numerous bankruptcies; that competition was unfair and standards were lowered.

Among large numbers of Germans the new system was regarded with great favor despite an admitted increase in bankruptcies. The American contention that the removal of the severe limitations on business activity would have a constructive influence toward establishing democratic foundations in German life appeared to have validity. However, the pressure exerted by the entrenched interests was

331

such that, despite the support of American military government and during the latter period of the occupation by HICOG, frequent inroads were made. Whether, with the return to German sovereignty, any progress made in freeing Germany from the control of the guilds will remain is problematical. Left to a free vote of the people it was possible, and even probable, that the new economic freedom would be retained, but under the existing political process it was not always popular sentiment which controlled.

ATTEMPTS TO REFORM THE GERMAN CIVIL SERVICE

From the early days of the occupation, the Americans believed that the German civil service required a thorough overhauling. They contended that the failure to reform the civil service in an adequate manner during the period of the Weimar Republic contributed to the basic weakness of that first essay on the part of the Germans into the field of democratic government. Moreover, it was pointed out that the undemocratic civil service had offered little or no support for the Weimar Republic during its critical fight for survival and that many of the senior civil servants had gone over to the Nazis without much persuasion in 1933, even if they had not flirted with the National Socialists earlier.

The United States provided for a civil service section of military government from the beginning, and various persons working in this field issued manuals, recommendations, and proposals for action. Early actions led to the banning of titles and uniforms for the hordes of lesser civil servants. But the chief goal of the American civil service experts, among whom E. C. Wolfsperger and H. P. Jones probably had the greatest influence, was the reconstruction of the German civil service somewhat along American lines. The great gulf separating the rank and file of lower civil servants from the smaller number of senior civil servants was regarded as undemocratic, and it was proposed to extend more equal pay scales, greater tenure, more adequate provisions for retirement and vacations, and so forth, to most if not all of the public employees. Entry into the senior civil service largely through the avenue of legal training was to be modified to include those who had taken their university work in political science, public administration, social work, economics, and other related fields. Mod-

332

ern public personnel practices familiar in the United States were to be introduced as far as applicable to German public service.

During the military government period, the United States had full authority to do what it thought desirable for civil service, but this period was so confused as far as re-establishing a German governmental structure was concerned that the scope was actually severely limited. Not until the West German Federal Government came into operation was there an opportunity to apply civil service reforms on a broad scale, and under the Occupation Statute the United States lacked the full authority in this area enjoyed earlier. In the meantime, the group of old higher civil servants became more or less entrenched and naturally vigorously opposed civil service reconstruction along the lines proposed by the American experts, mainly because their own positions would be considerably weakened.

The West German Federal Government found itself under considerable moral pressure to do something about civil service reform despite the lack of enthusiastic support which the American experts could stir up among their British and French colleagues. But it delayed and delayed taking any final action, maintaining that time would be required to enact a definitive civil service statute. When the act was finally passed, it contained some of the provisions urged by the Americans, but by and large it seemed to leave the senior civil servants substantially in their old positions, widely separated from the rank and file of ordinary public employees.

Several years will be required before it is at all clear what the actual effect of the new statute may be and consequently to what extent American efforts in this field have been effective.[8] However, it seems improbable that the entrance to the public service will have been broadened appreciably and that preparation in political science and other social sciences will be substituted for legal training in any large measure in the foreseeable future. Films designed to show the obnoxious and often absurd behavior of petty civil servants had a fairly wide showing among the Germans and evoked laughter, but their actual influence is difficult to predict. Perhaps the most valuable contribution made by the American occupation authorities was in connection with the organization of a German association of public

---

[8] The best treatment of civil service developments is that of Arnold Brecht in E. H. Litchfield, ed., *Governing Postwar Germany*.

personnel officials. The exchanges program enabled a number of these officials to observe civil service administration in the United States and various quite impressive reports were prepared on the basis of their visits which seem to indicate a progressive attitude on the part of at least some of the younger public personnel officers. Were it not for the deep hostility and vigorous opposition to reform on the part of the German senior civil servants who feel that they are fighting for their professional privileges and rights, the future would appear more promising.

CITIZEN PARTICIPATION PROGRAM

Although the main emphasis of the United States in attempting to prepare the Germans for democracy at least during the military government period seemed to be along the lines of drafting constitutions, holding elections, and the like, some attention was given to the stimulation of interest on the part of the German citizens and to the encouragement of more active participation by the citizens in their local governments.[9] Thirteen pamphlets bearing such titles as "The Citizen and the Public Authorities," "The Citizen and the City Council," "What Does Self-Government Mean?" "The State Legislature," "From Subject to Free Citizen," "You and Your Local Government," "You Are Not Interested in Politics?" "The Individual and the State," and "It's Your Turn to Speak" were prepared by the Division of Internal and Governmental Affairs of the HICOG Office of Political Affairs, and these were circulated to the extent of 20,000 each. Much of the time of the *Kreis* resident officers under HICOG during the period 1949-1951 was given to organizing citizens' committees, conducting public affairs forums, promoting the active participation of women in local affairs, and related programs.

These activities were diversely regarded by American authorities in Germany as well as by the German people. Many American officials considered such programs as of the "do-gooder" type and at least privately held the view that they served no useful purpose. It was frequently remarked that they represented "boon-doggling" in an extreme form. The local German officials often had a most disparaging attitude which even became venomous at times, but in their

---

[9] For the details of the HICOG program, see *Program to Foster Citizen Participation in Germany*, a monograph put out by that agency in 1951.

case it was to some extent at least motivated by an apprehension lest their personal power be undermined. Officials in the British and French zones where such activities were not undertaken often expressed themselves critically on the American program in this field.

The dropping of the American *Kreis* resident officers in late 1951 and 1952 largely put an end to these American activities, though the Germans were encouraged to continue them. Since the period covered by such a program was brief and the time and money at the command of the resident officers for such a purpose were not very adequate, there is some question as to whether as much was accomplished as could have been. If one examines the record, it is apparent that the results varied widely, depending on the ability and efforts of the resident officer and his wife, upon the response of local German communities, upon the opposition of local leaders, and other factors. In certain communities the movement really never got under way; in others it never reached the stage of stirring up much local interest; but in a number of places extraordinary interest was stimulated and at least for a time there was considerable activity in connection with the citizen committees, the public affairs forums, the town-meeting projects, the women's program, and so forth. In Württemberg-Baden more than 700 citizen committees were organized among the some 1,500 villages (*Gemeinden*) in that state. Of these it was reported in August 1951 that approximately 150 were "active." [10] It is interesting to note the reactions of certain British and French resident officers who spent a week or thereabouts observing the work of their American colleagues in a particular *Kreis*. Usually arriving with little respect for such American activities, several of these reported later that they had been favorably impressed by what they saw.

POLITICAL PARTIES

The Joint Chiefs of Staff directive 1067 reflected the somewhat suspicious attitude of the American military toward political parties in postwar Germany. It was stipulated: "No political activities of any kind shall be countenanced unless authorized by you. You will assure that your military government does not become committed to any

---

[10] For a more detailed treatment of this program, see H. P. Pilgert, *Community and Group Life in West Germany*, in the Historical Series of the Office of the U. S. High Commissioner of Germany (1952), especially Chaps. 5 and 6.

335

political group." [11] However, the Potsdam Agreement provided that "all democratic political parties with rights of assembly and of public discussion shall be allowed and encouraged throughout Germany." [12] This was probably the result of Russian action in June 1945, under which antifascist parties were authorized in the Russian Zone and in Berlin, four such political parties being licensed at once. The Americans and British had to take cognizance of such an existing situation and at least on paper accord such privileges in their zones.

American military government was in somewhat of a quandary as a result of the conflict between the basic go-slow attitude of the American top-brass and the provision of the Potsdam Agreement noted above. To begin with, there was a very real apprehension of the Communist party and its designs on Germany. It was known that the Communists had gone underground following the collapse of the Weimar Republic and that it was the only political party which had been able to maintain some semblance of an organization during the Hitler regime. Not unnaturally, military officials were wary of any step which might give the Communists an opportunity to move ahead toward their objectives. Nevertheless, with the policy of the Russians as regards political parties known among the German people and the provision of the Potsdam Agreement in August 1945, some action had to be taken. Accordingly, permission was given political groups of an anti-Nazi, non-Fascist character to carry on activities in the villages (*Gemeinden*) and counties (*Kreise*) of the American Zone during the summer of 1945. When it was apparent that the Communist menace was less great than had been anticipated, such permission was extended to the state level in the autumn of 1945.

The political parties early found that it was not satisfactory to operate on a *Kreis* or even on a *Land* basis, and pressure developed to allow political party activity throughout the American Zone. This was granted in February 1946. Permission was not an automatic affair but was rather given after application and review in each instance in the form of a license. It is to be noted, however, that the hand of the reluctant American military government officials was more or less forced after the initial step had been taken. After forming local organizations, the political parties moved ahead rapidly toward state

[11] Pt. I, Sec. 9, a.
[12] Pt. II, Sec. A, paragraph 9.

336

and even zonal activities; and the extensions mentioned above which took place in the fall of 1945 and the early part of 1946 actually recognized what had already transpired.

The Potsdam Agreement anticipated Allied action which would result in uniform policies as regards political parties throughout Germany; but, since the Allied Control Authority found it difficult if not impossible to act in accord, each zone became a little world of its own and the American military government handled the licensing of political parties as it saw fit.[13] Despite the large State Department staff which formed the Political Affairs subdivision of the Office of Military Government, the attitude of American military government toward political parties remained largely negative for some time. The Russians displayed great energy in pushing the advancement of political parties of the Communist variety, but the Americans had no corresponding program as far as the democratic parties were concerned. It has been noted that the attitude of the generals seemed to be one of distrust of political parties in general. The Foreign Service Officers, who in certain cases at least had more knowledge of German political party history, were either indifferent or unable to exert their influence —some of them were primarily concerned with checking the Communist party. Mr. Scammon succinctly summarizes the situation thus: "Interference by occupation authorities was not infrequent in the earliest days of German political activity, and many of these interferences seem on later examination to have been improper and arbitrary." He goes on to add: "Most of these activities, however, were the product of a lack of thorough political training and lack of understanding rather than a deliberate policy, and they had virtually vanished by the ending of the political licensing system."[14]

After the German political parties became well established on an interzonal basis throughout Western Germany, it was not infrequently charged that the United States favored the somewhat conservative Christian Democratic party and opposed or at least distrusted the Social Democratic party which, being based on the mass of industrial workers, was regarded by some as the hope of any vital democratic development in Germany. There may be some basis for such claims,

---

[13] A more detailed discussion of the development of political parties in the American Zone is to be found in R. M. Scammon's contribution to E. H. Litchfield, ed., *Governing Postwar Germany*.

[14] See *ibid.*, p. 479.

though they seem to be exaggerated. The fact that the Christian Democratic party along with its much weaker sister parties, the Free Democratic party and the German party (and later the All-German Bloc [Refugee] party), controlled the West German Federal Government until the end of the occupation naturally contributed to somewhat closer American relations with that party. Nevertheless, Mr. McCloy as High Commissioner made a very real effort to maintain regular contacts with the Social Democrats and spent many hours discussing matters with Dr. Schumacher and others of its leaders. The basis for the charge of American preference for the Christian Democratic party lies in part in statements made by certain high ranking Americans in Washington prior to the election of 1953 which indicated that they hoped for a Christian Democratic victory.*

It has also been alleged that the underlying conservative sympathy of the United States was such that it gave preference to the Christian Democrats rather than to the Social Democrats who were supposedly the favorites of the British. Individual British officials perhaps did have more of a common meeting ground with the Social Democrats than most Americans, and during the years of the Labor government, 1945-1951, the official British policies at home were closer to those advocated by the Social Democrats in Germany. The same situation may have applied to the Americans and the Christian Democrats to a lesser degree, though not all of the actions of the Christian Democrats were consonant with American policies. However, as American attention was more and more focused on bringing West Germany into the western defense alliance, the fact that the Christian Democratic party supported the integration of Germany into such a grouping and the Social Democrats held back, if they did not actually oppose, made for more cordial American relations with the former.

Even a casual observer of German political parties must be impressed by the progress made during the relatively brief period since 1945. The national election campaign in 1953 indicated that the German political parties do not lag behind political parties in the United States and Britain insofar as effective campaign techniques are a gauge.[15] Their use of sound trucks, loud-speaker apparatus, parades,

---

* Secretary of State Dulles contributed the most publicized statement to this effect.
[15] An illuminating first-hand analysis of this election is presented in J. K. Pollock et al., *German Democracy at Work* (University of Michigan Press, Ann Arbor, 1955).

338

placards, posters, banners, radio broadcasts, handbills, and the like, reminded one of the United States. The turnout of voters at the elections exceeds that to be noted in the United States: the 1953 national election brought out more than 80 per cent of those qualified to vote, and state and local elections usually draw 70 per cent or more of the voters.[16] But as to whether the German political parties have become democratized, there is a wide difference of opinion. Some observers believe that they are substantially as democratic as political parties in the United States or any other of the democratic countries. Others see little in the existing political parties of Germany which suggests any fundamental advance over the parties of the German Empire or the Weimar Republic. The fact that, instead of the shifting multiple party system which characterized the Weimar Republic, there is now what seems to be a stable system of parties, with two, the Christian Democrats and Social Democrats, so far ahead of the others as to resemble a biparty rather than a multiple-party setup, apparently has little significance to this latter group. It is too early to attempt a conclusive evaluation. Political parties, like other elements of the political system of Germany during the years of the occupation, were in a formative stage. The real tests are ahead as Germany re-enters the family of sovereign nations. Only the meeting of these tests will determine the extent to which democratic traditions have actually been incorporated into the political parties of West Germany.[17]

---

[16] For a discussion of elections and electoral processes, see R. M. Scammon's second chapter in *Governing Postwar Germany*.

[17] For additional discussion of the political parties, see G. A. Almond, "The Political Ideas of Christian Democracy," *Journal of Politics*, Nov. 1948; J. P. C. Carey, "Political Organization of the Refugees and Expellees in West Germany," *Political Science Quarterly*, June 1951; V. Franke-Eliasberg, "Political Party Developments," in G. A. Almond, ed., *The Struggle for Democracy in Germany* (University of North Carolina Press, Chapel Hill, 1949); F. A. Hermens, *Europe between Democracy and Anarchy* (University of Notre Dame, Notre Dame, Ind., 1951); E. W. Meyer, *Political Parties in Western Germany* (Library of Congress, Washington, 1951); R. G. Neumann, "The New Political Parties of Germany," *American Political Science Review*, Sept. 1946; S. Neumann's section on Germany in *Modern Political Parties* (University of Chicago Press, Chicago, 1956); L. Bergstrasser, "Political Parties in Germany," *Contemporary Review* (London), Aug. 1947; H. Meyerhoff, "Parties and Classes in Postwar Germany," *South Atlantic Quarterly*, Jan. 1947; OMGUS, *Political Parties in Western Germany* (1949); H. Price and C. E. Schorske, *The Problem of Germany* (Council on Foreign Relations, New York, 1947), pp. 93-111; "The Radical Right," *7th Quarterly Report of the U. S. High Commissioner for Germany;* HICOG, *Elections and Political Parties in Germany, 1945-1952* (Bad Godesberg, 1952); R. Wildenmann, *Partei und Fraktion* (Meisenhaim, 1954); W. Mommsen, *Deutsche Partei programme der Gegenwart* (Munich, 1954); L. Bergstrasser, *Geschichte den politische Parteien in Deutschland* (Munich, 1955).

24

The Special Problem of Berlin

Even before the surrender of the Germans, Berlin presented a special problem to the Allies. This great city not only had been the political capital of Germany, but it had been a cultural, educational, and financial center, with an outstanding place in German history. Associated as it was with Hitler and the Nazi regime, though Munich had been the real home of the National Socialists, and with other aspects of extreme nationalism, there was a serious question in the minds of some Allied leaders whether Berlin should be given a place of any unusual importance in the postwar period. It had been very badly bombed by Allied planes and suffered further serious damage from the artillery fire and bitter street-to-street fighting which took place during the Russian siege. Some argued that it should be left in its ruined state as a monument to past German folly and that a new site could be selected on the borders between the western and the Russian zones for a capital.

However, for various reasons it was decided to retain Berlin as the chief city in Germany, despite its location deep within the Russian Zone—it was actually nearer the Polish border on the east than to the western zones, being approximately one hundred miles from the latter. The European Advisory Commission agreed that Berlin should be set aside within the Russian Zone as an Allied center to be administered by the military commanders of the Allies, and this was approved by the Yalta Conference. In issuing in early June 1945 the document drafted by the European Advisory Commission, the military commanders appropriately met in Berlin,[1] though it was some weeks later before the Russians permitted their Allies to establish military government headquarters in Berlin and to begin the quadripartite administration of the city. In the meantime the Russians had set up a city government along their own lines and with Communist officials.

---

[1] For a first-hand description of this event, see L. D. Clay, *Decision in Germany*, pp. 20-23.

The Special Problem of Berlin

Although American military leaders are usually almost ultra-sensitive to the most minute provisions for maintaining communication lines, the agreement relating to the use of Berlin as a quadripartite headquarters for the administration of an occupied Germany contained no clear provisions for communication lines from Berlin to the western zones. The European Advisory Commission had top-ranking military advisers, and it was strange that they did not insist on adequate communication guarantees. Moreover, the agreement was considered at Yalta where again senior military representatives of the United States were present in sizable numbers. It was finally approved by the respective Allied governments and in the case of the United States must have received the attention of the Joint Chiefs of Staff. Even after all of these steps, the military commanders, according to General Clay, apparently did not regard the document as absolutely fixed and, after the commanders reached Berlin in June 1945, a deletion was made at the request of the Russians on the authority of the military commanders themselves.[2] Yet the provisions for communications between Berlin and the West remained vague and in the last analysis depended on the good will of the Russians. The curious explanation offered to justify such a strange lack of foresight on the part of the military was that it seemed desirable at the time to display faith in the Russians.

After the American, British, and French were permitted by the Russians to send military government forces into Berlin in the mid-summer of 1945, a *Kommandatura* was organized to administer Berlin. A Communist city government had already been established by the Russians, as noted above, and the *Kommandatura* had the difficult job of trying to control this instrumentality of the Russians. How impossible a job it was, soon became apparent. Prior to the German surrender the United States had made provision for a military government detachment to function in Berlin—indeed more than a single provision was actually made and this occasioned some confusion and conflict. The American military government contingent which finally arrived in Berlin was part of the military force under General Floyd Parks. It consisted of some 500 officers and enlisted men under Colonel Frank L. Howley. The British had made a similar provision; and the French, only recently in a position to take steps of any charac-

---

[2] See L. D. Clay, *Decision in Germany*, p. 22.

ALLIED KOMMANDATURA, BERLIN

ORGANIZATIONAL CHART

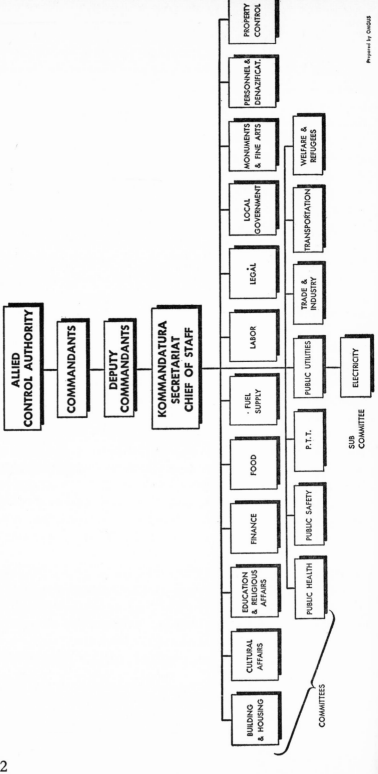

Prepared by OMGUS

ter, were rather less well provided for. Each of the four occupying powers was at first represented on the Berlin *Kommandatura* by its chief military representative in charge of Berlin forces rather than by the head of its military government setup, but the latter served as deputy and, along with his chief assistants in the military government organization, attended *Kommandatura* meetings. A comparatively intact building in the American Sector was designated as *Kommandatura* headquarters, and here meetings of the representatives of the four Allies were held. Each of the four Allied commanders took turns in serving as head of the *Kommandatura*, rotating every month, and a corresponding provision was made in the case of the head of the secretariat.

The meetings of the *Kommandatura* were held each week and were stormy affairs from the beginning. The Russians started out with the notion that they were hosts to the other Allies in Berlin and consequently occupied a preferred position. It seemed quite appropriate to them that they should have the main responsibility for Berlin affairs and that the Americans, British, and French should acquiesce in whatever they thought desirable, even to the point of supporting a Communist regime in the city administration. The other Allies naturally did not accept such a Russian view and regarded themselves as equally responsible with the Russians for Berlin control. Under such circumstances it was not surprising that the meetings of the *Kommandatura* should have been characterized by considerable disagreement.[3] The Russians never changed their original stand and persistently sought to maintain their privileged position as far as Berlin was concerned. When they failed to gain their way in the *Kommandatura*, they did not hesitate to go behind the scenes and give their own orders to Berlin officials, even though these directly countermanded *Kommandatura* policies.

Nevertheless, the Russians maintained straight faces in going through the motions of participating in the sessions of the Berlin *Kommandatura*. Although they had no intention of abiding by the decisions of the *Kommandatura* unless they wanted to, they seemed to take great pleasure in presenting their views in great detail and with

---

[3] A first-hand account of the situation by the American deputy and later Berlin military governor is to be found in Frank L. Howley, *Berlin Command* (Putnam, New York, 1950).

unusual eloquence and force. Indeed the meetings of the *Kommandatura*, like certain sessions of United Nations bodies, seemed to be regarded by the Russians as opportunities to talk at great length about their own rightness and the evil character of their associates. At first it was rather interesting to observe the Russians in the *Kommandatura* meetings. They often expressed themselves well, they were frequently colorful as individuals, the interpreting was better than average, and the chamber where the sessions were held lent an air of distinction. But the Russians repeated the same old story again and again and their charges aimed at the western Allies soon became tiresome. But more than anything else, the western representatives resented the Russian practice of ignoring the actions of the *Kommandatura* and their treachery in going behind the backs of other Allied representatives to give their own orders to the Berlin city government.

It was not until October 1946, more than a year after the *Kommandatura* had been organized, that the western Allies were able to force an election for the purpose of choosing Berlin city officials. By hook and crook the Russians had managed prior to this time to keep their own stooges in charge of Berlin. Seeking to make their program more palatable to the Germans, the Russians had engineered a marriage of the Social Democrats and the Communists under the name of the Socialist Unity party which had its main success in the Soviet Sector of Berlin, since most of the Social Democrats of the western sectors of Berlin refused to be forced into such a shot-gun sort of marriage. The results of the election held on October 20, 1946, were extremely gratifying to the Americans, British, and French, and deeply resented by the Russians. The Social Democrats, who had defied the Russians by refusing to enter the Socialist Unity party, polled almost half of the votes, with 48.7 per cent; whereas the Christian Democrats and the Liberal Democrats, both far from friendly with the Russians, received 22 per cent and 9 per cent, respectively. Despite all of the Russian assistance, the Socialist Unity candidates received only 19.8 per cent of the votes. A Social Democratic administration was installed and Dr. Otto Ostrowski, a Social Democrat, was chosen as *Oberbürgermeister* (mayor).

The Russians, having lost the election, attempted to nullify the election results by maintaining that art. 36 of the Temporary Berlin Constitution required *Kommandatura* approval of elected officials.

344

Moreover, they insisted that the new Berlin government could not oust the Communists whom they had appointed earlier to various municipal posts. The result was that the sessions of the *Kommandatura* became even stormier than before. The western Allies were forced to regard the Russians as determined to have their way at any price and despite any steps taken by the *Kommandatura*. When in February 1947 the *Oberbürgermeister* under pressure from the Russians was discovered to have made a deal with the Socialist Unity minority, great indignation developed among the western Allies and the rank and file of the Berliners. Dr. Ostrowski, being disavowed by a vote of 85 to 20 in the City Assembly, resigned. The City Assembly then elected Dr. Ernst Reuter, one of the ablest and most forceful public officials to be found anywhere in postwar Germany, as his successor by a vote of 89 to 17. But the Russians refused to approve and the office of mayor remained vacant for two years until the election of 1948. An acting mayor, Dr. Louise Schroeder, filled the unexpired term.[4]

When the time approached for a new election in 1948, the relations of the West with the Russians had become very strained indeed and Berlin was under the famous blockade. By September of 1948 it seemed unlikely that the Russians would sanction any elections in Berlin under the existing circumstances The election regulations agreed upon by the City Assembly on September 6, 1948, were not vetoed by the Russians outright, but the reply of the Russian commandant laid down conditions which were not acceptable either to the Germans or the western Allies. The election originally scheduled for November 14, 1948, was postponed until December 5. A provision had been made that if the Russians permitted no elections to be held in their sector, the representatives chosen from that sector in 1946 could continue to occupy seats in the City Assembly. The Russians did not countenance elections in their sector, and consequently the results of the election reflected only the desires of the people of the western sectors. This vote gave the Social Democrats 64.5 per cent of the ballots, the Christian Democrats 19.4 per cent, and the Liberal Democrats 16.1 per cent. Professor Reuter was elected mayor, and he proposed a coalition government representing his own party, the

---

[4] This and other material relating to Berlin government is taken largely from Elmer Plischke, *Berlin: Development of Its Government and Administration*, a monograph in the Historical Series of the Office of the U. S. High Commissioner for Germany (1952).

Social Democrats, and the Christian and Liberal Democrats, though the Social Democrats with 76 seats in the City Assembly out of 130 had a clear majority.

THE BERLIN BLOCKADE

If one episode in the complex events of the occupation of Germany during the years 1944-1955 had to be selected as the most spectacular, it is probable that the blockade of Berlin and the resulting western Allied airlift would be accorded priority. Indeed the breaking of the Russian blockade of Berlin may well go down in history as one of the most striking events of the mid-twentieth century.

The blockade of Berlin was instituted by the Russians in the spring of 1948 as a result of their dissatisfaction with their Allies and their insistence on having their own way. At the last meeting of the Allied Control Council held in Berlin on March 20, 1948, the Russian delegation had made drastic charges against the western Allies and, after making various demands, suddenly walked out in the midst of the session. It seemed apparent that this action was not taken on the spur of the moment as a result of sudden anger but rather represented a prearranged plan. In leaving the meeting the Russian chief representative, Marshal Sokolovsky, said: "I see no sense in continuing this meeting, and I declare it adjourned." [5] The Russian commander, as chairman of the Allied Control Council for March, should have fixed a date for the March 30th meeting at the meeting on March 20, but he failed to do this and did not subsequently issue such a call during the month of March. It seemed clear that the Russians did not desire further meetings of the Allied Control Council. The Russians also walked out of the Berlin *Kommandatura*.

During the days following the Russian walkout, there were daily interferences with traffic bound to and from Berlin and the western zones. On March 31 the Russians issued an order which prevented military passenger trains from moving from the western zones to Berlin unless passengers and baggage were checked by Russian agents. This represented a violation of an agreement made with General Zhukov and constituted a serious and intolerable interference with American, British, and French communications with Berlin. Thinking that there

[5] L. D. Clay, *Decision in Germany*, p. 356.

346

might be some misunderstanding, General Clay sent a train across the border to see whether the Russians would enforce their order. This train was shunted to a siding and after remaining there several days had to return to the West. Shortly thereafter the Russians stopped passenger trains from leaving Berlin for the western zones. Berlin therefore was shut off from the West under a Russian blockade.[6]

The Russians apparently believed, or at least hoped, that the western Allies would decide to withdraw from Berlin under this threat, but General Clay and the commanders of the British and French forces in Berlin refused to be forced out and were supported by their governments. To supply the American, British, and French forces in Berlin, an airlift of rather modest proportions was started. In May the Russians took steps to make the movement of ordinary civilian traffic into Berlin difficult if not impossible, and on June 18 movement of all civilian freight and passenger trains between Berlin and the western zones was stopped by orders of the Russians because of alleged bad roadbed conditions. By early August the blockade had been extended to highway and canal traffic, completely cutting off surface transportation between Berlin and the West. In addition to making repairs on rail lines, the Russians also maintained that it was necessary to close the borders of their zone to traffic from the West in order to prevent injury to the economy of their zone resulting from currency reform in the western zones. Since most traffic had stopped before currency reform went into effect in the West and currency reform was not to apply in Berlin, such an explanation received little credence. On June 23 the Russians introduced their own new currency for Berlin and the western Allies followed the next day by making the DM legal currency in Berlin, though leaving the door open for negotiation by giving the new west mark the same value as the east mark.

The blockade imposed by the Russians left some 2,500,000 Germans residing in the western sectors of Berlin in a very precarious position. Since the Russians had not been willing to allow food supplies, fuel, and other necessities to be taken from the Russian Zone economy to feed these people, it had been necessary for the western Allies to furnish supplies from the West. Now such supplies could not be moved. Reserves had been built up to meet emergencies, but obviously these would not suffice to meet the needs of two and a half

---

[6] This account follows that given by General Clay in his *Decision in Germany*, Chap. 19.

million people very long. The Russians doubtless thought that they had the western Allies and particularly the United States, whom they blamed perhaps more than Britain and France for their troubles, in an impossible situation where they could be dealt with as the Russians pleased. The modest airlift which had been set up earlier to bring supplies to the Allied forces in Berlin could do little or nothing to feed, clothe, and warm two and a half million Germans.

The decision of the United States, Britain, and France to do everything possible to counteract the Russian threat shows the western democracies in a most favorable light. Instead of following a cautious line of expediency, they set out on a course which was strikingly courageous and which many thought could be brought to a successful termination only through miracles. The United States had only some 100 transport planes in the European Theatre at this time, and they were small C-47s carrying only about two and a half tons of cargo each. Britain had less in the way of transport planes, and the French had none available. Such facilities would have hardly been able to bring in more than the proverbial drop in the bucket to meet the needs of Berlin. But General Clay asked for 160 C-54s with a capacity of ten tons each from the National Security Council in Washington, and these were supplied without undue delay. The British furnished as many transport planes as they could scare up. While hoping to move about 8,000 tons of supplies into Berlin daily and thus meet the most essential needs of the Germans, "Operation Vittles" actually at its height was able to deliver nearly 13,000 tons every day to the three airports in the western sectors. Planes were arriving in such a split-second succession that if one was even slightly off schedule it had difficulty in landing. With the bad weather that is to be expected in northern Europe in the autumn and winter, the problem became even greater, and elaborate radar techniques had to be developed. General Clay asked that the number of C-54s be upped from 160 to 224. Airports in Berlin had to be rebuilt to take care of the traffic. Careful preparations were required in the western zones to collect the supplies and load them. The airlift went on month after month through the long winter of 1948-1949. It was not until May 1949 that the Russians finally were forced to admit that their plans had failed and that the western Allies had broken the Berlin blockade.

The impact of the breaking of the blockade was by no means

348

limited to Berlin. True, the Berliners were immensely encouraged as a result of the impressive airlift; but in East Germany, throughout West Germany, in other parts of Europe, and indeed more or less throughout the world, notice was taken of the resolution and daring on the part of the western democracies which had led to the failure of the Russians in what seemed an almost sure move. Few if any actions or programs on the part of the United States, Britain, or France have made anything like the deep impression on people both within and outside of Germany occasioned by the breaking of the Berlin blockade. An exact measuring of its impact is not possible, but it seems probable that it, along with currency reform, did more to get Germany back on its feet than any other steps.

THE PERIOD AFTER 1949

With the breaking of the blockade, American relations with the Russians never resumed even the unsatisfactory character of the 1945-1948 period. West Berlin increasingly became a western outpost in the Russian Zone and in the German People's Republic, with only geographical proximity to East Berlin. A new Berlin constitution was put into effect on October 1, 1950, which provided in detail for the governmental structure of West Berlin.[7] The relations of the United States with this government have usually been cordial and there has been a high degree of cooperation between the two. Under this constitution, West Berlin has a quasi-status as a state (*Land*) of the West German Federal Republic, with seats in its Bundestag and Bundesrat. However, since the legal status of West Berlin is such that it cannot be brought under the West German Republic without jeopardizing its existence, it cannot be allowed full status as a state and its parliamentary representatives have no vote.

Cut off as it is from West Germany, the economic position of West Berlin is always precarious. Trade is carried on between West Berlin and the West, but it is subject to various handicaps which are serious obstacles. The result is that unemployment has usually been a major problem of West Berlin and far greater than in West Germany.[8] It

---

[7] For the text of this constitution, see Plischke, *op. cit.*, Appendix 18.

[8] However, unemployment dropped from 312,902 in 1950 to 125,000 in July, 1955. See the *New York Times*, August 10, 1955.

is impossible for the government of West Berlin to raise sufficient taxes to meet its obligations, and the United States and the West German Federal Government have regularly made special financial grants to its treasury.

In order to strengthen West Berlin, the United States has given special attention to ECA programs which involved this little island in the Russian orbit. A large-scale, work-relief program was supported out of American funds to relieve unemployment for several years. ECA aid has been given in large amounts to assist in the rebuilding of West Berlin industrial plants, housing, and physical plant.[9] Loans have been made to enable hotel construction. Efforts have been made to have the American Army place contracts for supplies manufactured in Berlin. The HICOG housing project in Frankfurt was furnished with furniture produced in Berlin. During the period 1949-1955 a total of 2,400,000,000 DM ($571,421,000) was given in counterpart funds by the United States to assist Berlin.

But the United States recognized the need for more than economic assistance in West Berlin. Indeed, nowhere in Germany have cultural and informational programs received as great emphasis as here. Perhaps the chief American memorial in all Germany is the large public library constructed with American money in West Berlin. Great interest has been displayed in the Free University in West Berlin, and its phenomenal growth has been the result in some measure at least of the support received directly or indirectly from the United States. The Ford Foundation provided a large grant to enable it to build up its library and to strengthen its work in political science. Funds were made available by HICOG for the purchase of equipment and library books, to reconstruct buildings, to set up research institutes, and to furnish school meals to supplement the inadequate rations of its students. The West Berlin school system has received particular attention from American officials and has been reconstructed to a greater extent than any other German educational system.

The United States has operated its chief broadcasting station, RIAS, in West Berlin. Through this station many programs have been available to the people of West Berlin as well as to those living

---

[9] A detailed discussion of the economic assistance program is included in H. G. Schmidt, *Economic Assistance to West Berlin, 1949-1951*, a volume of the Historical Series of the Office of the U. S. High Commissioner for Germany (1952) (Restricted).

in the German People's Republic and other Russian-dominated areas. One of the three editions of *Die Neue Zeitung*, the daily newspaper published under American auspices in Germany, was published in West Berlin. This was continued for a time even after the Frankfurt and Munich editions were dropped. The American information programs, including America Houses, have been especially outstanding in West Berlin.[10]

In order to promote cultural life in West Berlin, efforts have been made to strengthen the Municipal Opera House and several theatres through providing equipment and operating subsidies and bringing in visiting performers. At the end of each summer a much-publicized and widely attended cultural festival is held in West Berlin under American, British, and French auspices. Here international films are exhibited, visiting dramatic and musical companies perform, and other cultural events are scheduled. A large hall has been constructed with American aid to provide more adequate facilities for festival programs.

Since West Berlin is occupied by the western Allies under the proclamation made by the military commanders of the four powers in 1945, it continues under Allied supervision despite the end of the occupation in 1955. Any step to incorporate it into West Germany and thus end the occupation would give the Russians an excuse to declare that the legal basis for the independence of West Berlin from the German People's Republic had been broken. Therefore, while the West Berlin government is in practice given more or less full freedom in handling its affairs, the United States, Britain, and France maintain military forces and other offices there until the time comes when some definite agreement of acceptable character can be reached with the Russians. In the meantime, the West German Federal Government has proclaimed its intention to restore Berlin as the capital of a united Germany.

---

[10] For a detailed treatment, see Elmer Plischke and H. P. Pilgert, *U. S. Information Programs in Berlin*, a monograph in the Historical Series of the Office of the U. S. High Commissioner for Germany (1953).

25

The Occupation in Retrospect

In looking back over the occupation as a whole there are various queries which more or less inevitably present themselves. Was the duration unduly long? Was too much or too little attempted? Was the type of organization as effective as could be devised? These are of course all controversial questions to which there are no categorical answers. Nevertheless, in concluding this study of the American record in Germany during the years 1944-1955, some attention to these questions may serve a useful purpose.

THE QUESTION OF DURATION

A cardinal principle which has often been mentioned in connection with discussion of military government involving the United States is that the duration should not be too extended, that such a responsibility should be regarded as of emergency character to be completed at an early date. Military government and occupation are of course not identical, but they are necessarily closely related. The occupation of Germany following World War II lasted in excess of ten years, and that is hardly to be regarded as a short time under any conditions. The early thinking in high places on the subject may be indicated by the statement by President Franklin D. Roosevelt at the Yalta Conference to the effect that it seemed doubtful whether American troops could be maintained in Germany for much longer than two years after the conclusion of the war.[1] General Eisenhower's advice to the War Department shortly after the surrender, noting the desirability of bringing military government to an end as soon as possible, also is significant.[2] The latter involved of course the termina-

---

[1] State Department, *Foreign Relations of the U. S., Diplomatic Papers, 1945,* "Conferences at Malta and Yalta," Bohlen Minutes of Second Plenary Meeting, p. 617.

[2] D. D. Eisenhower, *Crusade in Europe* (Doubleday, New York, 1948), pp. 434-435.

tion of military government rather than the end of the occupation. In contrast, there were those who maintained that the American occupation of Germany should extend over a period of half a century or so, certainly at the very least 25 years. President Roosevelt's statement at Yalta was apparently based on the assumption that public opinion in the United States would not tolerate the keeping of American military forces on European soil beyond a comparatively brief period after the conclusion of the fighting. The advocates of an extended occupation were not primarily concerned with such a practical problem at home, but founded their estimate on the magnitude of the job to be done in Germany.

It is interesting to recall that many, though not all, of the American occupation personnel during the early period in Germany felt that a period of from ten to fifteen years would be about right. Some of those who were concentrating only on the emergency tasks of getting water supplies re-established, electric current available, sanitary facilities of a sort operating, and the like, argued for a shorter period if they displayed any interest in the problem of timing at all. And there were those, particularly in such fields as education, who maintained that 25 years or more would be required to do a worthwhile job. But a large proportion stood in a position between these two extremes, pointing out that neither German nor American public opinion would support an occupation extending over a quarter of a century or more and that the complexities facing the occupation ruled out a period of less than a decade. It is sometimes stated that the people engaged in an enterprise have so little perspective that their opinions are worth little when it comes to judging the larger aspects of that enterprise; but, at least as far as German experience goes, it would seem that these limitations were not controlling. At any rate the predictions of those actually handling the job of occupation turned out to be nearer the truth than those of top political leaders in Washington or the White-Morgenthau group. This may have been more or less of an accident, it is true. Certainly few if any Americans anywhere could foresee the full extent of the development of relations involving the Russians.

Any consideration of the duration of the occupation brings to focus the relations between the United States and the Soviet Union. It seems probable that many aspects of the occupation would have been different, and possibly radically different, had American and Russian relations even approached a normal basis. Perhaps under such circumstances American public opinion would have demanded the withdrawal of American military forces from European soil at an early date after the German surrender, as President Roosevelt predicted, thus making an end of the occupation necessary, irrespective of anything else. Certainly it seems altogether probable that the recommendation of General Eisenhower looking toward an early conclusion of the military government phase would have been followed had the Russians displayed willingness to cooperate. At the same time, it was the unsatisfactory relations with the Russians which motivated the western Allies in seeking to bring the West Germans as partners into a European defense alliance, and this of course had an important bearing on the termination of the occupation. Consequently, the Russian factor worked two ways: during the early years it undoubtedly pushed the occupation beyond what otherwise might have been its limits, and during the later years it served to urge the western Allies toward a restoration of German sovereignty and the end of the occupation.

Coming finally to the direct query as to whether the occupation was unduly prolonged or not, it is clear that an answer which is based on a vacuum would be meaningless. Theoretically one might argue for a duration of five years or 50 years, but unless one takes into account the actual situation in Germany, in the United States, and indeed in the world, an answer has no validity. In such terms it would seem that the duration of the occupation was reasonably satisfactory. A termination at the end of eight years might have been better for the United States and Germany, but it would have left France in a frame of mind which might in the long run have proved costly. The psychology of the Germans would certainly have been more favorable had the end of the occupation come in 1952 or 1953. Progress toward building up a defense against Russian aggression, so much desired by the United States, would also presumably have been accelerated by an ending of the German occupation in 1952 or 1953.

A period much shorter than eight years would seem untenable if one accepts the premise that the United States should carry forward the program which it had prepared for Germany. Supporters of some of the elements of the American program devised for Germany would

354

certainly argue that the duration of the occupation was definitely too short; anything less than another decade or so would not have suited them. It seems probable, however, that those favoring a longer occupation fell into the error of forgetting the stresses and strains built up under an occupation. Except for the threat of the Russians, it seems altogether likely that German attitudes would have been more intensely resentful during the later years of the occupation. How effective would any constructive program in the education, cultural relations, economic assistance, or other fields have been in an atmosphere of extreme bitterness, sullen resentment, and the like? It seems improbable that much could have been accomplished. It is quite possible that achievements already gained would have been jeopardized by a longer occupation.

THE QUESTION OF SCOPE OF ACTIVITIES

The questions of whether the United States attempted too much or too little in Germany and whether what it attempted was wisely conceived are perhaps the most important of all queries relating to the occupation. Here, as in the matter of duration, there is great disparity of viewpoints. Some have labeled the program of the United States in Germany as "grandiose," "unrealistic," "a vast waste of energy and money," "an indication of megalomania," and the like. Others have regarded it as "too narrow," "unduly cautious," "lacking in imagination," and "involving a niggardly outlay." Still others would approve some segments of the undertaking, but rule out others as unworthy and ill-conceived. Another group sees in the occupation the embodiment of noble aims, unusual wisdom, and remarkable execution. With such divergent evaluations, it may seem hopeless to attempt a definite answer to the question as to whether too much or too little was included in the American program, to say nothing of the soundness of particular activities. Nevertheless, this question must be faced in a study of this kind.

Those who have regarded the scope of the American activities in Germany as too broad approach the question from various positions. There are the White-Morgenthau group who rule out the constructive activities and concentrate on punishment and isolation. There are those like Professor Hocking who apparently sincerely believe that

355

German achievements have been so brilliant and socially valuable that it is a travesty to seek in any way to modify German patterns—the Allies should instead have gone to Germany to learn and benefit. Then there are certain men who conceive of war as one of man's chief pastimes and who argue that anything beyond maintaining order and providing emergency services among a conquered people pending a settlement is unnecessary and a waste of energy.

American activities in Germany were by no means few in number or modest in scope. Even those who have spent some years on the military or civil staffs of the United States in Germany frequently do not realize just how elaborate an overall program was drafted. Those who have conceived of the American occupation in terms of "wine, women, and song," a large staff with little or nothing to do, and similar corruptions must have almost unbelievable skill in blinding themselves to the far-flung activities. There is perhaps no other instance where one country has attempted as much in a conquered country to strengthen existing institutions, to reconstruct without discarding, to bolster up local efforts, though there are of course cases where countries, such as the Soviet Union, have taken advantage of their victories to throw overboard the political, economic, and social institutions.

The activities of the United States in Germany have assumed such a labyrinthine character that considerable skill is required to follow them. Even after some years of study one is likely to find a new activity or at least a new aspect of an activity which has hitherto escaped attention. How much of this extended activity on the part of the United States was the result of the almost unbelievable penetration of every nook and corner of German life by Nazi fanaticism and how much came from a combination of American energy, personal empire building, and idealism, it is difficult to ascertain. There can be little doubt that the explanation of the extended efforts on the part of the United States lies to a considerable extent in an attempt to root out the cancer of Nazism in Germany. At the same time, the fact that the United States tried to do more than either Britain or France regarded as necessary or desirable and often applied itself to its goals with a vigor exceeding that of its Allies cannot be ignored.

Did the United States then take on too much in Germany? It seems fair to say that in some instances it did. While there may be honest differences of opinion, there is evidence that the denazification program for one was ill-conceived and literally impossible of execution, though, of course, some steps were required in this field. The program involving a reconstruction of the German education system and curriculum along American lines may be cited as another instance beyond the limits of common sense, despite the weaknesses exhibited by the German schools. The dismantling program, though never implemented in the American Zone as it was in the Russian and British Zones, represents another activity which in retrospect seems definitely unjustifiable. Decartelization and deconcentration may have required American attention—certainly not everything was as it should have been in certain areas of German economic life—but the complications were such and the probability of success so slight that such projects are questionable. While the directives relating to democratization were sufficiently vague that they were not taken too seriously and no attempt was made to draft a master plan for bringing democracy to Germany, the wisdom of any formal stipulations in this field may be questionable. At the same time it is only fair to note the valuable work done on a limited scale in curtailing the power of the guilds, promoting the activity of women in public affairs, and scheduling adult education groups to study local affairs as well as the personal influence exerted by American officials in HICOG.

Since there was hardly a phase of German life in which the United States did not display some interest, it would be difficult to cite a field in which the United States might have carried on activity with profit but failed to do so. But it is possible to note that some activities seemed to receive more support than could be easily justified, while others of equal or even greater significance found themselves fighting for recognition. The education effort during the early period received comparatively little support, despite the probability that it could have made good use of additional facilities to assist German educational institutions—this was before the grandiose scheme to rebuild the German system along American lines. The information program is another activity which was not adequately supported during the early years and which, even during the later period, received less financial underpinning than other activities of no greater and probably minor significance. The priorities accorded political party and labor union reconstruction in the American Zone during the early period of the

357

occupation were below those given in the British and Russian Zones and would seem to represent American shortcomings. The youth program is another which, considering the dire condition of the German youth following the Nazi debacle, might very well have received greater emphasis.

Did the plans drafted by the United States in the multiplicity of fields embody the soundest and wisest elements which human beings can be expected to conceive? A few uncritical Americans would maintain that everything was almost if not absolutely perfect, but most persons of intelligence or knowledge would admit a good many imperfections. But were these imperfections the sort which are avoidable under a system manned by human beings? To what extent were these shortcomings of the variety which are apparent in retrospect but which could not have been expected to be recognized at the time? Some of the criticism which has been directed at certain of the American activities in Germany does seem to be based on hindsight and on ideal standards, but by no means all. The education, denazification and economic fields were perhaps the outstanding ones in which there was too little sound common sense displayed at certain stages of the occupation.

THE QUESTION OF TYPE OF ORGANIZATION

In looking at the organization set up by the United States for the occupation of Germany, there are perhaps fewer ramifications than in the preceding question, but no less controversy. As to whether the body of military government officials should have been organized as an integral part of the Army, the evidence is conflicting. Tactical personnel frequently did not regard the military government staff as an integral part of the military forces whether it was legally so or not. By organizing military government as a direct part of the armed forces it was of course necessary to accept military rules in regard to recruiting personnel, following command channels, basing assignments on rank, and the like. A heavy burden which sometimes almost seemed crippling resulted. Misfits and rejects from other military units had to be accepted for duty in military government under such a system, though it is true some commissioning of specialists direct from civilian life was permitted. A great deal of the poor reputation of military

358

government staffs in the tactical units and headquarters grew out of this weakness. It can hardly be doubted that military government could have provided more competent persons for many positions had it been able to go outside such places as the replacement depots. As integral parts of the Army, military government units had to be subjected to the regulations, the promotion system, and so forth, of the Army and these frequently did not apply very well to their job and resulted in waste, poor morale, and the like.

It can hardly be questioned that military government organizations must be closely related to the armed forces, but does that mean that it is desirable to make them an integral part of the latter? The experience in Germany seems to many who have given some attention to the problem to indicate that there would be definite advantages in following the pattern of such organizations as the Office of Strategic Services and the Office of War Information. Under such an arrangement military government would have had, at least to begin with, military officers, though not necessarily professional soldiers, at the head as commanders. In certain lower echelons where the work called for military status this could have been provided, as in OSS and OWI, but the rank and file of officials would have been civilians in uniform rather than commissioned officers. Greater flexibility would almost certainly have resulted. This would not only have made it possible to get the experts needed for such jobs as monuments, fine arts, archives, and governmental affairs who are not ordinarily available in the armed forces in adequate numbers, but after appointment these officials would have been in a better position to get their jobs done. They could have been appointed only when needed, instead of being brought to the European Theatre a year or so before they were required because of space priorities among military personnel, with resulting damage to morale. They could perhaps have been permitted to move about with some measure of freedom and to communicate readily with their associates which, under military regulations, was not possible. This alone would have increased their effectiveness materially. Such an organization might have developed a tradition which would have more nearly suited the assignment in Germany and obviated some of the difficulties experienced by OMGUS after its staff had become predominantly civilian. In both the OSS and the OWI, primary emphasis was placed on the job to be done and a traditional military system did not develop—there was an informality which contributed to a good morale and to initiative which military government often lacked.

The second aspect of the question of organization involves the change-over from military government to civil administration. As noted earlier, this was delayed in Germany. Should the State Department have proceeded with its original plans to take over the non-security responsibilities in Germany, say in 1946? This would have cut down the military government period from four or five years to half of that period. It might have instigated a more workable policy directive a considerable time before 1947. And theoretically a fairly strong case could be presented for it, even though confusion might have resulted because of the lack of preparedness and inexperience on the part of the State Department. However, in retrospect it is difficult to see how such a change could have been made with the relations between the Russians and the Americans so strained and the picture so unclear as to the future. Until the Russians had actually staged the blockade of Berlin, walked out of the Allied Control Council, and otherwise clearly demonstrated their unwillingness to cooperate with the western Allies, it is doubtful whether the French at least would have sanctioned an Allied High Commission. Nor was German public opinion apparently ready for as drastic a step as going ahead in the West without the Russians. An American civil administration set up in 1946 might have been able to work with the French military government and perhaps would have had a British civil agency to serve as a counterpart. Nevertheless, it is not easy under the existing circumstances to see how an American civil administration could have operated in 1946, 1947, or 1948.

CONCLUDING COMMENTS

In concluding this survey of the American occupation of Germany during the years 1944-1955, it may be said that the record in general seems to warrant a large measure of commendation. Despite the serious shortcomings of the early policy relating to denazification and economic reconstruction, the United States pushed ahead as best it could under the vigorous leadership of General Clay. As the situation developed, clearer thinking characterized both Washington and the field, and the negative aspects were crowded more and more into the background by the positive aspects of the program. Able High Commissioners in the persons of John J. McCloy and James B. Conant were given the job of representing the United States in Germany, and both with the support of their staffs contributed in no small way to the German achievements to be noted since 1949. The overriding question as to the wisdom of the American policy in bringing West Germany into a European defense community and the North Atlantic Treaty Organization remains and cannot be answered until world developments move forward. In retrospect the American occupation of Germany seems to compare favorably with other occupation experiences of the United States. Indeed there is some basis for concluding that it surpassed any previous occupation in effectiveness and achievements.

Bibliography

COLLECTIONS OF DOCUMENTS

Department of State, *Germany, 1947-1949; The Story in Documents* (Washington, 1950).
Dokumente der Deutsche Politik und Geschichte, Vols. 6-8 (Berlin, 1946-1955).
Office of Military Government of the U.S., *Constitutions of the German Länder* (Berlin, 1947).
Office of Military Government of the U.S., *Documents on the Creation of the German Federal Constitution* (Berlin, 1949).
Pollock, J. K., Meisel, James H., and Bretton, H. L., *Germany under Occupation, Illustrative Materials and Documents* (rev. ed., Wahr, Ann Arbor, 1949).
Ruhm von Oppen, B., ed., *Documents on Germany under Occupation, 1945-1954* (Oxford University Press, London, 1955).

OFFICIAL REPORTS

Information Bulletin, issued under OMGUS and HICOG until March 1953.
Quarterly Reports of the U.S. High Commissioner for Germany, issued until 1951.
Report on Germany, September 21, 1949-July 31, 1952, Office of the U.S. High Commissioner for Germany (1952).
Reports of the major divisions of the Office of Military Governor, including Civil Administration, Law, Economics, etc.
Reports of the Military Governor, issued on a monthly basis during the early period of the occupation and later on a quarterly basis.

OTHER OFFICIAL PUBLICATIONS[1]

Allied Control Council, *Official Gazette of the Control Council.*
Allied High Commission for Germany, *Official Gazette of the Allied High Commission for Germany.*
American Military Government, *Military Government Gazette Germany.*
Frederiksen, O. J., *The American Military Occupation of Germany, 1945-1953*, Historical Division, Headquarters, U.S. Army, Europe (1953).
Handbook for Military Government in Germany (1944).
Office of Military Government of the U.S., *Chronological Tables on Germany, 1947-1949.*
Office of Military Government of the U.S., *Political Parties in Western Germany* (1949).

---

[1] For a more detailed list of official publications, see R. W. Miller, *United States Policy towards Germany 1945-1955—U.S. Government Documents on Germany* (Forschungsinstitut der Deutschen Gesellschaft für Auswärtige Politik, Frankfurt, 1956).

Bibliography

Office of the U.S. High Commissioner for Germany, *Elections and Political Parties in Germany, 1945-1952* (1952).

HISTORICAL MONOGRAPHS OF THE OFFICE OF THE
U.S. HIGH COMMISSIONER FOR GERMANY

Brauer, A. E., "The German Housing Program and U.S. Aid," mimeographed (1953).

Gillen, J. F. J., "Deconcentration and Decartelization in West Germany, 1945-1953," mimeographed (1953).

———, *The Employment of German Nationals by the Office of the U.S. High Commissioner for Germany* (1952) (Restricted).

———, *Labor Problems in West Germany with Special Reference to the Policies and Programs of the Office of Labor Affairs of the Office of the U.S. High Commissioner for Germany* (1952).

———, *The Special Projects Program of the Office of the U.S. High Commissioner for Germany* (1952).

———, *State and Local Government in West Germany, 1945-1953* (1953).

Korman, J. G., "U.S. Denazification Policy in Germany, 1944-1950," multilithed (1952).

Lee, G. A., ed., *Documents on Field Organization of the Office of the U.S. High Commissioner for Germany* (1952).

———, *The Establishment of the Office of the U.S. High Commissioner for Germany* (1951) (Restricted).

———, *Field Organization of the Office of the U.S. High Commissioner for Germany, 1949-1951* (1952) (Restricted).

———, *Guide to Studies of the Historical Division of the Office of the U.S. High Commissioner for Germany* (1953).

Loehr, R. C., *The West German Banking System* (1952) (Restricted).

McClaskey, B. R., *The Free German Youth and the Deutschlandtreffen* (1951) (Restricted).

———, *The History of U.S. Policy and Program in the Field of Religious Affairs under the Office of the U.S. High Commissioner for Germany* (1951).

Pilgert, H. P., *Community and Group Life in West Germany* (1952).

———, *The Exchange of Persons Program in Western Germany* (1951).

———, *The History of the Development of Information Services through Information Centers and Documentary Films* (1951).

———, *Press, Radio, and Film in West Germany, 1945-1953* (1953).

———, *The West German Educational System* (1953).

———, *Women in West Germany* (1952).

Plischke, E., *The Allied High Commission for Germany* (1953).

———, *Allied High Commission Relations with the West German Government* (1952) (Restricted).

———, *Berlin: Development of Its Government and Administration* (1952).

———, *History of the Allied High Commission for Germany: Its Establishment, Structure, and Procedures* (1951).

————, *Revision of the Occupation Statute for Germany* (1952) (Restricted).

————, *The West German Federal Government* (1952).

————, and Pilgert, H. P., "U.S. Information Programs in Berlin," mimeographed (1953).

Schmidt, H. G., ed., "Documents on the Reorganization of the West German Coal and Iron and Steel Industries under the Allied High Commission for Germany, 1949-1952," mimeographed (1952).

————, *Economic Assistance to West Berlin, 1949-1951* (1952) (Restricted).

————, *Food and Agricultural Programs in West Germany, 1949-1951* (1952).

————, *The Liberalization of West German Foreign Trade, 1949-1951* (1952) (Restricted).

GENERAL TREATISES

Almond, G. A., ed., *Struggle for Democracy in Germany* (University of North Carolina Press, Chapel Hill, 1949).

Annals of the American Academy of Political and Social Science, Nov. 1948 issue devoted to "Postwar Reconstruction in Western Germany," with articles by German writers.

————, Jan. 1950 issue devoted to "Military Government."

Balfour, M., and Mair, J., *Four-Power Control in Germany and Austria, 1945-1946* (Oxford University Press, London, 1956).

Bourthoumieux, C., *La politique et le régime interallies d'occupation de l'Allemagne de 1945-1949* (Paris, 1950).

Brandt, K., *Germany: Key to Peace in Europe* (Claremont Colleges, Claremont, 1949).

————, *Is There Still a Chance for Germany* (Regnery, Chicago, 1948).

Brecht, A., *Federalism and Regionalism in Germany* (Cornell University Press, Ithaca, 1945).

Butz, Otto, *Germany: Dilemma for American Foreign Policy* (Doubleday, New York, 1954).

Byrnes, J. F., *Speaking Frankly* (Harper, New York, 1947).

Clay, L. D., *Decision in Germany* (Doubleday, New York, 1950).

————, *Germany and the Fight for Freedom* (Harvard University Press, Cambridge, 1950).

Friedmann, W., *Allied Military Government of Germany* (Stevens, London, 1947).

Friedrich, C. J., and associates, *American Experiences in Military Government in World War II* (Rinehart, New York, 1948).

Grosser, A., *Colossus Again: Western Germany from Defeat to Rearmament* (trans. from French, Praeger, New York, 1955).

Holborn, H., *American Military Government; Its Origins and Policies* (Infantry Journal, Washington, 1947).

Johnsen, J. E., comp., *Dilemma of Postwar Germany* (Wilson, New York, 1948).

Knappen, M. M., *And Call It Peace* (University of Chicago Press, Chicago, 1947).

364

Bibliography

Litchfield, E. H., ed., *Governing Postwar Germany* (Cornell University Press, Ithaca, 1953).

Mehnert, K., and Schultze, H., eds., *Deutschland-Jahrbuch, 1949* (Essen, 1949).

Moennig, R., *Die amerikanische Deutschlandpolitik 1945-1955* (Bonn, 1956).

Morgenthau, Hans, ed., *Germany and the Future of Europe* (University of Chicago Press, Chicago, 1951).

Morgenthau, H. J., *Germany Is Our Problem* (Harper, New York, 1945).

Neumann, S., *Germany, Promise and Perils*, Headline Series, Foreign Policy Association, 1950.

Nizer, L., *What to Do with Germany* (Ziff-Davis, New York, 1944).

Pollock, J. K., ed., *Change and Crisis in European Government* (Rinehart, New York, 1947).

Pollock, J. K., and Thomas, H., *Germany in Power and Eclipse* (Van Nostrand, New York, 1952).

Price, H., and Schorske, C. E., *Problem of Germany* (Council on Foreign Relations, New York, 1947).

Rodnick, D., *Postwar Germans* (Yale University Press, New Haven, 1948).

Stolper, G., *German Realities* (Reynal, New York, 1948).

Warburg, J. P., *Germany, Bridge and Battleground* (Harcourt, Brace, New York, 1947).

———, *Germany: Key to Peace* (Harvard University Press, Cambridge, 1953).

Zink, H., *American Military Government in Germany* (Macmillan, New York, 1947).

Reports by Journalists

Clark, D., *Again the Goose Step* (Bobbs-Merrill, Indianapolis, 1949).

Habe, H., *Our Love Affair with Germany* (Putnam, New York, 1953).

Middleton, D., *Struggle for Germany* (Bobbs-Merrill, Indianapolis, 1949).

Settel, A., ed., *This Is Germany* (Sloane, New York, 1950).

West, R., *Train of Powder* (Viking, New York, 1955).

White, W. L., *Report on the Germans* (Harcourt, Brace, New York, 1947).

Monographs and Specialized Treatises

Ambruster, H. W., *Treason's Peace* (Beechhurst, New York, 1947).

Bathurst, M. E., and Simpson, J. L., *Germany and the North Atlantic Community: A Legal Survey* (Stevens, London, 1956).

Belgion, M., *Victor's Justice* (Regnery, Chicago, 1949).

Bernstein, V. H., *Final Judgment* (Boni and Gaer, New York, 1947).

Glueck, S., *The Nuremberg Trials and Aggressive War* (Knopf, New York, 1946).

Hallstein, W., *Die Wiederherstellung des Privatrechts* (Tübingen, 1946).

Hocking, W. E., *Experiment in Education; What We Can Learn from Teaching Germany* (Regnery, Chicago, 1954).

Howe, T. C., *Salt Mines and Castles* (Bobbs-Merrill, Indianapolis, 1946).

Howley, F. L., *Berlin Command* (Putnam, New York, 1950).

365

Institut zur Förderung offentlicher Angelegenheiten, *Millionen ohne Heimat* (Frankfurt, 1950).

Institute for Social Research, *Learning Across Cultures, A Study of Germans Visiting America* (University of Michigan Press, Ann Arbor, 1955).

Jackson, R. M., *The Nuremberg Trial* (Knopf, New York, 1947).

Kaiser, J. H., *Der Landtag* (Hochschule für Politische Wissenschaften, Munich, 1951).

————, *Die Repraesentation organisierter Interessen* (Berlin, 1956).

Lewis, H. O., *New Constitutions in Occupied Germany* (Foundation for Foreign Affairs, Washington, 1948).

Liddell, H., *Education in Occupied Germany* (Columbia University Press, New York, 1949).

Loewenstein, K., "Law and the Legislative Process in Occupied Germany," *Yale Law Journal*, 1948.

————, "Reconstruction of the Administration of Justice in American-Occupied Germany," *Harvard Law Review*, 1948.

Mangoldt, H. von, *Das Bonner Grundgesetz* (Berlin-Frankfurt, 1950).

Martin, J. S., *All Honorable Men* (Little, Brown, Boston, 1950).

Nettl, J. P., *The Eastern Zone and Soviet Policy in Germany, 1945-1950* (Oxford University Press, New York, 1951).

Norman, A., *Our German Policy: Propaganda and Culture* (Vantage, New York, 1951).

Pollock, J. K., ed., *German Democracy* (University of Michigan Press, Ann Arbor, 1955).

Ratchford, B. U., and Ross, W. D., *Berlin Reparation Assignment* (University of North Carolina Press, Chapel Hill, 1947).

Salomon, E. von, *Frägebogen* (Eng. trans., Putnam, New York, 1954).

Taylor, T., *Nuremberg Trials, War Crimes, and International Law* (Carnegie Endowment, New York, 1949).

Utley, F., *High Cost of Vengeance* (Regnery, Chicago, 1949).

Weber, W., *Weimarer Verfassung und Bonner Grundgesetz* (Göttingen, 1949).

Wolff, K., "German Attempts at Picturing Germany: Texts" (Ohio State University, Columbus, 1955).

———— and Etzkorn, K. P., "Hans Vogel: A Case Study of a Young German Farmer on a Visit to the United States" (Ohio State University, Columbus, 1954).

———— and Roth, G., "The American Denazification of Germany" (Ohio State University, Columbus, 1954).

Index

Adenauer, Dr. Konrad, 78, 79, 190, 191.
Administrative Code, 309.
Administrative courts, 309.
A. F. of L., 287.
Agricultural activities of the U. S., 300-303.
Alcoholics, problem of, 76.
Alexander, Thomas, 200.
All-German Bloc, 338.
Allied Control Authority, 29, 106, 107, 108, 116, 117, 166, 170, 265, 270, 272, 273, 281, 283, 307, 330.
Allied Control Council. *See* Allied Control Authority.
Allied High Commission, 56, 114, 115, 119, 191, 195, 306, 307, 308.
America Houses, 225, 245-250.
American Embassy in Germany, 55.
American Forces Network, 241.
American Zone decided upon by European Advisory Commission, 177-178.
Amerika Dienst, 239.
Amerikanische Rundschau, 240.
Armies, place of, in military government, 34-35.
Army Groups, place of, in military government, 34-35.
Army Specialized Training Program, 14-15.
Augsburg, 214, 245.

Bank deutscher Länder, 276, 277.
Banking reorganization, 275-278.
Barnes, R. P., 324.
Barrows, Arthur, 252.
Bavaria, 237, 275.
Bell, Laird, 252.
Berlin, 210, 214, 226, 241, 242, 245, 249, 340-351.
Berlin Blockade, 97, 99, 345, 346-349.
Berlin Element of HICOG, 63.
Berlin *Kommandatura,* 109, 341-345.
Bernstein, Colonel B., 21, 154.

Biddle, Francis, 145.
Big Six Banks, 267.
Bizonal Economic Council, 183.
Bizonal High Court, 183.
Bizonia, 113-114, 182-183, 255, 283, 297.
Black, white, and gray lists, 171, 172.
Black-marketing, problem of, 138-140.
Boeckler, Hans, 284.
Bonn, as capital of West Germany, 190.
Bonn Basic Law, 186-188.
Bonn Constitution. *See* Bonn Basic Law.
Bookmobiles, 246.
Books, program relating to publication of, 239-241.
Border police, 305.
Bormann, Martin, 145.
Boston University, 11.
Bowie, R. R., 81-82.
Boyd, James, 252.
Bremen, 210, 214, 226, 241, 245, 249.
Bremerhaven, 214, 245.
British, American relations with, 3, 110-116.
British Control Commission, 29, 109, 112, 131.
Bromage, Arthur, 16.
Brown, Harvey W., 81, 289.
Brown, Irving, 287.
Bruchsal, 214.
Bürgermeister, 171-173.
Burns, R. A., 222.
Buttenwieser, Benjamin, 80.
Byrnes, Secretary of State J. F., 43, 93, 95-96, 328.
Byroade, Colonel Henry, 122.

Carey, J. B., 287.
Case Subcommittee, 163.
Cattier, Jean, 81.
CDU. *See* Christian Democratic Union.
Chicago University, 11.
Christian Democratic Union, 337, 338-339, 344, 345.

Christian Science Monitor, 90.
Citizen participation program, 334-335.
City government, 170-175.
Civil Affairs Division, 3, 6, 7, 8, 9.
Civil Affairs Training Schools, 11.
Civil-military relations, problem of, 121-131.
Civil service, problem of reform of, 332-334.
Civil War, 5.
Clay, General Lucius D., 3, 27, 29, 31, 32, 50, 68-71, 84, 94-95, 96, 97, 112, 124, 160, 161, 162, 164, 165, 179, 181, 188, 195, 254, 255, 257, 287, 298, 330, 341, 347, 360.
Coburg, 245.
Co-determination, 291-292.
Collective bargaining, 285-286, 290-291.
Collisson, N. H., 257-258.
Colm-Dodge-Goldsmith Report, 273.
Combined Civil Affairs Committee, 19.
Command-channels, problem of, in military government, 33-34.
Commanding General of U. S. Forces, 127, 128.
Commerce, Department of, 90.
Committees of Allied High Commission, 56-57.
Commodity Credit Corporation, 261.
Communist party, 336, 337, 344.
Conant, James B., 76, 78-79, 85, 361.
Constituent assemblies, at the state level, 179-181; at the national level, 185-188.
Constitutional conventions. *See* Constituent assemblies.
Constitutions of the *Länder*, 179-181; of the West German Federal Republic, 186-188.
Contractual Agreement, 58.
Council of States, 181-182.
Councils of Christians and Jews, 325.
Counter Intelligence Corps, 159.
Counterpart funds, 207-208.
County government, 170-175.
Courts, reorganization of, 308-310.
Cuba, 1.
Currency reform, 259-260, 273-275.

Dachau trials, 146-147.
Darmstadt, 245.

Davies, John Paton, 81.
Dawson, Colonel William, 73.
Debevoise, E. W., 81-82.
Decartelization, 264-268.
Deconcentration, 264-268.
Demilitarization, 67.
Democratization, problem of, directive relating to, 326-328; abolition of Prussia, 329-330; freedom of choice of occupation, 330-332; civil service reform, 332-334; citizen participation program, 334-335; political parties, 335-339.
DENA, 239.
Denazification, development of U. S. policy, 151-156; American activities, 157-160; German denazification tribunals, 161-164; record in American Zone compared with other zones, 165-167; evaluation, 167-168.
Denazification tribunals, 161-163.
Department of the Army. *See* Civil Affairs Division; Provost Marshal General, Office of.
Deputy Military Governor, 26-27, 67.
Dermody, Patricia J., 51.
Der Monat, 240.
Detachments, military government, 37-39.
Deutsche Genossenschaftskasse, 278.
Die Neue Zeitung, 235, 238-239.
Dismantling program, 256-258.
Displaced persons, 27.
Documentary film program, 244-245.
Doenitz, Admiral K., 145.
Doenitz Government, 169.
Doherty, W. C., 287.
Donnelly, W. J., 76-77, 78.
Dorn, Walter L., 158.
Draper, Major General W. H., 70, 73.
Dubinski, David, 287.

Eastbourne military government training center, 16.
Economic Affairs Division of OMGUS, 27, 251.
Economic Affairs, Office of, of HICOG, 52, 56.
Economic Cooperation Administration, 225, 237, 238, 301.

Index

Economic reconstruction, early period, 251-255; Joint Export-Import Agency, 255-256; dismantling, 256-258; level-of-industry provisions, 258-259; currency reform, 259-261; direct U. S. aid, 260-264; decartelization and deconcentration programs, 264-268.

Education Adviser of OMGUS, 201.

Education, American activities in the field of, period 1945-1947, 196-199; period 1947-1950, 199-207; period 1950-1955, 207-208; concluding comments, 208-214.

Education and Cultural Affairs Division of OMGUS, 199-207.

Education Branch of OMGUS, 195-199.

Education Branch of HICOG, 207-208.

Education Service Centers, 214.

Eisenhower, General D. D., 18, 43, 67, 111, 122, 123, 134, 157.

Elections, 179-180.

Empie, P. C., 324.

Erlangen, 245, 249.

Essen, 214, 245.

European Advisory Commission, 21-24, 104-105, 320, 340, 341.

European Civil Affairs Division, 16.

European Defense Community, 192.

European Payments Union, 262.

European Recovery Program, 262-263.

Exchanges Branch of OMGUS, 216, 217.

Exchanges Division of HICOG, 217-227.

Exchanges program of U. S., basis of, 216-217; machinery of administration, 217-223; types of, 223-225; selection process, 225-227; evaluation of, 227-233.

Executive Secretary, Office of, of HICOG, 54, 56.

Expellees, 27.

Fahy, Charles, 74-75.

Farben Industrie, 266-267.

FDP. See Free Democratic party.

Federal Chancellor, 190-191.

Federal Civil Service Act of 1953, 333.

Federal constitution. See Bonn Basic Law.

Federal Constitutional Tribunal, 309, 310.

Federalism, emphasis on, by U. S., 185-188.

Fertilizer, problem of, 300-301.

Field Division of HICOG, 54.

Field organization of military government, 36-42.

Film program, 243-245.

Finance Division of OMGUS, 27.

Food, problem of, 293-300.

Food rationing, 296-299.

Ford Foundation, 211, 212, 350.

Foreign Economic Administration, 253.

Foreign Service Officers, 122.

Fort Custer military government center, 11-13.

Fragebogen, 159, 160, 161.

François-Poncet, A., 119-120.

Frankfurt, 235, 241, 245, 249, 292.

Frankfurt Enclave, 177.

Frankfurter Rundschau, 235.

Fraternization, problem of, 133-136.

Free Democratic party, 330.

Free German Youth, 311-312.

Free University in Berlin, 211, 350.

Freiberg i. Br., 214.

French relations with U. S., 116-120.

Freitag, W., 284.

Friedmann, W., 165.

Fulda, 245.

G-5, SHAEF, 19, 21.

G-5, USFET, 28-29.

GARIOA, 263.

Gemeinde, 170-175.

General Counsel, Office of, of HICOG, 53, 55, 56.

Gerhardt, Colonel H. A., 46, 50, 80.

German Country Unit, 18-21, 104, 105, 110, 111, 151-152.

German employees of U. S., 30-31, 84.

German Federation of Labor Unions, 288.

German party, 338.

German Peoples Republic, 349, 351.

German press, activities of U. S. relating to, 235-239.

German Youth Assistance Centers, 312-313.

Gestapo, 305.

Giessen, 245.

Goering, Field Marshal H., 145.
Government reconstruction, at local level, 170-175; at regional level, 175-182; at bizonal level, 182-183; at national level, 183-192.
Grace, Alonzo G., 204-207.
Gross, Major General C. P., 79.
Gusev, F. T., 23.

Hamburg, 214, 245, 272.
Handbook of Military Government in Germany, 21, 293.
Hanes, R. M., 81, 82.
Hanover, 214, 245.
Harris, M. S., 81.
Harrison, G. M., 287.
Harvard University, 11.
Hay, John, 81.
Hays, Major General George P., 46, 47, 50, 51, 80.
Health, problem of, 298-299.
Heath, Donald R., 74.
Heidelberg, 214, 245, 249.
Heilbronn, 245.
Hess, Rudolf, 145.
Hesse, 177-178, 211, 237, 275.
Hesse crown jewels theft, 136.
Heuss, Dr. Theodor, quoted, 326n.
Heute, 240.
HICOG. *See* Office of the U. S. High Commissioner for Germany.
Higgins, Father G. C., 324.
High Commissioners of the U. S. in Germany, 76-79.
Hilldring, Major General J. H., 122.
Hillman, Sidney, 287.
Hocking, W. E., 193, 208, 355-356.
Hoff, Hans vom, 284.
Hoover, Calvin, 75.
Hoover, Herbert, 297.
Howley, Brigadier General F. L., 341.
Hull, Secretary of State Cordell, 87.
Humphrey, G. M., 257.
Hunt, Colonel L. L., 12.
Hunt Report, 12.
Hunting and fishing, problem of, 129-130.

Illegitimate children, 137-138.
Income tax, 272.

Information program of U. S., the press, 235-239; other publishing fields, 239-241; the radio, 241-242; films, 243-245; America Houses, 245-250.
Information and Exchange Survey Mission, 217-220.
Information Control Division of OMGUS, 27.
Intelligence, Office, of HICOG, 53, 55.
Interallied relations, 103-120.
International Authority of the Ruhr, 185.

Jackson, Mr. Justice Robert, 145, 147.
Japan, occupation of, 1-2, 6, 103.
JCS 1067, 27, 91-92, 93-96, 101, 155-156, 157, 252, 253-254, 261, 326-327, 335-336.
JCS 1779, 96-97.
Jeff, Captain (Navy) C. R., 79.
JEIA. *See* Joint Export-Import Agency.
Jodl, General Alfred, 145.
Joint Chiefs of Staff, 24, 90, 91, 94, 327, 341.
Joint Export-Import Agency, 255-256.
Jones, Howard P., 82, 322.

Kaiserlautern, 214.
Karlsruhe, 214, 245.
Kassel, 214, 245.
Keenan, Joe, 282.
Keitel, Field Marshal W., 145.
Kempner, R. M. W., 145.
Kiel, 214.
Kimball, Arthur, 46.
King, James E., Jr., 80.
Knappen, Marshall, 196, 321.
Koblenz, 214.
KPD. *See* Communist party.
Kreis, 170-175.
Kreis Resident Officers, 63-65, 83-84.
Krimminalpolizei, 305.

Labor Affairs, Office of, of HICOG, 53, 55, 285, 288-290.
Labor courts, 286.
Labor, Department of, 90.
Labor Front, 280-281.
Labor unions, 280-292.
Länder, reorganization of, 175-181.

Index

La Follette, C. M., 73, 286-287.
Land Central Banks, 275-276.
Land Commissioners, 59, 79-80.
Land government, 175-182.
Landkreis, 170-175.
Land observers, 80.
Land Offices of HICOG, 59-62.
Land Offices of military government, 35-36.
Landrat, 170-175.
Landtag, 307.
Landwirtschaftliche Rentenbank, 278.
Language instruction, problem of, 13-14, 15-16.
Law for Liberation of National Socialism and Militarism, 161, 162.
Law, problem of revising, 306-308.
Leaders exchange program, 223-224.
Legal Division of OMGUS, 27, 145.
Level-of-industry provisions, 258-259.
Liaison and security teams, 41-42.
Licensing of press, 236-238.
Litchfield, E. H., 49, 70, 73-74.
"Little Americas," 140-142.
Local government, reorganization of, 170-175.
London Conference of Foreign Ministers 1947, 184.
London Conference of Foreign Ministers 1948, 44-45, 184-185.
Looting, problem of, 136.
Lyon, Cecil, 82.

MacArthur, General Douglas, 2, 33.
Madden, J. W., 74-75.
Malmedy case, 147, 148.
Manchester military government training center, 16.
Mannheim, 214, 245.
Manpower and organized labor, military government period, 282-287; High Commission period, 288-292.
Manpower Division of OMGUS, 27, 284-285, 286.
Marburg, 245, 249.
Marsh, Colonel John, 74-75.
Marshall, General George C., 44, 97, 121-122, 261.
Marshall Plan, 261-262.
Mayors, 171-173.

McCloy, John J., 31, 45, 46, 68, 76-78, 85, 125, 191, 195, 267, 292, 316, 338, 361.
McCloy, Mrs. John J., 36, 318.
McLain, C. A., 81-82.
McManus, Father W. E., 324.
McNarney, General J. T., 67-68.
Michigan University, 11.
Military government organization of the U. S. in Germany, U. S. Group, Control Council for Germany, 26-29; OMGUS, 29-34; regional, 34-36; field detachments, 36-42.
Military government specialist officers, 9-10.
Military governors of the U. S. in Germany, 67-71.
Military mark notes, 269-270.
Military Security Board, 53-54, 56.
Minister Presidents, 178-179.
Morgenthau, Henry, Jr., 153, 154.
Morgenthau Plan, 21, 87, 155.
Moriarity, P. J., 312-313.
Morse, David, 75.
Moscow Conference of 1947, 257.
Mosley, P. E., 23.
Mott, Rodney, 271.
Muccio, John J., 74.
Muelder, Milton, 201-202.
Munich, 214, 241, 245.
Murphy, Robert D., 74.

National Security Council, 90, 91.
National Socialist party, liquidation of, 156.
NATO. *See* North Atlantic Treaty Organization.
Neue Auslese, 240.
Newman, J. R., 79.
Newspapers in American Zone, 235-239.
New York Times, 90, 221-222.
Nonfraternization, problem of, 133-136.
North Atlantic Treaty Organization, 100.
Northwestern University, 11.
Nuremberg, 214, 245, 249.
Nuremberg trials, 145-146.

Occupation Statute, 58, 188-190, 191, 259, 265, 288, 307, 333.

371

Oder-Neisse Line, 95.
Office of Military Government of the U. S. for Germany, 29-34, 113, 124, 125, 215-216.
Office of Strategic Services, 17, 122, 153, 171, 172, 173, 178, 359.
Office of the U. S. High Commissioner for Germany, establishment of, 43-46; headquarters office, 46-55; functions of headquarters office, 56-59; *Land* offices, 59-63; *Kreis* offices, 63-65.
Office of War Information, 359.
OMGUS. *See* Office of Military Government of the U. S. for Germany.
Organization for European Economic Cooperation, 262.
OSS. *See* Office of Strategic Services.
Ostrowski, Dr. Otto, 344, 345.
OWI. *See* Office of War Information.
Oxnam, Bishop G. Bromley, 323.

Papen, Franz von, 145, 146.
Parker, Chauncey, 46, 55.
Parker, John J., 145.
Parkman, Brigadier General Henry, 73, 82.
Parks, Major General Floyd, 341.
Parliamentary Council, 186-188.
Patch, Lieutenant General A. M., 71-72.
Patton, General George, Jr., 71-72, 158.
Personnel, problem of, in military government, 67-79; under HICOG, 76-84; conclusions, 84-85.
Petersberg Protocol, 257.
Philippines, 1.
Physical training program, 14.
Pittsburgh University, 11.
Planning for the occupation, 18-25.
Police, 304-306.
Policy of the U. S. in the occupation of Germany, development of, 86; 1945-1947, 93-96; mid-1947 to Berlin Blockade, 96-98; Berlin Blockade to 1955, 98-100.
Political Advisers, 33, 123.
Political Affairs Division of OMGUS, 33.
Political Affairs, Office of, of HICOG, 52-53, 56.
Political parties, 335-339.

Political Science in German universities, 211.
Pollock, J. K., 75, 182.
Potsdam Agreement, 94, 107, 165-166, 254, 256, 270, 281, 331, 337.
Potsdam Conference, 257.
Pressure groups in state legislatures, 307.
Provost Marshal General, Office of, 6, 7, 8, 9, 11.
Prussia, abolition of, 329-330.
Public Affairs, Office of, of HICOG, 51-52, 58-59.
Public debt, 272, 274.
Public finance, U. S. activities relating to, 271-273.
Public Law No. 402, 217.
Public safety, activities of U. S. relating to, 304-306.
Quebec Conference, Second, 92, 155-156.
Quinn, Father E. E., 324.

Radio, U. S. activities relating to, 241-242.
Railway police, 305.
Rape, problem of, 137.
Raymond, Colonel John, 74-75.
Reber, Samuel, Jr., 81, 82.
Reconstruction Loan Corporation, 277-278.
Refugees, 27.
Regensburg, 214, 245.
Regierungsbezirk, 175-181.
Regional government, 175-181.
Reichsbank, 275-277.
Religious affairs, U. S. activities relating to, 320-325.
Religious Affairs Branch of HICOG, 322.
Religious Affairs Section of OMGUS, 321-322.
Religious press, 325.
Requisitioning of German property, problem of, 129.
Reuter, Dr. Ernst, 345.
Review of German legislation, 307-308.
Revision Committee, 308.
Rhineland, occupation of, 1.
RIAS, 234, 241-242, 350-351.

Index

Ribbentrop, Foreign Minister J. von, 145.
Riddleberger, James, 74, 81.
Rockwell, Alvin, 74-75.
Roosevelt, President Franklin D., 2, 21, 29, 70, 87, 88, 92, 104, 121, 154, 167, 352, 353, 354.
Ross, Michail, 287.
Russians, relations of U. S. with, 2-3, 103, 104-110.

Scammon, R. M., 337.
Schacht, Dr. H., 145, 146.
Schaeffer, Dr. F., 178.
Schmidt, A., 284.
School of Military Government at Charlottesville, 11-13.
Schumacher, Dr. Kurt, 78, 338.
SED. See Socialist Unity party.
Seventh Army, 35.
Sexual problem in the occupation, 137-138.
SHAEF, 19.
Shrivenham military government center, 15-16.
Shuster, George N., 79-80.
Shute, B. H., 81.
Sicherheitspolizei, 305.
Simons, Dr. Hans, 186-187.
Smith, General W. Bedell, 28.
Social Democratic party, 337, 338, 339, 344, 345.
Social insurance, 286.
Socialist Unity party, 344.
Sokolovsky, Marshal V., 346.
South Baden, 177.
Southwest state, 177.
Spanish-American War, 5.
SPD. See Social Democratic party.
Special Branches, 159.
Special Projects Fund, 211.
Stadtkreis, 170-175.
Stanford University, 11.
State Department, 43-44, 70, 86, 90, 95, 99, 122, 123, 195, 207, 218, 219-220, 221, 222, 230.
State government, 175-182.
State legislatures in American Zone, 307.
State, War, Navy Coordinating Committee, 31, 90.

States. See Länder.
Stimson, Henry L., 157.
Stone, Shepard, 81, 82, 316.
Strang, Sir William, 21, 105.
Student exchange program, 223-224.
Stuttgart, 214, 245, 249, 266-267.
Sundquist, J. L., 46.
Supreme Headquarters of the Allied Expeditionary Forces, 19.
SWNCC. See State, War, Navy Coordinating Committee.

Taxes, 271-273.
Taylor, John, 196, 200.
Taylor, General Maxwell D., 82.
Taylor, Brigadier General Telford, 145, 146.
Teachers College, Columbia University, 198.
Teen-age exchange program, 225, 229.
Textbooks, problem of, 198-199.
Third Army, 35.
Treasury Department, 90.
Trizonal Fusion Agreement, 114.
Truman, President H. S., 89.
Turck, C. J., 12.
Turnover tax, 272-273.

UFA, 243.
Ulm, 245.
Unemployment, problem of, 287, 289-290.
UNESCO. See United Nations Educational, Scientific and Cultural Organization.
Unification of Germany, problem of, 100.
United Nations Educational, Scientific and Cultural Organization, 206.
U. S. Commander, Berlin, 63.
USFET. See U. S. Forces, European Theatre.
U. S. Forces, European Theatre, 28-29.
U. S. Group, Control Council for Germany, 24-25, 26-29, 104, 106, 112, 113, 151.
U. S. Information Centers. See America Houses.
U. S. relations with its Allies, with the Soviet Union, 104-110; with Britain, 110-116; with France, 116-120.

Village government, 170-175.
Visiting civilian experts, 224-225, 232-233.

War brides, 4.
War crimes trials, 145-146.
War Department. *See* Civil Affairs Division; Joint Chiefs of Staff; and Provost Marshal General, Office of.
Warburg, James P., 100, 101-102.
Washington Three-Power Meeting of April 1949, 45.
Water, problem of chlorination of, 130.
Water-protection police, 305.
Weimar constitution, 180-181, 187.
Welfare services, 286.
Wells, H. B., 200-203.
West Berlin, 349-351.
"Welt im Film," 243.
Western European Union, 99.
Western Reserve University, 11.
West German Federal Republic, 183-191, 263, 266, 267, 272, 273, 278-279, 288, 302, 305, 314, 329, 333, 338.
White, Harry Dexter, 153.
White-Morgenthau group, 2, 20, 87, 153, 154, 353, 355.
Wickersham, Major General C. W., 24, 27.

Wiesbaden, 214, 245.
Wilson, Orlando, 75.
Winant, J. G., 21.
Wisconsin University, 11.
Wolfe, Glenn G., 46, 80-81.
Wolfsperger, E. C., 332.
Women's activities of the U. S., 317-319.
Women's Affairs Branch of HICOG, 318-319.
Women's Affairs Section of OMGUS, 317-318.
Works councils, 283.
Workshops, educational, 213-214.
World Council of Churches, 324.
World War I, 5.
Württemberg-Baden, 177-178, 211, 237, 275, 286, 335.
Württemberg-Hohenzollern, 177.
Würzburg, 245, 249.

Yale University, 11.
Yalta Conference, 23, 105-106.
Youth program of U. S., 311-317.

Zones, four national, in occupation of Germany, 22-23.
Zhukov, Marshal G., 107, 346.